The Darksome Bounds of a Failing World

The Darksome Bounds of a Failing World

The Sinking of the *Titanic* and the End of the Edwardian Era

Gareth Russell

WILLIAM COLLINS

William Collins
An imprint of HarperCollins*Publishers*
1 London Bridge Street
London SE1 9GF

WilliamCollinsBooks.com

First published in Great Britain in 2019 by William Collins

1

Copyright © Gareth Russell 2019

Gareth Russell asserts the moral right to be identified as the author of this
work in accordance with the Copyright, Designs and Patents Act 1988

A catalogue record for this book is available from the British Library

ISBN 978-0-00-826316-4 (hardback)
ISBN 978-0-00-829678-0 (trade paperback)

Typeset by Palimpsest Book Production Ltd, Falkirk, Stirlingshire
Printed and bound in Great Britain by CPI Group (UK) Ltd, Croydon CR0 4YY

For my great-grandparents,
Thomas Hutton and Elizabeth Johnston-Clarke,
The first to tell me stories of the Titanic,
And my father,
Who encouraged me to write them.

CONTENTS

Dramatis Personae   xi

Author's Note   xv

1. The Lords Act   1

2. The Sash My Father Wore   24

3. Southampton   46

4. A Contest of Sea Giants   63

5. A Safe Harbour for Ships   80

6. The Lucky Holdup   89

7. A Decent Wee Man   103

8. A Kind of Hieroglyphic World   119

9. Its Own Appointed Limits Keep   143

10. Two More Boilers   170

11. A Thousand Uneasy Sparks of Light   182

12. Going Up to See the Fun   203

13. Music in the First-Class Lounge   212

14. Vox faucibus haesit   223

15. Be British   242

16. Over the Top Together   255

17. The Awful Spectacle   261

18. Grip Fast   268

19. Where's Daddy?   274

20. Extend Heartfelt Sympathy to All   293

21. The Spinner of the Years   315

Glossary   339

Acknowledgements   341

Notes   343

Bibliography   399

Image Credits   423

Index   425

DRAMATIS PERSONAE

THE COUNTESS OF ROTHES

Lucy-Noëlle-Martha Leslie, Countess of Rothes
Norman Leslie, 19th Earl of Rothes, her husband
Malcolm, Viscount Leslie, their eldest son, later 20th Earl
  of Rothes
The Honourable John Leslie, their youngest son
Gladys Cherry, the Earl's cousin and the Countess's
  travelling companion
Clementina and Thomas Dyer-Edwardes, the Countess's
  parents
Roberta ('Cissy') Maioni, the Countess's lady's maid

THOMAS ANDREWS

Thomas Andrews, Managing Director of the Harland and
  Wolff shipyard
Helen Andrews, his wife
Elizabeth Andrews, their daughter
William, 1st Lord Pirrie, Thomas's uncle, Chairman of
  Harland and Wolff

THE STRAUSES

IDA STRAUS, a philanthropist
ISIDOR STRAUS, Ida's husband, a former congressman for
    New York and co-owner of Macy's department store
ELLEN BIRD, Ida's lady's maid
JOHN FARTHING, Isidor's valet

JESSE STRAUS
CLARENCE STRAUS
PERCY STRAUS
SARA HESS } Ida and Isidor's children
MINNIE WEIL
HERBERT STRAUS
VIVIAN SCHEFTEL

THE THAYERS

JOHN BORLAND THAYER, Second Vice-President of the
    Pennsylvania Railroad
MARIAN THAYER, his wife
JOHN BORLAND THAYER III ('JACK'), their eldest child
MARGARET FLEMING, Marian's lady's maid

FREDERICK THAYER
MARGARET THAYER (LATER TALBOTT) } The Thayers'
PAULINE THAYER (LATER DOLAN) younger children

DOROTHY GIBSON

DOROTHY GIBSON, an actress
PAULINE GIBSON, her mother
GEORGE BATTIER, Dorothy's husband
JULES BRULATOUR, a movie producer and Dorothy's lover
LEONARD GIBSON, Dorothy's stepfather

OTHER RELEVANT PASSENGERS

RHODA ABBOTT, a Salvation Army officer, travelling in Third Class

MADELEINE and COLONEL JOHN JACOB ASTOR IV

ALGERNON BARKWORTH, a landowner from Yorkshire

LAWRENCE BEESLEY, a science teacher, travelling in Second Class, subsequently author of *The Loss of the S.S. Titanic*

MAJOR ARCHIBALD BUTT, Military Aide to President William Howard Taft

CHARLOTTE DRAKE CARDEZA, a socialite from Pennsylvania

ELEANOR CASSEBEER, returning home to New York

LUCY, LADY DUFF GORDON, a fashion designer

ELIZABETH EUSTIS and MARTHA STEPHENSON, sisters and neighbours of the Thayers

COLONEL ARCHIBALD GRACIE IV, an historian and friend of the Strauses

J. BRUCE ISMAY, Managing Director of the White Star Line

FRANCIS ('FRANK') MILLET, a painter, author and sculptor

ALFRED NOURNEY, a car salesman travelling under the pseudonym of a German baron

EMILY and ARTHUR RYERSON, friends of the Thayers, returning home after their son's death

FREDERIC SEWARD, a New York-based lawyer and a bridge partner of Dorothy Gibson

WILLIAM SLOPER, an American stockbroker, who also played bridge with Dorothy Gibson

ELEANOR and GEORGE WIDENER, prominent members of Philadelphia Society and friends of the Thayers

RELEVANT MEMBERS OF THE CREW

HAROLD BRIDE, the *Titanic*'s Junior Wireless Operator

HARRY ETCHES, a steward in First Class

VIOLET JESSOP, a stewardess in First Class

THOMAS JONES, Able Seaman, put in charge of Lifeboat 8
MARY SLOAN, a stewardess in First Class
ANNIE ROBINSON, a stewardess in First Class
CAPTAIN EDWARD J. SMITH, Commander of the *Titanic*
CAPTAIN ARTHUR ROSTRON, Commander of the *Carpathia*
DR FRANCIS ('FRANK') McGEE, the *Carpathia's* Surgeon
DR WILLIAM O'LOUGHLIN, the *Titanic's* Surgeon

HENRY WILDE, the *Titanic's* Chief Officer
WILLIAM MURDOCH, the *Titanic's* First Officer
CHARLES LIGHTOLLER, the *Titanic's* Second Officer
HERBERT PITMAN, the *Titanic's* Third Officer
JOSEPH BOXHALL, the *Titanic's* Fourth Officer
HAROLD LOWE, the *Titanic's* Fifth Officer
JAMES MOODY, the *Titanic's* Sixth Officer

AUTHOR'S NOTE

On Sunday 14 April 1912, at about 11.40 p.m., the *Titanic*, an ocean liner operated by a British shipping company with American owners, struck an iceberg. Two hours and forty minutes later, she sank with a loss of life that was variably estimated at 1,502, 1,503, 1,512, 1,517 and 1,522 but which has recently been established at 1,496.[1] A total of 712 survivors in lifeboats were rescued by another British ship, the *Carpathia*, between two and six hours after the *Titanic* disappeared. Two inquiries were held, in each of her homelands, and they reached broadly similar conclusions about what had been done in the past and should be done in the future. In 1985, the wreck of the *Titanic* was discovered 2½ miles under by an expedition led by American oceanographer Robert Ballard.[2]

These are the bare facts surrounding a ship that is, arguably, the most famous vessel in history. When compared to nearly any other contender for that epithet, the *Titanic*'s popular appeal outstrips that of Cleopatra's barge, the *Mayflower*, the *Lusitania* and perhaps even Noah's Ark. Her name has become a synonym for catastrophe. The story of the largest and most luxurious ship ever built, racing across the Atlantic Ocean in an attempt to break the record for that journey, ignoring numerous ice warnings and then sinking with the loss of thousands, is an entrenched narrative, the belittling of which is surprisingly easy, if one is so inclined. Had she survived her first voyage, the *Titanic* would have dated like other ocean liners. While she was the largest man-made moving object when she eased off from her Southampton pier in 1912, she would only have held that accolade for the next thirteen months, until the arrival of a German passenger liner with room for a thousand more passengers amid 6,000 more tons.[3] Some of the *Titanic*'s second-class passengers preferred the accommodation on the *Mauretania*.[4] Before she sank, the *Titanic* was eclipsed in fame by her elder and slightly smaller sister ship, the *Olympic*, which had captured the attention of the world's press when she set sail a year earlier.[5] Her passenger quarters, while splendid in many places, were soon surpassed – the march of comfort on the sea lanes did not halt in the spring of 1912.

The exceptionalism of the *Titanic* can be rubbished in other ways. On a more macabre note, she was neither the only great seafaring tragedy of the Edwardian era – two years after her, the *Empress of Ireland* sank following a collision with another ship as she departed Quebec City, with the loss of just over a thousand lives.[6] Nor, arguably, was she the most important. In 1915, the *Titanic*'s one-time rival, the *Lusitania*, foundered off the coast of Ireland with marginally fewer casualties, but far greater and more tangible a political impact. The attack on the *Lusitania* by the German submarine *U-20* irrevocably hardened attitudes towards Imperial Germany in the United States at the height of the First World War, forcing an emergency meeting of the Crown Council in Berlin which effectively altered German naval policy for the next eighteen months and prepared the mood that would bring America into the war against Germany two years later.[7]

However, although the *Titanic*'s dreadful allure may be easy to unpick, it is impossible to dispel. There are societies dedicated to the study of the *Titanic* across the world, along with numerous museums, souvenirs, novels, musicals, children's cartoons, computer games, television shows and movies. The first *Titanic* motion picture was produced in the weeks immediately after the sinking, another silent movie was produced in Germany later that same year, and an early 'talkie', *Atlantic*, appeared in 1929, heavily inspired by the sinking but with the ship's name and appearance altered after the *Titanic*'s still-operational owners, the White Star Line, allegedly threatened a lawsuit.[8] A project in the late 1930s between David O. Selznick and Alfred Hitchcock to dramatise the disaster never moved beyond pre-production, with the result that after *Atlantic* it was another fourteen years before a motion picture that was both filmed in sound and unambiguously about the *Titanic* appeared.[9]

On 30 April 1943, Josef Goebbels, the Nazi Minister of Propaganda, banned the movie *Titanic*, the production of which he had initially authorised.[10] Following the outbreak of the Second World War, Goebbels had overseen a series of anti-British costume dramas that were released in Germany and then, despite some concerns about their potential impact, in various Nazi-occupied territories. *Titanic* proved to be the last of this politicised genre, which had begun with 1940's *Der Fuchs von Glenarvon* and 1941's *Mein Leben für Irland*, both dramatising the Irish struggle for independence from Britain. They were joined by *Ohm Krüger*, set during the Boer wars, and by a biographical drama loosely based on the life of Mary, Queen of Scots, with her English kinswoman, Elizabeth I, cast as a villain who was manipulative to the point of depravity. By the time *Titanic* went into production, American entry into the war on the Allied side had widened the target of these historical didactics, for which the sinking of the Anglo-American *Titanic* offered seemingly perfect fodder. The allocated budget made *Titanic* one of the most expensive motion pictures produced thus far in Germany, dozens of naval personnel were transferred from active duty at the front to serve as extras, and the decommissioned German passenger liner *Cap Arcona* was provided as a set for much of the filming. Prior to the war, the *Cap Arcona* had been the most luxurious ship to ply the route to South America, sailing from Hamburg to Buenos Aires, but like many vessels she had been removed from commercial service upon the outbreak of hostilities.

Goebbels wanted *Titanic* to depict Teutonic heroism, to which end a fictional German officer was inserted into the ship's roster and shown in the final scenes dashing bravely through flooding corridors to rescue trapped children, but the movie was also intended to highlight the corruption of Germany's enemies. In one particularly memorable scene, showing a dinner during the *Titanic's* voyage, the shipping line's owner, J. Bruce Ismay, gives a speech to the Dining Saloon boasting of the liner's record-breaking speed. At his announcement, several American financiers scuttle away from their tables to send telegrams ordering their brokers to buy shares in the White Star Line while, back in the Saloon, the *Titanic's* privileged passengers stand as the ship's orchestra plays 'God Save the King'. As a depiction of German perceptions of British arrogance and American greed, the scene had all the subtlety of a sledgehammer – although that, of course, was not the reason Goebbels vetoed his own creation.

Filming had been plagued with difficulties from the start. The director, Herbert Selpin, privately complained about the military extras' sexual harassment of the actresses, comments that may have widened into criticism of the armed forces. The scriptwriter reported Selpin's comments to the Gestapo, who had him arrested and imprisoned, at which point Goebbels almost certainly gave the order that Selpin was to be found hanged in his cell, as if from suicide. Certainly, almost nobody believed Selpin had died by his own hand.[11] Back on set, the production costs were spiralling beyond the generous allowance and several Allied bombing raids on nearby towns intermittently disrupted filming. By the time Goebbels saw the movie at a private screening, those bombing raids had helped turn the tide of the war against Nazi Germany and Goebbels was concerned that the scenes of passengers screaming in panic during the evacuation would remind too many moviegoers of their own experiences during the air raids. He also allegedly worried that German civilians might sympathise with the plight of the British and American passengers as they struggled to escape the *Titanic*, no matter how repugnant their on-screen leaders.[12] *Titanic* was the last of the anti-British Nazi historical dramas, after which productions shrank as the Reich stuttered towards oblivion.[13]

During the regime's depraved unravelling, the *Cap Arcona* was once again pressed into service, this time to move 9,000 people from Nazi Poland, most of them prisoners from local camps. Whether the SS knew that the *Cap Arcona* had been identified as a target by the Royal Air Force before they herded the prisoners on board and if that was the reason they herded all the prisoners below deck to make sure the British pilots did not cease fire is unclear. According to the fullest modern account of the *Cap Arcona*'s career, the surviving evidence suggests that if the British aeroplanes had not turned up as expected to attack the ship the SS would have bombed it themselves and placed the blame on the Allies, the main reason for moving the prisoners on to known targets being the guards' hopes of destroying living evidence of the existence of the neighbouring concentration camps.[14] As the RAF attacked the ship, small German boats near by evacuated only fleeing camp guards and SS personnel, who were also the only passengers to have been provided with lifebelts. The *Cap Arcona* burned, capsized and sank with the lost of about 5,000 lives, meaning that the *Titanic*'s one-time cinematic stand-in became the first ship to break her record for the greatest loss of life at sea.

Goebbels' *Titanic* is one of the least-known if most repellently intriguing interpretations of the *Titanic* as both a symbol of Anglo-American cooperation and a damning indictment of its elites. Although no subsequent dramatisations of the disaster have mined the depths of national stereotypes seen in the 1943 version, the story of the *Titanic*'s owners pushing her to break the record for the fastest crossing of the Atlantic has been replicated ad nauseam. Where Goebbels sought to excoriate, others have sympathised or simply remained fascinated. As a child growing up in Belfast, I heard stories from my great-grandfather, who had seen the *Titanic*'s construction and departure from the city and remembered men and women weeping in the streets when the news broke of the sinking. For him, something had shattered, some certainty had vanished, in that moment. He had never seen his father cry before that morning and he did not remember seeing him do so again. Admittedly, many are unimpressed by the allure of the *Titanic* to its own or subsequent generations. When he edited the memoirs of one of the *Titanic*'s surviving crew members, Stewardess Violet Jessop, the late historian John Maxtone-Graham was unmoved by the liner's appeal, positing, 'Ostensibly sinkable in life, she has proved positively unsinkable posthumously . . . My sense is that we should view the vessel as neither symbol nor metaphor but merely an imprudently captained vessel lost at sea. Leave *Titanic* as she was, one of hundreds of wrecks littering the Atlantic depths.'[15]

With respect to a fine historian, this sounds unduly curmudgeonly. The *Titanic* has become both cultural touchstone and looking glass. There is an enduring sense that what happened to the *Titanic* in April 1912 was somehow totemic, a process which began during her construction, when the *Titanic* was woven into a political debate over the future of the United Kingdom. The *Titanic*, like her sister ships, was a child of Anglo-American capitalism. In response to the disaster, King George V sent a public telegram of condolence to President Taft in which he expressed how he and his wife were 'anxious to assure you and the American nation of the great sorrow which we experienced at the terrible loss of life that has occurred among the American citizens, as well as many of my own subjects, by the foundering of the *Titanic*. Our two countries are so intimately allied by ties of friendship and brotherhood that any misfortunes which affect the one must necessarily affect the other, and on the present terrible occasion they are both equally sufferers.'[16]

The 2012 centenary of the disaster significantly increased the corpus of *Titanic* literature, with several excellent panoramic accounts of the voyage appearing in print, including the immensely thorough *On a Sea of Glass*, product of the research and authorship of Tad Fitch, J. Kent Layton and Bill Wormstedt. In the strictest sense, *The Darksome Bounds of a Failing World* is not solely an account of the *Titanic* disaster, nor a striving to replace the works of earlier scholars who examined the catastrophe as a whole. As its subtitle suggests, it is an attempt to look at her sinking as a *fin de siècle*, with a deliberate exploration of the voyage as a microcosm of the unsettled world of the Edwardian upper classes. With the admittedly dubious benefit of hindsight, the *Titanic*'s story functions like the Lady of Shalott's mirror, reflecting shadows of the world around it, its splendours and injustices. Since its maiden voyage, the ship has been inextricably linked in popular culture with the question of class. British taste and American money built the *Titanic*, which had room for more first-class passengers, even as a percentage, than almost any other ship then at sea, and the perceived symbiosis between the *Titanic* and the elites who designed her and sailed on her is compelling.[17] In the years before the *Titanic*'s creation, the Industrial Revolution and the corresponding expansions of both the British Empire and the American economy had created new kinds of wealth. Modernity had shaken the class system. There were many different kinds of privilege in pre-war Britain and America, the *Titanic*'s respective spiritual and economic homelands, and all of these elites would be, as individuals and a class, changed by the decade that lay ahead.

The focus of this narrative is six first-class passengers and their families: a British aristocrat, a patriotic maritime architect, an American plutocrat and his son, a first-generation American philanthropist, and one of the first movie stars. By examining its story through the experiences of these six first-class passengers, it is not only possible to explore the ways in which the upper classes were changing by 1912 but also to reflect on how the isolation created by privilege left many of them unaware or indifferent to the coming danger, until it was too late. Some first-class passengers did not realise anything was seriously wrong with the *Titanic* until they spotted pyjama legs poking from beneath the trousers of the White Star Line's normally fastidiously well-dressed

Managing Director. Others belatedly guessed that a crisis was looming when they realised that some of the people standing next to them on the Promenade Deck were from Third Class. The *Titanic*'s only commercial voyage is a window into a world that was by turns victim and author of the tragedies that overtook it.

Sources from the *Titanic*'s passengers and crew are numerous. There are inevitable problems in reliability arising from eyewitness testimonies by those who were participants in something deeply traumatic. It is not always possible or advisable to construct a precise chronology of what happened between the *Titanic*'s collision with the iceberg and the rescue of her survivors. One can, however, query the improbable or dismiss the impossible and, by comparing eyewitness accounts with modern research, particularly after the discovery of the *Titanic*'s wreck, offer a convincing account of the *Titanic*'s short career.

1

The Lords Act

In a dream I saw territories,
So broad, so rich and handsome,
Lapped by the blue sea,
Rimmed by mountains' crest.

And at the centre of the territories
Stood a tall oak tree,
Of venerable appearance,
Almost as old as its country.

Storms and weather
Had already taken their toll;
Almost bare of leaves it was,
Its bark rough and shaggy.

Only its crown on high
Had not been blown away,
Woven of parched twigs,
Skeleton of former splendour . . .

Elisabeth of Bavaria (1837–98), Empress of Austria and
Queen of Hungary, 'Neujahrsnacht 1887'

FLOWING IN FROM NORTH AND WEST, WEAVING PAST Roman and Celtic monuments of obscure purpose, two streams joined with the River Leven to ring the 'magnificently wooded gardens' of Leslie House, the thirty-seven-bedroom country seat of Norman Leslie, 19th Earl of Rothes.* Nestling in 10,000 acres of 'excellent arable land', in 1911 Leslie House dominated the encircling parish, as it had for centuries. The minister of the local Church of Scotland drew his salary from the Earl's coffers. So complete was the Leslie family's influence in this part of eastern Scotland that the parish's ancient recorded name of Fetkill had faded to become the parish of Leslie.

It had been predominantly a benign local absolutism. When an amateur historian arrived in Leslie in the 1830s, in the hope of unearthing grisly anecdotes from the village archives, he was, in his own words, distressed to find 'nothing generally interesting in them', with no perceptible drama having occurred in Leslie over the course of the last 300 years. The 800-seat chapel was built, the flax mills spun, whisky houses and inns were opened, closed and renamed, and local legend had it that King James V had written his poem 'Christ's Kirk on the Green', in celebration of a Caledonian pastoral idyll, after his hunting trip near the village in the 1530s.[1]

As the Edwardian era drew to its close, the then Countess of Rothes, Lucy Noëlle Martha Leslie, had busied herself with the renovation and preservation of Leslie House. Given the spiralling cost of maintaining a stately home, expansion, in the hope of restoring the house to what it had been in the previous centuries, would have been financially lunatic, although even at that the young Countess had sunk nearly £11,000 of her natal family's money into the preservation and beautification of her husband's ancestral home.[2] She had married into the Leslie family on a 'delightfully bright and genial' day in 1900, with a service at St Mary Abbots Church in Kensington,

---

* Pronounced 'Rothiz'. Each time a peerage is created, the incumbents are numbered. If the title falls into disuse and is subsequently revived, the numbering starts anew.

near the London townhouse of her parents where the future countess had been born on Christmas Day twenty-two years earlier.[3]
Christ's Nativity gave Lucy Dyer-Edwardes the first of her two
middle names, Noël (the spelling on her birth certificate, but
commonly spelled in Society columns and by various relatives as
Noëlle); the other was Martha. These names and spellings were
used variably throughout her life, although by adulthood she increasingly seemed to prefer her middle name of Noëlle. Her education
had been entrusted to governesses and tutors who moved with the
family as they oscillated between the Kensington house, their château
in Normandy and their favourite home, Prinknash Park, the Dyer-
Edwardeses' country seat in Gloucestershire. Prinknash, pronounced
'Prinnage' as one of the thousands of anti-phonetic nomenclatures
that form the pleasurable minefield of English place names, was
originally a Benedictine monastery founded, with spectacularly poor
luck on the Order's part, only thirteen years before England's break
with Rome. Secularised and sold by the Tudors, Prinknash Park had
become a beautiful stately pile in idyllic countryside, where Noëlle's
father, Thomas, was free to pursue his fascination with his home's
long-dead original owners and, bit by bit, their Catholic faith, to
the distress of his wife, who regarded the Church of Rome as a
foreigner's creed.[4]

An only child and thus sole heiress to a substantial fortune,
Noëlle also had the added benefit of blossoming into what one
family member called 'a true English rose beauty' by the time she
turned eighteen and could be launched into the ballrooms and
on to the marriage market of the upper classes as part of the
debutante Season. After a formal presentation at Buckingham
Palace, which marked their 'coming out' into Society, the debutantes were, in the words of an Irish peer's daughter, paraded 'to
shooting and tennis parties, polo matches, tea with the Viceroy
in Dublin' or, in Noëlle's case, with the who's who of the London
beau monde.[5] The ultimate goal of this whirlwind of merrymaking
was a wedding announcement in *The Times*, but although Noëlle
was a popular 'deb', she resisted many of the offers of marriage

3

that came her way until she met Norman Leslie, 19th Earl of Rothes, an infantry officer with a 'pleasant face and manners', who proposed to her in 1899.[6]

The Countess of Rothes

'One of the most beautiful young women seen at the Court this season': the Countess of Rothes, shortly after her marriage.

Married the following spring in 'a pretty gown of white satin covered with exquisite Brussels lace' and carrying a bouquet of carnations and white heather, Noëlle honeymooned on the Isle of Wight, before returning to London for her first audience at Court as the new Countess of Rothes.[7] A young, wealthy and good-looking couple, who were clearly very much in love, the Rotheses became a fixture in Society columns. The aristocracy were obsessive points of interest for the British, and certain sections of the American, press – the 'beautiful people' of the era, according to a critical study of their long decline.[8] It made the press's job easier when, like Noëlle, the subject actually was physically beautiful, with even the *Washington Post* informing its readers, 3,000 miles away, that on her second trip to Buckingham Palace when she curtseyed to the Princess of Wales for the first time as a countess Noëlle was, by general agreement, 'one of the most beautiful young women seen at the Court this season'.[9]

After their honeymoon, the newlyweds had spent most of their time at the Rotheses' country house in Devonshire and their mansion in Chelsea, where their first son, Malcolm, was born on 8 February 1902 and the couple attended King Edward VII's coronation in the capital on 9 August of that year. By the time their second son, John, was born in December 1909, the death of Norman's great-uncle had freed up Leslie House for their use and Noëlle was enraptured with her husband's fiefdom. With the piqued pride of a jilted friend who cannot quite believe the world exists beyond the sparkle of London, the *Bystander* reported that the Countess of Rothes, who had been the toast of the capital at the time of Edward VII's succession, was now 'so devoted to her Scottish home, Leslie House, that neither she nor Lord Rothes are often to be seen in London or anywhere else [where] the world of amusement foregathers'.[10] A journalist from the *Scotsman* observed that within a few years of her residency at Leslie House 'not a Christmastide passed but the Countess celebrated her birthday, Dec. 25, by treating all the children in the parish to an entertainment in Leslie Town Hall, and presenting each with a Christmas gift'.[11] Convinced of the benefits created by clean air, Noëlle organised trips for young women employed in local factories to visit the beach or the countryside. She funded the creation of Fife's first ambulance corps, the Countess of Rothes Voluntary Aid Detachment, she paid for the neighbouring parish of Kinglassie's first clinic, organised parties to raise money for veterans from her husband's regiment, and two years after John's birth she began training with the Red Cross as a nurse.

Despite the *Bystander*'s gripes, London was not quite abandoned by the Rotheses and Noëlle often returned for the Season. She joined the committee that organised the Royal Caledonian Ball, an annual highlight for the capital's socialites with its insistence on proper Highland attire and music. The funds raised were channelled to the Royal Caledonian Educational Trust's care for Scottish orphanages.[12] She worked for the YMCA Bazaar and the

Children's Guild; she sat on the foundation boards for the Randolph Wemyss Memorial Hospital and the Queen Victoria School in Dunblane, which taught the sons of Scottish military personnel, and her passion for preserving a rural way of life in Britain brought her to serve the Village Clubs Association. The young Countess's charitable activities were a mixture of the more glittering variety of philanthropy and intense hands-on work, and the former solidified many of her relationships with fellow like-minded aristocrats – Evelyn Cavendish, Duchess of Devonshire, Consuelo Spencer-Churchill (née Vanderbilt), Duchess of Marlborough, Kathleen Wellesley, Duchess of Wellington, and Constance Sackville, the Dowager Countess De La Warr, became close friends. With Millicent Leveson-Gower, Duchess of Sutherland, Noëlle helped raise a substantial amount of money for the National Milk Hostels' quest to provide 'wholesome milk for poor families', through a series of Society masquerade balls and garden parties, at which tickets were costly and donations firmly encouraged.[13]

One of Noëlle's philanthropic connections was Louise, Duchess of Fife, who alone of King Edward VII's daughters had married into the native aristocracy.[14] Through her, Noëlle met, and was sincerely liked by, King Edward's daughter-in-law Mary, Princess of Wales. Her friendships within the Royal Family added a personal affection to the feudal obligations that brought Norman and Noëlle to most major state occasions, including the funeral of Edward VII, after his death at Buckingham Palace was announced on 6 May 1910. Over the course of the next three days, a quarter of a million people filed past the royal coffin to pay their respects. Despite a reign of only nine years, Edward VII had, in his Foreign Secretary's observation, grown 'intensely and increasingly popular' and grief at his passing was judged stronger than the mourning surrounding Queen Victoria's death nine years earlier.[15] The first people in the queue to pass King Edward's bier, 'guarded by household cavalry, soldiers of the line and men from Indian and Colonial contingents, all in the characteristic pose of mourning, that is with bowed heads with their hands crossed over rifle butts and the hilts of their swords', had been 'three women of the seamstress class: very poorly dressed and very reverent'.[16] When the Liberal Prime Minister, Herbert Asquith, was caught leaning against a pillar during the lying in state, courtiers judged 'his attitude and general demeanour rather offensive' and concluded that he must have been tipsy to behave so atrociously or, as one of them put it with leaden subtext, 'I fear he had dined well.'[17]

There were no comparable faux pas at the funeral procession three days later. Many of the mourners had camped out overnight to vouchsafe their place in the crowds, which in places stood 100 yards deep, to watch Edward VII's body being conducted from Westminster Hall to Windsor. As the catafalque passed Hyde Park, where nearly 300,000 had congregated, cigarettes were stubbed out and a forest of caps rose into the air. After the body, the first being to receive these gestures of deference was Caesar, Edward VII's white terrier, who with the Queen Mother's permission trotted by his dead master's side.[18] Caesar was followed by nine monarchs on horseback, leading perhaps the largest gathering of royalty in history, with one of the emperors joking that this was the first time in his life he had yielded precedence to a canine.[19] Monarchy, the cause in which Edward VII had been such a devout believer, had come to inter 'the uncle of Europe'. His son and heir, now George V, rode with two of the late King's brothers-in-law, Denmark's Frederick VIII and Greece's George I, with one of his sons-in-law, King Haakon VII of Norway, and with two of his nephews – one by birth, the other by marriage, both heroically moustached – the German Kaiser Wilhelm II and King Alfonso XIII of Spain. They and their glinting medals were joined by the young Portuguese and Belgian sovereigns, Manuel II and Albert I, both on their respective thrones for less than two years. If Prime Minister Asquith's slouching had been noted at the lying in state, so too were other things that mattered deeply to the Edwardian upper classes – it was observed by one civil servant that the rotund Tsar Ferdinand of Bulgaria had the worst seat on a horse of any royal present; the phrase 'like a sack' was tossed around with uncharitable accuracy.[20]

Affection rippled through the crowd as the fantastic spectacle of the Golden State Coach trundled into view, carrying four women transformed into black pillars by clouds of mourning lace and veil. Edward VII's sixty-five-year-old widow, Alexandra of Denmark, one of the most consistently popular members of the British Royal Family since her arrival in 1863, had borne five children and buried two, but she retained the slender beauty of a person twenty or thirty years her junior. The Prime Minister's daughter-in-law, who watched as Alexandra went by and saw her later at the interment, wrote in her diary that evening, 'She has the finest carriage and walks better than anyone of our time and not only has she grace, charm and real beauty but all the atmosphere of a fascinating female queen for whom men and women die.'[21] Joined in the coach by her younger sister the Dowager Empress of Russia, her daughter Queen Maud of Norway and her daughter-in-law the new Queen consort, Alexandra was so moved by the sight of the crowds that at Hyde Park she broke with protocol by lifting her veil to bow her head to them, at which point hundreds of people began shouting variations of 'God bless you!'[22] Most unusually in a country that still prided itself on its proverbial stiff upper lip when in public, the Queen Mother's gesture produced sobbing from dozens, if not hundreds, of people.[23] Behind her carriage came coaches attended by scarlet-liveried footmen and transporting the men who were one day expected to inherit the thrones of Austria-Hungary, the Ottoman Empire, Greece, Romania, Serbia and Montenegro. They were followed by representatives from the reigning houses of Russia, China, Italy, Japan, the Netherlands, Persia and Siam. With this dynastic confraternity sat members of the deposed royal houses of France and Brazil, as proudly and conspicuously as if their families still reigned from the Tuileries and São Cristóvão – as though nothing had ever really changed and the republics that had toppled them were an aberration, a nightmarish blip from which the world might soon recover. Noëlle's husband marched with the dukes, marquesses and earls of Edward's nobilities, custodians of the hereditary compact that stretched back to before the three British kingdoms and one principality had been ruled by a single house.* Far behind these princes and potentates, America's President Theodore Roosevelt rode with delegates sent by other republics, in a horse-drawn carriage without gilding and manned by footmen in a duller colour of livery. The French republic's Foreign Minister was incandescent at the slight; Roosevelt, at least publicly, insisted that he did not care.[24]

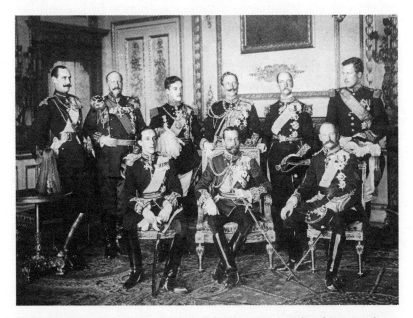

After the funeral: the monarchs who gathered to mourn Edward VII, standing from left to right King Haakon VII of Norway, Tsar Ferdinand of Bulgaria, King Manuel II of Portugal, Germany's Kaiser Wilhelm II, Greece's King George I and King Albert I of the Belgians. Sitting from left to right are kings Alfonso XIII of Spain, George V of the United Kingdom and Frederick VIII of Denmark.

---

* The three kingdoms were England, Ireland and Scotland. Wales was a princi-pality, the importance of which is reflected in the bestowal of the title of Prince of Wales on the heir-designate to the throne of the others.

With the benefit of hindsight, Edward VII's funeral took on the appearance of an entire world gathering to bury itself alongside the man whose name had been given to their era, but at the time it appeared instead as the appropriate grief of an immutable order. When a peer who had taken his little daughter to watch the royal funeral asked her to say her prayers before bedtime, she replied, 'It won't be any use. God will be too busy unpacking King Edward.'[25]

Nonetheless, Edward VII's death heightened the general sense of unease in his country. The King's passing could not have come at a more politically delicate moment for Britain, one that Edward's subtle influence and considerable experience had, rightly or wrongly, been trusted by many to ameliorate. Seven months before bronchitis took Edward VII, the United Kingdom had collided with a constitutional crisis through the deployment of their veto by the House of Lords, the upper chamber of Parliament consisting of the Lords Spiritual, the bishops of the devolved branches of the Anglican churches in England, Scotland, and Wales, and the Lords Temporal, the hereditary peers. The Lords' use of the veto was well within their constitutional rights, but their decision to wield it against the Liberal government's Budget was vibrant testament to the difference between the permissible and the sensible. The House of Lords had not vetoed any financial Bill sent to them by the elected House of Commons since the seventeenth century and so their decision to do so in the winter of 1909 focused attention on whether the veto should have survived into the twentieth.

The new Budget raised taxes substantially on the wealthiest of King Edward's subjects, ostensibly in furtherance of the aim of providing funds for old age pensions and to meet the cost of naval rearmament. The surtax of 2.5 per cent on the amount by which all incomes of £5,000 or more exceeded £3,000 might seem laughably low today, but the four new kinds of tax levied on land struck the peers as a deliberate piece of class warfare, with the majority of the shrapnel aimed squarely at those whose ancient privileges were tied to their positions as landowners. That taxes were not being raised as significantly on those made rich by the factories of the Industrial Revolution did not go unnoticed; likewise invoked were dark mutterings that the Budget represented a grossly untenable expansion of the state's powers. The upper chamber's rejection of the Budget forced the King to call another election at which, incredibly, the Lords seemed to receive some limited form of popular approval when the Conservatives, who dominated the hereditary Lords but had lost their majority in the elected Commons, won back 100 of the seats they had lost in the 1906 election. The Liberals had, however, still won enough to be returned to office and they immediately allied themselves with two smaller parties, Labour and the Irish Parliamentary Party, to outnumber the Tories decisively in the House of Commons. In a victorious mood, the Liberal coalition tabled three resolutions to prevent a repeat of 1909 – firstly, the Lords would lose the right to amend or reject a financial Bill; secondly, the lifespan of a Parliament was decreased from seven years to five, thus enabling more frequent elections; and, finally, the Lords' veto was to vanish, to be replaced by the right to delay by a maximum of twenty-five months any piece of legislation passed in the Commons.

It was as this dilemma over the greatest change to the British Constitution accelerated that Edward VII died. Expectations that his reactionary son would lend royal support to the nobility were crushed when George V made it clear that he saw his job as brokering a peaceful settlement rather than favouring one side against the other, whatever his personal opinions might be. Lord Haldane, the Liberal government's Secretary of State for War, who had initially expected subtle Tory politicking from the new monarch, was touched and impressed by how George V walked the tightrope of his first few steps as monarch: 'I have in these days come to greatly admire the King. He has shown himself to have far more of his father's qualities of tact and judgement than I supposed. He is being bombarded by Tory extremists with all sorts of suggestions.'[26] The proposal that George V should withhold the Royal Assent, something which had not been done since the reign of his distant predecessor Queen Anne, was shot down by the King, who rightly predicted it would divide the nation even further.[27]

Noëlle's husband Norman threw himself into working with the bloc in the Lords who opposed the impending Parliament Bill, or the 'Lords Act' as it was more generally known.[28] At first, cold logic dictated that the House of Lords had one immeasurable advantage in their favour: to pass this Bill neutering them, Prime Minister Asquith needed the victims' acquiescence. They, fairly obviously, were expected to veto the Parliament Bill with savage alacrity, piously arguing that not to do so would ensure that their legacies 'would be degraded by our failure to be faithful to our trust'.[29] Asquith and his allies threatened to pull the monarchy into the maelstrom by pressuring the King who was, after all, the hereditary guardian of the elected government; they wanted him to flood the House of Lords with an unprecedented number of newly created peerages, all awarded to prominent Liberal sympa-thisers. Privately, George V regarded Asquith's plan as 'a dirty, low-down trick', but practically he had no intention of seeing the Crown dragged into the mire of an ugly political quarrel, particu-larly after one fraught prime ministerial audience at the Palace, during which Asquith reiterated that, if his demands were not met, 'I should immediately resign and at the next election should make the cry, "The King and the Peers against the people."'[30] This threat to the monarchy reawakened feelings of chivalric loyalty in a sufficient number of peers, including Noëlle's husband and her friend's husband, the Duke of Sutherland, who fell on their swords for their king by agreeing either to abstain or vote for the Bill that would castrate them. A less charitable interpretation of their actions might be that they chose to surrender decorously only once they realised they could not win at anything but the most pyrrhic of costs.

The Lords Act was a critical moment in the decline of the British aristocracy, indeed arguably its most significant single event. Their power had been waning since 1832, thanks to a series of prerogative-clipping Reform Acts, while a sustained period of agricultural recession, beginning in the 1870s, had caused irreparable damage to a caste that still generally drew most of its income from the rural economies. There was also a sense of malaise and victimhood within the aristocracy that accelerated, and perhaps secured, their decline, while the rise of capitalism had left many of them confused and, for the first time, familiar with the uncomfortable sensation of not being the chief beneficiaries of the passing of the ages. Noëlle Rothes had a political mind which, like her husband's, leaned strongly towards Toryism. She was also a supporter of the suffragettes, a cause she shared with her friend Edith Vane-Tempest-Stewart, Viscountess Castlereagh, whose husband Charles was heir to the marquessate of Londonderry, one of the most prestigious peerages in Ireland. Edith, like Noëlle, was aghast at the Lords Act, not just because

Lafayette

Lady Rothes in the outfit she wore to George V's coronation.

it was their class's legislative equivalent of seppuku, but also for what it meant to the other great crisis of Edwardian Britain – Irish Home Rule, the movement born in the nineteenth century that sought some form of governmental independence for Ireland. Initially, the proposal had called for a Dublin Parliament that had jurisdiction over local matters, within a system that remained tied to Britain through foreign policy, which was to be left to the London Parliament at Westminster, and through the Crown, with the King and his heirs remaining kings and queens of Ireland.

This seemingly mild proposal was hugely popular in Ireland's southern three provinces and intensely feared in most of Ulster, Ireland's northern segment. The Irish branch of the aristocracy, often referred to as the Ascendancy, were similarly alarmed, seeing in the Home Rule movement the first whisper of their requiem; as a result, the House of Lords had twice vetoed Home Rule Bills. Now, with that power of destruction softened simply to one of delay, Asquith had promised his Irish nationalist allies a Third Home Rule Bill which this time would almost certainly pass. Plans to prevent Home Rule being granted to any part of Ireland now looked hopeless, resulting in Ulster unionists adjusting their focus to populist agitation in the north of Ireland and, if necessary, arming their supporters as part of the new 'Save Ulster' campaign, the de facto headquarters of which were to be the north's industrial centre, the city of Belfast.

The Parliament Bill was reintroduced to the House of Commons on 21 February 1911 and it had passed all its necessary stages there by 15 May. A brief lull in proceedings ensued, generated by cross-party deference for the kaleidoscope of patriotic festivities surrounding the opening of the Festival of Empire in London and George V's coronation at Westminster Abbey five weeks later, alongside his Anglo-German wife, Mary of Teck, the first British queen consort to be born in the country since Katherine Parr, four centuries earlier.[31] As the morning of the coronation dawned, with his typical pragmatism the King noted in his diary that it was 'Overcast and cloudy, with some showers and a strongish cool breeze, but better for the people than great heat'.[32] By the time Noëlle and her husband boarded the train to return north to Leslie House for the start of the grouse-shooting season on 12 August, the King had signed the Bill, the Home Rule crisis was one step closer and the British aristocracy's greatest remaining form of tangible political clout was dead.

*

Between the Festival of Empire and the coronation, Belfast, the nexus of the coming crisis, celebrated the launch of a ship. Two minutes before she slid into the Lagan river for the first time, the *Titanic* claimed her sixth victim.[33] As workers wove in and out beneath the 26,000-ton hull, knocking away the massive timber supports which had cradled the *Titanic*'s belly during her construction, one collapsed on to James Dobbin, shattering his pelvis. The forty-three-year-old shipwright had worked at the Harland and Wolff shipyards for nearly two decades; he was carried to the company car, which rushed him to the Royal Victoria Hospital, recently completed thanks to the fund-raising of Harland and Wolff's owner William, Lord Pirrie.[34] Pirrie himself, unaware that one of his employees was fatally haemorrhaging, remained in the specially erected stands with the 100,000-strong crowd, an extraordinary turn-out considering it was nearly one-third the size of the total population of Belfast; they had gathered to watch the launching ceremony of what would, within a year, become the largest moving object in human history.[35] Flags spelling out the word 'SUCCESS' fluttered from the grandstand.[36] Proceeds from ticket sales for the launch would be gifted to the hospital where James Dobbin was now fighting for his life.[37] Within twenty-four hours, Dobbin was another subject for the grim joke that did the rounds at Harland and Wolff when a colleague perished on the job: 'He's gone to another yard.'[38]

Joining Pirrie at the launch were his wife Margaret; his nephew Thomas Andrews, the yard's Managing Director and a man largely responsible for designing the ship; the slender Joseph Bruce Ismay, Managing Director of the White Star Line, the new vessel's operators; Ismay's New York-born wife Florence, who had never quite accustomed herself to giving up a life spent shuttling pleasurably between homes on Madison Avenue and Tuxedo Park for residency in the Ismays' faux-baronial pile outside Liverpool, and the *Titanic*'s de facto owner, the imposing American financier J. Pierpont Morgan, in declining health and painfully conscious of the inflammation of his nose caused by rhinophyma.[39] Morgan's cabal of shipping companies, the International Mercantile Marine, had bought the White Star Line as the jewel in its crown in 1903, after several years of bumper revenue for the transatlantic passenger trade.[40] Eight years on, Morgan's capital had created the *Titanic*, the second in a three-ship design that would give IMM the largest and most luxurious vessels in the world, operating a weekly run between Britain and America. Her elder sister, the *Olympic*, would be handed over from builders to owners that same afternoon, in preparation for her maiden voyage from Southampton to New York two weeks later.[41]

Despite their American ownership, White Star ships were still

'Down to the river with a grace and dignity': the launch of the *Titanic*.

built by a British firm, were staffed predominantly by British crews and flew the British flag. The *Titanic* was thus the most recent child of Anglo-American cooperation, a product of British sensibilities and American money or, as the *Belfast News-Letter* put it, a demonstration of how the empire and 'the mighty Republic in the West' had produced a 'pre-eminent example of the vitality and the progressive instincts of the Anglo-Saxon race'.[42] Keeping with White Star tradition of no inaugural speech or shattering-on-the-bow champagne, at 12.13 p.m. a firework streaked into 'the glow of the turquoise sky, from which the piercing rays of the sun descended, making the heat exceedingly trying'.[43] With the signal given, two foremen turned the release valve. It took sixty-two seconds for the *Titanic's* 882-foot hull to move through 21 tons of lubricating tallow as she 'glided down to the river with a grace and dignity which for the moment gave one the impression that she was conscious of her own strength and beauty'.[44]

Cheers erupted from the onlookers, hats and handkerchiefs were waved in the air; small river craft sounded their sirens, as chains created enough drag to stop the *Titanic* slamming into the other side of the river.[45] With no funnels or masts and empty interiors, she came to a gentle stop in the water and attention turned to the completed *Olympic*, which the *Titanic* would one day so closely resemble. A journalist from the *Shipbuilder*, the industry's most respected trade journal, waxed lyrical about White Star's new flagship, half as heavy again as the previous record holder, the Cunard Line's *Mauretania*:

The *Olympic* is the most beautiful boat ever built on Queen's Island. The grace and harmony of her lines were admired by the thousands of enthusiasts who saw her on the day of her launch, but since then the work on her has been advanced, and her four massive funnels seem to add immeasurably to her splendour and dignity. Her majestic proportions and her unparalleled dimensions tend to enhance her picturesqueness and power, and one can well understand the interest with which the builders and owners are anticipating her maiden voyage . . . In her equipment she possesses features that are not to be found on any other boat.[46]

Among the new features celebrated in the press, the *Olympic* offered the first lift for second-class passengers and the first swimming pool at sea, in First Class.[47] Three weeks later, she arrived to a rapturous welcome in New York, returning eastward on 28 June with a record-breaking number of first-class passengers.[48] Both the *Olympic* and the *Titanic* had nearly as many berths for first-class travellers as for Third, a reflection of the growing number of wealthy people travelling across the North Atlantic on a regular basis, apparently justifying the White Star Line's investment in the future earning potential of the privileged. For all the talk of an assault on the established order, the world spun onwards, simultaneously contented in the accumulated treasures of a century of economic progress and tense at the uncertainty of what lay ahead. When the grouse-shooting season was over, the King and Queen sailed to India for a theatrical and manufactured ceremony at which they were crowned Emperor and Empress of India. One peer's daughter in attendance marvelled at the maharajahs' jewels as 'a thing to dream of – great ropes of pearls and emeralds as large as pigeon eggs such as I have never seen before', though she thought it 'so strange to see them adorning men'.[49] The old boys' network flourished in the King's absence when, to the surprise of many, including himself, the recently elected MP Sir Robert Sanders was invited to become one of the Conservative and Unionist whips. In his diary, he stated with crushing self-honesty, 'I believe I owe it mainly to the fact that I was a successful Master of the Devon and Somerset [Staghounds].'[50]

In Russia, the Tsar's eldest daughter, the Grand Duchess Olga, made her debut into Society with a 140-guest candlelight supper at her family's Crimean summer palace. At the ball that followed, wearing her first floor-length evening gown, its sash pinned by roses, the Grand Duchess was partnered in her first waltz by her father. The sixteen-year-old had her first sip of champagne and one of her mother's ladies-in-waiting rhapsodised over 'the music of the unseen orchestra floating in from the rose garden like a breath of its own wondrous fragrance. It was a perfect night, clear and warm, and the gowns and jewels of the women and the brilliant uniforms of the men made a striking spectacle under the blaze of the electric lights.'[51]

In Austria, hat-wear changed as usual with the Vienna Derby marking the point at which it became de rigueur for gentlemen to switch from derbies to summer boaters, while later in the Season the country's octogenarian Emperor, Franz Josef, was seen in a rare public good mood when he visited the village of Schwarzau for the wedding of his great-nephew, the twenty-four-year-old Archduke Karl, to Princess Zita of Bourbon-Parma.[52] That evening, cheering villagers processed in torchlight celebration past the imperial couple as a prelude to a fireworks display over the castle.[53] Born in Italy to a French family, educated at a Catholic boarding school in Britain, fluent in six languages, walked down the aisle by the Duke of Madrid, married by the Pope's personal representative, granddaughter of a king of Portugal, great-great-granddaughter of the last Bourbon king of France, first cousin of the Queen consort of the Belgians and sister-in-law of the Bulgarian Tsar, the new Archduchess Zita was a reassuring return to marital form for a Habsburg heir, after the first in line had caused collective palpitations a decade earlier by proposing to a commoner.[54] She had been a countess, but to the Habsburgs he might as well have walked up the aisle with Rosa Luxemburg.

As summer bled into autumn and winter, the great migrations began. After 'two terrible years' watching her marriage disintegrate under the strain of her husband's mental ill-health, the American novelist Edith Wharton went skiing in St Moritz, where she was joined by her friend, the Italian nobleman Prince Alfonso Doria-Pamphilj.[55] The new American Ambassador to Germany, a former vice-president of Carnegie Steel, invited the

Second Vice-President of the Pennsylvania Railroad and his wife to visit him and the Consul General in Berlin. Crossing the Atlantic not long after them was the co-owner of Macy's department store and his wife, fleeing the Manhattan blizzards for the restorative warmth of Cannes. They arrived in France as another of their compatriots was leaving it: the London dinner-party circuit had it that the American socialite Gladys Deacon had quit Paris to rent an apartment at 11 Savile Row in London, above Huntsman the Tailor, fuelling rumours of a reconciliation with her unhappily married lover, the Duke of Marlborough.[56]

Noëlle and Lord Rothes spent a week as guests at a hunting party given by their friend the Marquess of Bute and they hosted their own autumnal shooting weekends at Leslie House as usual.[57] It was a splendid home for entertaining and despite the recent financial and political pressures on the aristocracy, to outward appearances it remained as majestic and tranquil as it had been for centuries. Leslie House had, within a generation of its construction in the seventeenth century, been referred to as a palace by visitors, who favourably compared it to William III's residence at Kensington Palace and his controversial imitation of Versailles, for which he had ordered the demolition of half of the original Tudor wings at Hampton Court Palace.[58] Leslie House had boasted two courtyards, an entrance hall 'pav'd with black and white Marble', and one of the finest private libraries in Great Britain. Then, early in the reign of George III, much of that splendour went up in flames.[59] Snow was falling as three-quarters of Leslie House burned in the night air, immolating one of the courtyards and the entirety of the library. Some sources give the date of the fire as Christmas Day 1763; others say it was three days later, on the Feast of the Holy Innocents. Either way, there is a general agreement of a Yuletide conflagration.

One feature that survived the 1763 Leslie House fire was a magnificent gallery, three feet longer than its counterpart at Edinburgh's Palace of Holyroodhouse, the Royal Family's official residence in Scotland. There, in paint and tapestry and silver, unfurled the genealogical and political history of the Leslies. Like most ancient aristocratic families, the Leslies have their own contested origin myth in the mist-shrouded centuries of document-deficient antiquity. In their case, that a Flemish or Hungarian baron called Bartholomew arrived in Scotland in the entourage of Margaret of Wessex, an eleventh-century English princess and subsequent saint, who had been raised in exile in Hungary before her marriage to King Malcolm III, and a series of legends arose about his subsequent career in Scotland.* Much of the more lovely nonsense associated with Bartholomew's life was politely disbelieved by many of the later Leslies themselves who, in 1910, submitted evidence to *The Scots Peerage* that their first recorded grant of land had arrived at some respectably distant juncture in the 1170s, when a Malcolm Leslie, traditionally described as Bartholomew's son, had been a recipient of royal largesse from William the Lion, King of Scots.[60]

From there, a fusion of family legend and historical evidence placed a Leslie on the Crusades, another pledging allegiance to Robert the Bruce in his quarrel with England's Edward Longshanks, and others representing Scotland on diplomatic missions to the courts of Pope John XXII and King Edward III of England. A spirit of ferocious devotion to the Crown, seemingly equally nurtured by loyalty and ambition, had pushed the Leslies upwards as the centuries wore on. The first recorded mention of them in possession of the earldom of Rothes dates from March 1458, after they supported King James II in his torturous dispute over the earldom of Mar. In the next generation, they continued to aid the consolidation of royal authority under the Stewart monarchs, who ruled Scotland from 1371 to 1714. The 3rd Earl of Rothes fell in combat at the Battle of Flodden, while supporting James IV's failed invasion of England; his son, the 4th Earl, himself tussled unsuccessfully with Henry VIII's armies, this time at the Battle of Solway Moss in 1542, but survived to attend James V

---

* Malcolm III (c.1031–93) was the historical inspiration for the prince whose military victory provides the denouement in *Macbeth*.

at his deathbed, and later represented his kingdom at the Parisian wedding of Mary, Queen of Scots, to the future King François II of France. That Earl's death, on his way home, from food poisoning was, probably erroneously, attributed to the French family of Scotland's Queen Mother, Marie de Guise, in retribution for the Leslies' vigorous involvement in the assassination of her adviser, Cardinal Beaton. The dagger used to stab His Eminence was still, in 1911, mounted in the Leslie House gallery, next to a portrait of the accidentally poisoned Earl's son, the 5th Earl of Rothes, who had ended the family's brief flirtation with disloyalty by holding his allegiance to Mary, Queen of Scots, long after her deposition and despite finding themselves on different sides of the confessional aisle created by the Protestant Reformation.

A generation later, when Mary's son, James VI, inherited the English and Irish thrones as their King James I, the Leslies' fidelity to the reigning house eventually catapulted them into the national trauma that English histories refer to as 'the English Civil War', but which might more properly be remembered by its British name of 'the War of the Three Kingdoms', given its appalling impacts on all the constituent parts of what later became the United Kingdom. The Leslies supported King Charles I even as the monarchy entered freefall. Also mounted on their gallery walls was the Sword of State carried by the 7th Earl at the first coronation of King Charles II at Scone in 1651, after Scotland had refused to accept the legality of Charles I's execution or the English republican regime that had arisen in its wake. Ruinously fined for their loyalty to the deposed royals, the restoration of the monarchy in 1660 brought the Leslies back into the sunlight of governmental favour. Next to the portrait of the 7th Earl and his monarchy-affirming sword, the gallery boasted, near one of Rembrandt's self-portraits, a likeness of Mary of Modena, the last Catholic queen consort in Britain.[61] In recognition of their steadfastness to the royalist cause, Charles II had granted the 'able and magnificent' 7th Earl of Rothes the unusual honour of allowing his title to descend through or to the female line. This royal gratitude had prevented the Leslies from stuttering into oblivion thanks to the lack of a Y-chromosome, on which rock so many other noble families had perished. Through the 7th Earl's over-zealous defence of royal-led Anglicanism in Scotland in the seventeenth century, his immediate descendants' refusal to support either of the Jacobite rebellions in the eighteenth, or the service of the 10th Earl – rendered for the gallery's posterity by the brush of Joshua Reynolds – who had accompanied George II as one of his generals to the Battle of Dettingen, the Leslies had remained conspicuously loyal to the British monarchy, regardless of the gender of the head of the family. Also in the gallery was a beautiful old tapestry that recreated the mythical, fatal voyage of Leander, crossing a darkened, storm-struck stretch of sea in pursuit of Hero.[62]

Clan Leslie and the Rothes earldom had a history that tied them to the developments of the Scottish kingdom, then Great Britain, the United Kingdom and its empire. They had faced many obstacles over the centuries and it was clear that after 1911 they would face more. To maintain Leslie House, not only had Noëlle invested a substantial amount of her own inheritance but Norman had sold various parcels of land and considered other income-generating projects. After the frantic social whirl surrounding the coronation, Norman planned to skip the next London Season with a prolonged trip to America where he would undertake a fact-finding mission for the British government and also explore the possibility of investing in the New World.

2

The Sash My Father Wore

Cursèd be he that curses his mother. I cannot be
Anyone else than what this land engendered me:
. . . I can say Ireland is hooey, Ireland is
A gallery of fake tapestries,
But I cannot deny my past to which my self is wed,
The woven figure cannot undo its thread.

Louis MacNeice, 'Valediction' (1934)

I N THE SMALL HOURS OF THE MORNING OF TUESDAY 2
April 1912, before the electric trams with their recently added
roofs commenced their shuttle into the city centre, a Renault
motor car waited on tree-lined Windsor Avenue in south Belfast.[1]
The residential street, full of alternating white and redbrick
mansions, ran between the Lisburn and Malone roads, the axis
of upwardly mobile prosperity that was both child and parent of
the city's most affluent suburb. Like Windsor Avenue's homage
to Britain's most famous castle, many of Malone's public spaces
had adopted royally inspired names which proclaimed the area's
loyalty to the throne along with, perhaps, a faint sense of self-
identified social kinship with its incumbent. Twenty years earlier,
the residents had ditched the workaday address of Stockman's

Lane, at the bottom of the Malone Road, to rechristen it Balmoral Avenue, in a nod to Queen Victoria's favourite home.[2] Near by, various streets and stations were named in honour of Adelaide of Saxe-Meiningen, William IV's queen; Belvoir and Deramore honoured a late Tory baron; the Annadale embankment, which lines the slow-flowing waters of the Lagan river where young medical students practised their rowing on weekend mornings, was named for another deceased local aristocrat, Anne Wellesley, Countess of Mornington.[3] Later, when a school was founded near the Annadale embankment, it was called Wellington after Anne Wellesley's son, the 1st Duke of Wellington.[4] Shaftesbury Square, the urban gateway to south Belfast, bore the name of an earldom with historic influence in the north of Ireland, while multiple streets and buildings paid tribute to the Chichester family and their marquessate of Donegall.* There were various parks, roads and avenues with the prefix of Osborne in honour of Queen Victoria's former summer house on the Isle of Wight, while Sans Souci Park, near the top of the Malone Road, widened the geography of homage, if not the class, by choosing as its inspiration the baroque palace built for King Friedrich the Great of Prussia.

In neighbouring Stranmillis, the suburb that intersects Malone, newly completed streets were given the name Pretoria to commemorate imperial victories in southern Africa. On the other side of the river, the Ormeau neighbourhood created roads called Agra, Baroda and Delhi, after areas of the British Empire in India. Botanic, the final stretch of land before south Belfast gave way to the city centre, contained new avenues after seventeenth-century British generals or, like Candahar Street, to celebrate successful colonial expeditions into Afghanistan.[5]

From his home on Windsor Avenue, Thomas Andrews, the thirty-nine-year-old Managing Director of the Harland and Wolff shipyards,

---

* Created as the earldom of Donegall by Charles I in 1647 and elevated to a marquessate by George III in 1791, the title retains the antique spelling of 'Donegall', though the county itself is usually spelled 'Donegal' in English today. The heir uses the courtesy title of Earl of Belfast.

stepped into his waiting car before it turned towards the Malone Road.[6] He left behind his wife of four years, Helen, and their two-year-old daughter, Elizabeth. Andrews, who would be gone for several weeks supervising the maiden voyage of the *Titanic*, was ambitious and almost fanatically dedicated to his career, but when he travelled he suffered dreadfully from homesickness, particularly after the arrival of little Elizabeth.[7] One of the five servants they employed was a nurse for the toddler.[8] His car turned left on to Malone to continue its journey towards east Belfast, where the *Titanic* was docked in preparation for her sea trials.

Thomas Andrews, c.1912.

Tall and softly handsome, with a trim build, dark hair and brown eyes, Andrews – known as Tommy to his family and closest friends – had the elegant manners and unfailing kindness with which even

the most exacting of aristocratic etiquette experts would have struggled to find fault. His work in the shipyards brought him into
regular contact with men from all walks of life – be they industrialists, like his uncle Lord Pirrie, or semi-literate labourers from
east Belfast, some of whom brought their seven- or eight-year-old
sons to work in the shipyard because they could not afford to send
them to school. Andrews' total lack of snobbery, his sense of fairness
and his gentle tone in conversation endeared him to most of his
colleagues and helped spare him from accusations of nepotism.[9]

As Andrews' automobile moved down the gentle slope that
marked the end of the Malone Road, he passed the still-slumbering
accommodation of the 400 or so students of Methodist College.[10]
A boarding school with a white Maltese cross for its crest, 'Methody',
as it was known by locals and alumni, had a stellar reputation for
academics and sports. Two weeks earlier, its rugby team had
competed in the Ulster Schools' Cup Final, a match held annually
in Belfast on St Patrick's Day, in which the two best squads in the
north of Ireland played against one another. That March, rather
gratifyingly for Tommy Andrews, Methody had played and lost 11–3
against his own alma mater, the Royal Belfast Academical Institute.[11]

'Inst', as it was and is referred to for reasons of ease, laziness and
affection, lay less than a mile from Methody. Tommy Andrews, like
his brothers John, James and William, was proud of their status as
'Old Instonians', regularly contributing to fund-raising for the school
sports and prizes. Cricket had been one of Andrews' favourite clubs
as a pupil and he retained a keen interest in the sport.[12] Between
them, Methody, Inst and Victoria, the all-girls school which then
had its campus halfway between them, were consciously turning
out sons and daughters of the British Empire.[13] It was one generation's duty to prepare the next. In east Belfast, the late textile magnate
Henry Campbell had left a bequest to found an all-boys college
that bore his name. Every year, Campbell College, which operated
an Officer Training Corps as part of its extracurricular activities,
celebrated Empire Day, during which the head prefect would plant
a tree in the school grounds, symbolising with each passing year

and each new tree the empire's continued growth and the shelter it would provide to its obedient subjects. Its founder's will stated that Campbell was 'to be used as a College for the purpose of giving there a superior liberal Protestant education' and, flowing from all the schools that dotted the emerging or established suburbs of middle- and upper-class Belfast, there was a steady stream of young men and women who would 'Fear God and serve the King'.[14]

Tommy Andrews had benefited from this kind of education that inculcated Protestantism, patriotism and propriety in almost equal measure. Like many residents of Malone in 1912, Andrews displayed the easy-going grace popularly associated with the patrician classes but, again like Malone itself, he was in reality a product rendered in its final form by the plutocracy, the expansion of the British Empire and its Industrial Revolution. The other prominent families in Malone were, like Andrews, tied to trade. His wife, Helen, came from the Barbour family of linen merchants. The Johnstons and MacNeices had been made rich by tea; the Andrewses' immediate neighbours, the Corrys, were in timber. The Stevensons ran Ireland's largest printing press and its second-largest glue factory. The McDonnells, father, son and grandson, were lawyers. Most of Maryville Park's grand homes were occupied by Andrews' similarly well-paid colleagues from Harland and Wolff. The former south Belfast home of Lord Deramore was now rented by the Wilsons, who had made their fortune in the property boom of the 1890s. By 1912, the aristocracy's influence in the day-to-day life of Belfast looked set to contract to matters of taste and prestige by proxy.

It was a trend in time that had worked in the Andrewses' favour. Tommy had learned to ride to hounds, becoming a skilled horseman and hunter, and he had played cricket at his local club – where his love of the sea earned him the nickname 'the Admiral' – but despite these activities neither he nor his ancestors had ever been part of the Ascendancy.[15] The family had been based in the village of Comber, 11 miles outside Belfast, since the seventeenth century, when another Thomas Andrews had established the local corn mill, which turned near their pretty house, Ardara, product of its profits. By the time Tommy Andrews was born at Ardara in 1873, the house and its lawns had acquired a mature grace, reached by an avenue lined with rhododendrons leading down to the gleaming waters of Strangford Lough.[16] The Andrewses' sustained upward trajectory over the course of the nineteenth century had been part of Britain's quiet revolution in local government, as the increasing complexity and size of modern bureaucracy saw power shift permanently from the hands of the landed classes to those of useful local businessmen, who became loyal politicians. Along with ownership of the mill and serving as Chairman of the Belfast and County Down Railway Company, Tommy's father was High Sheriff of the county, Chairman of the Down County Council and President of the Ulster Liberal Unionist Association.[17] His uncle, William Andrews, was a judge in the Irish High Court; both had been made Privy Councillors during the celebrations for Queen Victoria's Diamond Jubilee in 1897.[18] Tommy's maternal uncle, Lord Pirrie, remained Chairman of Harland and Wolff while being twice elected Lord Mayor of Belfast and elevated to the peerage for his philanthropy, and Edward VII had approved his induction into the Most Illustrious Order of St Patrick, a chivalric order of knighthood once reserved for sons of the Hibernian nobility.[19]

Tommy's car progressed from the quiet avenues of Malone to a city centre dominated by sprawling temples to commerce. During working hours, this part of Belfast was a hive of activity, described by *The Industries of Ireland* as a place of 'crowded rushing thoroughfares [where] we find the pulsing heart of a mighty commercial organisation, whose vitality is ever augmenting, and whose influence is already world-wide'.[20] No other town in Ireland had benefited so significantly and unambiguously from the successes of the British Empire. As Britannia's boundaries were set 'wider still and wider', Belfast had boomed and its growth seemed only to accelerate. Its population had risen seventeen-fold over the nineteenth century, with the biggest spurt occurring in the final twenty-five years, when it had doubled.[21] From a town that still, in 1800, had operated as a fiefdom of the marquesses of Donegall, Belfast had, by 1900, become one of the largest urban centres in the United Kingdom, dominated and defined by its industries.[22] Granted city status in 1888, a mere three years later Belfast had outstripped Dublin in terms of population and living standards.[23] To celebrate, Belfast's City Council, with the hungry and gaudy vitality of a newly enfranchised adolescent, approved the construction of a Grand Opera House, where audiences sat beneath a dome decorated with paintings of cheerfully obedient life throughout Queen Victoria's Indian dominions as goldleafed elephants gazed down from the front-facing corners of the proscenium arch.[24]

The Opera House had been part of a building mania that swept Belfast in the twenty years preceding the *Titanic*'s construction. The spires of the seven-year-old Protestant St Anne's Cathedral were visible as Tommy Andrews' car turned right from his former school to motor down Wellington Place and pass the new City Hall, a looming quadrangle in Portland stone, with ornamental gardens, stained-glass windows, turrets and a soaring copper dome. Completed two years after St Anne's, the City Hall had cost more than £350,000, a sum that had not been without controversy, especially for some of the city's more parsimonious Presbyterians. But there were many more, including Belfast's Chamber of Commerce, who had applauded the council's extravagance on the grounds that a powerhouse like Belfast, 'a great, wide, vigorous, prosperous, growing city', needed to be represented with appropriate splendour.[25]

As a younger man, Andrews had been there to witness the surge of capitalist confidence in Belfast's heartlands. The journey from Comber to the city was too long for the early-morning starts required by the shipyards, so after he had secured his apprenticeship aged sixteen Andrews became a boarder in the home of a middle-aged dressmaker and her sister on Wellington Place.[26] From there, he had witnessed the construction of the City Hall in the same years as Belfast inaugurated its new Customs House, a Water Office built to imitate an Italian Renaissance palazzo, and four banking headquarters.

30

Belfast's Donegall Square North. Robinson and Cleaver is on the left.

Directly in front of City Hall, between its imposing entrance and its wrought-iron gates, a statue of Queen Victoria stared unseeing towards the sandstone turrets of Robinson and Cleaver, one of the most expensive and prestigious department stores in the United Kingdom. Inside the 'Harrods of Ireland', 3,000 square feet of polished mirrors lined the shop's interiors, spread over four working floors, all connected by white marble staircases, at the top of which stood statues of Britannia.[27] Belfast's well-heeled customers flocked to Robinson and Cleaver, as did prosperous members of county Society, who were prepared to pay for goods shipped 'from every corner of His Majesty's Empire'. Reflected in Robinson and Cleaver's mirrors were busts of the store's most august clients, including the late Lady Lily Beresford and Hariot Hamilton-Temple-Blackwood, one of the bluest of the Ascendancy's blue bloods as Marchioness of Dufferin and Ava, who had used her time in India as wife of the British Viceroy to campaign for better medical care for Indian women and introduce Robinson and Cleaver's produce to the Maharajah of Cooch-Behar, who now also stood beside her in bust form, along with Queen Victoria's German grandson, Kaiser Wilhelm II, and his consort, Augusta Victoria of Schleswig-Holstein, who had temporarily overcome her pathological hatred of Britain to place repeated orders with the firm.[28]

Many of the craftsmen who worked on the construction and decoration of Robinson and Cleaver, and then on the interiors of City Hall, had also laboured on the ships designed by Tommy Andrews for Harland and Wolff.[29] His car passed the earliest rising of these workers as they travelled on foot, by bicycle or by tram over the bridges linking the city centre to the east, Queen's Island, and the shipyards. The majority of these dawn risers were on their way to work on Andrews' latest and grandest creation, the *Britannic*, whose hull had been laid amid the driving Belfast winter rains six months earlier.[30] As the journey of a million miles

End of the day: workers from Harland and Wolff with an under-construction *Titanic* in the background.

begins with a single step, the foundation of the largest ship built on British soil for the next two decades was already taking shape in her embryonic form. *Britannic* was not scheduled to grace the waters of Belfast Lough for another two years and her maiden voyage to New York was timetabled for the spring of 1915, at which point she would become the flagship of the White Star Line, completing the *Olympic*-class.[31]

The relationship with White Star Line was a source of pride to many in Belfast, which was hardly surprising considering the employment and revenue it generated, both of which were regularly cited in speeches by city officials and businessmen as among the many reasons for Belfast's superiority over other Irish cities, a conclusion with which Andrews wholeheartedly concurred.[32] Even in the very poorest parts of Belfast, all houses were single-occupancy units for families. Unlike Dublin or Cork, Belfast's leaders had worked hard to avoid the horrors associated with the special strain of poverty bred in tenements. Alongside the thick brogue of natives, Scottish and English accents could be heard in the jostling crowds that poured from the Protestant working-class neighbourhoods, their owners lured to Ulster by promises of affordable, good-quality housing through jobs at Harland and Wolff, in one of Belfast's 192 linen manufacturers or in its behemoth-like rope or tobacco factories.[33] Belfast had one of the lowest urban rates of infant mortality in the British Empire; with eighty-two state-funded schools, it also had the highest rate of literacy for any area in Ireland, and it implemented provisions for the care of the deaf and dumb long before most other towns.[34] As its two synagogues, built by the migrant-turned-merchant-turned-city mayor Sir Otto Jaffe, attested, Belfast was also so far the only section of Ireland to welcome and nurture a Jewish community.[35] In the eyes of the loyal, all this was abundant proof that Belfast had benefited from the spirit of dynamic, self-fulfilling conservatism that guided its civic authorities and indelibly separated it – in spirit and soon, God willing, in law – from the south.[36]

Five years earlier, this march of progress and prosperity had been interrupted by strikes that erupted in Harland and Wolff and then spread to the adjacent dockyards. For Protestants to protest was, by 1907, an event so remarkable it shocked even seasoned observers. The dock riots erupted as work on the first of the *Olympic*-class was due to commence. Tommy Andrews, while concerned about his timetable being disrupted, was also protective of the workers who turned his projects into a reality.[37] He was appalled by some of the conditions in the yard, particularly on the gantries, where men too often fell to their deaths, lost limbs in preventable accidents or were dismissed when they burned themselves badly on the rivets. His argument that paternalism must remedy the situation before socialism seized it had been ignored by his superiors and by his uncle Lord Pirrie, though he took no pleasure in being proved right.[38] At the height of the dispute, about 3,500 workers were on strike, most of them organised by the charismatic trade union leader James Larkin.[39] Initially, the demonstrations had looked for support from their cousins across the Irish Sea – the 1907 dock protesters voiced many left-wing sentiments, but they did so in the spirit of British social democracy, expressing implicit faith in British trade unionism, rather than Irish republicanism. However, cries of 'Go back to work!' and even 'Traitors!' grew louder after the strike's opponents, aided by most of Belfast's newspapers, painted the protest as furthering a crypto-nationalist agenda which could lethally weaken Ulster's economy, ultimately leaving it at the mercy of the Home Rule movement. These conspiracy politics were given regrettable credibility by the behaviour of certain Irish nationalist politicians, particularly west Belfast's Joseph Devlin, who actively attempted to turn the protests into displays of anti-British sentiment.[40] The strike collapsed and Larkin left Ireland, repulsed by the sight of people in working-class districts taking to their streets to celebrate the strike's defeat. The passing years did not lessen the contempt directed at those who had betrayed the side by striking. Weeks after the *Titanic*'s completion, 600 'rotten Prods' were driven from their jobs at Harland and Wolff by their own colleagues for daring to sympathise with left-wing movements that allegedly threatened the productivity of the yard and, through it, Ulster's unchecked evolution further and further away from the agrarian economies of the southern three provinces.[41] Incredibly, given its position as a major industrial city, there was no serious interest in trade unionism from Belfast for another twenty years. It was seen as somehow disloyal, destructive of the greater good. Nor were the 600 rotten Prods of 1912 expelled alone. At the same time, a sectarian pogrom in employment forced the shipyard's 2,400 Catholic employees to quit.[42]

Belfast's growth was as remarkable as it was undeniable, but to pretend that the fruits of that progress were evenly distributed is absurd. There were no laws in Edwardian Ulster that mandated discrimination against the province's Catholic minority, but equally there were none to stop it and this left Protestants free to hire those of their own preference who were, overwhelmingly, their co-religionists. Protestant jobs were often marginally better paid and nearly always significantly more secure than a northern Catholic's. As the Home Rule crisis accelerated, so too did Protestants' antipathy towards their Catholic neighbours, resulting in appalling events like the aforementioned expulsion of thousands from their jobs at Harland and Wolff. Belfast's reputation for anti-Catholic discrimination was so widespread that San Francisco's civic authorities refused to name one of their streets in the city's honour, despite a petition from Ulster-born immigrants.[43]

From the route Andrews' car took, just visible on the horizon was the spire of the Church of the Most Holy Redeemer, another product of the construction bonanza, but one which a man like Tommy would likely never see save from a distance. Located in west Belfast, Holy Redeemer was described at the time of its completion as 'a noble Church in the most Catholic quarter of a bitterly Protestant city'.[44] The two communities' decisions to congregate themselves into working-class neighbourhoods in the west and east was a prophylactic kind of social engineering, which, like all such things, had the potential to fail.

Religion gave a toxic, defining flavour to this political quarrel.

It was true, as many in the north of Ireland so strenuously insisted, that the troubles of their region were not caused by religion, in so far as no one ever rioted in defence of consubstantiation or tossed a brick over whether there are seven sacraments or two. But that is to miss the point, in that religious affiliation defined the boundaries of division. Although it was not universally true, overwhelmingly Protestants favoured retaining union with Britain, while Catholics hoped for the opposite. The years preceding the *Titanic's* construction had witnessed an intensification of this trend. A series of mid- and late nineteenth-century evangelical missions into the working-class areas of Belfast had deliberately solidified a view of Catholicism as backward, tyrannical and superstitious.[45] Just as they pointedly began to eschew the adjective 'Irish' in favour of 'northern Irish' or simply 'British', many of the more zealous Ulster Protestants began to redefine the etymology of the word 'Christian' to mean axiomatically, and solely, 'Protestant'. When a Catholic converted to Protestantism, the phrase 'He has become a Christian' was launched with depressing frequency. Meanwhile, the Gaelic Revival, a rejuvenated and sustained interest in the Celtic culture of Ireland, created a series of societies that defined being Irish in opposition to that which was British, right the way down to what sports should be played.[46] Some of these groups made an effort to reach out to Irish Protestants, others made an effort to do the exact opposite by helping 'to embed the myth that Ireland was a religiously and ethnically homogeneous society'.[47] This idea that to be Irish meant being Catholic played into the hands of unionists in the north who claimed that a compromise with Home Rule would be tantamount to collective suicide, particularly since unionists insisted that the moderate proposals for Home Rule would inevitably result in full independence. The nineteenth century's torturous preoccupation with race birthed apparently 'scientific' justification of each side's respective prejudice; the 'Two Nations Theory' insisted that there were insuperable racial, moral, cultural and intellectual differences between Irish Catholics and Protestants. Even academic publications like the *Ulster Journal of*

Archaeology promulgated the idea that Irish Protestants, particularly those in the north, were essentially Anglo-Saxon, while Irish Catholics were predominantly Celtic, giving both a distinct set of characteristics which made political union between them an absurdity. Protestants were hard-working, law abiding and stalwart; Catholics, as Celts, were lazy, dishonest and prone to drunkenness. Nationalists often accepted this racial hogwash, but rejigged it to class Hibernian Catholics as hospitable, artistic and passionate, while Protestants were dour, miserly and cruel.[48]

By the time the *Titanic* had been completed, the question of Irish independence, whether in part or in full, was the blood seeping beneath a closed door in Belfast. Fear of it preoccupied everybody, including Thomas Andrews. In his own political views, Andrews was described by family friends as 'an Imperialist, loving peace and consequently in favour of an unchallengeable Navy. He was a firm Unionist, being convinced that Home Rule would spell financial ruin to Ireland.' However, he was uneasy with the perceptible drift towards Irish politics being governed by 'passion rather than by means of reasoned argument'.[49] Many Ulster Protestants sincerely believed, and were proved correct in their suspicions, that Irish independence would constitute a major triumph for Catholicism in the island, with an Irish government choosing to grant special status to the Catholic faith.[50] Ironically, the north's fevered insistence on absenting itself from independence was the behaviour of Laius after the Oracle since Ulster's secession would mean the removal of the majority of Irish Protestants from a future Irish state, whatever the strength of that state's ties to Britain, thus enabling many of the events they claimed to fear. As a southern lawyer practising in Belfast tried in vain to warn his unionist friends, if the predominantly Protestant north separated from the predominantly Catholic south, 'you would have not one, but two, oppressed minorities'.[51]

Protestant fears of being outnumbered and thus overruled by their Catholic compatriots were lent unfortunate credence by Pope Pius X's issuing of the *Ne Temere* decree of 1907. The decree ruled that any marriage between a Catholic and a Protestant was invalid unless it was witnessed by a priest, implicit within that stipulation and often explicit in its application being a priest's refusal to officiate unless an undertaking was given that any children born to that couple were raised Catholic. *Ne Temere* seemed particularly unhelpful in the Irish context because it negated a papal rescript, issued by Pius VI in 1785, which had allowed for the legality of mixed marriages in Ireland, even if they were not solemnised before a Catholic priest.[52] Viewed as pastoral care by its defenders and lambasted by critics as prejudice by stealth, *Ne Temere* resulted four years later in the McCann case, when the marriage between a Belfast man called Alexander McCann, a Catholic, and his Protestant wife Agnes fell apart. A private sorrow became a public circus when McCann's local priest allegedly encouraged the separation and certainly helped Mr McCann gain sole custody of his children, despite the fact that the McCanns had married before the publication of *Ne Temere*. Agnes McCann went to her local minister, Reverend William Corkey, who had already regularly waxed apoplectic in his sermons about the 'foul' *Ne Temere* decree and saw in the McCann case the inevitable fruition of Pius X's edict.[53] As such things often did in Edwardian Belfast, the issue moved from the pulpit to the press to protests, the latter of which spread from Belfast to London, Dublin and Glasgow.[54] At one rally, the McCanns' marriage certificate was held up before the crowd, as a Presbyterian clergyman roared, 'I hold in my hand a marriage certificate bearing the seal of the British Empire, and recording the marriage of Alexander McCann and Agnes Jane Barclay. This certificate declares that according to the law of Britain these two are husband and wife. This Papal decree says their marriage is "no marriage at all". Which law is going to be supreme in Great Britain?'[55] The pursuit of the answer had already fractured lifelong friendships and it looked, in 1912, as if it had the potential to destabilise an empire.

*

As he boarded the *Titanic*, Andrews received a note from one of his colleagues in the engine rooms saying that there was a problem in one of the boiler rooms. Since this was their first full run, that was to be expected. A fire had started raging when some of the coal stored in one of the bunkers had caught fire and there was no chance of putting it out before the ship was due to start her tests. Should they postpone them? No, not if the fire in question could be contained. An extra squadron of stokers and firemen was deployed to monitor the troubled boiler room, the others were fired up and, without fanfare, the *Titanic* took to the ocean for the first time, beginning six hours of technical manoeuvres and trials.

The sea trial had originally been scheduled for the previous day, but was postponed in the face of high winds which would have made it impossible to vet properly the *Titanic*'s speed, turning and stopping capabilities in calm seas. The winds had since died down, allowing for the leviathan to undertake manoeuvres which saw her tested at a variety of speeds, ranging from 11 to 21½ knots, the latter being close to her expected full speed. She was also halted at 18 knots, coming to a stop three minutes and fifteen seconds later, at just three and a half times her own length which, for a ship of her size travelling at that velocity, was judged yet another encouraging indicator of her safety.[56] On board, Andrews meticulously watched each manoeuvre, joined by some of the colleagues who knew the ship almost as well as he did, chief among them Francis Carruthers, the British Board of Trade's on-site surveyor, and Edward Wilding, the yard's Senior Naval Architect. As the Board's eyes at Harland and Wolff, Carruthers had made hundreds of trips to the *Titanic* over the course of her construction. Wilding, like Carruthers an Englishman who had relocated to Ireland for his job, was not just a colleague but a friend, who had been a guest at Andrews' wedding in 1910. Together, the three men had watched *Titanic*'s 'vast shape slowly assuming the beauty and symmetry'. She was, thus far, the crowning glory of Andrews' and Wilding's careers, 'an evolution rather than a creation', according to one of their contemporaries, 'triumphant product of numberless experiments, a perfection embodying who knows what endeavour, from this a little, from that a little more, of human brain and hand and imagination'.[57]

The *Titanic* in Belfast Lough during her sea trials.

On her way back into Belfast, *Titanic* passed the seaside town of middle-class Holywood on one side of the Belfast Lough and working-class Carrickfergus on the other. In both towns, it was time for local chapters of the Orange Order to be out on the streets practising their music, hymns and configurations in preparation for the start of marching season, an annual series of parades held to commemorate the anniversary of King William III's victory over his Catholic uncle at the Battle of the Boyne in 1690 and the ensuing establishment of a legal Protestant ascendancy in Ireland for the next century. The Orange Order, founded as that ascendancy had cracked open in defeat at the end of the eighteenth century, organised itself somewhere between masonic and military lines, claiming nearly one-third of northern Protestant men as members.[58] Each was required, by oath, to 'love, uphold, and defend the Protestant religion, and sincerely desire and endeavour to propagate its doctrines and precepts [and] strenuously oppose and protest against the errors and doctrines of the Church of Rome; he should, by all lawful means, resist the ascendancy of that church'. A later extension to the formula, added in 1860, prohibited members from ever attending a Roman Catholic religious service.*[59]

Disruption, intimidation and violence at Order events had resulted in legislation curtailing its parades in the middle of the nineteenth century, and its reputation for disruptiveness had lasted, even among many Protestants, until the 1870s.[60] By 1912, however, its influence in the north of Ireland was enormous. Even politicians and clergymen who were indifferent or hostile to the Order's aims, like the MP Sir Edward Carson who privately compared it to an ancient Egyptian mummy, a preserved and desiccated corpse of something that had mattered long ago, 'all old bones and rotten rags', felt that they had to join if they stood any chance of appealing to working-class voters.[61] Andrews and his brothers came from a family with a long association with the Order who marched with its orange sashes around their necks, every year.[62] Andrews would be back in Belfast by the time of the Order's parades at the high point of marching season, 12 July.† Each lodge had their own banner, depicting a vividly rendered moment in Irish Protestant history – a particular favourite was an image of drowning settlers, usually women and children, piously clutching a cross as they were butchered, with the slogan 'My Faith Looks Up to Thee', victims of anti-Protestant massacres

---

* As of 2018, these injunctions remain in place.

† This is sometimes colloquially known as 'the Glorious Twelfth' in the north of Ireland, although the term originally applied to the start of the grouse-shooting season for the landed classes on 12 August. Whether the appropriation of this nickname for 12 July originated as a joke or a mistake is unclear.

carried out in 1641. On the reverse of all banners, long-dead King William forded the waters of the Boyne river atop his white steed, his sword already drawn for the children of the Glorious Revolution and their descendants, who would defend its legacy. As the Order's most famous song proclaimed:

> For those brave men who crossed the Boyne have not
>   fought or died in vain,
> Our Unity, Religion, Laws, and Freedom to maintain,
> If the call should come we'll follow the drum, and cross
>   that river once more
> That tomorrow's Ulsterman may wear the sash my
>   father wore!

By April 1912, the Order had helped rebrand Home Rule as 'Rome Rule'. On the day the *Titanic* conducted her trials, a letter to the *Belfast News-Letter* from a local headmaster opined, 'Under Rome Rule, there is no possible future for unionists, but despairing servitude or its preferable alternative – annihilation.'[63] Hysteria had trumped civic virtues. Rome was on the march. Upper-class Protestants had forgotten their fears of the radicalised workers and had instead given themselves over to the giddy novelty of Protestants straining together in common cause, as they had in days of old – or so the banners of the Orange Order told them. A paramilitary organisation, the Ulster Volunteer Force, was formed with thousands of recruits training on aristocratic estates as guns were smuggled into the island to arm them. One of Andrews' compatriots wrote with moist-eyed pride that it was 'indeed a wonderful time. Every county had its organisation; every down and district had its own corps. The young manhood of Ulster had enlisted and gone into training. Men of all ranks and occupations met together, in the evenings, for drill. This resulted in a great comradeship. Barriers of class were broken down or forgotten entirely. Protestant Ulster had become a fellowship.'[64]

The sound of these flute-serenaded battle cries followed the

Titanic in and out of her home waters. She was born in this heartland of an industrial miracle, with its rich and explosive confusion. We might look back now and think it unutterably bizarre that Ulster was prepared to immolate itself to prevent a quasi-independence that might never have matured to full secession if the north had chosen to be a part of it, but to the participants in this quarrel they were contenders in a Manichean struggle for the very soul of Ireland. In London, the new King was frantically trying to organise a preventative peace conference at Buckingham Palace, hopeful of exploiting unionism's atavistic attachment to the Crown to force its adherents back into line, and three days before the *Titanic* left Belfast the constitutional nationalist Sir John Redmond, leader of the Irish Parliamentary Party, gave a speech in Dublin, squarely aimed at his compatriots in the north – 'We have not one word of reproach or one word of bitter feeling,' he promised. 'We have one feeling in our hearts, and this is an earnest longing for the arrival of the day of reconciliation.'[65]

No one was listening. It was a man of action who flourished in April 1912, drowning out men of prudence. Unionism was now dominated by leaders like the lawyer Edward Carson, who had once served as the prosecuting counsel against Oscar Wilde, and the Andrewses' family friend, the ferociously uncompromising Sir James Craig. To make explicit how far they were prepared to go if Home Rule was extended to Ulster, the Ulster Volunteer Force, the Orange Order and the heads of the north's major industries were organising one of the largest mobilisations of political sentiment in Irish history, a covenant due to be paraded through the province to an enormous final rally outside Belfast City Hall.[66] Agents were sent out to help those who wanted to sign in the smaller towns and countryside. Tommy Andrews and the men in his family intended to sign this declaration:

being convinced in our consciences that Home Rule would be disastrous to the material well-being of Ulster as well as of the whole of Ireland, subversive to our civil and religious freedom, destructive of our citizenship, and perilous to the unity of the Empire, we, whose names are underwritten, men of Ulster, loyal subjects of His Gracious Majesty King George V., humbly relying on God whom our fathers in days of stress and trial confidently trusted, do hereby pledge ourselves in solemn Covenant, throughout this our time of threatened calamity, to stand by one another in defending, for ourselves and our children, our cherished position of equal citizenship in the United Kingdom, and in using all means which may be found necessary to defeat the present conspiracy to set a Home Rule Parliament in Ireland. And in the event of such a Parliament being forced upon us, we further solemnly and mutually pledge ourselves to refuse to recognise its authority. In sure confidence that God will defend the right . . . [67]

Partly from despair and frustration that unionism would never willingly give so much as an inch in compromise and partly in tune with the mounting radicalisation of nationalist politics across Europe, Irish nationalism was evolving and splitting into republicanism, itself increasingly shaped by die-hards like Pádraig Pearse. Moderation had become a tarnished virtue, a tired or even pathetic concept. Although he begged his followers to 'restrain the hotheads', Edward Carson simultaneously urged them to 'prepare for the worst and hope for the best. For God and Ulster! God Save the King!'[68] On the other side of the soon actualised barricades, Pearse urged his followers to hope for civil war, to pray for rebellion and for all of British Ireland to vanish in flames regardless of the human cost, because 'Blood is a cleansing and sanctifying thing, and the nation that regards it as the final horror has lost its manhood.'[69] From their respective demagogues, all sides in Ireland heard the sibyl cry of their pasts, promising them the future glory of a war without ambiguity. Protestant and Catholic, loyalist and nationalist, Ireland would willingly wrestle itself off a cliff edge, plunging the entire island into the unknown.

The head of the police service, the Royal Irish Constabulary, told the Chief Secretary of Ireland, 'I am convinced that there will be serious loss of life and wholesale destruction of property in Belfast on the passing of the Home Rule bill.'[70]

When he arrived back in Belfast that night, after the sea trials, Andrews sent a note to his wife in Malone. Everything had gone well; there were one or two problems, which would no doubt be fixed by the time the ship reached Southampton three days later. Francis Carruthers had been duly satisfied by Titanic's performance and he had granted her the Board of Trade's standard twelve-month certificate as a passenger ship.[71] Andrews and Wilding spent the night on board, to prepare for the early-morning departure to England. The Union Jack fluttered from one of the Titanic's flagpoles as the sun set around the slumbering leviathan with the fire burning unchecked within her interiors.

3

Southampton

[The *Titanic*] was so much larger than one even expected; she looked so solidly constructed, as one knew she must be, and her interior arrangements and appointments were so palatial that one forgot now and then that she was a ship at all. She seemed to be a spacious regal home of princes.

Ernest Townley, interview given to the
Daily Express (16 April 1912)

ONE WEEK AFTER HER MIDNIGHT ARRIVAL AT Southampton, the *Titanic*'s main mast ran the company's red flag with its eponymous white star, fluttering over final preparations for her first commercial voyage.[1] The day of departure, Wednesday 10 April, was overcast in the south of England, with the sun occasionally appearing from behind the scudding clouds to provide a mild temperature of about 9 degrees centigrade as the crew, numbering about 900, were divided into three groups for the muster. Firemen, seamen and those assigned to care for the soon-to-board passengers went through their final medical checks and a head count, carried out under the watchful eye of another representative of the Board of Trade, who then proceeded to observe as two of the ship's twenty lifeboats were lowered down the side with eight trained crew wearing their lifejackets. Typically, this inspection would involve the tested lifeboats unfurling their sails, but an uncooperative breeze put pay to that, so the white-painted wooden craft were successfully raised back on to deck and into their davits, with their virgin sails left unfurled. Vast quantities of luggage were being manoeuvred on board. Pieces bound for the first-class quarters bore White Star-provided labels with variants of 'CABIN' or 'STATEROOM', to indicate that they should be taken to the passenger's bedroom; 'BAGGAGE ROOM' or 'WANTED', if they were not to go immediately to their accommodation but contained items which might be required later in the voyage, a helpful utilisation of space given the upper classes' minimum requirement of three outfit changes daily; and 'NOT WANTED', if the pieces were to go into the hold until disembarking.[2]

Thomas Andrews had arrived on board half an hour or so after dawn that morning, checking out from his interim accommodation at the nearby South-Western Hotel, where he had stayed in the week since leaving Belfast.[3] The days in between had been spent overseeing the last touches to the *Titanic*'s accommodation, which produced the kind of productive mania at which Andrews excelled. The ship's schedule had already been altered, and then squeezed, by her elder sister's accident in the Southampton waters a few months earlier when, moments after departure, the *Olympic* had collided with the British warship *Hawke*.[4] Mercifully, there had been no serious injuries, but a trip to Belfast for repairs was required, with the result that construction on the *Titanic* temporarily halted for a few days, tightening the preparation time allowed for the maiden voyage. Andrews himself did not doubt that 'the ship will clean up all right before sailing on Wednesday', but with the door hinges and paint still being applied to the *Titanic*'s Parisian-style café on Wednesday morning, White Star had ordered in vast quantities of fresh flowers which went straight into *Titanic*'s cold storage to be brought out over the course of the voyage to disguise any lingering smell of varnish.[5] Fixtures in some of the second-class lavatories needed to be attached, furniture bought from firms in England had to be delivered, the furniture in the Café Parisian still was not the right shade of green, and the pebbledashing in two of First Class's most expensive private suites was too dark.[6] Andrews had overseen everything he could. His secretary, Thompson Hamilton, who had joined him from Belfast for the week, noticed, 'He would himself put in their place such things as racks, tables, chairs, berth ladders, electric fans, saying that except he saw everything right he could not be satisfied.'[7] Meanwhile, a hose was working away on the contained fire in one of Boiler Room 5's coal bunkers, with the source expected to be extinguished in the next few days.[8] By the evening of the 9th, everything of note had apparently been taken care of and Andrews could write to his wife, 'The *Titanic* is now about complete and will I think do the old Firm credit to-morrow when we sail.'[9]

With their tasks accomplished, Andrews said a temporary farewell to colleagues, like Edward Wilding, whose work on *Titanic* ended in Southampton, and his secretary, Thompson Hamilton, who was travelling back to Belfast to handle any correspondence during Andrews' absence. 'Remember now,' Andrews told Hamilton, with that second word ubiquitous to an Ulster dialect, 'and keep Mrs Andrews informed of any news of the vessel.'[10] From the deck, Andrews could see other ships, moored together in greater numbers than usual. The British Miners' Federation had voted to end a six-week strike only four days earlier and the impact on an industry as dependent on coal as shipping had been temporarily significant – many smaller liners had their voyages rescheduled to facilitate coal being reallocated for the on-time departures of the leviathans.[11] The red-, white- and blue-capped funnels of the American Line's *St Louis*, *Philadelphia* and *New York* were moored next to White Star's *Majestic* and *Oceanic*. After twenty-two years at sea, the *Majestic* had been withdrawn from regular service and designated a reserve ship, while the *Philadelphia* and *New York* were about to have their first-class quarters removed entirely for an increase of second- and third-class, as the drift of first-class clientele to larger, more modern ships had rendered them superfluous.[12] For Andrews, the most significant of the slumbering ships in the harbour was White Star's former flagship, the *Oceanic*, berthed alongside the *New York*. After working his way up from his post-school apprenticeship at Harland and Wolff, Andrews had first been given charge of a design for the White Star Line in the late 1890s, helping to produce the *Oceanic*, praised then and later as a 'ship of outstanding elegance both inside and out'.[13] The *Oceanic* was still in service in April 1912, but shipbuilding's technological strides in the thirteen years since her debut had left that pretty ship far behind; the *Titanic* was nearly three times heavier than Andrews' first ship, with room for almost twice as many passengers and crew.

Far below, the process of boarding the third-class passengers began shortly after the crew's muster was completed. Since many in Third Class travelled as emigrating families, there were usually more children, necessitating a longer boarding process, combined with the delay-inducing medical inspections required by American immigration authorities.[14] Those on the dock that day were a few hundred of the 23,000 immigrants who would sail on White Star ships to America over the course of 1912–13.[15] Although it was, and is, often used to describe this collective, the word 'steerage' did not apply to those in *Titanic*'s Third Class. The noun sprang from the earlier days of mass migration to the United States and it could still in 1912 apply to the cheaper class of accommodation offered by other, often less prestigious travel companies, but there was an appreciable difference. Hamburg-Amerika's soon to be launched *Imperator* would provide four classes of travel, delineating Third and Steerage as two different sections of the ship.[16] To qualify as steerage, there had to be communal dormitories, something that the *Titanic* did not offer. Every third-class passenger was in a cabin, albeit with bunk beds and, if travelling on their own, typically shared with others of their own gender. The White Star Line had a reputation for offering the best third-class accommodation then available, with the result that tickets on the *Titanic* or the *Olympic* could cost as much as Second Class on other liners.[17]

Thus a contemporary travel guide could confidently assert that the White Star Line carried 'a better class of emigrant'.[18]

Nonetheless, following a cholera epidemic among immigrants at the German port of Hamburg twenty years earlier, the United States had introduced firm policies on who could be admitted at Ellis Island.[19] This meant that all third-class passengers had to undergo medical examinations at embarkation and that there could be no contact between them and the two more expensive classes, because if there was, those passengers would also have to be inspected before leaving the ship in New York.[20] For first- and second-class passengers this meant that barring any glances from their promenade decks down to the outdoor areas at the stern for Third Class, boarding was likely to be the only time they had a sustained opportunity to see third-class passengers. Even leaving aside the quarantine issues set by the American government, contemporary travel guides insisted that it was the height of bad manners for a first-class passenger to play the tourist by asking to see the third-class public rooms during the voyage: 'it cannot be urged too strongly that it is a gross breach of the etiquette of the sea life, and a shocking exhibition of bad manners and low inquisitiveness, for passengers to visit unasked the quarters of an inferior class . . . the third-class passengers would be within their rights in objecting to their presence . . . they expect to have the privileges and privacy of their quarters respected also.'[21]

Unlike passengers who could afford to cross the ocean annually or travel far and wide for their holidays, a third-class ticket was usually a one-way experience, a fact which produced particularly heartrending scenes on the dock. While viewing the boarding process of another of the 'floating palaces' in 1912, the contemporary travel writer R. A. Fletcher asked one of the crew for the reasons behind a much longer embarkation window for Third Class, which the latter explained had something to do with how often immigrants ran back across the gangplank to embrace loved ones who had come to wave them off. 'It's a nuisance, you know,' the crew member remarked, when you want to be off, but after all its [sic] human nature and you can't blame them. If I were a woman I'd be as bad myself. You see, it comes harder to a married woman to pull up stakes and to make a new home in a new country than it does to a man or children. A man makes a new home and the children grow up in new surroundings and become accustomed to them; but God help most of the mothers. They go for the sake of husbands and children, but they leave their hearts behind them, in another sense, as often as not.[22]

For the Countess of Rothes, the purpose of her transatlantic jaunt was also for the sake of her husband, albeit in happier and less permanent circumstances. The Earl had been in the United States since February, when he had sailed from Liverpool on the *Lusitania*, to go on a fact-finding mission, comparing the efficiency of the privately operated American telegraph system with that of its publicly owned British equivalent. After his work was finished, Norman took the opportunity to tour and he had invited Noëlle to join him in the United States to celebrate their twelfth wedding anniversary with a visit that would culminate with a stay in a rented cottage on an orange grove in Pasadena, California, one of the properties Norman was allegedly interested in purchasing.[23]

Trading the inconsistent loveliness of an English spring for the beautiful monotony of California's had not presented Lady Rothes with an easy task when it came to packing. She had been piecing together a new wardrobe for her American sojourn up until the day before she left London, including a last-minute dash to Zyrot et Cie, a milliner's near her townhouse on Hanover Square, where she picked out some new hats and motoring veils.[24] Most of those would go into one of the two steamer trunks that Noëlle would not need during the voyage, slumbering in the cavernous chill of the hold until they reached Manhattan. London was wrapped in its own brand of unseasonable frigidity with the result that most of Noëlle's fellow passengers had boarded the train that morning wearing top coats and hats.[25]

Noëlle was boarding *en famille* in a travelling cabal held together by affection, vaguely complementing itineraries and curiosity about the *Titanic*. Her companion as far as New York was her husband's cousin Gladys, a vivacious and unmarried fixture of the London social scene who had decided to keep Noëlle company for the voyage and visit her brother, Charles Cherry, an aspiring theatre actor who had moved to New York two years earlier. Gladys and Noëlle were friends and, following the convention of most families at the time, referred to each other as 'my cousin' after Noëlle and Norman's marriage. They were joined by Noëlle's parents, Thomas and Clementina Dyer-Edwardes. Thomas had taken long voyages before – indeed, arguably one of the longest possible when he had sailed from England to Australia in the 1860s to spend ten years increasing the family's fortune – but this trip on the *Titanic* was not to add to the roster of his far-flung travels. He and Clementina were only going as far as the *Titanic*'s first port of call, the town of Cherbourg in north-western France. From there, they would travel to Château de Rétival, their eighteenth-century house in Normandy, which they were opening up for the summer. Since they usually made the first annual trip to expel Rétival's dust covers in spring, the Dyer-Edwardeses had decided to combine their cross-Channel trip with Noëlle's departure for America. It would be a chance to wish their only child Godspeed before she was gone for several months, with the added attraction of travelling, however briefly, on the inaugural voyage of the world's largest liner. There seems to have been a slight delay with the boat train from Waterloo, which did not reach Southampton until about 11.30, thirty minutes before the ship's scheduled departure.[26]

When the train came to a halt on tracks running parallel to the *Titanic*'s towering hull, the Countess's party stepped out into a large shed, nearly 700 feet in length, where a small industrious army of porters were dealing with the last of the ship's cargo and luggage.[27] Noëlle's steamer trunks were added to their task as she, her parents, Gladys and Noëlle's lady's maid, Cissy Maioni, crossed under the skylights and up the stairs to an enclosed balcony, where they presented their tickets.[28] They were ushered over the 28 feet of the gangplank from which, turning right, they could see the second-class walkway, on the same level but 500 or so feet aft, and one of the third-class gangways, three decks below.

The view from the first-class gangplank on departure day. Those used by Second (above) and Third Class (below) can be seen in the distance.

They arrived to see crew members waiting for them in a white-panelled vestibule with a black-and-white-patterned floor, which had such a gleaming finish that some passengers initially mistook it for marble.[29] Several of the *Titanic's* officers were required to be on meet-and-greet duty for the first-class passengers, a piece of etiquette that had survived in transmogrified form from the days of sail when the owners of ships had often escorted prominent passengers on board themselves.[30] However, it was the stewards and stewardesses, not the officers, who offered practical help by escorting the passengers to their rooms. Since they were only going as far as France, Noëlle's parents had a ticket which entitled them to lunch and afternoon tea, but no cabin. Noëlle herself and Gladys were to spend six or seven nights as roommates in cabin C-37.[31]

The *Titanic*'s decks were labelled with alphabetical efficiency. Unlike many other liners, where decks were often given a name indicating their purpose, like 'Shelter', 'Saloon' or 'Upper', the *Titanic*'s top deck, which was open to the elements and housed her lifeboats, was called the 'Boat Deck', but after that her levels were ranked in consecutive descent from A- through to G-Deck, the final point accessible to passengers, below which were the boiler and engine rooms.[32] A common misconception about the allocation of space for the respective traveller classes was that the liners' architecture directly replicated the idea of social hierarchy, with First Class occupying the top decks and Third spread over the lowest. In reality, the most stable parts of a liner are amidships, since they are the least prone to pitching during inclement weather. On *Titanic*, First and Second Class were located amidships, running downward through the ship and linked for the crew by various corridors. Both classes had access to the air on the Boat Deck, with a low dividing rail separating Second Class's aft promenade from First's more expansive, forward-facing space. First-class cabins, generally referred to by the slightly grander adjective of 'stateroom', ran from A- to E-Deck, while the public rooms were dotted around from the Gymnasium, through a door off the Boat Deck, to the Swimming Pool, Racquet Court and Turkish Baths down on F-Deck. The public rooms generally lay on either side of the two sets of staircases, one forward and one aft, running through every level of first-class accommodation. The space between the staircases was connected by the stateroom corridors.

Every passenger with a first-class ticket had access to the same amenities and food included in the tariff, but there were significant gradations of luxury and corresponding cost when it came to the staterooms. The most expensive single class of ticket on the *Titanic*, one of the two suites with their own private verandahs, were located on B-Deck, and it was on B- and C-Deck that the ship's most lavish accommodation was located. The only noticeable difference between the two decks' staterooms was their windows – B-Deck was the lowest level of the *Titanic*'s white-painted superstructure, enabling her cabins and suites to offer rectangular windows. Immediately below and also painted white, C-Deck was the highest deck in the *Titanic*'s otherwise black hull; all cabin windows in the hull were the more traditional nautical portholes.

At Southampton, the Countess of Rothes and the other first-class travellers boarded straight on to B-Deck and, having confirmed their cabin numbers, were escorted by stewards from the vestibule, immediately turning right. They would then either have walked down the stairs or, less probably given how short the distance was, taken one of the three lifts to C-Deck. It was possible for first-class passengers travelling with their own serv-ants, as Noëlle was with Cissy Maioni, to book them into cabins in Second Class, but Noëlle had evidently decided that that was rather mean-spirited, with the result that Cissy was to occupy a first-class cabin of her own, two levels below, on E-Deck.[33]

Between the train and the gangplank, the Countess had been asked for a comment by the English correspondent of a foreign gossip column, who wanted to know what the doyenne of the beau monde felt about 'leaving London Society for a California fruit farm'. With her imperturbable no-nonsense cheer, the Countess had smiled back, 'I am full of joyful expectation.'[34] Unfortunately, joyful expectation experienced its first stutter when the door to C-37 was opened for them. The *Titanic*'s surviving deck plans give several possible reasons for Noëlle's request to be moved – the first being C-37's location so close to the stairwell and lifts. It was located in the corridor immediately leading off from them, which may have made Noëlle worry unnecessarily about possible noise and disturbance. There was also the issue of C-37's size, which offered comfortable if standard first-class accommodation, different to the more splendid options profiled in the White Star Line's advertising.[35] It has been suggested that Lady Rothes' parents decided to treat their daughter and her companion to an upgrade; it has also been suggested that the room was unsuitable for the Countess. The two explanations are not wholly contradictory. The Purser's Office was on the same deck and requests to be moved were not uncommon. An admiring captain with the Cunard Line thought that pursers and their staff on board the great liners 'do most of the clerical work of this floating city; the purser's office is a kind of "enquire within" bureau for passengers; it is a reception office; it is the place where complaints are ventilated, and where official oil is poured on the sometimes troubled waters that are bound to occur in a ship that carries, as she often does, thirty different nationalities – including people of widely different tastes, customs, temperaments and requirements'.[36] Upon hearing that the request for a new room concerned Lady Rothes, Purser McElroy seems to have moved with breakneck speed.

They were escorted past the staircase, the Purser's Office and its Enquiry Desk, which functioned much like the reception of a modern hotel, and into long white-panelled corridors leading to stateroom C-77. It was a particularly convenient relocation for Cissy, since her employer's new room was opposite the small but comfortable special dining room set aside for maids, valets and other servants travelling with their employers.[37] Lady Rothes was, by European standards, the highest-ranking person on the ship, a silken-voiced embodiment of the empire of manners which

The parlour in the Strauses' suite was identical on the *Titanic* and the *Olympic*. The desk where Ida wrote her letter to Lilian Burbidge can be seen on the far left.

the British aristocracy still commanded. With her caste's social influence still tangible, Noëlle was not an anachronism on the *Titanic*, but she was an anomaly in being the only member of the nobility on board.[38] An old world silently passed a new one as the Countess's party walked among the self-made millionaires and plutocrats who occupied most of the other C-Deck staterooms.

Ten doors up from the Countess's new stateroom, sixty-three-year-old Ida Straus, travelling with her husband Isidor, a former Democratic Senator for New York and co-owner of Macy's department store, was thrilled with her quarters. The Strauses had taken a parlour suite, which gave them a bedroom, a drawing room, a bathroom and ample wardrobe space. The layout of their rooms, C-55 and C-57, was almost identical to the same suite on the *Olympic*, from which several photographs fortunately survive showing in detail the parlour and bedroom occupied by Ida Straus and her husband.*[39] The drawing room was decorated in an Edwardian take on the Regency era, with three-armed candelabra mounted throughout on the room's mahogany walls, flecked with interweaving gold leaf. A tapestry of a pastoral scene, vaguely in the style of Fragonard, was displayed between two curtain-draped portholes and above the fireplace with its electric heater. On a table in the centre of the room, a large bouquet of flowers had been waiting for Ida when she arrived, a gift from Lilian Burbidge, wife of Richard Burbidge, Managing Director of Harrods. The two couples had spent some time together during the Strauses' recent stay in London, during which the Burbidges had taken them to theatre and supper, favours which Ida planned to repay when the British couple visited New York the following summer.

---

* The counterpart of their suite on the *Olympic* was later offered to the future King Edward VIII when he returned on board from his visit to the United States in 1924. He asked to be moved to another room, because it was 'too pretty for me'. The rooms were then assigned to the Prince's Groom-in-Waiting, Brigadier-General Gerald Trotter. Why the Prince felt this way is unclear, given that his famous future home in the Bois de Boulogne did not exactly reek of the spirit of Sparta.

The Atlantic Ocean had framed Ida and Isidor Straus's life together. Both were first-generation Americans, emigrating to the United States as children – in Isidor's case from the kingdom of Bavaria and in Ida's from the grand duchy of Hesse-Darmstadt, two decades before both territories were incorporated with varying degrees of unwillingness into a unified Imperial Germany. Transatlantic travel then had been fraught with possible dangers and certain discomfort, but it had already begun its meteoric sequences of improvement when the couple first met in New York in the 1860s, at a time when their families were on opposite sides of the American Civil War and Isidor, who had then lived in Georgia, was preparing to sail back to Europe to work as a blockade runner for the Confederacy. He had called on old friends of his family in New York, including the young Ida Blun's parents, before booking passage to England, while maintaining the pretence of being a Northerner under which he had arrived. By the time they met again and fell in love, the Confederacy as a political actuality had been wiped from the face of the earth and the Strauses had emigrated once more, this time trading Georgia for New York. Since then, there had been numerous trips across the Atlantic for the couple, initially because of Isidor's desire to remain in touch with his German relatives and to visit London, a city he had fallen in love with during his time there in the 1860s.[40] Ida preferred Paris, partly thanks to her love of shopping; her husband tolerated rather than enjoyed their stays there.[41]

Isidor remained fascinated by liners and their technology, so the couple made their way on deck for the send-off, stopping at the end of their corridor to chat with a stewardess, who had once attended to them on the *Olympic* and thought them 'a delightful old couple – old in years and young in character – whom we were always happy to see join us'.[42] When they reached the deck, they fell into conversation with their friend Colonel Archibald Gracie IV, who like Isidor came from Confederate stock – his father, General Archibald Gracie III, had been killed by a Union shell at the Siege of Petersburg in 1864.[43] Knowing that mail would be taken off the ship at Cherbourg in a few hours' time, Ida wanted to make sure she sent a prompt thank-you note to Lilian Burbidge for the flowers and, since the Strauses had been spending the winters in Europe away from their New York home every year since 1899, the anchors-away moment no longer held much of a thrill for Ida.[44] While Isidor stayed up top with Gracie, Ida, by 1912 plump and elegant with a cloud of dark hair beginning to show streaks of grey, with a prominent flesh-coloured mole on the lower left-hand side of her face and a warm smile which many people considered her best feature, made her way back to their suite, sitting at its little escritoire beneath one of the portholes, while her new maid, Ellen Bird, and Isidor's English valet, John Farthing, began the long process of unpacking.[45] Ida was a particularly hands-on housewife, who was almost alone among the wealthy women of Manhattan in never having hired a housekeeper; Isidor was constantly urging her to take on fewer responsibilities.[46] It had been a series of nervous complaints and then problems with Ida's heart, flaring up with regularity over the previous three years, that had turned their annual migration to the French Riviera into something approaching a necessity. When they could not spend too much time away from America, Ida had gone to relax at their beach house in New Jersey and once to California.[47] That year, they had left New York in January aboard the Cunard Line's *Caronia*, which plied the route from Manhattan to the Mediterranean, and spent most of their holiday at a quiet hotel in Cannes, which Ida in a letter home to her married daughter, Minnie, had described as 'a lovely spot for old people'.[48] But Ida had made something of a poor swap, since New York had one of the mildest winters that anyone could remember, while the Riviera was pelted by rain for most of February and March.*

---

* There remains some confusion about the Strauses' itinerary that spring, with several modern accounts stating that they also visited Jerusalem and Palestine. However, it was Ida's brother-in-law, Nathan Straus, who made the trip to Jerusalem in 1912, with his wife, Lina. En route, they stopped to spend several days with Ida

From five decks beneath her, the *Titanic*'s engines roared to life, producing a quiet hum beneath Ida's feet and in the walls around her. Many of the passengers would remark later that the ship was so well designed that they were barely aware of the vibrations, although they certainly noticed them when they stopped, since the engines muffled much of the noise flowing between the relatively thin walls of the cabins.[49] The Strauses' rooms, like the Countess's, were on the *Titanic*'s starboard side, facing away from the pier, but the noise would have given Ida a general idea of what was going on. Far above her, the scream of the ship's whistles and the cheers of the crowd announced that it was time for the *Titanic* to make her midday departure, only a few minutes late.[50] Then, a silence fell as the engines cut out and the *Titanic* floated adrift in the River Test, until the reassuring growls of the machinery eventually returned and the journey continued.

An explanation for this arrived when her husband returned. Sixty-seven years old, bald, with a well-trimmed white beard and occasional pain in his legs, Isidor told Ida that, as the *Titanic* set

This photograph caught from the pier shows just how close the *New York* came to colliding with the *Titanic*.

---

and Isidor, but there was no time for the latter to join them as they travelled further east. They were still in Cannes when Ida and Isidor's youngest daughter, Vivian Scheftel, briefly joined them with her husband and children.

off, the suction from her three enormous propellers had caused the *New York* to break free from her moorings and drift towards her. A quarter of a century earlier, Isidor had sailed on the *New York*'s maiden voyage from Liverpool, when she had been considered 'the last word in shipbuilding'.[51] In a harbour overcrowded by ships laid up by the miners' strike, the coils of the ropes mooring the *New York* had snapped with a noise like gunfire, whipping back on to the docks to lacerate a woman in the crowd who had to be rushed away to receive medical attention. For one horrible moment, it looked as if there would be a repetition of the *Olympic*'s accident the previous year, with a smaller ship sucked into a voyage-cancelling collision.[52] The *Titanic*'s Captain had moved quickly to halt the churning of the propellers, giving those in the guiding tugboats time to manoeuvre the *New York* back to safety.[53]

The *Titanic*'s schedule had been dented before she even left her home waters, but she was intact. Later, many chose to re-interpret the near miss as an omen, such as the large flock of seagulls that Cissy Maioni noticed following the *Titanic* overhead as the ship resumed her journey.[54] Ida, however, turned back to her letter to Lilian Burbidge, as the waters of the Test became the Solent and then the Channel:

On Board R.M.S. Titanic
Wednesday

Dear Mrs Burbidge,

You cannot imagine how pleased I was to find your exquisite basket of flowers in our sitting-room on the steamer. The roses and carnations are all so beautiful in color and as fresh as though they had just been cut. Thank you so much for your sweet attention which we both appreciate very much.

But what a ship! So huge and so magnificently appointed. Our rooms are furnished in the best of taste and most luxuriously and they are really rooms not cabins. But size seems to bring its troubles – Mr. Straus, who was on deck when the start was made, said that at one time it stroked painfully near to the repetition of the Olympian's [*sic*] experience on her first trip out of the harbor, but the danger was soon averted and we are now well on to our course across the channel to Cherbourg.

Again thanking you and Mr. Burbidge for your lovely attention and good wishes and in the pleasant anticipation of seeing you with us next summer. I am with cordial greetings in which Mr. Straus heartily joins,

Very sincerely yours,

Ida R. Straus[55]

4

A Contest of Sea Giants

To the battle of Transatlantic passenger service, the *Titanic* adds a
new and important factor, of value to the aristocracy and the plutocracy attracted from East to West and West to East. With the
Mauretania and the *Lusitania* of the Cunard, the *Olympic* and *Titanic*
of the White Star, the *Imperator* and *Kronprinzessin Cecilie* of the
Hamburg-Amerika, in the fight during the coming season, there will
be a scent of battle all the way from New York to the shores of this
country – a contest of sea giants in which the *Titanic* will doubtless
take high honours.

The Standard (5 April 1912)

PASSENGERS WAITING TO BOARD THE *TITANIC* AT
Cherbourg, the first of two European ports of call after
Southampton, were told of the delay that had arisen as a
result of the *New York* incident by Nicholas Martin, Manager of
the White Star Line's main French office, who had accompanied
the firm's boat train from Paris earlier that day.[1] He broke the
news in an uncomfortably pitching tender, the *Nomadic*, built in
Belfast two years earlier and boasting several decorative features
like bronze grilles on the doors as aesthetic anticipations to the
interiors of her destinations – either the *Olympic* or *Titanic*, both

too large to dock in Cherbourg's harbour. First- and second-class passengers were ferried to the waiting liners on the *Nomadic*; Third Class and mail were brought out by her partner, the *Traffic*.[2] Embarkation had been tentatively rescheduled by about ninety minutes for about half-past five at which time, despite the fact that the *Titanic* had still not actually come into view, the *Nomadic's* skipper moved her off from the little quay and out into the break-water, where it unhappily became clear that the lovely spring weather had obscured a strong breeze and equally lively currents. Many of the *Nomadic's* 172 passengers became nauseous, either from the pitch or from the enforced cosiness of the crowded boat.[3] Several false sightings of the *Titanic* raised hopes whose disappointment nurtured irritation. Those with better sea legs distracted themselves with a 'slight and passing interest in a fishing boat – [then] more waiting'.[4]

Grouped together in the *Nomadic's* stultifying saloon were names that had already earned the *Titanic's* crossing a press-created nickname of 'the Millionaire's Special' – Astors on the final stretch of their honeymoon, a Guggenheim ending his winter on the Riviera, a presidential adviser emerging from a recuperative stay in Rome and a celebrated art historian returning to fractious negotiations about the design of the proposed Washington DC memorial to President Lincoln. By a considerable margin, Americans constituted the majority of the *Titanic's* first-class ticket holders and the reason for this lay in the approaching summer Season. The East Coast upper class's Season in the United States fell at about the same time as that of their British counterparts, but with far greater precision, lasting from Memorial Day, then commemorated on 30 May, until Labor Day on the first Monday in September, at which point wearing white slipped from a proc-lamation of belonging to an advertisement of bad taste. Well serviced by railways from the Paris terminals, Cherbourg proved a convenient point of embarkation for those who had spent their winters in the south of France or, equally popular with travelling Americans, Italy.

John Thayer, Second Vice-President of the
Pennsylvania Railroad Company.

Heavy jawed, thickly but tidily mustachioed and eleven days
short of his fiftieth birthday, John Borland Thayer Sr, Second
Vice-President of the Pennsylvania Railroad, was, like many on
the *Nomadic* that afternoon, a beneficiary of, and participant in,
perhaps the greatest sustained economic expansion in recorded
history. The assets of the most fantastically beneficed courtier at
Versailles in the middle of the eighteenth century would have
paled in comparison to the wealth of the American industrialists
created in the nineteenth. The first few generations of American
millionaires had led the surge that took their country from the
British Empire's most rebellious child to become its competitor
and, in the years after 1912, its successor – in 1800, American
factories produced just one-sixth the amount churned out in Great
Britain; by the time the *Titanic* sailed, they were making 230 per
cent more, accounting for 32 per cent of global industrial production, compared to 14 per cent from the admittedly far smaller
Britain.[5] This growth had been sustained, at least initially, by an
appalling humanitarian cost to America's labourers – 'the cost of
lives snuffed out, of energies overtaxed and broken, the fearful

physical and spiritual cost to the men and women and children upon whom the dead weight and burden of it all has fallen piti-lessly', in the words of Woodrow Wilson, the soon to be Democratic nominee for the US presidency.[6] When the heir to the Austrian throne, the Archduke Franz Ferdinand, visited the United States in 1893 he had praised the Great Republic's federalist structure but expressed horror at the treatment of the country's workers, who, he believed, endured conditions far worse than anything seen in the more technically unequal kingdoms and empires of Europe. It was after his stay in New York that Franz Ferdinand wrote home that in America, it seemed to him, 'For the working class, freedom means freedom to starve.'[7] The Archduke's depressing conclusions were unknowingly corroborated by one of his uncle's former subjects, an immigrant to New York called Faustina Wiśniewska, who wrote home to her parents in the same year to tell them that 'here they exploit the people as they did the Jews in Pharaoh's time', and by several prominent American industrialists, like bosses at the Carnegie steel conglomerate who issued advice to avoid placing orders with foreign factories, not for any reasons of national loyalty, but because foreigners, particu-larly the British, were 'great sticklers for high wages, small production, and strikes'.[8]

By the turn of the century, many of the children and grandchil-dren of the plutocratic pioneers had sought to beautify and perhaps exorcise their legacy with a gilding borrowed from the once rejected hierarchies across the Atlantic. Palatial homes were built in imita-tion of the Trianon, Grand and Petit, albeit with modern plumbing, wiring and far better heating. The tribe was demarcated with rules as rigid as Habsburg Spain's and a similar sense of worth. One of the Astors boarding the *Titanic* was a son of the famous socialite whose ballroom's capacity of 400 had set the parameters of what constituted polite New York Society, known thereafter as 'the Four Hundred' – 'If you go outside that number you strike people who are either not at ease in a ballroom or else make other people not at ease,' explained one member of the sacred band. In that rarefied milieu, Mrs Astor had been compared by one admirer to Dante's version of the Virgin Mary in *The Divine Comedy*, only here the 'circulated melody' surrounding the blessed lady was the Manhattan elite rather than the heavenly host, and the sparkle of the twelve celestial stars in the Virgin's crown had been replaced by so many family diamonds that Mrs Astor was likened to a chandelier by a guest at one of her annual January balls. There she greeted guests sitting in a throne-like chair before a life-size portrait of herself, with her Fifth Avenue mansion staffed by footmen dressed head to toe in a livery inspired by those worn by the British Royal Family's servants at Windsor Castle.[9] The fashions, sports and manners taught at Eton, Harrow and Winchester were imported and applauded, as were countless art treasures which were bought, shipped and quite probably saved from crumbling European palazzos, manors, castles and monasteries.

Following the Anglophile trend had come easily for John Thayer. Both he and his wife Marian, ten years his junior, were scions of old-money families from Philadelphia, America's first capital, where Society predated the War of Independence. There had been born a class that would later jokingly be dubbed the acronymic WASPs, since they were all white and nearly all Anglo-Saxon Protestants. Thayer's life had played out along the paths paved by this self-created aristocracy, beginning with prep schools and then an Ivy League education, where he had excelled at lacrosse. His summers had been divided between the family's main home on the outskirts of Philadelphia and their sprawling mansion-sized cottage by the beach. He had pursued his love of cricket at their local club, Marion, in Haverford, which he represented in 1884 on a team sent to compete in England. That trip had apparently solidified Thayer's belief that it was only in Europe that one could learn the 'correct' way of doing things. After he and Marian Morris married in 1893, jaunts across the Atlantic had become a regular part of their annual routine. That year, they had been accompanied by their eldest son, John Thayer III, known as 'Jack' in the family.[10] Seventeen years old, tall, blond, athletic and an excellent swimmer,

Jack was sitting next to his parents on the *Nomadic*, returning to his three younger siblings and home, where as a student of the nearby Haverford School he would begin the application process for Princeton, after which he would be sent back to Europe for a few years of apprenticeship in private banking. In his words, 'It could be planned. It was a certainty.'[11]

As the *Nomadic* and the *Traffic* made their way slowly towards the arriving *Titanic*, Tommy Andrews watched from the deck, anxiously inspecting their progress. A year earlier, the White Star Line had retired their antiquated tenders in favour of new constructions from Harland and Wolff to service the *Olympic's* maiden stop at Cherbourg.[12] Relieved that the ferries still seemed to be working as expected, Andrews went back to his cabin to pen a brief letter to his wife, containing the observation, 'We reached here in nice time and took on board quite a number of passengers. The two little tenders looked well, you will remember we built them a year ago. We expect to arrive at Queenstown about 10.30 a.m. to-morrow. The weather is fine and everything shaping for a good voyage.'[13]

The *Titanic* arrived just at the dying of the afternoon light with the sun setting behind her, and by the time of the last embarkation the liner's decks, windows and portholes were illuminated against the night. As they approached, Edith Rosenbaum, an American fashion journalist returning from the Paris spring shows, observed, 'In the dusk, her decks were 11 tiers of glittering electric lights. She was less a ship than a floating city, pennants streaming from her halyards like carnival in Nice.' One of the Astors opined, 'She's unsinkable. A modern shipbuilding miracle.'[14] The *Nomadic's* passengers gazed up at a ship weighing just over 46,000 tons, nearly 883 feet long and 92 feet wide, rising roughly to the height of an eleven-storey building beneath four funnels, their top quarters painted black and the rest in the buff yellow that constituted the White Star Line's livery.[15] The last of those funnels was a dummy, used for ventilation, obviating the need to build as many on-deck ventilation shafts as were required on other ships. This decision by Andrews and his team had helped create in the *Titanic* and her sisters three extraordinarily elegant ships. They had more in common with the smooth lines of the private yachts of European royalty than with their often bulky commercial rivals. Particularly when seen in profile, the *Olympic*-class liners were blessed with a clean and appealing gracefulness, a fact frequently praised in shipbuilding journals and contemporary travel guides.[16] The earliest designs for the *Titanic* had apparently suggested only three funnels, but the White Star Line concluded that four were indelibly associated with great ships in the travelling public's mind, thanks largely to a class of ships that had emerged from the Thayers' last stop before Cherbourg.[17]

*

Prior to boarding the *Titanic*, John Thayer and his wife had spent some time visiting Berlin as guests of both the US Consul General, Alexander Montgomery Thackara, and the new American Ambassador, John Leishman, who had previously served as the US representative to Switzerland, the Ottoman Empire and Italy. Although it had existed for hundreds of years as Prussia's capital, as Germany's Berlin remained new, high on hustle and low in majesty, with most traces of the provincial capital vanishing in pursuit of modernity. Berlin, like Belfast, seemed ever expanding; Mark Twain had once quipped, 'Next to it, Chicago would appear venerable.'[18] Nonetheless, it was European and, like Thayer, Leishman was persuaded of the European way of doing things, at least when it came to manners if not to business. Unhappily, by the time the Thayers arrived as guests of the embassy the Ambassador had run aground on some of the Old World's less appealing attributes. His eldest daughter had already married a French count when her younger sister, Nancy, received a proposal from the Prince von Croÿ, who was in the happy and increasingly unusual position of possessing both a fortune and a pedigree like Midas'. Nancy, as an American and a commoner, was counted as defective on two fronts by the Prince's formidable aunt, the Archduchess Isabella of Austria and in her crusade to prevent the nuptials, the Archduchess enlisted the help of the German Kaiser, who was traditionally required to give his blessing to the marriage of a subject as high-ranking as von Croÿ.[19] This the Kaiser declined to give, causing a rupture with the American Ambassador, who was understandably mortified by the insult to his daughter. As the newspapers buzzed with the scandal, relations between the Kaiser and the Ambassador deteriorated to the extent that, after Nancy and the Prince married without imperial permission in October 1913, Leishman felt he had no choice but to resign.[20]

For the Thayers, their trip to Germany had also offered an opportunity to see one of the world's most prosperous states. With plenty of fertile agricultural land, huge natural reserves of coal and iron ore, and population growth sustained by an increasingly excellent healthcare system, Imperial Germany also stood at the forefront of new industries like electrical engineering as well as steel and chemical production. Germany's public education system was superior to those in Britain, France or America, while conditions for its working classes, particularly after the development of its sophisticated welfare state, meant that a German factory worker's average life expectancy was about five years longer than their British equivalents' and nearly two decades longer than a Russian's. This spate of progress was rendered all the more remarkable by the fact that Germany had existed as a political entity for only forty-one years by the time the *Titanic* sailed on her maiden voyage.

The recession of Habsburg influence in Germany after the Napoleonic Wars had allowed the northern kingdom of Prussia, ruled by the House of Hohenzollern, to assume primacy and eventually, in 1871, to unite the many kingdoms, grand duchies, principalities and states into the Second Reich, with the King of Prussia installed as hereditary German Emperor.[21] The other pre-unification German rulers kept their wealth, titles, prestige and varying degrees of regional influence, but it was the culture of Prussia – confident, militarist and expansionist – that dominated the new empire. This caused particular concern in London, Paris and eventually St Petersburg. Despite being the son of a British princess, upon his succession to the German throne in 1888 Kaiser Wilhelm II did little to allay British fears and much to exacerbate them. In some way, the *Titanic*'s genesis lay with the Kaiser's dichotomy when it came to his mother's homeland – devout emulation jarring with suspicious competition. Wilhelm II's passionate interest in the mercantile marine had, in fact, begun thanks to a White Star liner, the *Teutonic*, when, during the Kaiser's 1889 visit to the United Kingdom, she had been picked to underscore Britain's commercial and military dominance of the oceans. Wilhelm had been invited to a naval review at Spithead and then, in the company of his uncle, the future Edward VII, offered a tour of the *Teutonic*. If the intention had been to intimidate the German Emperor, or gloat, it backfired spectacularly. Instead, as he viewed the *Teutonic*, the Kaiser was apparently heard to remark, 'We must have some of these.'[22] In 1897, imperial encouragement, the sustained economic miracle of the Second Reich and a booming eastern European migrant trade for which the German ports proved more convenient points of embarkation to America than their rivals in Italy, France or England, wove together to create the *Kaiser Wilhelm der Große*, the first transatlantic liner with the soon to be iconic four funnels. Christened after the Kaiser's late grandfather, the ship was a sensation – hugely popular with all classes of travellers, particularly European emigrants and affluent Americans – and lavishly decorated with the fantastically overwrought designs of Johann Poppe. A contemporary joke described the aesthetic as 'two of everything but the kitchen range, and then gilded'.[23] Six months after her maiden voyage, she took the Blue Riband, the award for the fastest commercial crossing of the North Atlantic.[24] Her success was sufficient to inspire her owners, the Norddeutscher Lloyd, to commission three running mates over the next decade, all likewise named for, and launched in the presence of, members of the German Imperial Family.[25] A testament to how important these ships were to the German Empire's sense of self was delivered

71

via *Our Future Lies upon the Water*, a large allegorical mural painted for the first-class Smoking Room of the *Kronprinz Wilhelm*; it depicted conquering sea gods in aquatic chariots, holding aloft tridents and a banner that looked suspiciously like the German flag.[26] There seems to be no truth in the story that the last of the quadruplets, the *Kronprinzessin Cecilie*, bearing the name of the Kaiser's daughter-in-law, Cecilia of Mecklenburg-Schwerin, which should logically have been the largest of the four, had her gross tonnage registered as one ton less than that of the third ship in the series, the *Kaiser Wilhelm II*, in deference to the Kaiser's enormous yet fragile ego. In fact, the *Kronprinzessin Cecilie* was publicly listed as the heaviest of the four sister ships, with 19,400 tons against the *Kaiser Wilhelm II*'s marginally smaller 19,361.[27]

The first of the greyhounds: the *Kaiser Wilhelm der Große*.

Nicknamed 'the German greyhounds' and 'the Hohenzollerns of Hoboken' after Norddeutscher Lloyd's piers on the Hudson, the *Kaiser*-class transformed the transatlantic trade by proving the idea of the commercially viable super-ship.[28] Norddeutscher Lloyd's home-grown rivals, the Hamburg-Amerika Line, retaliated with their own four-stacker speed queen, the *Deutschland*.

Reflecting on the race thirty years later, the maritime historian Gerald Aylmer wrote, 'By 1903 Germany possessed the four fastest and best appointed merchant ships afloat, with another on order. This state of affairs was not palatable, to put it mildly, to Britain, a country which had always prided itself on its steamship construction and speed.'[29] Aylmer was right; the success of the *Kaiser*-class inflamed within the British a fear born of the belief that their place in the world was tied inextricably to mastery of the sea lanes, which had as much to do with their passenger and cargo ships as it did with their dreadnoughts and destroyers. During the Second Boer War, between 1899 and 1902, the White Star Line had donated several of its ships to temporary military service with the Royal Navy, which, combined with unease at the success of the German greyhounds, helps explain the British reaction when White Star was purchased by J. P. Morgan's conglomerate in 1903.[30]

A few years earlier, the writer and apostle of British imperialism J. A. Froude had sounded like the voice of Cassandra when he warned his compatriots, 'Take away her merchant fleets, take away the navy that guards them; her empire will come to an end; her colonies will fall off like leaves from a withered tree; and Britain will become once more an insignificant island in the North Sea.'[31] In 1903, despite assurances that it was only White Star shares and not her ships that were passing into American control, the sale was sufficiently worrying to inspire speeches in Parliament, a mood turned brilliantly to their advantage by White Star's main British competitors, the Cunard Line, who intimated that they too were considering joining Morgan's International Mercantile Marine. Suppressing the news that they had in fact already passed on a too low offer from Morgan, Cunard presented themselves as the firm who could gladly recapture Britain's seagoing pride if only they had sufficient funds to prevent the ugly necessity of selling out to an American.[32] The government and the press took the bait. To help with their plan to outshine the *Kaiser*-class, Parliament voted Cunard a £2.5 million loan to be repaid over the next twenty years at 2.75 per cent interest, materially and obviously below the base rate of 3–4 per cent, coupled with an annual £150,000 operating subsidy.[33] In the autumn of 1907, Cunard delivered on the investment with the creation of the Scottish-built *Lusitania* and then her English-constructed sister, the *Mauretania*.[34] The latter was marginally larger and ultimately proved slightly faster as well, but with both sisters weighing in at about 32,000 tons, each was almost twice as heavy as the largest of the German grey-hounds.[35] For the next three years, the *Lucy* and the *Maury*, as they were nicknamed by their legions of loyal customers and ship enthusiasts, cheerfully passed the Blue Riband between them until, in 1910, the *Mauretania* decisively took the prize with a crossing time of four days, ten hours and forty-one minutes, a record she would hold for the next nineteen years.[36]

Outflanked by the Germans and then by Cunard, Morgan and the White Star Line felt called upon to respond in similarly bombastic fashion, with three floating palaces to Cunard's two, each of which was to be half as heavy again as the *Mauretania*. Thus were the *Olympic*-class born. In retaliation, Cunard had ordered a third behemoth, the *Aquitania*, due to sail from Liverpool to New York for the first time in 1914. Piqued and hitherto over-looked, the Compagnie Générale Transatlantique was preparing to unveil their 'château of the Atlantic', the *France*, on her maiden voyage a few weeks after the *Titanic*'s, around the same time as the Kaiser planned to travel north to Bremerhaven to launch the *Imperator* which, a year later, would pluck the sobriquet of 'world's largest ship' from the *Titanic* by a margin of 6,000 tons, a devel-opment that had forced a change of name for the *Titanic*'s youngest sister, even as she was being built in Belfast. Just as the names of Cunard ships, prior to the 1930s, ended with *-ia* thanks to the company's policy of making use of provinces of the Roman Empire, White Star vessels were typically branded with an adjective trans-formed into a noun, ending with *-ic*. The *Titanic* and her two sisters were called after great species in Greek myth, respectively the gods of Olympus, the titans and the giants. However, the original name of *Gigantic* for the third sister never made it past a few provisional poster ideas and excitable press articles. In May 1912, the White Star Line filed the necessary papers to reserve the off-theme but patriotic name *Britannic* for their forthcoming flagship.

For decades, this shift has popularly been attributed to White Star's desire to distance the third sister from the tragedy of the second by abandoning a too similar name. This is a logical explanation for how the *Gigantic* became the *Britannic*, especially in light of White Star officially filing for the new name a few weeks after the *Titanic* sank, but it is also incorrect. The alternative name of *Gigantic* seems to have been genuinely considered by the White Star Line only at the earliest stages in the vessel's development and some of their contractors continued to use it, even after it had been abandoned – the order books for the English firm that made the liner's anchors referenced her as *Gigantic* as late as 20 February 1912 – as did several Harland and Wolff employees, who remembered the original name in interviews given in the 1950s. Rumours that the ship was to be christened *Gigantic* were current and firmly denied by the White Star's Managing Director, both in his testimony to the American inquiry into the loss of the *Titanic* and subsequently in a letter to a British newspaper.[37] Those printed denials may have been the company's response to letters they had received from concerned members of the public, begging them not to tempt fate by giving the new ship a name so similar to the *Titanic*'s, although at least one of the latter's survivors was sufficiently hardy to dismiss that as superstitious nonsense, 'almost as if we were back in the Middle Ages'.[38] More prosaically, it was almost certainly the *Imperator* that prompted the rechristening. Since, by 1915, the *Britannic* would 'only' be the third largest ship afloat, behind the *Imperator* and her 1914-projected running mate, the *Vaterland*, to call her *Gigantic* under those circumstances seemed foolhardy.[39]

The *Titanic*'s looming black-painted hull, summoned into being by capitalist competition and the diplomatic thrombosis of pre-war

Europe, greeted the Thayers as the *Nomadic* at last docked alongside the *Titanic*. The tender's gangplank could not safely reach
the B-Deck embarkation doors used at Southampton and so
Tommy Andrews had designed another, two decks lower, reaching
a vestibule which opened on to the first-class Reception Room,
where stewards waited to guide first-class passengers to their
cabins and second-class aft to their section of the ship. Standing
in front of the Thayers as they boarded was J. Bruce Ismay, son
of the White Star Line's late founder and Managing Director
since its merger with the IMM. If the *Titanic*'s legend has a two-
dimensional caricature, it is Ismay, cast as both vulpine villain
and a serial weakling in the hysterical aftermath of the sinking.
So complete was Ismay's historiographical evisceration that when
a consultant first saw the script for what became a multi-Oscar-
winning cinematic romance set on the *Titanic* and queried the
characterisation of Ismay as a megalomaniacal moron, butt of
penis-envy jokes he cannot understand and shameless manipulator
of the Captain in the dangerous quest for more speed, he was
told there was no point in changing it because 'the public expects'
a heinous Ismay.[40] That is not to say that Ismay was incapable of
moments of mind-boggling stupidity, but he was also astute,
devoted to his company and, like Tommy Andrews, obsessed with
detail.[41] A complex man whose inherent shyness produced acts
of great kindness and flinch-inducing obtuseness, Ismay's thought-
fulness had won out on 10 April as he bore down on the Thayers'
travelling companions and lifelong friends, Arthur and Emily
Ryerson, who were returning home to America unexpectedly after
hearing that their son, Arthur Junior, had been killed in a car
accident during his sophomore spring at Yale. He had gone home
to Bryn Mawr in Pennsylvania for the Easter weekend where he
had died, along with his classmate, John Hoffman, two days before
the *Titanic* sailed.[42] Ismay took over from the Thayers as temporary chaperon of the grief-stricken by informing the Ryersons,
who were travelling with their three younger children, a maid and
a governess, that he had arranged for them to be given an extra

stateroom adjoining those they had already booked, along with a personal steward to look after them during the voyage.[43] A broken Emily Ryerson intended to spend the trip in her cabin with her family, avoiding everyone else on board except the Thayers.

Less solemnly, a middle-aged New York widow, Ella White, was carried past the boarding passengers. She had fallen and sprained her ankle as the gangplank swayed in the winds.[44] A few stewards had been summoned to help Mrs White's chauffeur lift her to her C-Deck stateroom, the same deck where the Thayers were also settling into their accommodation on the opposite corridor to the Strauses and the Countess of Rothes. The latter escorted her parents down to the Reception Room to see them off on to the *Nomadic*. Noëlle, Thomas and Clementina descended the staircase into the Reception Room. Directly ahead of that, they turned left at a wall mounted with a reproduction of the *Chasse de Guise* tapestry, depicting a hunting party, the original of which had been owned by the French aristocratic family unfairly accused of poisoning the 4th Earl of Rothes in the sixteenth century.[45] From two sets of double doors leading off the Reception Room into the Dining Saloon, the Countess and her parents heard hundreds of passengers tucking into their second meal of the voyage. They walked over dark Axminster carpets, past settees, armchairs, white cane chairs with green side pillows, potted palms and a Steinway piano, one of six on board, into the small vestibule that opened on to the gangplank and the night air.[46] Thomas and Clementina said their farewells, but at the last minute the normally reserved Clementina turned on impulse and dashed back to give her daughter a final embrace.[47] When the Dyer-Edwardeses joined the *Titanic*'s thirteen other cross-Channel ticket holders in the tender, the gangplank was disengaged and the boarding doors were closed. After they had been locked, crew members pulled wrought-iron gates back into place to shield the utilitarian steel from the passengers' view.

The usual expectations governing dinner, including the formal dress code, were typically eschewed on the first night out.[48]

Wearing the dress in which she had boarded, Noëlle left the vestibule for the Saloon, which has since become one of the *Titanic*'s most recognisable rooms thanks to its frequent depiction in silver-screen dramatisations of the voyage.[49] Meals in the Saloon were run on the same lines as they might be in a country house on shore, with limited options, generous portions, set times for each course every evening except the first, and *placement* decided by the host – in this case, the ship's Purser, who assigned passengers to one of the 115 tables which variably sat two, three, four, five, six, eight, ten or twelve. His decisions with this social roulette could introduce a passenger to delightful week-long shipboard acquaintances or purgatorial companionship in a multi-course dinner that moved with the sprightliness of a state funeral. You could, of course, ask the Purser's Office to move you to another table if you found the company particularly stultifying but, as a passenger on the *Queen Mary* noted later, 'the cost of [which] would be the contempt of those still seated at the table you had spurned, and the frozen stares with which they'd greet you on deck for the rest of the trip'.[50]

Where to put a countess and her companion would have been one of Purser McElroy's main priorities and it seems, from a letter sent by one of their stewards, that they won the lottery in their three gastronomic companions. A steward was assigned to every three diners and it was considered proper for those in his care to leave a gratuity at the end of the voyage, the amount of which very often outpaced his wages. The Countess's Steward, Ewart Burr, described her group as being 'very nice to run'. He was particularly pleased to have an aristocrat at his table and he made a point of mentioning it in the note he penned to his wife that evening, writing, 'I know, darling, you will be glad to know this. I have got a five table, one being the Countess of Rothes, [who is] nice and young.' Burr predicted that they would be generous at journey's end or, as he put it, 'I shall have a good show.'[51]

The decor in the Dining Saloon was loosely inspired by Elizabeth I's childhood home at Hatfield Palace and the dukes of Rutland's house at Haddon Hall. Despite both those buildings being Elizabethan and the Tudor roses in scrollwork on the Saloon's roof, trade journals described the *Titanic*'s Saloon as reflective of 'early Jacobean times'.[52] The green-leather chairs with their oak frames were heavy enough for White Star to do away with the bolted-to-the-floor chairs used on the *Kaiser*-class and the Cunard sisters. This was the only significant innovation in a room that several industry experts dismissed as conventional almost to the point of staid. One admittedly biased observer was Leonard Peskett, designer of the *Lusitania* and *Mauretania*, whose disapproval was laced with a vigorous dose of delight when he saw the near-identical Dining Saloon during his tour of the *Olympic* in 1911. The *Titanic*'s Dining Saloon may have been the largest room afloat but it was not, by any stretch of the imagination, the finest, at least not in Peskett's view or that of many of his colleagues, especially when compared to the two-storeyed domed Rococo equivalent on the *Lusitania*.* There was also a problem of over-heating caused by the Saloon's 404 light bulbs, although the chill outside meant that this was unlikely to be a problem on 10 April.[53]

Stewards served the first course on the fine bone-china plates, edged with 22-carat gold and bearing the White Star logo at the centre, setting them down amid the small forest of silver-plated cutlery, while water was poured and wine decanted into crystal glassware.[54] At ten minutes past eight, some diners began to debate when they would leave Cherbourg; their Steward leaned in to inform them politely, 'We have been outside the breakwater for more than ten minutes, Sir.'[55]

---

* Peskett's assertion that the first-class cabins were similarly inferior to the Cunarders' did not, however, meet with general agreement.

A Safe Harbour for Ships

And doesn't old Cobh look charming there
Watching the wild waves' motion,
Leaning her back up against the hills,
And the tip of her toes in the ocean.

John Locke, 'Morning on the Irish Coast' (1877)

T O REDUCE THE DELAY CAUSED BY THE LONDON BOAT
trains and then by the *New York*, the *Titanic*'s speed was
increased as she made her night-time crossing of the Celtic
Sea from France to Ireland.[1] Twenty of her twenty-nine boilers
were eventually operational that evening, during which the
Captain stayed on the Bridge, rather than make an appearance
at his table in the Dining Saloon.[2] He did not, apparently, miss
much. Even the smoothest of travel days are liable to produce
their own special brand of fatigue and many passengers retired
early, abandoning the *Titanic*'s main after-dinner haunts like the
Reception and the Lounge, three decks above, long before their
respective closing times of 11 and 11.30 p.m.[3] One passenger
recalled later that their day had been spent 'unpacking, making
the cabin homelike, getting the lay of the public rooms, trying to
determine fore and aft, port and starboard [and] getting the feel

of the ship . . . many passengers are so exhausted with farewell parties and preparations for the voyage'.[4]

At bedtime, those who wanted a restored shine on their shoes left them to be collected from the stateroom corridors, a service that was not required by Ida Straus's husband as he was travelling with his own valet, Farthing, a man with several years' service to the Strauses.[5] Such familiarity was not yet possible for Ida with her maid, Ellen Bird, who had celebrated her thirty-first birthday two days earlier while packing for a new chapter of her life, in America, after Ida's maid, Marie, had quit to marry a barber she had met during the Strauses' winter holiday on the French Riviera. The weeks during which Marie served out her notice had not apparently been pleasant for anyone involved and the normally magnanimous Isidor was offended on his wife's behalf since, as Ida told a relative, Marie had begun 'behaving very badly over here. When Papa sours on a girl you know there is good cause, and he is disgusted with her.'[6] She had intended to replace Marie with another French lady's maid, but none could be found by the time the couple reached Britain, where, after another was retained and quit upon changing her mind about moving to America, Ida had hired Ellen on the recommendation of the housekeeper at Claridge's, their hotel during their London stay. Like the Countess of Rothes' maid, Cissy Maioni, Ellen came from a family with a history in domestic service and she had been a maid in various households since her early twenties. Although Ida remained worried, as she had been with Marie, about 'whether I can count on her', so far she was pleased with Ellen, whom she described in a letter home as a 'nice English girl'.[7] Ellen helped prepare Ida for bed, then left for her own cabin which was in First Class and on the same corridor as the Strauses'.[8]

The Strauses' bedroom, located between their parlour and private bathrooms, was decorated in the style of the First Napoleonic Empire, to which any curve left ungilded was regarded as a curve wasted. They slept in two single beds on opposite sides of the room, separated by the door to the parlour and a marble washstand; there was a dressing table on the other side of the room, along the wall that led to their wardrobe and bathrooms. At sea, as on land, many upper-class couples had separate bedrooms and so to put them in a double bed when they were travelling was considered *infra dig*. The Strauses' decision to share a cabin, if not a bed, thus emphasises their closeness rather than the opposite. They had shared a room on their previous crossing on the seven-year-old *Caronia*, which still had bunk beds in some of its best first-class accommodation. Isidor had taken the top berth and, one morning after he had risen, its corner fell missing Ida's head by inches. The ship's Purser attributed its collapse to 'some peculiar bend or twist of the ship', although the fact that bunks existed at all on the *Caronia* showed how far ocean liners' accommodation had evolved in a relatively short period.[9]

Their mattresses on the *Titanic* were firm, on the instructions of J. Bruce Ismay who had ordered a change throughout First Class after sailing on the maiden voyage of the *Olympic*, when he had observed, 'The only trouble of any consequence on board the ship arose from the springs of the bed being too "springy"; this, in conjunction with the spring mattresses, accentuated the pulsation in the ship to such an extent as to seriously interfere with passengers sleeping.'[10] All first-class cabins were located amidships, where the ship was most stable, but this was also directly above, albeit far above, most of her elephantine engines, hence Ismay's insistence on a new type of bedding to cushion any vibrations when the *Titanic* ran at high speed, as she incrementally began to do after Cherbourg. That evening, the extinguishing of the lamps installed over most of the *Titanic*'s first-class beds left a nocturnal gloom gently pierced by the glow from the electric heaters provided in every stateroom. The cold in London and the breeze in Cherbourg had followed the *Titanic* and combined to strengthen.[11] In cabins with portholes or windows, even if closed and latched, the chill was felt to some degree and so the heaters hummed in successful combat.[12] Fortunately, even as the wind whistled around their temporary home, few of the *Titanic*'s inhabitants experienced seasickness – she remained on an even keel.* As one of them put it a few days later, they slept contentedly thanks to 'the lordly contempt of the *Titanic* for anything less than a hurricane'.[13]

This beacon of lordly contempt was sailing between Land's End in Cornwall and the Scilly Isles when the sun rose through broken clouds; around the same time, nearly fifty of the ship's clocks swung in silent unison from about 5.40 to 5.15 a.m.[14] As the ship sailed westward, two master clocks in her Chart Room, both displaying time to the second, were adjusted for the crossing of the time zones. Clocks throughout the crew's quarters and the passengers' public rooms were linked to these master clocks and adjusted automatically with them. Known as the Magneta system, it did away with the need for crew members to move through the ship manually adjusting individual timepieces.[15] Usually the reclaiming of an hour was calculated and implemented for about midnight during the voyage, but in 1912 Ireland operated under Dublin Mean Time, twenty-five minutes behind Greenwich, and the *Titanic* did not clear English waters until sunrise or shortly after.† As the ship awoke, a small battalion of stewards and stewardesses brought morning tea to the staterooms or breakfast trays for those, like Ida Straus, who had the option of taking the first meal of the day in their private parlours.[16] For the rest, the Dining Saloon revived for a two-hour window, beginning at eight o'clock.[17]

*

Shortly after breakfast, south-eastern Ireland came into view with 'the brilliant morning sun showing up the green hillsides and

---

* An early exception was Lady Rothes' maid, who felt queasy shortly after departure from Cherbourg.
† Dublin Mean Time was abolished in 1916 after it had caused confusion in relation to reports and reactions to an anti-British uprising in Dublin, generally known later and today as the Easter Rising. France also operated under its own time zone, until 1978, which was nine minutes and twenty-one seconds ahead of Greenwich Mean Time.

picking out groups of dwellings dotted here and there above the rugged grey cliffs that fringed the coast', according to one passenger's memoirs.[18] The port they were heading for had first been referred to as 'the Cove of Cork', its nearest city, in the middle of the eighteenth century, which had inspired the town's subsequent name of Cóbh, an Irish rendering of the English 'cove' and pronounced in the same way.[19] Following a visit by the young Queen Victoria in 1849, Cóbh had been rechristened Queenstown. However, opponents of the Union with Britain continued to refer to the town by its pre-Victorian name, which was legally restored following Irish independence in the 1920s. Queenstown's motto, *Statio Fidissima Classi* ('A Safe Harbour for Ships'), reflected its long history as a busy port, particularly as it became the main boarding point for the millions who emigrated from Ireland in the nineteenth century. By 1912, the Irish diaspora to America had slowed to a steady trickle compared to the anguished flood of previous decades and the *Titanic's* call at Queenstown had more to do with fulfilling the obligations of White Star's mail contract, through which the ship gained her prestigious prefix of RMS, or Royal Mail Steamer.[20]

Ports like Liverpool, New York and Southampton had frequently been dredged to accommodate the recent leaps in liner size, but Queenstown, like Cherbourg, still relied on tenders. The *Ireland* and the *America* beetled out into waters turned a murky brown as the seabed sand was churned to the surface by the *Titanic's* slowing propellers.[21] Sacks of mail, luggage and 191 new passengers were moved from tenders to ship, while those taking the air on the *Titanic's* Boat or Promenade decks joked about the minuscule size of the ferries, 'tossing up and down like corks' in the swell.[22] Many admired the view of Queenstown, particularly the turrets, buttresses and 300-foot spire of its Catholic cathedral, St Colman's, a generation-long endeavour then seven years from completion.[23] This idyllic vista, particularly the green hills hugging Queenstown and running to the shore, justified Ireland's nickname as the Emerald Isle, a phrase allegedly first committed to paper by one of Tommy Andrews' maternal ancestors, the republican writer William Drennan, who had, to the embarrassment of his Edwardian descendants, sided with the ill-fated 1798 rebellion against the Crown and launched the famous moniker in his poem, 'When Erin First Rose'.[24]

At anchor off Queenstown: many of the passengers visible on the stern were Irish immigrants who had boarded the *Titanic* in Third Class that morning.

The stop at Queenstown vacated cabin A-37, directly opposite Andrews' A-36 and occupied by a devout Irish Catholic, thirty-two-year-old Francis Browne, a charming amateur photographer who had gone to boarding school with James Joyce and was later immortalised as 'Mr Browne the Jesuit' in Joyce's novel *Finnegans Wake*.[25] Browne evidently had not lost his ability to make an impression, since at dinner the previous evening two of his companions in the Saloon, a wealthy couple from New York, had been so captivated by his eloquence that they offered to pay his fare if he wished to remain on the ship and at their table until America. Browne, who was reading Theology in Dublin with the aim of pursuing a vocation as a priest, had to ask his superior for the necessary permission to miss his studies for a few weeks. He received a sharply worded reply in telegram form, 'Get off that ship'.[26] Had the Jesuit professor reached the opposite decision, Andrews might have grown accustomed to seeing Browne's face throughout the voyage. As it was, the trainee priest was up as early as the ship's designer to snap away on his camera, mostly in the better lighting provided on the Boat Deck.[27]

Andrews' morning produced less picturesque sights, particularly through his inspection of the watertight doors between the ship's subterranean boiler rooms.[28] The doors had already been repeatedly tested in Belfast, but a subsequent trial at sea was considered sensible. Almost in unison, the heavy mechanised doors slid into place, sealing the *Titanic*'s sixteen watertight compartments off from one another, as they would if the hull was ever breached. Joined by the ship's Chief Officer, Henry Wilde, Andrews then watched to see if the crew could open and close the watertight doors manually with a large specially purposed spanner, in the event of the failure of the doors' electric controls operated from the Bridge. This too was successfully executed, removing another item from Andrews' and Wilde's to-do list.[29] The latter's posting to the *Titanic* had been very much last minute and it was attributed to his service in the same role on the *Olympic*, where he had been liked and trusted by Captain Smith, who had also been transferred to the *Titanic*. It may have been Smith's friendship that prompted Wilde's appointment only seven days before the *Titanic* sailed from Southampton, bumping William Murdoch down to First Officer and Charles Lightoller to Second. There were six officer posts on the *Titanic*, but since the Third Officer's task functioned largely as an apprenticeship to serving as Second Officer, this meant the previous Second Officer, David Blair, had become surplus to requirements upon Wilde's arrival. Wilde, who preferred the *Olympic* and said he had a 'queer feeling' about the *Titanic*, was no more happy at being summoned than Blair was at leaving 'a magnificent ship. I feel *very* disappointed I am not to make the first voyage.'[30] This reshuffling of command had an important, if subsequently exaggerated, impact in the Crow's Nest, the vantage point on the forward mast. As theirs had not yet arrived, Blair had offered to lend the lookouts his binoculars, which he innocently took with him when he left. When this was brought to Wilde's attention, he hunted around the ship but there did not seem to be any permanent spare pair to loan to the Crow's Nest for the duration of the voyage. Some of the lookouts refused to let the matter drop and approached Second Officer Lightoller, around the time the ship reached Queenstown. Lightoller agreed that binoculars would be helpful and went searching for an extra set, though with the same lack of success as Wilde. Other crew members, however, thought the lookouts were creating a fuss over nothing, that one's eyes ought to be sharp enough to do without them or that binoculars would be a hindrance rather than an aid, since they might seduce a lookout into a sense of complacency or encourage undue focus on a far away point at the expense of more immediate dangers.

The notoriety of the *Titanic*'s failure to provide binoculars entered the popular mythology of the tragedy as another potent example of incompetence-laced hubris. The origins of that claim lay with one of the surviving lookouts, Frederick Fleet, who insisted at both subsequent inquiries into the disaster that if he had been provided with binoculars it would have given him more time to warn the Bridge, perhaps 'enough to get out of the way'.[31] However, modern tests conducted in similar conditions seem to corroborate the views of contemporary seamen who countered Fleet's testimony by stating that on dark and cold nights on open water binoculars are ineffective to the point of uselessness in spotting objects, particularly ones that are already dark, like a growler iceberg.[32]

While the *Titanic*'s anchors remained dropped at Queenstown, journalists from local newspapers and enthusiastic members of the Royal Cork Yacht Club skimmed out in crafts to photograph and admire the liner before, at half-past one, her anchors were raised, the seabed sand was disturbed again as the triple-screw propellers spun back into motion and she turned slowly to point her prow to the Atlantic. By the time afternoon tea was served, three hours later, the coast of Ireland was fading from view.[33] There were four venues in which first-class passengers could take tea, one of which afforded spectacular views towards the stern.[34] The Verandah Café, split into two rooms, one that allowed smoking and the other, particularly popular with mothers and their children, that did not, was located on A-Deck as the furthest aft of the first-class public rooms. Inspired by the 'winter gardens' popular on the German greyhounds, the Verandah was lined with bronze-framed windows and green trellises covered in growing plants. White wicker chairs and tables cluttered the room, reminiscent of a conservatory on land. As Ireland melted into the horizon, a passenger who had boarded there went up on to the Poop Deck, the area at the stern used as the promenade for Third Class. There, on his uilleann pipes, an Irish instrument similar to the Highlands' bagpipes, the young man played 'Erin's Lament' and 'A Nation Once More', paeans to the Irish quest for independence and, in the case of the former, sharply critical of the landed classes.[35] It is unlikely that anyone at tea heard him; the doors into the Verandah were designed to stifle a chill breeze and any sounds from the outside.[36]

The Lucky Holdup

Eustacia Vye was the raw material of divinity. On Olympus she would have done well with little preparation. She had the passions and instincts which make a model goddess . . .

Thomas Hardy, *The Return of the Native* (1878)

AFTER DINNER ON THE DAY THE *TITANIC* VISITED Queenstown, printed copies of her passenger list were delivered to the first-class staterooms facilitating, for those so inclined, an eagle-eyed hunt for on-board friends, established or intended.*[1] Showing only those travelling in First Class, the manifest was printed alphabetically, running in this case from twenty-nine-year-old Elisabeth Allen, returning to her native Missouri to pack up her life in preparation for her forthcoming marriage to a British doctor, through to New Yorker Marie Young, who had once taught music to President Theodore Roosevelt's youngest, and allegedly favourite, daughter Ethel and was returning from her European vacation as a companion to her relative Ella White, she who had sprained her ankle while

---

* An equivalent list was also passed out in Second Class although, according to the recollections of passenger Kate Buss, it was not issued there until just after the next day's breakfast.

boarding at Cherbourg.[2] Few subsequent accounts of the *Titanic*'s career agree on her passenger capacity and the quest for a precise figure is in some sense a fool's errand. Some of these discrepancies arise from the facts that both First and Second Class had blocs of their cheapest cabins which could, in moments of high capacity, be reassigned to the class below them and that several cabins had room for a cot or child's bed, adding a further variance.[3] Broadly speaking, the *Titanic* had room for about 900 passengers in First Class, 550 in Second and 1,100 in Third. The lists passed out in First Class on 11 April confirmed that there were 324 travelling in the most expensive part of the ship. Despite the fact that the *Titanic* is described as fully booked in several dramatisations and popular accounts of her voyage, the reason why Purser McElroy had been able to move the Countess of Rothes with such ease at Southampton was because nearly two-thirds of *Titanic*'s first-class cabins were unoccupied.[4] Second Class was about half empty and Third Class just under two-thirds occupied once the full complement was on board after departure from Queenstown. With 891 crew members, this meant that about 2,208 people were on the *Titanic* after Thursday the 11th, not allowing for stowaways, if any had avoided the ship's eagle-eyed officers.

Different reasons for the 'Queen of the Ocean' sailing at about 50 per cent of commercial capacity have been suggested, with the recent British miners' strike popularly identified as having caused enough uncertainty in the travelling public that many decided to wait until the coal-dependent steamers were certain to sail.[5] Equally possible is the fact that the *Titanic* sailed in spring, just before the more popular summer season, which might explain the dip in occupancy. Eastward crossings at that time of year, back from New York, also seem generally to have been busier than those westward – a comparison with the *Olympic*'s maiden crossings a year early shows broadly similar numbers with 489, 263 and 561 in the respective classes from Europe compared to 731, 495 and 1,095 for the return trip.[6]

For John Thayer, a glance at the roster was unlikely to produce too many surprises. The majority of Americans in First Class had, like the Thayers, boarded at Cherbourg via the *Nomadic*. There was another railway tycoon in Charles Hays, the American-born General Manager of Canada's Grand Trunk Pacific Railway, who was travelling home from a Board of Directors' meeting in England in time for the opening of his company's new railway hotel, the Château Laurier, in Ottawa.[7] There was also a healthy number of fellow Pennsylvanians, nearly all of whom were friends of the Thayers, including George Widener and his family, sailing in a C-Deck suite a few doors down from theirs. The Wideners' money came from banking, which had been used by George as the springboard to a Philadelphia streetcar monopoly, while the bulk of the family fortune remained with his seemingly immortal father, Peter. The richest man on board, by a considerable margin, was Colonel John Jacob Astor IV; his military rank came from his service in the Spanish-American War of 1898, and his $87 million bank balance, broadly equivalent to just over $2 billion in 2019, from being born into a family who owned so much of the city that they were nicknamed 'the landlords of New York'.

If the sight of Lady Rothes' name on the passenger list excited those attracted to the allure of the titled, a similar thrill was generated for devotees of the emerging cult of celluloid celebrity by the name of Dorothy Gibson, sandwiched in the passenger list between her redoubtable mother and Arthur Gee, the British-born manager of a printworks in southern Mexico.[8] Dorothy's most recent movie, *The Lucky Holdup*, was released in the USA and France on the day the *Titanic* left Queenstown. Ordinarily, Dorothy tried to turn up at her various premieres, the first actor to make a regular habit of doing so, but she had been so busy and successful in recent months that she could afford to skip the promotions for her latest opus. Even to those unfamiliar with the burgeoning movie industry, Dorothy Gibson had made an impression since boarding at Cherbourg the previous evening. Unaware of her name, the Washington DC-based socialite and author Helen

Candee, having spotted Dorothy when they were sequestered on the *Nomadic*, was almost certainly referring to her when she wrote later of 'the most beautiful girl' and perhaps when she recalled the 'indispensable American girl'.[9] Publicly, Dorothy was self-deprecating about her appearance, but in private a colleague confirmed that she considered it almost a gift from God 'by the grace of which she earns an honest living'.[10]

Dorothy Gibson, photographed c.1911.

To describe Dorothy's career as 'an honest living' implied a humbleness as theatrically misleading as her demure claims regarding her looks. At five weeks short of her twenty-third birthday, Dorothy was one of the highest-paid actresses in the world on a weekly salary of $275, nearly double that of her most prominent competitor, 'America's Sweetheart' Mary Pickford.[11] It was, to her relief, an income that had taken Dorothy far from her comfortable lower-middle-class childhood in Hoboken, New Jersey, which, fittingly for a woman who was to forge her first great successes by marketing herself as the 'all-American girl', was also 'the birthplace of baseball, the Tootsie Roll and the ice cream cone', in the charming phrase of one of her modern biographers, Randy Bryan Bigham. Her Scottish-born father, John Brown, had been a contract builder until his death aged twenty-five in February 1891, when Dorothy, his only child, was twenty-one months old. Brown's death certificate gives the cause of death as bronchopneumonia at the family home on Bloomfield Street in Hoboken.[12] Almost exactly three years later, his twenty-seven-year-old widow, Pauline, married an Irish shopkeeper, Leonard Gibson, who adopted Dorothy, at which point she was given his surname.[13] She was eight when the *Kaiser Wilhelm der Große* docked in her home city at the end of its first crossing of the Atlantic and over the next decade the Hohenzollerns of Hoboken came and went from a city with a thriving German immigrant community. Dorothy grew into a popular child and teenager, who was praised at parties given by family friends for her beautiful singing voice. In a later interview with a journalist, she claimed, 'It was singing that I loved. But I had not the slightest inkling of the stage as a profession. In those days, a girl was expected to act in amateur theatricals for charity but never was she to think of it as an occupation, and I didn't.'[14]

This particular claim does not entirely convince when one considers that Dorothy made her Broadway debut at the age of sixteen. Her stepfather, a devout Baptist, insisted that Pauline act as a chaperone at their daughter's rehearsals and evening performances, a task at which she proved so woefully inadequate that one can only suspect her apparent negligence was deliberate strategy. As a further sop to her nervous stepfather, who had upped sticks and moved the family from New Jersey to New York to launch the career of the allegedly reluctant Dorothy, she initially appeared under the stage name of 'Polly Stanley', which she later misremembered as 'Polly Stanton'. Polly Stanley was abandoned in favour of Dorothy's real name around the time her early vaudeville performances caught the attention of one of the great theatrical producers of the era, Charles Frohman. Sickly, slender and brilliant, Frohman offered Dorothy a part in *The Dairymaids*, a show he was then in the process of bringing over from London for its Broadway premiere, which she accepted, landing her first review in the *New York Times*.

Despite that review's praise, Dorothy's professional relationship with Charles Frohman ended after *The Dairymaids*. Why remains unclear, although subsequent accounts of her career have hypothesised that Frohman's notoriously obsessive attitude towards the morality of his female actors may have caused the rupture. Dorothy was flirtatious and well liked. The most serious of her beaux was a young pharmacist from Memphis, Tennessee, George Battier, who delivered gifts to her dressing room, something which may not have sat well with Frohman. It did not matter. Her career had already started its upward swing. On the back of the show's success, and the compliments of the *New York Times*, Dorothy was signed by the Shubert Brothers agency, who launched the eighteen-year-old into a manic schedule of theatrical tours throughout 1907 and 1908, and then again in 1909 when she was asked to reprise her role in a comedy titled *The Mayor and the Manicure*. It was not exactly her Ophelia, but, like her next play, *Sporting Days*, in Dorothy's words, 'It was a hit.' Her wonderful singing landed her another tour in 1910, this time to Boston and Philadelphia with the Metropolitan Comic Opera Company. She and her mother were thrilled with her success, but she remained refreshingly unpretentious about the kind of plays she was doing – 'all we did', she joked, 'was stand around in pretty hats, lean on our parasols and purr through some ditties.' On 10 February 1910, she married George Battier and they moved into an apartment in Manhattan. By summer, she had left him. The religious zeal she admired in her stepfather proved suffocating in her husband, a fervent evangelical who was both possessive and perpetually suspicious of her.

She was back to standing, leaning, purring and being applauded in *A Trip to Japan* when there was another knock on her dressing-room door. She remembered that the caller, Harrison Fisher, arrived with no gifts and shook her hand, rather than kiss it. She appreciated that, especially in light of his opening offer of 'Miss Gibson, I admire your face. May I paint it?' She laughed, but consented once she realised he was serious. Fisher was already known as 'the king of the magazine covers' and, according to *Harper's Bazaar*, he was 'the greatest portrayer of American womanhood'. His paintings offered the country a fantasy of idealised femininity, full of beautiful clothes in everyday scenarios, by turns playful, alluring, romantic and doe-eyed. Fisher's critics characterised his work as so sweet it could induce cavities, but he was phenomenally successful and Dorothy was impressed with his 'very gentlemanly and businesslike' attitude towards her. Gossip swirled, then and later, that she and Fisher were lovers, but there is no evidence for that or for most of the other stories in circulation about the pair, such as the deliciously absurd claim that at their first meeting, far from a handshake, Fisher 'went down on his knees and begged the lovely Miss Dorothy to come away to his studio so that he might at once commit to canvas her gorgeous features, glorious curves and glamorous youth. She consented and resigned her post on the spot to become Mr. Fisher's latest muse.'

As she had been with her plays, Dorothy was dismissive about her modelling career, describing the whole thing as 'a terrific bore' and joking, 'I believe I have a permanent crick in my neck from the strain' of having frozen so often in poses of head-tilting adoration. However, as with her professed nonchalance towards her roles on Broadway, it is difficult to believe that Dorothy was as indifferent as she claimed about becoming one of the most recognisable models in America. She was certainly peeved when other 'Harrison Fisher girls' were given precedence over her and incensed when, for one cover, Fisher merged some of her features with those of another model, Rita Rasmussen. Later, she saw the humour in it – she told journalists, 'The first picture I recall seeing my features mixed up with hers in was one where I was in furs with a pug dog to my chin' – and she was pragmatic enough to let Fisher ply his trade without too much interference. When he put her on the cover of the *Saturday Evening Post* in April 1911, her face was sent out to over a million readers and in both June and July of that year she was in radiant isolation on the cover of *Cosmopolitan* magazine. The June cover became one of her most memorable incarnations – her blue eyes gazed at the unseen artist, her lightened blonde hair was caught up beneath a huge beribboned hat, she wore a white afternoon gown and sipped sarsaparilla through a straw. It was Americana, in a haute couture hat, and it inadvertently took her back to New Jersey when she received an offer of work from the Independent Motion Picture Company.

It was not, initially, a happy exchange. After the attention she had deservedly received for her work in the theatre, Dorothy was surprised and then distressed to realise that her new employers wished to harvest her fame for their advertising, while relegating her to the life of a glorified extra. She signed a new contract with the Lubin Studios in Philadelphia, where the press office twice confused her work with that of another actress on their books with the same surname. The main American movie studios were still on the East Coast in 1911, with the great move west several years off, which brought the Société Française des Films et Cinématographes Éclair to Fort Lee when they decided to establish their first American base. They were already celebrated for their work in Europe, where they had merged highbrow historical pieces with commercial success. Their new studio in Fort Lee, New Jersey, was the largest in the United States, serving as the base for the company's self-proclaimed mission to 'marry the appeal of American acting with French technical mastery'. For their first American-made picture, Éclair hit upon the ingenious idea of producing a costume drama chronicling the founding moment of Franco-American cooperation – Louis XVI's support for the War of Independence. There was a frenzy of competition among actors to be seen by Éclair, from which Dorothy remained majestically aloof since she had already been offered a contract after securing a private interview with Harry Raver, one of Éclair's American administrators. She quit her unsatisfactory job at Lubin and left Philadelphia for a larger salary and better exposure.

For its time, *Hands Across the Sea* was, as described in a review by the *Motion Picture News*, one of the 'masterpieces of motion picture photography and intelligent artistic production'. It recreated for impressed audiences George Washington's fêtes at Mount Vernon, Benjamin Franklin's reception by the French Royal Family and the revolutionary battles of Monmouth, Brandywine and Yorktown. In an early section of the movie, Dorothy glittered on the screen in jewels, a wig and a ballgown, cast as the most beautiful noblewoman at Versailles, dramatising an historical incident when Louis XVI and Marie Antoinette had honoured Benjamin Franklin by permitting a court belle to crown the first American Ambassador with laurel leaves.[15] In the second segment, Dorothy appeared as Molly Pitcher, an iconic if possibly apocryphal American revolutionary war widow who fought at the Battle of Monmouth.[16] Elsewhere in the reel, Dorothy played the victim of attempted rape by theatrically villainous Redcoats and then a politician's wife who, wholly fictitiously, catches the eye of George Washington.

Dorothy's lover, Jules Brulatour.

Hands Across the Sea, sometimes advertised as *Hands Across the Sea in '76*, was a triumph both for Éclair and for its star. The movie was still playing to packed houses across the country, with some cinemas requesting extra reels to mount two or three showings simultaneously, when Dorothy accompanied Harry Raver to the Motion Picture Distributing and Sales Company ball in October 1911. What it lacked in a catchy name, the party more than made up for in glamour and amusement. At the ball, Dorothy was introduced to Jules Brulatour, a forty-one-year-old producer at Éclair whom she had not yet had the opportunity to meet. Brulatour was tall with dark eyes and a strong physique. He had been brought up in New Orleans and retained the accent. He also carried with him an unsavoury reputation for blackmail and double-dealing in furthering his career, but he could be charming, as he was at his first meeting with Dorothy in the Alhambra's ballroom. He complimented her on introduction with the remark that he recognised her from her 'lovely photo in the papers'. They struck up a conversation and Dorothy lost interest in Raver's company or anybody else's – 'It was', she said, 'the kind of immediate acquaintance where no one else exists.' Their romance began almost immediately, with discreet rendezvous at the St Regis and Great Northern hotels in the city.

Somebody else did exist, however, namely Mrs Brulatour, who had, on the night of the ball, been at home with their three children, sixteen-year-old Marie, six-year-old Ruth and their four-year-old brother, Claude. Despite the fact that she too was still legally married to the pious Battier, Dorothy was unwilling to accept that her love affair with Brulatour should remain adulterous and covert. During filming for her next picture, a Society-set comedy called *Miss Masquerader*, she initiated her own divorce proceedings and Brulatour promised he would do likewise, when the time was right. There was no denying that the pair were infatuated. She nicknamed him 'Julie', a teasing pun on Jules, and he called her 'Mutsie'. Pauline Gibson knew all about her daughter's liaison and actively encouraged it; Brulatour had made a fortune in his previous job as a distributor for the Eastman Kodak Company.

It would, however, be wrong to suggest, as some have, that the next stage of Dorothy's career was simply the result of her affair with Brulatour. She was already established and admired when they met. If anything, the relationship nearly derailed her success. *Miss Masquerader* was another triumph, with a syndicated column in the Hearst press singling out the comic ability of Éclair's 'new leading lady, Miss Dorothy Gibson', and she was again compared to Pickford for the naturalism of their performances, eschewing the typical melodramatic gestures of most other silent movie actors, a style which Dorothy seemed to regard as demented puppetry on the part of her fellow actors. More offers came and were accepted. Even accounting for their reduced running length, with many popular films lasting no longer than ten or fifteen minutes, it is hard to fully appreciate the speed with which movies were made, produced and distributed in 1911 and 1912. Over the course of a few months, Dorothy appeared as a fairy godmother in *The Musician's Daughter*, a sweatshop-trapped widow in *The Wrong Bottle*, wives respectively suspicious of adultery and guilty of it in *Mamie Bolton* and *Divorcons*, a down-on-her-luck debutante in *Love Finds a Way*, wounded love interests in *The Awakening* and *The Guardian Angel*, a gambling addict in *Bridge*, an unlikeable snob in the didactic domestic drama *It Pays to Be Kind* and, in art mirroring life, a young woman who falls in love with an older man for *A Living Memory*. These were followed by a return to her natural strength, comedy, for *Getting Dad Married* and *The Kodak Contest*. Her salary had doubled and she was queen of the Éclair lot, hosting numerous parties for the studio's staff and talent, but by the spring of 1912, when she played a lovelorn cooking teacher in *The White Aprons*, she was also exhausted. A real shove towards a nervous breakdown came when Jules turned up to one of her soirées with his wife, Clara, as his plus one.

Unravelling under the pressure of a frenetic work schedule and torturously confusing private life, Dorothy's performance in *Brooms and Dustpans* was panned as 'flat and absurd' by the formerly admiring critics at the *Dramatic Mirror*. Brulatour, perhaps remorseful for his behaviour at the party, was worried about Dorothy's health, as was her mother. Dorothy arranged another tête-à-tête with her friend and erstwhile boss Harry Raver to impress upon him her need for a vacation. During their meeting, she became so upset that she expressed a seemingly sincere desire to quit permanently. Raver, in a fairly repugnant display of manipulation, promised to release her temporarily from her contract only on condition that she film three more comedies before she left. Victim of a tiredness that had crept into her bones, Dorothy agreed and raced through half-hearted performances in *The Easter Bonnet*, *The Revenge of the Silk Masks* and *The Lucky Holdup*, the last being a Gilded Age take on Romeo and Juliet, with a happier ending. Brulatour was handling the logistics of her proposed trip to Europe and Egypt, with her mother as a companion, when Dorothy discovered Raver had snuck a fourth movie on to her schedule, the second screen adaptation of Washington Irving's *The Legend of Sleepy Hollow*. She filmed it and left for New York from which, as the city's Irish community were celebrating St Patrick's Day, she and her mother sailed in choppy weather for France.

No one can know for certain if Dorothy's journey to Europe was motivated more by her professional or personal considerations. Given her fatigue, it is highly unlikely that she herself could have known for certain. It was later suggested by some of those who knew the couple that, after the embarrassment of the party and his foot-dragging over his divorce, Dorothy engineered the entire trip to re-inspire Brulatour's pursuit of her through pain at her absence. This assessment of Dorothy's motives seems unnecessarily suspicious, especially in light of her distress at the schedule inflicted upon her by Harry Raver. However, that Brulatour remained Dorothy's priority is suggested by a telegram he sent to her when, after a week spent in Venice, she and Pauline reached

Genoa on Monday 8 April. Although her recuperation was supposed to have lasted months, Dorothy agreed to Jules' suggestion that she return to New Jersey so they could make a movie together. Her trips to Naples and Egypt were cancelled and the Gibson women moved with lightning speed to return to the United States. The journey from Genoa to Paris required at least two trains and one of those overnight, but they had arrived in time for a shopping spree on the Rue de la Paix on Tuesday the 9th and caught the boat train to Cherbourg the following day. On the train journey from Paris, she told one of her companions that she was 'overjoyed' to be travelling home on the *Titanic*.[17]

As famous as she was, Dorothy was still part of a nascent industry and the considerable wealth enjoyed by movie stars was nearly a decade away. A salary of $275 was huge to most of Dorothy's generation, but not to many of the *Titanic*'s other first-class passengers. Tellingly, she remained preoccupied with a need for permanent security, for which she looked to marriage and not her career, which she always, perhaps not unfairly, regarded as inherently and terrifyingly unstable.

Dorothy and her mother shared cabin E-22, one of the cheapest rooms available in First Class. The Countess of Rothes' maid was travelling on the same corridor. Nonetheless, Dorothy was impressed by the *Titanic*, which she described as 'glorious'. The three manned lifts for First Class, running from A- through E-Deck, opened on the latter opposite the ladies' bathroom since, like most of the *Titanic*'s cabins, even in First Class, the Gibsons' room did not have its own lavatory. Sinks were provided in all first-class staterooms, but only a few of the suites on B- and C-Deck, like the Strauses', had their own private bathrooms. Communal toilet facilities, similar to those in a restaurant, were provided in lieu and this was to remain the norm in First Class until the arrival in 1938 of a Dutch luxury liner, the *Nieuw Amsterdam*, after which en-suites throughout First Class came to be expected.[18] Accessible from a small corridor within the E-Deck lavatory bloc were two ladies' bath-rooms, which could be reserved by passing on a request to one's steward or stewardess, who would in their turn talk to the ship's Bath Steward about booking a slot on the passenger's behalf.[19] Immediately around the corner from this bloc was Dorothy and Pauline Gibson's two-berth white-panelled cabin, with its oak dressing table, wardrobe and chest of drawers, over which their porthole looked out to the sea.[20] The voyage would offer Dorothy her final few days of rest before she met 'Julie' for another bout of filming. At Cherbourg, she had assured a reporter from the *Moving Picture News* that she felt 'like a new woman' and 'so happy at the prospect' of getting back to America that 'I couldn't think.'

Well versed in the hyperbolic politesse of the movie industry, Dorothy had also once assured a journalist, 'I am a daughter of Hoboken. There is a pride in that.' Only she, and perhaps her mother, ever knew how much truth there was in that statement. On another occasion, Dorothy contrasted her stepfather's evangelicalism with her ambition in what sounds like a more frank admission of why she had struck out from the paths expected of a girl from her background in Hoboken: 'My father is a great man of the spirit and is contented with the simple life. But I and my mother are bohemians and we find the pleasures of this lovely world irresistible!'[21] Whether she would find permanent access to the pleasures of the world through the career she had won for herself or the marriage she wanted remained to be seen.

7

A Decent Wee Man

Life is for living and working at. If you find anything or anyone a
bore, the fault is yours.

Cecilia Bowes-Lyon, Countess of Strathmore
and Kinghorne (1862–1938)

RIDAY 12 APRIL, THE VOYAGE'S FIRST FULL DAY WITHOUT
a port of call, arrived clear, calm and 'fresh', as the Daily
Chart informed the passengers, along with the information
that, by noon, the ship had travelled 386 miles from Queenstown.[1]
Along with the company pennant on her aft mast, the *Titanic* flew
both the Stars and Stripes and the Blue Ensign. Until the outbreak
of the First World War, British passenger ships typically displayed
the national flag of their ultimate destination; shortly before arrival,
the Union Jack would be rehoisted. On the *Titanic*, this meant
that for most of the trip her forward mast flew an American flag
with forty-six stars since, although New Mexico and Arizona had
been admitted as the forty-seventh and forty-eighth states of the
Union earlier that year, their stars would not officially be added
to the flag until the Fourth of July. The Blue Ensign was a mark
of distinction, flown from the stern with Admiralty permission on
any ship with a captain who was a member of the Royal Navy

Reserve, which the *Titanic*'s commander, Captain Smith, had been for years.[2] That afternoon, he ordered a new boiler, the twenty-first, opened up to test an increase in speed, around the same time as the ship received her first warning of 'thick ice' ahead from Captain Caussin of the French liner *La Touraine*, who signed off his telegram with 'best regards and bon voyage'.[3]

Friday was an opportunity for Jack Thayer to start exploring 'all over the ship'. Moving through the first-class quarters on the *Titanic* while his parents socialised with their friends, seventeen-year-old Jack was in awe of the 'palatial' ship, although so far as we can tell his favourite activity remained firmly centred on meal times.[4] There were some rooms to which he did not have access, namely the Smoking Room, on account of his age, and the Reading and Writing Room, on account of his gender. The latter had been designed with his mother and all the other women of First Class in mind since, according to an industry magazine, 'the pure white walls and elegant furniture show us that this is essentially a ladies' room'. Mahogany doors opened into a bay-windowed drawing room with thick rose-coloured carpet and floral-patterned chairs and armchairs. Writing desks and potted plants dotted the room. With everything in its design geared towards solitude, the Writing Room was not a social space. Apart from the turn of a magazine or book page or the scratch of a nib on the White Star-embossed stationery, the only intended noise was the tick of the Magneta-linked clock above the electric-grate fireplace. Unfortunately, the equivalent room on the *Olympic* had not been without its teething problems, particularly with the excessive use of electric light points. After an afternoon spent there, a passenger had complained in a spirit of magisterial disapproval that 'one cannot contemplate spending a couple of hours under this illumination, with even the most enticing of novels, without anticipating the burning eyes that must surely result from the glare from the dazzling points of light above'.[5]

The ship's publicity material described the Writing Room as a tribute to the late Georgian period, as was the male-only Smoking Room on the same deck. The gender-neutral Lounge was apparently 'decorated in the style which was in vogue in France when Louis XV was on the throne, when social intercourse was the finest of fine arts'.[6] With far less historical precision, the ship's Turkish Baths, located as part of a complex on F-Deck that also contained a swimming pool and electric baths, an early form of the tanning bed, was described as conveying 'something of the grandeur of the mysterious East'.[7] The *Titanic* was, like the era that created her, somewhere between nostalgia and experiment, with the latter spirit reflected in her technology but banished from her accommodation. Her interiors conspicuously eschewed anything that smacked of the outré. As with most of her contemporary counterparts, the *Titanic*'s renderings of historical styles were distinctly sanitised and improved, inspiring a contemporary travel guide for first-class passengers to joke good-naturedly of the *Olympic*-class, 'When you board . . . you enter the reception-room, which is Jacobean English in style, but so modernised and improved that even King James might be forgiven if he did not identify it.'[8] Despite subsequent claims for the daring, unparalleled cutting-edge modernity of the *Titanic*, the governing prescription for the interiors of the White Star sisters was conservative splendour. It was not until the unveiling of the *Île de France* in 1927 that transatlantic liners began to have a uniform internal decorating scheme and started to influence architecture on land, rather than vice versa.[9] A year after the *Titanic*'s voyage, Richard Fletcher wrote in his study-cum-travel guide, *Travelling Palaces*, that when it came to the great liners:

> In the dining-rooms every ornamental historical period has been resuscitated. You may sleep in a bed depicting one ruler's fancy, breakfast under another dynasty altogether, lunch under a different flag and furniture scheme, play cards or smoke, or indulge in music under three other monarchs, have your afternoon cup of tea in a verandah which is essentially modern and cosmopolitan, and return to one of the historical periods experienced earlier in the day for your dinner in the evening at which meal, whatever be the imperial

style or the degree of Colonial simplicity, you will appear in very modern evening dress.[10]

Like Jack Thayer, Thomas Andrews spent most of his Friday inspecting the ship. Unlike Jack, there were no rooms to which he did not have access. Although it was only the second day of the voyage for most of the *Titanic*'s passengers, Andrews had been working almost non-stop since the previous Tuesday. He was at the head of the nine-man 'Guarantee Group' from Harland and Wolff, who were tasked with inspecting any issues arising on the maiden voyage, be they big or small, fixing what they could and writing detailed reports for the yard back in Belfast. It had been eighteen months since Andrews' boss and uncle, Lord Pirrie, issued a directive that his nephew 'should be present on board all steamers built by us while undergoing their trials and accompany them on the run round to the cross-channel or other port to which they are ordered from Belfast'.[11] As with the *Olympic*, the maiden voyage of a ship as prestigious as the *Titanic* required Andrews to go beyond his uncle's stipulation by staying on board until the final port of call. It was not a task he relished and, by Friday, he was painfully homesick.[12]

Depending on one's interpretation of good fortune, Andrews was therefore lucky in having more than enough to keep him occupied. A stewardess recalled that 'If anything went wrong it was always to Mr. Andrews one went. Even when a fan stuck in a stateroom, one would say, "Wait for Mr. Andrews, he'll soon see to it," and you would find him settling even the little quarrels that arose between ourselves.' Perhaps a more pleasurable set of interruptions were the numerous passengers who sought Andrews out to congratulate him on his latest creation; Jack Thayer was not the only one who thought the *Titanic* was 'splendid'. However, if he was in a hurry and wished to avoid his admirers, Andrews could travel through the ship via Scotland Road, a long corridor which ran along E-Deck and allowed the crew to move quickly from one area of the *Titanic* to the other. Named after a street in Liverpool, it linked the respective classes of accommodation, and many of the ship's first- and second-class stewards were housed in bunk-filled cabins lining the route.[13] Jenny, the ship's cat, prowled the halls after delivering a litter of kittens shortly before departure and seeking out the company of a 'big, patient, overworked' scullion to whom she had taken a shine.[14] Scotland Road ended at the *Titanic*'s Potato Store, filled at Southampton with 1,420 tons of the tuberous crop.[15] Elsewhere on the same deck were the *Titanic*'s two hospital wards – one for recuperation, the other for quarantining the infectious. All of this was Tommy Andrews' design and all, apparently, was remembered and observed by him with uncanny precision.

A deck above Scotland Road, Andrews had placed the first- and second-class Dining Saloons on the same level, so that they could be both separated and served by the Galley, where some of the ship's 6,000–10,000 daily meals, depending on capacity, were cooked, and the Pantry, where these meals were prepared for service. Amid a mechanised forest of culinary equipment, the Galley's Duck Press stood out as 'most imposing' as it pulverised the dead fowls' bones and internal organs, the results of which were then added to a sauce that could be spooned over the meat. Unfortunately, not everything in the galleys was working so well and Andrews was trying to organise a repair of a galley's hot press on B-Deck.[16] Heating, in general, seemed to be the vessel's major teething problem by Friday afternoon. One ailing, if singularly loquacious, lady in Second Class had sent a dozen complaints to the Purser's Office in the course of thirty-six hours, demanding she be rehoused since the radiators in her cabin were not working.[17] At the same time as she fretted about being forced to recuperate in a furnished icebox, other second-class passengers had asked for their heating to be switched off entirely, as their radiators seemed stuck on the highest possible setting. Similar problems were being reported in a few of the third-class cabins and one stateroom in First Class had been unable to access hot running water. The button used to summon a steward was not working for Ann Isham, an American travelling in C-49.[18] Andrews' encyclopaedic eye for detail also led to him making notes to the effect that there were too many unsightly screws in the hat hooks in the first-class cabins. There had been a series of objections from the clerks who manned the Mail Room on G-Deck. Their quarters shared walls with the cabins reserved for single men travelling in Third Class and the clerks felt that, after the long shifts they worked, the resultant noise was too much to bear.[19]

The clerks' decision to approach Andrews with their concerns over their sleeping arrangements was a shrewd one, since he had a reputation for going above and beyond the call of duty in trying to make a crew's life comfortable, and central to that was where they slept. A crew member wrote later that Andrews could remember hundreds of names and details of employees' shifts and, no matter how busy, he would always find time for even the swiftest of friendly helloes.[20] Even while preparations for the *Titanic*'s sailing day had consumed his attention in Southampton, Andrews had sent a memo to a lower-ranking colleague, urging, 'I have always in mind a week's holiday due to you from last summer and shall be glad if you will make arrangements to take these on my return, as, although you may not desire to have them, I feel sure that a week's rest will do you good.'[21] Sincerely touched by the efforts he had gone to in improving their accommodation, the stewards had invited Andrews down to Scotland Road before departure, 'which he did to receive their warm-hearted thanks', wrote Stewardess Violet Jessop. 'His gentle face lit up with real pleasure, for he alone understood – nobody else had bothered to understand – how deeply these men feel to show any sentiment at all.' They had passed a vote of thanks to Andrews, something many of them had also done when they worked on the *Olympic*'s maiden voyage a year earlier, when they had clubbed together to present him with a walking cane as a token of their gratitude. His schedule at home when he was dashing around the shipyard and his at-sea inspections had already begun to take their toll on Andrews who, at thirty-nine, had started to develop varicose veins. They again produced a gift to accompany their thanks, but unfortunately the only surviving source, a stewardess's memoirs, does not specify what it was.[22]

This rather touching anecdote of improvements to the crew's

accommodation from the *Olympic* for the *Titanic* leads us tangentially to an historical theory so painfully ridiculous that one can only lament the thousands of trees which lost their lives to provide the paper on which it has been articulated. It originated with *The Riddle of the Titanic*, a book first published in 1995 and co-written by Dutch military historian Dan van der Vat and British engineer Robin Gardiner. The root of this conspiracy-heavy version of what happened to the *Titanic* in April 1912 lies with the *Olympic*'s previously mentioned collision with HMS *Hawke* in September 1911. The damage done to the *Olympic*'s hull was light enough that it could be temporarily mended until a week-long window could be found to send her to Harland and Wolff for more thorough repairs, which included replacing a propeller blade she had lost or 'thrown' mid-Atlantic. From 1 to 7 March 1912, the *Olympic* was docked alongside the *Titanic* in Belfast. For six days, the sisters sat next to one another as the *Titanic* was prepared to enter service and the *Olympic* was prepared to re-enter it.

The origin of the 'switch theory': the *Olympic* (left) and the *Titanic* side by side in Belfast for a few days in March 1912.

It was at this point, the story goes, that the *Olympic* allegedly became the *Titanic*. The story goes that the damage inflicted by the *Hawke* had belatedly been diagnosed as debilitating, making the *Olympic* such a bad investment for the White Star Line that the only logical thing to do was to commit the most audacious piece of insurance fraud in history. Since the *Olympic* was already damaged goods, the company decided to switch her with the unblemished and therefore insured-at-a-premium *Titanic*, which would be deliberately sailed into an iceberg on her maiden voyage in a few weeks' time. Several ships operated by other lines in the J. P. Morgan empire were to move into position around the predetermined crash site and, ostensibly by fortuitous coincidence, safely evacuate all the passengers and crew, before the *Olympic*, masquerading as the *Titanic*, sank beneath the waves and left her owners to collect a cheque from Lloyd's of London. The horrible loss of life was never planned but 'the ever-impetuous Smith gets it wrong and crashes early', so none of the IMM's pre-planned rescue party of ships was near enough to help.[23] The *Titanic*, rechristened as the *Olympic*, went on to have a long, successful seagoing career until the economic lugubriousness of the Great Depression forced her retirement in 1935.

Three years after *The Riddle of the Titanic* had been released, one of its authors, Robin Gardiner, went further with a solo effort, *Titanic: The Ship That Never Sank?*, in which he argued that there was no ice collision because 'steel, even of the quality in use in 1912, is very much harder than ice', an observation that has seemingly evaded generations of sailors and which must presumably come as a colossal surprise to the International Ice Patrol.[24] Gardiner instead argued, 'What lay in the *Titanic*'s path, however, was not an iceberg with its white fringe and line of phosphorescence at the waterline, but one of the rescue ships. This vessel had its lights out and had probably been damaged by the ice. For this reason *Titanic*'s lookouts, who were concentrating on searching the sea ahead of the ship for ice, failed to see the darkened silhouette of the blacked-out ship until it was too late to avoid the collision.'[25] The original theory, of an insurance-motivated charge into an iceberg, was the recipient of more undeserved attention in 2004 following a British documentary which culminated with grainy shots of the *Titanic's* wrecked bow as viewers were told, with the helpful use of some CGI, that the brass letters of the ship's nameplate had fallen away to reveal the M and P of *Olympic* beneath.[26] In reality, footage from an early exploration of the wreck in 1987 and HiDef filming in 2010 quite clearly show the name *Titanic* intact upon the bow, a situation aided no doubt by the fact that neither of the sisters ever had their names rendered in brass lettering. The names were inscribed into their hulls and then painted white, as hundreds of photographs testify.

A major plank of the argument that the sisters could be, and thus were, switched in the course of that week at Belfast in March 1912 is Gardiner's assertion that the *Titanic* was 'superficially identical to her sister except for her C Deck portholes'.[27] On the surface, there is some merit to this claim. The two liners had exactly the same dimensions, they were built from the same plans and their interior decorations were in many places a carbon copy of one another's. After the *Titanic* had sunk and there was a surge in demand for photographs of her, images of the *Olympic* were – and often still are – either deliberately substituted for the *Titanic* or innocently mislabelled as such. For the eagle-eyed, differentiating the sisters is relatively easy because of changes made to the first-class promenade areas on A- and B-Deck. The forward half of the *Titanic's* A-Deck Promenade was enclosed by glass windows, while aft was left open to the elements. On the *Olympic*, the whole deck remained open. This alteration has traditionally been attributed to the fact that during the *Olympic's* early crossings it became clear to her operators that the North Atlantic was often too cold or too blustery to justify an open promenade space. However, Mark Chirnside, author of the most thorough modern account of the *Olympic's* career, has conclusively proven that this could not have been the motivation. The *Olympic* had three promenade areas for her first-class passengers – their space on the Boat Deck, which as the top level of the ship was completely exposed to the elements, then the A-Deck Promenade, which had a roof but no windows, and below that a fully enclosed promenade on B-Deck. After observing that all three areas were generally underused on the *Olympic*, White Star decided that this was excessive. The B-Deck walkway was thus altered on the *Titanic* to allow for the installation of a new class of suites, with their own private promenade spaces, the creation of a Café Parisian and the expansion of an adjoining restaurant. The two types of promenade, enclosed and exposed, offered on different decks on the *Olympic* were merged in the *Titanic* on A-Deck, with windows added to the front half.

The *Olympic* (above) with the *Titanic* (below). The differences between their two A-Deck Promenades are particularly noticeable here – the *Olympic's* is completely open, compared to windows on the forward half of the *Titanic's*.

Supporters of van der Vat and Gardiner's version of events argue that all that was required was to change a few nameplates, add some windows to the A-Deck Promenade and race through alterations to B-Deck, which allegedly explains why parts of the *Titanic's* Café Parisian were still being painted en route from Belfast to Southampton. However, as the crewmen's gratitude to Thomas Andrews for their improved quarters suggests, there were in fact many more differences between the *Olympic* and the *Titanic* beyond the cosmetic issue of the Promenade Deck. The Restaurant was not the only room to be expanded between the *Olympic* and the *Titanic*; its popularity on the former had led to a larger Reception Room on the latter. The Bridge's bulwark was teak on the *Olympic* and steel on the *Titanic*. The Wheelhouses had different layouts. There were fewer windows in the younger ship's Chart Room. The barrier rails for the Officers' Promenade were further forward on the *Titanic*; their bedrooms were 9 feet aft. The size and shape of the sisters' on-deck ventilators were completely different from one another's. Water pipes ran higher up the *Titanic's* funnels; her hatch covers on the forecastle were in different places, as were the doors to her deck cranes. The C-Deck cabin portholes were in a different configuration, which Gardiner and van der Vat both acknowledged. The roofs of the first-class Smoking Room, Writing Room and Lounge were higher on the *Titanic*. The third-class General Room had a different porthole arrangement. Several styles of cabin were replicated but moved around and some, like Thomas Andrews' own bedroom of A-36, did not even exist on the *Olympic*. The layout of the Turkish Baths on F-Deck was significantly altered between the two sisters, and dives to the *Titanic's* wreck site confirmed that she sank with her own arrangement in the Baths intact, while photographs taken on the *Olympic* in 1911, before the alleged switch took place, and 1928, long afterwards, show that she kept the same configuration in the Turkish Baths throughout her career. The problems with the heating experienced by some of the *Titanic's* passengers and the non-functioning taps in several second-class bathrooms, which were not fixed until the ship reached Southampton from Belfast, are not issues that could have arisen on a ship that had already been in service for just under a year. The *Olympic* and *Titanic* were cosmetically similar, but in their minutiae they differed in dozens of points all of which, where access has been possible to submariners, have been confirmed by explorations of the *Titanic*'s wreck or, in other cases, by photographs from the *Olympic* before and after 1912.[28]

The ships had their own yard numbers during construction, respectively 400 and 401. At the time of writing, one of the *Titanic*'s propeller blades, jutting from the seafloor, still clearly displays the number 401. This is countered in *The Riddle of the Titanic* with the proposition, 'Yes; but the *Titanic* was cannibalized for parts when the *Olympic* was damaged: could this not have been one of them?'[29] Even if one charitably endows that fragile suggestion with strength, there is still the torrent of evidence that poured from the *Olympic*'s retirement auctions in 1935, when many of her fittings were removed to be sold before her scrapping, including the wood panelling that had been installed in 1911. In hundreds of cases, the number 400 was stamped on the back of those panels and can be seen in many of the pieces that survive to the present. To the objection that Belfast, a shipbuilding city, was not awash with rumours of what was going on as one liner was suspiciously traded for another, Gardiner and van der Vat proposed that the changes were 'surprisingly modest, perhaps as little as exchanging the ship's name-plates and the odd loose item such as lifebuoys (very few items bore the ships' names) – a task for a small team of men acting under the cover of all the work going on aboard other liners'.[30] In fact, this 'small team of men' would have needed to smelt away and then reinscribe the names, redesign the Wheelhouse, make a few changes to the funnels, switch at least one of the propeller blades and forget to remove the number 401 from it, alter the deck cranes and fore-castle hatches, move a deck rail, enclose half a promenade in glass, install a new set of ventilators, alter the roofs over three public rooms and the portholes in another, add in at least eight new cabins and move the officers', reconfigure the Turkish Baths and the Chart

Room, and rip out every piece of wood panelling to erase 401 and rebrand them all with the number 400 for an auction that no one then knew would take place, a quarter of a century later. All this, the unknown small group would have had to manage without anybody noticing, in the course of one week.

Even the foundation of the 'switch theory', that the *Olympic* was rendered a dud by her collision in 1911, is tempered by a passing contextual knowledge of the shipping industry at the time. Collisions like those between the *Olympic* and the *Hawke* were an unfortunate occupational hazard. The *Kaiser Wilhelm der Große* had been damaged by a dock fire in Hoboken in 1900 and hit a naval ram while navigating Cherbourg harbour in 1906.[31] In 1907, the White Star Line had been prepared to replace the entire bow of their *Suevic* after she ran aground off the coast of Cornwall, which suggests strongly that sinking their one-time flagship over something as minor as two damaged watertight compartments was unlikely to be viewed by them, or indeed most people, as a sensible plan. The *Olympic* had more *Hawke*-like collisions throughout her career, including an impact with another British warship, the *Audacious*, in October 1914, and she accidentally rammed and sank *LV-117*, one of the Nantucket lightships, in 1934. In none of those cases was the ship so damaged that it was in her owner's best interests to destroy her, rather than continue with her in operation.

Finally, beyond the overwhelming archaeological, photographic, logistical and contextual evidence that shows this theory of a switch in 1912 to be utter nonsense, we might also add common sense, the silver bullet to so many conspiracy theories. The moment these ships took on paying customers, particularly those in First Class, there was a solid chance that the insurance paid out to their owners would fail to cover both the loss of the ship and the compensation which the White Star Line, in their turn, would have to pay for the lost personal possessions of their passengers. When maritime historians Steve Hall, Bruce Beveridge and Art Braunschweiger examined Gardiner and van der Vat's arguments in 2012, they proffered the unanswerable conclusion that 'There simply was no profit in sinking *Titanic* on purpose, and even if there were, an elaborate switch scheme would have been unnecessary. One man, one box of matches and a drum of lamp oil is all that would have been needed.'[32] Fires while docked happened with brutal frequency – they had gutted the German ship *Saale* in 1900, they would destroy the French Line's *Paris* in 1939 and *Normandie* in 1942. If the *Olympic* was no longer commercially viable, and there is nothing to suggest that was the case and much to the contrary, her trip for repairs to Belfast in the spring of 1912 would have been the perfect opportunity for a devastating fire made to resemble an accident. As a risk to her owners, an orchestrated inferno would have been far less severe, and infinitely less stupid, than sailing her out into the middle of the Atlantic with thousands of people, and their luggage on board, and ramming her into an iceberg.[33]

*

Unaware of the dubious historiography that his creation would one day create, Tommy Andrews dressed for Friday dinner and walked down the three flights of stairs between his cabin and the Dining Saloon. As he descended into the Reception Room, Andrews did as most Irish people seem to do when travelling and found a few compatriots. Mary Sloan, a forty-three-year-old stewardess from Belfast, tall and thin with dark hair, was chatting to the *Titanic's* Surgeon, Dr William O'Loughlin, middle aged, genially rotund and sporting a Bismarckian moustache.* O'Loughlin had been orphaned as a young man, then taken in by an uncle who encouraged him to succeed in his ambition of becoming a doctor, firstly through undergraduate studies at Trinity College, Dublin, and then as a postgraduate at the Royal College of Surgeons in the same city. O'Loughlin was brilliant and well liked, and he and Andrews were

---

* In many accounts of the *Titanic* disaster, Mary Sloan's age is given as twenty-eight, the age she herself rather delightfully provided in several newspaper interviews given in 1912 and afterwards. The 1911 census of Ireland records Mary's age as forty-two.

old friends. They were close enough for O'Loughlin to call him by his familial nickname of Tommy. Mary Sloan knew Andrews less well but seemingly liked him just as much. If many of his colleagues admired Andrews deeply, his co-workers from the north of Ireland, in the words of one writer, 'loved him'.[34] Part of Andrews' attraction was that he conformed so obviously to the criteria set in northern Irish culture for measuring masculine goodness; as the Ulster-born poet Louis MacNeice put it when reflecting on his Edwardian childhood, 'their idea of goodness is summed up in the common phrase: "a decent wee man". The Decent Wee Man is unostentatious, sober, industrious, scrupulously honest, and genuinely charitable.'[35] In a letter to her family in Belfast, Mary Sloan wrote of Andrews, 'I was proud of him. He came from home and he made you feel on the ship that all was right.'[36]

O'Loughlin or, as Mary Sloan called him, 'the dear old Doctor', had been waiting for Andrews. The trio fell into conversation at the foot of the stairwell, unique among the *Titanic*'s stairwells in having an electric candelabra at its base. Mary assumed the two men would want to end the conversation as quickly as they could while remaining polite, so that they could go into dinner. Instead, Andrews evaded every opportunity to exit. He told them that he had written to his wife twice a day since he left Belfast, and when Mary complimented him on 'the beauty and perfection of the ship', Andrews answered that the only thing he had to complain about was that *Titanic* was taking him further and further away from home. O'Loughlin joked that he at least was grateful for the calm seas that had so far prevented any serious outbursts of seasickness. Throughout their conversation, Andrews failed to hide either his exhaustion or his homesickness well; he also mentioned that not only had his infant daughter been in poor health when he left Belfast, but his wife was unwell and his father quite seriously so. Mary wrote a few days later that during their conversation on Friday evening, 'Mr. Andrews seemed loath to go, he wanted to talk about home . . . I looked at him and his face struck me at the time as having a very sad expression.' Eventually, Andrews said goodbye to her and went through to the Saloon with Dr O'Loughlin for the start of a seven-course meal.[37]

A Kind of
Hieroglyphic World

The few hundred people who made up 'the world' never tired of meeting each other, always the same ones, to exchange congratulations on still existing.

Giuseppe Tomasi, Prince of Lampedusa,
The Leopard (1958)

DINNER IN THE SALOON THAT FRIDAY BEGAN WITH HORS d'oeuvres and oysters, then a soup course at which the choice was usually between a consommé and something heavier – in this case, a Consommé Sévigné or a Crème Condé. Halibut was served for the fish course, followed by a choice between duck and lobster Newburg. With the same course, a lighter, vegetarian option was also offered – mushroom vol-au-vent. For the next course, vegetables only appeared on the side of sirloin, a Surrey capon (rooster) with ox tongue or a haunch of mutton, before the salad course. Dessert was ice cream, Pineapple Royale or a friandise cake.[1] For some upper-class men and women who were keen to maintain a trim figure, the Saloon's determination to serve dinner with the same marathon number of courses as one might find at a British country house weekend inevitably proved trying, even if portions were generally kept relatively small. Several passengers skipped certain courses, grazed at those they did take, or trusted in the power of the corset. There were also those who had surrendered to permanent temptation and wore their resulting embonpoint with pride.

Dr O'Loughlin's joke to Tommy Andrews and Mary Sloan about how few passengers were suffering from *mal de mer* might not have raised a giggle from one of the unhappy few, the Countess of Rothes' maid, Cissy Maioni, who had been struggling with it since the *Titanic*'s first night out.[2] Elsewhere in First Class, a Swiss mother and daughter, a Canadian matriarch and her landowning compatriot from Manitoba were also feeling unwell, as were a similarly small handful in Second and Third Class. Most of them generally attributed their discomfort to unfamiliarity with the sea, rather than to the weather, which remained 'fresh' and 'so calm'. With the exception of the Swiss ladies, who lay bedridden as martyrs to nausea in their darkened cabins, the other passengers with shaky sea legs, including Cissy, were able to function.[3] In Cissy's case, that brought her to her employer's stateroom to help undress the Countess after dinner every evening and dress her for breakfast the next morning.[4]

Remembering her life in the Edwardian age, Lady Cynthia Asquith wrote later, 'A large fraction of our time was spent in changing our clothes . . . However small your dress allowance a different dinner dress for each night was considered necessary.'[5] The latter expectation applied only to visits, holidays or transatlantic voyages, which helps explain the mammoth quantity of luggage piled into the *Titanic* at her three ports of call. For the morning, ladies wore suits, often with narrow-heeled boots, since this was the outfit in which they would not just breakfast, but also take the air on the Boat or Promenade decks afterwards. These suits were a halfway nod to practicality, since the more fashion conscious donned the *en vogue* hobble skirt, which had tightened its grip as corsets loosened theirs. The French couturier Paul Poiret took dubious credit for the trend, remarking, 'Yes I freed the bust, but I shackled the legs.'[6] While it was considered extremely poor form for a man to keep his hat on indoors, the opposite was true for women, who were expected, when in company, to wear gloves and hats – by 1912 just slightly smaller than they had been in their gargantuan heyday in the summer of 1910 – until they changed for the evening meal. Contemporary maids later told stories of employers donning gloves with sixteen buttons, rising to past the elbow and taking nearly twenty minutes to put on. Admittedly, those were extreme examples, as most memorable anecdotes are, but gloves were a staple of a lady's wardrobe, usually changed throughout the first part of the day from the shorter, more practical ones for a morning walk to the longer pieces for lunch. In her quick stopover in Paris between Genoa and boarding the *Titanic*, Dorothy Gibson had as a treat bought dozens of pairs to equip herself for the voyage.[7] Along with hats for the trip, Lady Rothes had also purchased new gloves and boots, the latter from the Bond Street shop of a now defunct firm called Hook, Knowles & Co., who also made shoes for the Royal Family.[8]

This carousel of clothing was used by some contemporary commentators to diminish the standing of women since, then as now, there existed a curious belief that an interest in one's appearance automatically equated with a subpar moral worth or an indifference to intellect. In his memoirs *The House of Commons from Within, and Other Memories*, published that year, the former Liberal MP for West Aberdeenshire, Dr Robert Farquharson, chose to cite hats as evidence against the suffragettes' campaign, arguing that women were demonstrably unfit to vote on the grounds that 'Women seem inevitably to bring personal considerations into the discussion of larger questions, and appearance, manners, or even dress are apt to sway their opinions one way or the other . . . They possess a selfish and cynical indifference to the convenience and safety of others, as is shown by the preposterous erections they proudly bear on the top of their heads.'[9]

For Cissy Maioni, her employer's second outfit change of the day preceded lunch in the Saloon. By that point, many passengers had taken a walk on deck, where the Captain carried out his daily inspections between nine and eleven o'clock; at noon, the air was pierced by the sound of the testing of the whistles on the ship's three working funnels.[10] The afternoon was usually a quieter time, when many passengers relaxed in their cabins, read in the Lounge or in a steamer chair on deck, took tea or, depending on their gender, wrote letters from the Smoking Room or Writing Room – they could be delivered to the Purser's Office for posting in New York. Just as he had announced luncheon, the ship's twenty-five-year-old bugler, Percy Fletcher, moved through the ship's main public areas to give the passengers an hour's notice, and thus time to change, for dinner.[11] Fletcher's seagoing equivalent of the butler's ringing of the gong on land used the patriotic tune 'The Roast Beef of Old England', the unsung lyrics of which eulogised a happier time under Queen Elizabeth I when 'our soldiers were brave, and our courtiers were good' and the general population 'kept open house, with good cheer all day long' in a golden era when 'mighty roast beef was the Englishman's food'.

Women travelling without a lady's maid or companion could ring the in-cabin electric bell for the assistance of a stewardess, since it was impossible to dress oneself fully given the length, complexities and restrictions of Edwardian tailoring. Their surviving letters do not confirm one way or the other, but considering that Lady Rothes was accompanied by a servant it seems probable that Cissy helped dress both the Countess and her roommate. It would have crowded the cabin for Gladys to summon a stewardess every evening before dinner and, given the number of passengers who required a similar service, quite possibly a waste of time as well.

The bedroom shared by the Countess of Rothes and Gladys Cherry was beautiful, with white walls, a small chandelier, rose-pink duvets, mahogany wardrobes, armchairs, a sofa and a dressing table. It was decorated in the late Georgian style, one of the sixteen aesthetics employed throughout the *Olympic*-class first-class accommodation, with the layout of bedrooms and parlours replicated or mimicked between the sisters, albeit with the cabins in different locations between the two ships.[12] The Countess's stateroom on the *Titanic*, C-77, was more or less identical to the *Olympic*'s B-69, which was lovely enough for White Star to feature it in their early marketing campaigns for the *Olympic*. The only significant difference between them was that on the *Olympic*, as a B-Deck stateroom, the room had two windows, as shown in the surviving advertising prints, while on the *Titanic* the Countess and Gladys's dressing table was relocated against the interior wall, and one of their rose-pink quilted beds was placed below the cabin's two curtained portholes.[13]

It was here that Cissy spent hours of her time on the *Titanic*. Contemporary etiquette guides extolled the importance, rights and responsibilities of a lady's maid who, in an ideal situation, was to be:

> on call for her mistress from the moment of waking until she retires to bed. The principal responsibility of this role is to make sure every detail of her mistress's clothing is well presented at all times – only the Lady's Maid is permitted to touch her mistress's dressing tables – and that her hair is immaculately styled. Mending skills, tidiness and the ability to pack clothes correctly and speedily are essential. Being of good temper and reliability are vital qualities. A mistress will likely confide in her Maid, a privilege which requires absolute discretion . . . A Lady's Maid shall be expected to dress in a smart and modest manner at all times.[14]

There were tips on how to stand – 'Your toes should point straight ahead, never toe out . . . Hips should be at all times, walking or standing, folded down and under you in the same forward position you would assume to squeeze through a narrow space' – and how to carry one's chest, 'neither thrust forward in a strutting manner nor caved in like a broken reed'.[15]

If manuals like this continued to idealise the relationship between a lady and her maid as something sacred, by 1912 there were a dwindling number of acolytes as the centuries-old idea that a career in service was something honourable and enviable showed the first signs of unravelling. It remained the female occupation with the largest numbers, but in the previous decade there had been a 62 per cent drop in the number of young women, over the age of fourteen, who were embarking upon a career as a servant.[16] It became more difficult both to retain and to replace servants, particularly those with the requisite skills for the more prestigious and demanding jobs, leading to a higher turnover in positions like butlers, housekeepers, valets and lady's maids. Cissy was a case in point, since she had been with Lady Rothes for less than a year; thus far, it had been a happy relationship and Gladys, whose first real exposure to Cissy was during their time on the *Titanic*, thought she was tremendous at her job.[17] When she was not working, she loved listening to the ship's orchestra, struck up an at-sea friendship with an older gentleman travelling alone who, Cissy thought, 'seemed to suffer from loneliness' and even seemed to enjoy a flirtation with a crew member.[18]

Lady Rothes, *c*.1907, with her eldest son Malcolm, Viscount Leslie, who fell ill while she was on the *Titanic*.

The Countess's three days on board had been quiet, although not without worries. Around the time the *Titanic* left Queenstown, she had received a telegram bearing the unwelcome news that her eldest son, Malcolm, had fallen ill. Aged nine, Malcolm Leslie had been left at home in Scotland with his toddler brother John in the care of tutors and governesses, since even the most loving of Edwardian aristocratic mothers, which Noëlle seems to have been, did not generally take their children with them on long trips. The extant relevant letters do not specify the nature of Malcolm's illness and although it cannot have been particularly serious, nonetheless, it was unwelcome news to his mother.[19] She was confident that the servants at Leslie House would take care of him and it was a relief that Malcolm was not yet at boarding school. He was due to start at Eton, his father's alma mater, in two years' time; Norman's education there had been comparatively brief, truncated in 1893 when his grandmother's death brought him the earldom and enough corresponding responsibilities that he left after only three years to return to Scotland, where he was privately tutored.[20] That Noëlle's husband and eldest son were Etonians was a sign of privilege in the twentieth century, but to the careful observer of trends it was yet more proof of how long the rot had been working on the British aristocracy. When first established by Henry VI in the fifteenth century, Eton had been for the education of the poor, later the sons of merchants and then of the gentry. The great families of the nobility had endeavoured to teach their children at home, but as the influence of the gentry families grew and the royal court as a centre for establishing a network of useful companionship declined, boarding school increasingly became the preferred education for the sons of the aristocracy alongside families with more recently acquired influence. The last bastion of this trend to fall was the British Royal Family, who after 1955 abandoned tutors for the royal children under the modernising influence of Elizabeth II's consort, by which time even the most preciously blue-blooded families of the old guard had rebranded boarding school from something gauchely bourgeois into a mark of distinction.[21] The schools were also part of the reason why nearly all British aristocrats, regardless of their locality, spoke with the same accent. Lord Rothes, with his Scottish peerage, would have been taught the same form of heightened Received Pronunciation sociolect as the Irish dukes of Leinster, the English marquesses of Winchester and the Welsh viscounts Tredegar.

Although one of her relatives vividly recalled her temper – 'She could get quite cross, but she was so charming one soon forgot it' – Noëlle typified much of what was admirable in the British aristocracy and a glance at those she chose as friends suggests that she preferred to associate with like-minded individuals.[22] Two years earlier, when 136 miners were caught inside collapsed coal pits at Whitehaven, the mine's owner and the Rotheses' acquaintance, Lord Lonsdale, had clambered down into the pit himself, refusing to leave until he was convinced that the manager's assessment was correct and that the men were really dead. Lonsdale had then gone from door to door in the village built for the workers by his ancestors, breaking the news to each affected family. He had successfully petitioned George V to decorate fifty miners for their bravery in trying to free their trapped comrades.[23] Yet there were plenty of others in the British nobilities who behaved like wasps at the end of summer. They were viciously petty, small-minded, mendacious and steeped in greed, a trend that accelerated as the financial burdens of maintaining a Victorian standard of aristocratic living became difficult, improbable and finally impossible. In 1910, landowners in Norfolk had complained mightily after concluding that the Royal Family had forced a local wage hike when, upon taking control of his country house at Sandringham that summer, George V had issued a command that for workers on his estate there 'Everything [is] to be fair and more than fair; wages, cottages, everything.'[24] It was this kind of myopic selfishness that enabled the aristocracy's mounting number of critics to present them in their entirety as 'cruel, unreasonable, unfeeling and unpitying men'.[25] As well as the repulsive, the vile and the moribund, proximity with the aristocracy also required dodging the ridiculous. When hosting or attending the legion number of dinner parties, guests inevitably included 'young chaps', sent out into Society in search of a wife. Some were charming, some boring and many were braying incompetents, possessed of volume and intellect in apparently inverse proportion.

Both before and after the First World War, as the decline of the aristocracy accelerated, fictitious aristocrats peopled European literature attempting to capture the spectacle of a *Götterdämmerung*. These literary endeavours often offered readers aristocratic buffoons, loveable eccentrics and, most frequently, villains. There could be heroes such as the Duke of Dorset, possessor of 'Olympian wealth, rank, and intellect', in Sir Max Beerbohm's *Zuleika Dobson*, published the year before the *Titanic* set sail; self-acknowledged anachronisms like *The Leopard*'s Prince of Salina, incapable of competing in a world dominated by gauche *homo oeconomicus*; or the simply doomed, like the brittle and cruel Marie in *Pains of Youth* and the exquisitely useless Lord Sebastian Flyte of *Brideshead Revisited*.

Although most of these fictitious nobles are faced with problems created by being born into a class which had passed its prime and which clung to the trappings, if not the substance, of power, their final doom is nearly always a consequence of their own actions, or lack thereof. They are, like Salina and Sebastian Flyte, haunted by a self-fulfilling sense of futility. In this, they mirrored many actual nobles, on either side of the Great War, who would not or could not compete in a changing world and resigned themselves to failure. However, the diminishing of their class did not necessarily spell inevitable ruin for each individual born into it. There were plenty of patricians, like Noëlle, who remained committed to being useful, as shown by her philanthropy and recent training as a nurse for the Red Cross. Some of them could survive, even flourish, in the age of capitalism, if they had sufficient brains and inclination. They could invest in railways, industrial ports, and lead mines, like the late 7th Duke of

Devonshire, of whom an admiring *Vanity Fair* investigative piece concluded, 'had he not been a duke, he would have been a rare professor of mathematics'.[26] A diverse portfolio was often the key to survival in an age when reliance on the land alone had become suicidal folly, a stark reality in 1912 that explains Lord Rothes' possible interest in buying fruit farms in the United States. Noëlle and her husband dedicated themselves to increasing their income and reducing the debt of the previous generation, hoping to emulate the Earl of Carnarvon, who had been so successful in the task that he could safely funnel money into a decade-long archaeological dig which eventually uncovered the tomb of Tutankhamen.[27] The Edwardian aristocracy might not have been dealt as strong a hand as some of their ancestors, but that was no reason to fold.

Travelling with artefacts accumulated by their past was always a risk, which is why every evening Cissy made a trip to the Purser's Office and collected some of the jewels Lady Rothes had deposited in the Purser's safe at the start of the voyage. Conveniently, the Purser's Office was located at the end of the C-Deck cabin corridors and, on most evenings, Cissy would return the jewels for safety's sake. The Countess preferred more conservative gowns; part of her pre-holiday shopping had involved a trip to the premises of Francis, a dress designer on Grafton Street, where she had picked up several new dresses and a feather boa, then the height of fashion rather than the trough of whimsical kitsch. After helping the Countess into her dress for the evening, Cissy styled her mistress's hair and helped fasten on the jewellery selected for the evening. The Countess had come well equipped with pieces that would complement most of her seven evening gowns for the crossing and any dinners she might have to attend in America. She could choose from six rings, one a diamond marquise cut, one plain diamond, two in diamond and ruby, one pearl and one emerald; two diamond brooches, one butterfly and the other spray; another brooch, crafted with diamonds and emeralds; and three pairs of earrings, one in diamond and pearl, and two of amethyst.[28]

The Countess, with Gladys, proceeded in the same direction as the Thayers and the Strauses down a flight of stairs to the Reception Room and from there into the Dining Saloon. The *grande descente* to dinner was a staple vignette in the romance of the transatlantic crossing and, decades later, it inspired one of the most memorable scenes in motion-picture history, when James Cameron had his two fictional lovers meet for dinner at the base of the cherub-sporting Grand Staircase. In fact, that particular space on the *Titanic* would never have featured in the descent to dinner, since the dome-capped section of the stairwell was actually the entry from the Boat Deck and swooped down to A-Deck, where the first-class accommodation began. To descend by passing the clock, showing the allegorical figures of 'Honour and Glory Crowning Time', and then the cherub at the bottom of the stairs would have required passengers to dress for dinner in their rooms and then go up to the elements on deck and re-enter. The particularly beautiful cinematography of the scene, however, might argue for appreciation rather than pedantry when viewing it.

The Countess, the Strauses and the Thayers instead made their *grande descente* past the D-Deck staircase candelabra, while Dorothy ascended from her cabin on E-Deck. There was no tradition of a Captain's Table on White Star ships and Captain Smith had been placed at a small four-person table with the Thayers. History is full of the agony of the almost, and that the *Titanic*'s first voyage was intended to be Smith's last before retirement provides an enduring anecdote of the maybe. At sixty-two, he was the right age to retire, even if White Star had not emulated Cunard in setting a limit for its commanders to retire at sixty, which had caused confusion in a *New York Times* article of the previous year when it described Smith as having 'reached the age limit'.[29] With a career distinguished by its unremarkable character, Smith was a popular commodore who had seen the *Olympic* through her first year of service and some thought that he would be kept on until the maiden voyage of the *Britannic* in 1915.[30]

However, the White Star Line did not request a retraction from newspapers that suggested Smith had been due to retire in late 1911 and his retirement had thus probably been postponed for him to guide the *Titanic* through her inaugural season. Considering that Smith lived in England, he would presumably have been asked to captain the *Titanic* on her first return trip from New York and potentially for several other voyages, since no record survives of any officer or commander having received news that they would replace Smith on the *Titanic* in the near future. At the very most, the trip on which he lost his life would have been his penultimate voyage and, more probably, the opening scene of the final act in his career.

No menu for dinner on Saturday 13 April remains extant; those for the day before and the day after have survived only because a passenger accidentally folded them up in the pocket of an outfit they later wore in the evacuation or because they were among items retrieved later from the coats of several recovered corpses of the *Titanic*'s victims. The meal seems to have passed much as on the other evenings. Elmer Taylor, a successful paper manufacturer from Delaware, was entranced by what he saw in the 'beautifully lighted dining room . . . A smooth sea, clear skies and low temperature outside gave women passengers an opportunity to get out their latest Parisian gowns, their most brilliant jewels . . . It was a brilliant assembly – contentment and happiness prevailed. Conversations were perhaps animated by a social cocktail or two.'[31] After dinner, the passengers decamped into the Reception Room which, of all the public rooms on the *Titanic*, was the one referred to by the greatest number of alternative names by passengers: its decoration inspired several travellers to use the phrase the 'Palm Room'; it was also sometimes called the 'Lounge' (a name that properly applied to a different room on board), sometimes the 'Music Saloon' or the 'Ballroom' thanks to the after-dinner concerts performed there every evening, which proved extremely popular with first-class passengers.[32] The Strauses' Southern friend Colonel Gracie thought that one of the daily highlights of the voyage was when 'we adjourned to the Palm Room, with many others, for the usual coffee at individual tables where we listened to the always delightful music of the *Titanic*'s band. On these occasions full dress was always *en règle*; and it was a subject of both observation and admiration, that there were so many beautiful women – then especially in evidence – aboard the ship.'[33]

The eight-man band was headed by its lead violinist Wallace Hartley, a thirty-three-year-old Lincolnshire native and devout Methodist. Three cellists, a pianist, a bass player and two more violinists joined him for an hour and fifteen minutes, before they and their instruments went back over to Second Class to play for an hour. The musicians spent their days at sea moving between the two classes, playing in the second-class Entrance Foyer at ten o'clock every morning, then at the Grand Staircase's vestibule leading to the Boat Deck for First Class immediately afterwards, and at four o'clock in the Reception Room for tea, followed by another performance in Second Class, after which they ate dinner in the second-class Dining Saloon prior to their evening concert. On Saturday, as there had been every evening since Southampton, there was the possibility of dancing in First Class, and passengers, who had been provided with a White Star company song book listing each piece in the band's repertoire numbered for convenience, were encouraged to request tunes, which was the origin of referring to a song as a 'number'.[34]

Observing the collective bonhomie in the Reception Room that evening, the fashion designer Lucy, Lady Duff Gordon, accompanied by her magnificently staid husband, Sir Cosmo, was as captivated as Elmer Taylor and Colonel Gracie. Lady Duff Gordon, creator and proprietor of the eponymous fashion house Maison Lucille, was one of the most innovative and influential designers of her era. Along with easing the restrictiveness of corsets, which later led to their elimination as a staple in female wardrobes, she had also designed the trousseau for two British princesses,

Margaret of Connaught and Victoria-Eugenia of Battenberg, whose weddings respectively made them Crown Princess of Sweden and Queen of Spain.[35] Jack Thayer's mother was a friend and a client of Lady Duff Gordon, whose fame had increased significantly on the heels of her success in opening the new Parisian branch of her fashion house and following rave profiles in the pages of American *Vogue*. Another *Vogue* article, covering her Paris opening, was due to be published while she was still on the *Titanic*.[36] She and her husband were travelling to New York to open her first American store and, so that they could avoid the press attention while they worked for a few days after they disembarked, they were using the aliases of Mr and Mrs Morgan. Her initial reluctance to sail on the *Titanic* because it was a maiden voyage and 'I should not care to cross on a new ship' had been eased by the smoothness of the journey; she had enjoyed her trip tremendously, especially her 'pretty little cabin, with its electric heater and pink curtains', and breakfast, which prompted her to remark to her husband, 'Fancy strawberries in April, and in mid-ocean. The whole thing is positively uncanny. Why you should think you were at the Ritz.'[37] Despite their aliases in the Passenger Manifesto, nearly everyone in First Class knew who the Duff Gordons were. Even without her own prestige as a couturier, Lady Duff Gordon was also known for being the elder sister of the bestselling novelist Elinor Glyn, whose stories were both lambasted for, and hugely popular because of, their romantic and erotic scenes.

By the fourth night of the voyage, many of the more famous faces on board had become familiar to passengers who, like Elmer Taylor, confessed to 'indulging in gossip' – an Edwardian travel journalist joked that 'There is more gossip in a large passenger ship than at a parish sewing meeting' – and the best chance to see the noted names was during the after-dinner concerts, when most of the passengers congregated in the Reception Room.[38] Along with Lady Duff Gordon and Dorothy Gibson, the travelling celebrities included Karl Behr, the third highest-ranked tennis player in the US and a veteran of Wimbledon and the Davis Cup; Jacques Futrelle, author of a successful series of murder mysteries; and William Stead, a British newspaper editor and author, with a wide range of passions, including spiritualism and pacifism who, eleven years earlier, had published *The Americanisation of the World* which, as its name suggested, correctly predicted that the twentieth century would 'belong' as much to the United States as the nineteenth had to the United Kingdom. However, even at the distance of a quarter of a century from the act, Stead was far more famous, or infamous, for a series of articles he had penned in 1885, collectively entitled 'The Maiden Tribute of Modern Babylon'. While researching his story, Stead had gone to the East End of London where he had purchased the virginity of a thirteen-year-old girl from her mother. Stead briefly went to prison for this, even though he had entrusted the young girl, Eliza, unmolested into the care of an adopted family in France, via the Salvation Army, who became his main supporters in the quest to raise awareness of child prostitution. Prior to Stead's devastating articles, many Victorians, particularly the middle classes, seemed to believe that such things did not happen in England, and the resulting outcry was considered so damaging to public morale that the Home Secretary, Sir William Harcourt, begged Stead to desist from publishing any more, a plea he politely rejected. The momentum generated by the case resulted in the Criminal Law Amendment Act of 1885, which raised the age of consent in Britain from thirteen to sixteen. Popularly nicknamed the 'Stead Act', to Stead's mild distress the legislation was also harnessed by the Liberal MP Henry Labouchère to include an amendment criminalising all male homosexual activity in the British Isles, the legal noose that later destroyed the lives of Oscar Wilde and Alan Turing. Full sex between two adult males had been made a capital crime in England for the first time during the reign of Henry VIII and, although almost never enforced, the law had lasted until 1861. Even the Henrician legislation of 1533 had not criminalised other acts of homosexual intimacy, as the Labouchère Amendment did from 1885 until 1967, with the final flotsam and jetsam tidied up in 2003.

A less diligent publisher travelling on the *Titanic* was Henry Harper, indifferent heir to the Harper & Brothers publishing house, later to become HarperCollins. Harper and his wife were recognisable on board because they were frequently accompanied by their dragoman, Hamad Hassam Bureik, whom the couple had retained following their recent holiday to Egypt and who was generally agreed to be one of the most handsome men on the ship, and because they hated to be separated from their Pekingese Sun Yat-sen, named in honour of the republican politician who, a year earlier, had overthrown the Qing monarchy to become China's first president.[39] Victor de Peñasco, nephew of the Prime Minister of Spain, was on board with his wife, María-Josefa, as part of an impromptu extra leg of their honeymoon. The newlyweds had been in Paris when they spotted an advertisement for the *Titanic* and decided on a whim to buy tickets. They planned to tell Victor's mother by telegram only once they reached New York, since she was nervous about long journeys by sea. The couple were very obviously besotted with one another.[40] A passenger who had contacted the Purser's Office to pay for an upgrade from Second to First Class early in the voyage called himself 'Baron Alfred von Drachstedt', although the name on his Dutch birth certificate identified him as Alfred Nourney, who on land worked as a car salesman for Daimler-Benz in Germany. Others who had made themselves known to their fellow passengers by virtue of a memorable appearance included the 6 foot 1 Clarence Moore, a DC-based banker returning from a trip to buy hounds for the hunt he mastered on his family's estate in his native Virginia, and Quigg Baxter, a twenty-four-year-old Canadian sporting an eye patch after unintentionally offering up an eye in sacrifice to his national sport. An errant ice-hockey puck had exacted the tribute at a game in Montreal five years earlier, prompting Quigg to redirect his talents to coaching and promoting. He had organised one of the first international hockey tournaments during his recent stay in France. He, his younger sister and their Quebecois mother were occupying one of the most luxurious of the *Titanic*'s suites on B-Deck. A level below in C-90, unbeknown to his mother and sister, travelled Quigg's Belgian girlfriend, the cabaret singer Berthe Mayné. There had been a whirlwind romance during Quigg's visit to Brussels, where a local newspaper reported that Berthe was 'well known in Brussels in circles of pleasure, and was often seen in the company of people who like to wine and dine and enjoy life'.[41] Like the Duff Gordons, if for different reasons, Berthe Mayné was using an alias on the *Titanic*, 'Mrs de Villiers', a precaution likewise taken by Léontine Aubart, also a singer, from Paris rather than Brussels, and also involved in a covert romance.[42] In Aubart's case, she was the long-term mistress of Benjamin Guggenheim, a Philadelphian millionaire via inheritance from his father's mining empire. If Guggenheim's extramarital liaison was known to the Thayers or any of his other fellow Philadelphians on the *Titanic*, there was a polite code prohibiting anyone from mentioning it, and he and Aubart too had taken the precaution of reserving separate cabins.[43]

No such politesse prevented opinions being discreetly shared about another Pennsylvanian, Mrs Charlotte Drake Cardeza, the kind of person who felt the need to be the bride at every wedding and the corpse at every funeral. Possessed of impressive presence and volume, Mrs Cardeza was almost the archetype of the passenger warned against in travelling journals: 'It is necessary to remember that the ship's servants are human beings and need a little rest sometimes, and that a kindly word will do wonders; no one receives better attention by being ill-natured or swearing at them. If you have a sharp tongue and think you are witty when you are only unkind, just take that little weakness and drop it overboard.'[44] Dropping overboard was a phrase dancing through the heart of the Stewardess Violet Jessop when she realised she had been assigned to wait on Mrs Cardeza's suite.

She had barely recovered from the experience of dealing with her when she had crossed over to Europe on the *Olympic* a few months earlier. Two decades later, when she came to write her autobiography, Jessop had not forgotten – she referred to Cardeza, 'a certain well-known society woman', under a false name, but gave the game away, perhaps deliberately, by including a description of 'Miss Townsend's' Pekingese, Teeny Weeny. Jessop included the titbit that, despite her wealth and frequent custom, Cardeza had 'been blacklisted by another famous shipping line because of her utterly unreasonable behaviour and her demoralising effect on other passengers . . . Probably her happiest moments were spent watching the agonised struggles of a couple of perspiring stewards tackling the job' she had set them of rearranging her parlour's furniture within minutes of boarding.[45] As the aforementioned travel guide warned, 'People whom you offend have the knack of "getting their own back", and it is as easy to do this at sea as anywhere else, perhaps easier to those who know their way about. Besides, if you are selfish and want your own way badly, even if you inconvenience other people in the process, it is easier to get it by being polite, and you are less likely to experience revenge . . . It is necessary to treat your fellow-passengers with courtesy and civility.'[46] When private dinner and bridge parties were organised on board for those who knew each other from Washington DC and Philadelphia, Charlotte Cardeza was pointedly excluded.

The antithesis of Mrs Cardeza could be found in Helen Churchill Candee, a respected art historian after her recently self-published book on the history of interior design had won praise from relevant experts, as well as commissions to decorate from President Roosevelt and his Secretary of War, Henry Stimson.[47] A prominent presence in DC circles, Mrs Churchill Candee had kept her married name following her divorce from her physically abusive husband, an experience that had inspired her to write her most popular book, *How Women May Earn a Living*. It was unsurprising that, like the Countess of Rothes,

Helen Churchill Candee was an enthusiastic supporter of the suffragettes, serving as a board member for the national organisation's Washington chapter. Both intellectually and physically attractive, she was travelling by herself though not alone, having attracted a small coterie of admirers who joined her for walks on deck and dancing in the evening, including Mauritz Håkan Björnström-Steffansson, whose father owned most of the Swedish pulp industry and who was en route to Washington to study business. He was constantly attempting to quash rumours, on board and in the press, that he was in fact travelling to serve as a military attaché at the Swedish embassy in Washington. When she was not good-naturedly teasing her 'attaché', Churchill Candee often enjoyed the company of Hugh Woolner, a tall, charming, good-looking if questionably honest former broker who was emigrating to America after receiving a lifelong ban from the London Stock Exchange for illegal trades, part of a series of professional failures that had culminated in him declaring personal bankruptcy, which he had shed only in 1910.[48]

Woolner's embarrassment had been relatively public – his late father, Thomas, had been a famous sculptor – and the path from Marlborough College to Cambridge to the Stock Exchange had hardly been bereft of a network of privileged or influential acquaintances. Far more famous, if equally undesired, was the notoriety of James Smith, whose dinners on the *Titanic* had, so far, proved far more peaceful than the supper he had grabbed six years earlier at a rooftop restaurant in Madison Square Gardens. There he had been approached by his acquaintance, Harry Thaw, a millionaire and functioning cocaine addict who had offered to procure a prostitute for Smith as part of a *ménage à trois*. Whether Thaw intended to appear as the third starring party or to introduce two sex workers to the tryst is unclear. Smith icily refused this apparently unprompted suggestion and the conversation petered out. Thaw left the table, pulled out a gun and fatally shot Stanford White, an architect famous for designing the Fifth Avenue mansions of the Astors and the Vanderbilts. The ensuing trial turned into a circus, with Thaw's family utilising their considerable wealth to destroy White's reputation. Central to the defence's case was Thaw's insistence that, years earlier, White had sexually assaulted Thaw's future wife, the then model Evelyn Nesbitt, and their claim that discovery of this tragedy had caused temporary insanity in Thaw. Under the guise of concern for moral rectitude, the newspapers provided salacious details of unorthodox heterosexuality, including sex swings and bejewelled sadomasochistic whips in White's studio, all of which was used to paint a picture of depraved libidinousness at the heart of the artistic New York set. The media frenzy reached such a pitch that it was the first time in American history that a jury had to be sequestered. As the last person to speak to the accused before he murdered Stanford White, James Smith found himself the recipient of fevered interest from the press, something which was both distasteful and distressing to him. Thaw was found guilty but received a reduced sentence by reason of insanity, and Smith had spent much of the ensuing years living in Paris, returning home infrequently to visit his family on Long Island.[49]

There were also secrets that either were not discussed or could not be acknowledged in 1912. In the course of the voyage, John Thayer befriended Algernon Barkworth, a forty-seven-year-old unmarried squire from Yorkshire. Barkworth had championed improving the infrastructure in his home county, particularly through his service as a Justice of the Peace for the East Riding of Yorkshire. Family memories and the research of Northern Irish historian Gavin Bell confirm that for years Algernon Barkworth was romantically involved with his gardener, Walter, who later moved into Barkworth's ancestral home at Tranby House. One of Barkworth's collateral descendants recalls that no one assumed there was a platonic reason for inviting the gardener to live at the main house and 'people who worked at Tranby House were all

The Countess of
Rothes, after her
training as a Red
Cross nurse, which
encouraged her belief
that to be useful was
to be happy.

Thomas Andrews'
former home in south
Belfast, from which he
left to board the *Titanic*.

Andrews with his wife Helen and their
daughter Elizabeth, photographed in 1910,
shortly after Elizabeth's birth. As an adult, she
became Northern Ireland's first female pilot.

A poster advertising the *Olympic* and *Titanic* during
the publicity blitz for the sister ships in 1911–12.

Many industry experts considered the magnificent first-class Dining Saloon (*above*) on the rival *Lusitania* to be superior to the equivalent room on the *Titanic*. The *Titanic*'s (*below*) was inspired by Elizabeth I's childhood home and a country house belonging to the dukes of Rutland.

The last remaining White Star vessel: now docked permanently in Belfast, the *Nomadic* ferried the Thayers and Dorothy Gibson out to the *Titanic* at Cherbourg.

A 'clear-cut chap': Jack Thayer, aged seventeen, around the time he boarded the *Titanic* with his parents.

In 1911, Dorothy Gibson appeared twice on the cover of *Cosmopolitan* and her modelling career had soared thanks to her partnership with Harrison Fisher.

Cabin B-69 on the *Olympic*. The same style was replicated for C-77 on the *Titanic*, the room occupied by the Countess of Rothes and her friend, Gladys Cherry. B-Deck rooms had windows, as seen here, while on C-Deck they were replaced with more traditional portholes.

Despite having become one of the most famous rooms of the twentieth century, no known photographs of the *Titanic*'s Grand Staircase afloat are known to have survived. Her sister ship, the *Olympic*, had an almost identical feature, which was thankfully photographed on many occasions.

Rescue of the Survivors of the Titanic by the Carpathia, painted by Colin Campbell Cooper, an artist who was travelling on the latter when she intercepted the *Titanic*'s distress calls.

Luxuries Versus Lifeboats – in the aftermath of the disaster, many saw the *Titanic* as a grand moral lesson. In this poster, the Grim Reaper taunts, 'Why all this hue and cry about lifeboats? Have you not your veranda and Parisian cafés, palm-garden, squash-court, gymnasium, swimming-pool, Turkish baths, and à la carte restaurant?'

All that remains of the *Titanic*'s Grand Staircase. The chasm behind the chandelier is where the staircase once stood and shattered apart during the sinking.

After the 2009 fire, the derelict remains of Lady Rothes' favourite home, Leslie House.

aware of the situation there, though it wasn't talk[ed] about as many things weren't in those days'.[50] Harriette Crosby, in cabin B-26, had left her illegitimate daughter, Andrée-Catherine, at a boarding school in Paris until she could form a plan to bring her to live respectably with her in Michigan. Also hidden or at least covered in the silence of manners was the agony of Marie-Eugenie Spencer, a retired opera singer travelling in cabin B-78 and struggling with an opium addiction that would kill her a year later. Her British husband, William, was having an affair with one of her maids.[51]

Silence also cocooned the wealthiest couple on the *Titanic*, if for markedly different reasons. Almost no one was unaware of the honeymooning Colonel Astor and his wife. Astor's flamboyant fortune was not matched by his personality; he was a devout worshipper of the 'god of punctuality' according to the crushingly underwhelming compliment of his acquaintance Elizabeth Wharton Drexel.[52] He and his first wife, Ava, had gained freedom from their miserable marriage through their divorce in November 1909, following the death of Astor's redoubtable mother, to whom divorce had been anathema. The Astors' separation had shocked New York Society, although not nearly as much as the Colonel's subsequent marriage to Madeleine Force, a seventeen-year-old graduate of Miss Spence's School in Manhattan whom he had met at the upper-class summer retreat of Bar Harbor, Maine, a few months after his divorce had been finalised. Madeleine had allegedly been in love with a twenty-two-year-old family friend, William Dick, but once her name had been linked to Astor's her parents' ambition and genuine concern about their daughter's reputation resulted in her becoming the second Mrs Astor with a quiet ceremony in the ballroom at Beechwood, the Colonel's summer house in Newport, Rhode Island. Collective viciousness, expressed in silence, washed over the couple, with most of the Colonel's friends avoiding them, on their wedding day and after. To escape, they had embarked upon an extended honeymoon to Europe and Egypt from which they were returning on the *Titanic* after Madeleine had discovered she was pregnant. Once home, the Colonel planned to rewrite his will to provide for his on-the-way third child. Madeleine had spent much of the voyage so far in their suite on B-Deck, which, given the agony she had endured as a result of the observations of the serially unkind about her marriage, was probably a shyness born from painful experience. She had been regarded as a vivacious and intellectually preco-cious student during her time at Spence, traits which had been subsumed or hidden after her wedding. May Futrelle, travelling with her novelist husband, left a particularly sad recollection of the Astors' time on the *Titanic*: 'every other woman on board was curious about them . . . Perhaps they would have been rather glad to scrape up a few acquaintances. I used to think so when I saw her glance up from her reading at every one who passed. But, of course, the rest of us felt that it would have been rather presumptuous to make the first move.'[53] One of the ship's stewardesses, Violet Jessop, shared this curiosity but 'instead of the radiant woman of my imagination, one who had succeeded in overcoming much opposition and marrying the man she wanted, I saw a quiet, pale, sad-faced, in fact dull young woman arrive listlessly on the arm of her husband, appar-ently indifferent to everything around her'.[54]

One of the Astors' friends, Margaret Brown, was there to provide company. Occasionally known in her lifetime by the nickname of Maggie, she is better known today as Molly Brown, partly due to the success of the Broadway musical *The Unsinkable Molly Brown* and its subsequent film adaptation, for which Debbie Reynolds was nominated for an Academy Award.[55] As the title of the biographical musical suggests, Brown has become inextricably linked with her five days on the *Titanic*, frequently cast in dramatisations of the disaster as a breath of fresh air in the stultifying milieu of entrenched elitism. The hail and hearty

Molly functions in the *Titanic's* myth as the fun face of warm-hearted and carefree 'New Money' against the dour insularity of the Old. In fact, Maggie Brown was anything but indifferent to the nuances of Society. She was close enough to the Astors to have joined them briefly for a cruise up the Nile when their honeymoon took them to Egypt at the same time as she was vacationing there, and, in her own words, she gravitated towards 'exceedingly intellectual and much travelled acquaintances'.[56] As a young woman in Colorado, she had intended to marry for money, but changed her plans when she fell in love with Jim Brown, a struggling mining engineer. A few years after their wedding, Jim struck a thread of gold and the couple moved with their two young children into a mansion in Denver, with summer spent at a lodge just outside the city. Where the portrayal of Maggie as something of an outsider does hold true is in the way she was treated by the 'Sacred Thirty-Six', which was smaller Denver's equivalent of Manhattan's Astor-blessed Four Hundred. They refused to invite the Browns to their bridge or dinner parties, which understandably upset Maggie, although she soon eclipsed them all through her philanthropy. She was compulsively useful – founding, funding and serving in soup kitchens for the families of her husband's miners, working with local judges to help destitute children by establishing a juvenile court and, as a practising Catholic, raising money for the construction of Denver's Cathedral of the Immaculate Conception, due to celebrate its inaugural Mass that autumn, by which time Maggie would be back in Denver after another winter spent in Europe and the Middle East.

As the music and dancing came to an end, passengers finished their drinks and made their way back to their cabins. In his white tie and fronted piqué shirt with its imperial wing-tipped collar starched to a degree that would have won applause from an Elizabethan courtier, Tommy Andrews returned to his cabin and continued to work, poring over blueprints and his notes from that day's inspections. Elsewhere, most of the first-class passengers retired, as one of them put it, after another evening surrounded by 'the hum of the voices, the lilt of the German waltzes, the unheeding sounds of a small world bent on pleasure'.[57]

Its Own Appointed Limits Keep

Part of the afternoon had waned, but much of it was left, and what was left was of the finest and rarest quality. Real dusk would not arrive for many hours; but the flood of summer light had begun to ebb, the air had grown mellow, the shadows were long . . .

Henry James, *The Portrait of a Lady* (1880)

ON SUNDAYS AFTER BREAKFAST, STEWARDS PUSHED back several of the Dining Saloon's tables and rearranged chairs for a non-denominational service, led by the Captain since, like most ships at the time, the *Titanic* did not provide a designated chaplain. Amid the spiritual labyrinth of Protestant denominations, some differences are so slight as to be discernible only to a skilled theologian – Thomas Andrews' Presbyterianism, for instance, was technically Non-Subscribing Presbyterianism, a northern Irish creedal detour reached via rejection of the Westminster Confession of Faith of 1646, with its most significant theological deviation, the embracing of Unitarian as opposed to Trinitarian theology, making little difference to its everyday forms of worship. Others however are sufficiently distinct as to prevent any kind of meaningful ecumenicalism. There was very little by way of similarity between the typical Sunday worship of the Anglican-Episcopalian Thayers and Lady Rothes and the Baptist services attended by Dorothy Gibson and her mother. However, although the forty-five-minute religious service in First Class was pragmatically non-denominational, it was not non-confessional.[1] It was Protestant. Mass was celebrated in the second-class Library and afterwards in the General Room for Third Class, but it was not typically offered in British passenger liners' first-class quarters until the 1930s and it was offered on the *Titanic* only after a Catholic priest, travelling in Second Class, volunteered his services. Similarly, although kosher food was provided, no form of non-Christian worship was offered in the ship's public rooms.

Protestantism ringed and, to a large extent, defined the Anglo-American upper classes. There were a few old families in the British nobility, principally the Howard dukes of Norfolk, who had remained Catholic since the time of the Reformation, with their faith regarded either as an eccentric quirk by their Anglican peers or as grounds for disqualifying them from various positions in public service.[2] In rare instances, its oddity proved useful; prominent Catholic families in the British and American upper classes were often recruited to serve on diplomatic missions to the Vatican or Vienna.[3] However, while many Protestants from a similar background were quite happy to be friends or colleagues with Catholics or Jews, they drew the line at in-laws and there remained a feeling that, when it came to non-Protestants in the elite, they were 'not quite one of us'. So long as the outward signs were adhered to, a genuine lack of Protestant faith from those who publicly professed it did not carry the same subtle yet firm social penalties, which explains why Dorothy's mother Pauline had continued her regular attendance at the First Baptist Church of Hoboken, even after both of Dorothy's younger brothers died in infancy, a double tragedy that had dealt a body blow to Pauline's faith from which it never recovered. She had gone to church to placate her husband and to maintain her circle of friends, nearly all of whom were active in the spiritual and social organisations of Hoboken First Baptist.[4]

The two hymns sung in the first-class Saloon on Sunday 14 April were 'O God, Our Help in Ages Past' and 'Eternal Father, Strong to Save', both traditionally associated with the merchant and royal navies.[5] The latter is still known as the 'Hymn of Her Majesty's Armed Forces' and it has since been adopted and adapted by both the US Marine Corps and the US Coast Guard. With its place in maritime tradition, there was nothing unusual about 'Eternal Father, Strong to Save' being selected by Captain Smith that morning, but there is something unavoidably haunting in its opening verse:

> Eternal Father, strong to save,
> Whose arm hath bound the restless wave,
> Who bidd'st the mighty ocean deep
> Its own appointed limits keep;
> O, hear us when we cry to Thee,
> For those in peril on the sea![6]

Ida Straus and her husband were used to Protestantism's sacerdotal powers of bestowing respectability and demarcation. At the very least, organised Christianity had left a few bruises on the lives of most European and American Jews in the early 1900s. Isidor's youngest brother, Oscar, had been the first Jew to serve in the US Cabinet as Secretary of Commerce and Labour under the first Roosevelt administration; before that he had been a US Minister abroad, but initial suggestions of postings to Russia or Switzerland had to be rethought in light of the anti-Semitism prevalent in both countries. The Tsar would almost certainly have refused to receive Oscar and the Swiss government did not give Jewish businessmen or diplomats, even if American citizens, the same rights it extended to others.[7] Eventually, Oscar had represented his adopted country at the court of Sultan Abdul Hamid II in Constantinople, where the government under the Caliph of Islam proved more welcoming to a Jewish diplomat than either the Russian emperor or the secular cantons. On North American soil, Isidor's other brother, Nathan, had been denied a hotel room during a trip to Lakewood, New Jersey, and when Ida's youngest son, Herbert, applied to join the Triton Fish and Game Club near his Canadian summer home, he was blackballed on the grounds that a previous member had been 'objectionable and Jewish' and so they did not want another one.[8] The most personally aggrieving slight had come in 1909 when the Strauses' grandson was rejected as a prospective student from St Bernard's Academy. When Isidor, as a former senator and co-owner of New York's largest department store, took up his pen to lobby the Manhattan prep school into changing its mind, the headmaster had written back, 'I take it as a great compliment that you wish your grandchild to attend St. Bernard's. Though it is most painful to me, it seems only honest to tell you frankly that we dare not take a child of Hebrew parentage. I cannot say anything in extenuation, except that we have reason to know that we should lose our Gentile pupils were we to accept Hebrews . . . The writing of this letter to you gives me real distress.'[9]

Ida and Isidor Straus, photographed shortly before their trip on the *Titanic*.

For most of her time on the *Titanic*, Ida had tried to relax as much as possible. Her heart problem had flared up again that winter, despite the restorative powers expected of the French Riviera, and she had spent much of the voyage thus far indoors.[10] Her husband was worried about her and their business. As he had aged, Isidor had delegated more of his responsibilities at Macy's to their sons, but a renovation of the sixth floor, now offering cheaper goods than the others, had failed to turn a profit, even over the busy holiday season. Their son Jesse was due to take a break from Macy's to bring his wife and infant daughter, Beatrice, to visit relatives and begin familiarising the child with European languages. They planned to sail from New York on 11 April.[11] Rather than have them cancel their trip, Isidor decided to return early to see what could be done with the under-performing sixth floor.[12]

This change in the Strauses' schedule may explain the later story that they had originally booked passage home on one of the smaller liners temporarily laid up as a result of the British miners' strike. However, a letter Isidor wrote to his brother Oscar on 12 March mentions that he and Ida had taken a suite on the *Olympic*, which was due to make a westbound crossing from Southampton on 19 April. Jesse's impending departure for Germany and concerns about Macy's apparently prompted Isidor to switch their booking from the *Olympic* to the *Titanic*, scheduled to depart nine days earlier, thereby getting them home only two or three days after Jesse and his family left.[13] It may have been that the miners' strike removed from operation certain ships that the Strauses had considered because they had been timetabled to sail even earlier than the *Titanic*, but the easiest option would have been to switch to another White Star ship, with the *Titanic* as the obvious choice. The Strauses were in a hurry, if not quite a panic.

Jesse was travelling to Europe on the German liner *Amerika*, another creation of the Harland and Wolff shipyard and one which was to sail within range of the *Titanic*'s wireless that Sunday afternoon.[14] Passengers could pay at the Purser's Office to send personal telegrams to shore or other ships and Ida and Isidor planned to send one to Jesse, Irma and Beatrice. Until then, they went to the *Titanic*'s underused Lounge, which had been decorated as an homage to Versailles and was unfortunately sporting a similarly in-keeping feel of an abandoned state apartment.[15] No one criticised the appearance of the Lounge, described by a trade journal as 'a magnificent salon' and 'the finest room ever built on a ship'. In the centre of the room, a chandelier nestled in an oval cupola. Armchairs, sofas and settees with green silk-covered cushions were dotted across the green and gold carpet, and there was a small bar that served refreshments.[16] However, its location and utility had both been poorly thought out. The chief problem affecting the Lounge's popularity was that nearly everything it offered to passengers was provided in other rooms on board. Stewards collected letters from its ornamental post box, carrying them down to the Mail Room for sorting, and there were writing desks, stocked with pens and White Star-headed stationery, but elsewhere on the same deck there was a dedicated Writing Room and the men's Smoking Room, which likewise contained some desks and supplies for letter writing. Tea was served every afternoon in the Lounge, just as it was in the ship's two cafés, both of which had better views of the passing ocean, and while the Lounge stayed open late for after-dinner drinks, so did the Reception Room, which had the added benefits of playing host to the evening concerts and dances and of being adjacent to the Saloon, rather than three decks above. The Reception Room had proved popular enough on the *Olympic* to be expanded on the *Titanic*, while the Lounge remained of dubious utility and splendid appearance. Its only unique feature was its mahogany bookcase, which functioned as a lending library for first-class travellers and brought the Strauses regularly to the room, along with their friend Colonel Gracie, whom they saw there at about noon, before they sent their telegram to the *Amerika* and after he had sung and prayed in the Dining Saloon.[17] Gracie affectionately blamed the

Lounge and its collection of books for his uncharacteristic sloth since leaving Southampton: 'I had devoted my time to social enjoyment and to the reading of books taken from the ship's well-supplied library. I enjoyed myself as if I were in a summer palace on the seashore, surrounded with every comfort.'[18] By Sunday, Gracie had been sated by languor and rectified matters by getting up before breakfast to meet 'the professional racquet player in a half hour's warming up, preparatory for a swim in the six-foot deep tank of salt water, heated to a refreshing temperature'.[19]

Like Ida, the Colonel had boarded the *Titanic* in a state of fatigue. He had recently completed an enormous work of revisionist military history, *The Truth about Chickamauga*, a Civil War battle so bloody that the Tennessee river on whose banks it had been fought was briefly renamed 'the River of Death'. With 36,000 casualties, two Confederate generals had been suspended for refusing to carry out orders which they claimed would have substantially increased the body count to little tactical advantage. Colonel Gracie's father had served in the battle and his tome had garnered criticism for its failure to engage honestly with the split in the Confederate command and its strong antipathy towards the Union armies.[20] On the first day of the voyage, he had loaned a copy of his book to Isidor Straus, 'in which he expressed intense interest', and Isidor had finished reading it by the Sunday.[21] Since renewing their acquaintance during the departure from Southampton, when together they had witnessed the *New York* incident, Gracie and Isidor had taken daily walks on deck with their principal topic of conversation set by Gracie's admiring curiosity about Isidor's 'remarkable career, beginning with his early manhood in Georgia when, with the Confederate Government Commissioners, as an agent for the purchase of supplies, he ran the blockade of Europe. His friendship with President Cleveland, and how the latter had honoured him, were among the topics of daily conversation that interested me most.'[22] Isidor's family shared Gracie's fascination and, the previous spring, Jesse Straus had encouraged his father to write his memoirs, overcoming Isidor's objections that to do so would be self-indulgent and of limited interest to others.[23] Isidor had started the project in June, 'jotting down from time to time, as the spirit moved me, such occurrences as happened to present themselves to my mind', but left the manuscript in New York when he and Ida sailed for Europe in January.[24]

Decades later, one of Isidor's grandchildren remarked to an historian that Isidor and the first generation of Strauses to settle in America had lived a life that sounded, to him, like something from 'the world of *Gone with the Wind*'.[25] It was not a wholly inaccurate observation. *Gone with the Wind* provides a backstory for Gerald O'Hara, the fictional paterfamilias, which has him fleeing to the United States after running foul of an aristocratic agent in his native Ireland. Having been forced across the Atlantic by politics, Gerald initially enters a career in trade, migrating to the Southern state of Georgia where, over a game of cards, he wins an unloved plantation and a slave from a drunken opponent. Initially something of an outsider thanks to his Catholicism, Gerald is eventually accepted into the land- and slave-owning classes, who grow to like and trust him; he settles down, buys more slaves, raises a family and pledges allegiance to the Confederacy when, two decades later, Georgia secedes from the Union. Isidor's father, Lazarus Straus, came from a respected Jewish family in Otterberg, and he had sided with the uprisings of 1848, a wave of unrest that swept across Europe amid industrial downturn and political frustration. Unlike its Orléanist counterpart in France, the Bavarian monarchy weathered the crisis and retaliated by making life difficult for its former opponents. Later, both Isidor and his brother Oscar believed that this had been the direct cause of their father's emigration to America. Isidor wrote in his memoirs that 'My father, who was active in the revolution of 1848, finding life burdensome after the collapse of the movement, long contemplated emigrating, but his ties were so many that he found it most difficult to tear himself away, and not until the spring of 1852 could he bring himself to take this decisive step,' while Oscar, who was too young to remember the events personally, had been told of 'petty annoyances and discriminations which a reactionary government never fails to lay upon people who have revolted, and revolted in vain'.[26] However, historians who have written that Lazarus Straus had to move because of the hostility of the Bavarian government are perhaps taking too literally the brothers' recollections. Of the two accounts, Isidor's is the more restrained, mentioning only that his father's life in Otterberg became 'burdensome', while his citation of Lazarus' responsibilities as an explanation for why he did not emigrate until 1852 suggests that there were various reasons behind the Strauses' departure. The 1848 revolution had failed in Bavaria, but not completely; the collapse of the uprising did not equate with the simultaneous re-establishment of the status quo. In the immediate aftermath, the previous King of Bavaria, Ludwig I, had abdicated in favour of his son, Maximilian II, who initially attempted to pursue a moderate course between middle-class liberalism and the conservatism of the Catholic clergy and the aristocracy. It was not until 1852, when Lazarus Straus left Bavaria, that the powers of the police began to be increased to their pre-1848 levels and 1859 before the triumph of reaction with the garrotting of the electoral laws.[27] While life in Otterberg was less pleasant for Lazarus Straus after 1848, there is little in the history of the wider region to suggest he had to leave specifically because of his political views. There was an acrimonious inheritance dispute with several of his thirteen siblings, which may have been one of the 'many ties' vaguely remembered by Isidor. The argument seems to have soured relations with his family, making migration a potentially less wrenching prospect than it had been before.[28]

Lazarus left behind his wife, Sara, and their six children – Karolina, Isidor, Hermine, Nathan, Jakob and Oscar.[29] They were to follow when he had established a home and saved enough money to send for them. From his disembarkation at Philadelphia, Lazarus moved south to Georgia, where he found work as a pedlar, an integral part of the nascent American economy through its role in bringing goods to rural homesteads.[30] They were particularly necessary in the South, where plantations were often separated by significant distances from the nearest towns and stores. It was his father's experiences in the antebellum South that permanently convinced Isidor of the virtues of Southern hospitality and that anti-Semitism was both more pernicious and more widespread in the North. He told his own children that their grandfather had been:

> treated as an honoured guest and his visits were looked forward to with real pleasure. Another feature, which sounds almost like fiction, respecting the relationship between even the wealthiest and most aristocratic families and the comparatively humbler peddler, was the chivalrous spirit of hospitality that refused to take any pay for board and lodging of the man and made only a small charge for the feed of the horses, which gives an idea of the view entertained by the southern people regarding the proper conduct towards the stranger under his roof . . . [thus] a bond of friendship sprang up which in this part of the country and at this time seems difficult to understand.[31]

Within two years, Lazarus had saved enough to book passage for Sara and the children to sail from Le Havre to New York, and during the voyage the nine-year-old Isidor was excited to spot two icebergs in the distance.[32] The family settled in Talbotton, Georgia, where Lazarus opened a store and made friends.[33] Isidor's subsequent assertion that Jewish immigrants who settled north of the Mason–Dixon Line experienced more prejudice than those who migrated south is supported by most histories of Judaism in America.[34] The local Baptist and Methodist preachers were regular guests at the Strauses' dinner table, where they often discussed the risks of poor translations of the Old Testament from the original Hebrew and asked Lazarus for his help with the language.[35] Isidor remembered these meetings with fondness and continued

the tradition; by 1912, one of his closest friends was the episco-
palian Bishop of Tennessee, the Rt Rev. Thomas Gailor.[36] Privately,
Lazarus Straus and his youngest son, Oscar, always believed that
their acceptance into Southern society owed much to the fact
that the family's white skin trumped any other considerations.
The latter wrote in 1922 that Lazarus 'was treated by the owners
of the plantations with such a spirit of equality that is hard to
appreciate today. Then, too, the existence of slavery drew a distinct
line of demarcation between the white and black races. This gave
to the white a status of equality that probably otherwise he would
not have enjoyed to such a degree.'[37] Again, their interpretations
are supported by the research of later historians like Bertram
Korn, who argued that the caste system in the Old South was so
immeasurably weighted towards colour that 'this very fact goes a
long way towards accounting for the measurably higher social and
political status achieved by Jews in the South than the North'.[38]

One of the main conversational labours of the preachers who
befriended the Strauses was to convince them of the morality of
slavery.[39] Other German-Jewish immigrants to the region in the
1850s recalled being told that 'the peculiar institution' was 'not
so great a wrong as people believe. The Negroes were brought
here in a savage state; they captured and ate each other in their
African home. Here they were instructed to work, were civilized
and got religion, and were perfectly happy.'[40] In his memoirs,
Isidor passes over the issue almost in silence; Oscar wrote, decades
later, that neither of their parents had truly believed in slavery
and that they had first bought slaves after hiring them from another
plantation for a season's work in their home, whereupon the hired
slaves begged the Strauses to buy them, since they were treated
better by them.[41] The Strauses were well known later for their
kindness to those who worked for them which, when set in the
context of the brutality frequently experienced by slaves in other
households, lends some credence to Oscar's story. We know that
the Strauses taught their slaves a trade, as well as literacy, the
latter of which was vehemently opposed by most slave-owners.[42]

Secondly, by the 1850s, choosing to prioritise race over economics even in the face of mounting evidence that slavery was in fact retarding the South's economy, most Southern state legislatures had tightened legal restrictions on manumission until it was 'virtually impossible to free a slave except through stratagem or deceit'.[43] Finally, Lazarus Straus's initial opposition to slavery seems to have been worn down in the course of social interactions in his new home. A process by which he evolved through degrees of acceptance fits with hiring and then 'purchasing slaves one by one from their masters' because some begged him not to send them back to their previous owners.[44]

For Isidor and his siblings, the issue was less complicated. They arrived in the antebellum South as children where, in Oscar's words, 'as a boy brought up in the South I never questioned the rights or wrongs of slavery. Its existence I regarded as [a] matter of course, as most other customs or institutions. The grown people of the South, whatever they thought about it, would not, except in rare instances, speak against it.'[45] Where the family's later recollection of events is incomplete is in detailing how far their acceptance of slavery eventually went. It seems clear that Lazarus and his wife Sara participated in the slave-owning system reluctantly, but on at least one occasion, a teenaged Isidor and his middle brother, Nathan, were sent to represent their father at a slave auction, where they wrote home to inform their parents that they had nabbed a bargain in buying a pregnant slave; the phrase 'two for the price of one' dancing horribly in the image conjured by the letter.[46] By the time the 1860 census was conducted and the *rage militaire* was sweeping the Southern states, the Strauses have been described as owning thirteen slaves, although on closer inspection the relevant entry for the census seems to be referring to the age of one slave, rather than the overall size of the household.[47] Claims of a significant number of slaves by 1860 have been contested on the grounds that Oscar later mentioned that after the Civil War his parents took two of the slaves North with them because they 'were too young to look out for themselves, and so far as they knew they had no relatives'. However, that was by 1865 and elsewhere in his memoirs, he mentions several other slaves, including two men who were taught a trade – tailoring for one and cobbling for the other – on Lazarus' orders.[48] It may be that the Strauses' habit of hiring slaves from other masters explains, at least in part, the discrepancies in recollections about the size of the Strauses' household.[49]

The issue of Jewish involvement in the history of slavery, and then in the Confederacy, is a tortured one. Then and now, there were those who questioned how a community composed primarily of first-generation immigrants, most of whom were themselves fleeing varying degrees of state-sanctioned persecution, could have come to support a system of government under which the right to own human beings was presented as an inviolable part of the rights to private property. The Strauses' experience of being slowly convinced after moving to, or being raised in, a culture that increasingly came to define itself by the need to sustain the institution of slavery and which then, to a very large degree, willed itself into being as a nation and then into battle in order to defend it, was fairly common. There was also a slew of reasons that competed with the defence of slavery as motivation for enlistment in the Confederate armies after 1861. Another Jewish Southerner explained that he had volunteered because he was ashamed of staying at home while his compatriots went off to fight: 'I could no longer stand it. I could no longer look into the faces of the ladies.'[50] Others felt that the South was their home, it had been invaded and, regardless of one's personal views on slavery or any other political dispute with the North, duty required a fight under the banner of 'Death before dishonour'.[51] There were also those who hoped that Jewish service in the military would prevent the spread of various anti-Semitic tropes from Europe, principally the canard of the 'Wandering Jew', which perversely turned the centuries of diasporas and pogroms on their heads by suggesting that Jews were incapable of true loyalty to a country, as evidenced by the fact that they were always moving from one to the other. After the war, the Hebrew Ladies' Memorial Association for the

Confederate Dead justified their foundation, set up to care for the graves of dead Jewish Confederate soldiers, on the grounds that 'In time to come, when our grief shall have become, in a measure, silenced, and when the malicious tongue of slander, ever so ready to assail Israel, shall be raised against us, then, with feeling of mournful pride, will we point to this monument and say: "*There* is our reply."'[52]

None of these reasons was particularly different to the myriad that motivated American Christians to take up arms between 1861 and 1865. Approximately 3,000 Jewish Americans fought for the Confederacy, against 7,000 for the Union. As a split percentage, this was similar to that of Gentiles.[53] Just as there were anti-slavery Southern Jews who enlisted, several Confederate Christian generals whose families had been in the South for generations but who were themselves opposed to slavery felt that honour required them to fight for their home states. There were rabbis who exhorted their congregations to remember the Exodus and the plagues visited on Egypt for the sins of slave-owning; there were also preachers like Rabbi Morris J. Raphall, based in New York, who harangued abolitionists attending his synagogue, 'How dare you . . . denounce slaveholding as a sin? When you remember that Abraham, Isaac, Jacob, Job – the men with whom the Almighty conversed, with whose names he emphatically connects his own most holy name – all these men were slaveholders.'[54] Across the United States, there were priests, ministers, vicars and pastors who articulated the same dichotomy among Christians. Moses, Abraham, Isaac, Jacob and Job were once again woven into sermons, so were Christ, Noah and St Paul – the Lamb of God against the obedience demanded of a slave; mercy and free will against proper deference to the law of the land. Where the verses were needed, they could be found, mined, moulded and fired.

It was his service to the Confederacy that first brought Isidor into Ida's life. The Northern navy had blockaded most of the Southern harbours, slowly strangling a struggling economy and birthing the necessity of blockade runners, who soon counted

Isidor Straus among their number. Aged eighteen, Isidor, explaining to his worried mother that his decision to serve was prompted by 'my honor & due respect', made it out of Charleston on the *Alice*, a small steamer that carried him to Nassau.[55] From there, he sailed to Havana, where he hoped to catch a boat to England and the mills desperate for Confederate cotton. No ships were making the trip from Cuba and so Isidor, pretending to be a Northerner, bought a ticket on the *Trent*, a ship sailing to New York, where many transatlantic ships would be available to him. En route, the *Trent*'s occupants heard a garbled report of the Battle of Gettysburg, initially incorrectly relayed to them as a Confederate victory. For Isidor and another disguised blockade runner, the news 'produced such elation on the part of the two rebels on board that we had great difficulty in restraining ourselves from jubilation'.[56] They arrived in New York to newsboys shouting on the streets that it was the other American army that had triumphed at Gettysburg and that the Confederate forces under General Robert E. Lee were retreating south. Nearly 50,000 men lay dead on the battle-field in Pennsylvania and even the victorious Northerners had endured such heavy casualties that the federal government wanted to enforce a draft to replace those lost.[57]

Since crossing the Atlantic as a young boy, Isidor had been fascinated by the sea and he hoped to take advantage of the opportunity presented by being in New York to sail for England on the *Great Eastern*, then the largest ship in the world. In the meantime, he called discreetly on old family friends, the Bluns, at their home in midtown Manhattan, where he met their fourteen-year-old daughter, Rosalie Ida, who was nearly always known by the second of her two names. Ida's elder sister, Amanda, had married a Southerner and they had not seen her since the outbreak of hostilities. Isidor brought news from Amanda and best wishes from his parents, and impressed everyone with his exquisite Southern manners and his maturity, but it was a brief introduction as Isidor changed his booking to a smaller ship, timetabled to leave several days earlier than the *Great Eastern*. The collective mood in New York in the wake of Gettysburg had taken on an ugly, pained, vicious hysteria. Both the loss of life and the draft had presented different targets for the collective fury. One focus, fairly obviously, was against Southerners and Isidor could not count on his ruse of a Northern identity holding for much longer. Another, perhaps less predictably, was black people, whose liberation was now blamed by some in New York as the cause of the war and, thus, their suffering. Isidor left the city on the same evening as rioters torched a Fifth Avenue orphanage for African-American children and lynched black people in the streets.[58]

The defeat at Gettysburg was followed by a swift progression of disasters for the Confederacy. Vicksburg and Port Hudson fell to the advancing Union armies and, from what was reported in the British press, Isidor was sufficiently well informed to predict by the autumn of 1863 that the South would lose the war, with both the Confederacy and slavery vanishing in consequence. He was also well versed enough in history to appreciate the chaos that would ensue in the wake of societal disintegration. On 14 November 1863, he wrote a letter home in which he advised his family to 'Buy real estate, land, houses and lots. Don't buy *shwarze*,' a Yiddish word for black people.[59] Not everyone in the Confederacy seemed to appreciate the reckoning approaching with each new defeat. Brutality against slaves actually increased as the new republic unravelled. One particularly hideous anecdote among hundreds came from a Georgian general who told his wife that, after he had caught one of their slaves attempting to steal some food, he had personally inflicted the sentence of 400 lashes. 'Mollie,' he wrote, 'you better believe I tore his back and leg all to pieces.'[60]

Southern Jews too now found themselves the objects of collective prejudice. This was not exclusively from their Confederate compatriots. After a slew of victories, the Northern General Ulysses Grant issued a notorious order expelling all Jews from the military district under his command in Mississippi, Kentucky and Tennessee, claiming that Jews in the Northern-occupied areas were still trading with the Confederacy and that 'Jews, as a class,

[are] violating every regulation of trade established by the Trade Department.'[61] The order was rescinded only when the Jewish community in Paducah, Kentucky, invoked the protections of the Constitution through representatives they sent to speak directly with President Lincoln in Washington.[62] While General Grant punished Southern Jews for their alleged loyalty to the Confederacy, some in the South condemned them for supposed disloyalty. As the Confederate economy imploded and it became impossible for even blockade runners to get in or out, profiteering became a plague and then a target for public dissatisfaction. Rather than acknowledge it as a region-wide problem, several Southern communities insisted that it was a uniquely Jewish crime, including the Grand Jury of Talbot county in Georgia, where the Straus family lived. They issued a presentment lambasting Jews for their 'evil and unpatriotic' activities. Since Lazarus Straus was the head of the most prominent Jewish family living in the town of Talbotton, where the statement had first been published from the local court house, he took it as a personal insult. He sold his shop and announced his intention to move. Isidor, stranded in Europe with other Confederate blockade runners, only heard what happened later, recounting how the leading figures of Talbot county had assured Lazarus that they did not mean him, or any Jews they knew personally, and that they were distressed by his plan to leave:

> Father's action caused such a sensation in the whole county that he was waited on by every member of the grand jury, also by all the ministers of the different denominations, who assured him that nothing was further from the minds of those who drew up the presentment than to reflect on father, and that had anyone had the least suspicion that their action could be so construed, as they now saw clearly it might be construed, it would never have been permitted to be so worded.[63]

Their entreaties did not convince and by the time Isidor could return to America he found his family stranded at their new home in Columbus, Georgia, which they had moved to in time for the area to become part of the region desolated by the Union armies' 1864 'March to the Sea' through Georgia.

Although he always retained fond memories of his childhood in the South and its sense of community, Isidor never publicly indulged in nostalgia for the Confederacy after its final collapse in April and May 1865. By 1912, there were millions who did; Colonel Gracie being one of them. A school of historiography had arisen in the 1890s, first called the Objectivist movement and later the more revealing Reconciliationist approach.[64] Proponents of this interpretation of the recent American past objected strongly to the idea that the Confederacy was a republic christened by the tears of slaves and sustained by their blood. They underplayed both the necessary savagery of slavery and its importance as a motivating cause for secession. Instead, the South was presented as having been the custodian of the legacy of 1776, when the thirteen original colonies had seceded from the British Empire in objection to a central government felt to be unjustly expanding its authority. The 'Lost Cause' developed and gained traction, depicting the Old South as an agrarian civilisation doomed to collapse in the face of brute, industrialised Northern might. It inspired the erection of hundreds of rapidly produced monuments to Confederate warriors in public places, coinciding with the judicial strengthening of racial segregation in the South under the misnamed doctrine of 'Separate but Equal'. The Confederacy had become more enduring and successful in death than it ever had in life.

The only key tenet of the 'Lost Cause' myth to be rehabilitated by modern historians has been its depiction of the post-war South as an economic wasteland.[65] On his return from Britain, Isidor gradually took over their businesses from his father, who insisted the family work themselves to the point of exhaustion to raise enough money to settle their pre-war debts with Northern firms in New York and Philadelphia, most of whom had given up on ever receiving payments from those trapped in a scorched economy. The Strauses' actions were so admired that they never had subsequent problems securing credit; if they could pay back a loan after backing the losing side in a civil war, they could presumably be counted upon in most other circumstances. Isidor's trips to New York brought him back into regular contact with Ida Blun, who became 'as good a wife as ever man was blessed with' in a wedding at the home of Ida's parents on 12 July 1871, with their ceremony delayed by riots between Manhattan's Irish Protestant and Irish Catholic communities, which claimed the lives of thirty-two rioters and two police officers.[66]

As Isidor moved his parents and siblings to New York, worked for, befriended and bought out at his retirement the owner of Macy's department store, served as a Democratic senator for the state, became a political confidant to President Grover Cleveland and bankrolled his brother Oscar's burgeoning diplomatic career, Ida became the mother of seven children between 1872 and 1886 – Jesse, Clarence, Percy, Sara, Minnie, Herbert and Vivian.[67] Her greatest heartbreak came in 1876 when her second son, Clarence, died in her arms, shortly before his second birthday; years afterwards, his father concluded that the cause had been undiagnosed appendicitis.[68] Ida took great delight in her family, particularly their holidays, and when she and Isidor were apart they wrote to one another daily. After a fishing trip with their son Percy, during a summer when Isidor was serving as a senator for New York, Ida wrote to her husband, 'I with my own hands landed six trout. I am very proud of my achievement as I have to the best of my knowledge and belief broken all former records of ladies fishing. We remained all day and of course lunched out. This is one of the best parts of the fishing or of the excursion.'[69] When their children had grown up and married, they were all invited to dine once a week at their parents' homes with their respective spouses and children.[70] Ida also acquired a reputation in New York as a consummate hostess, who frequently invited to her dinner parties people whose achievements she had read about and been impressed by. One guest was Virginia Brooks McKelway, a graduate of the 1899 Women's Law Class of New York University, who thought Ida's 'hospitality was marked by generosity and elegance rather than by great elaboration. At her board one met with the finest minds of the day, people interested in the things which stand for progress, both Jew and Gentile.'[71] Another invitee, who became a close friend, was Julia Richman, first female District Superintendent of Schools for the Lower East Side.[72] Isidor, who had insisted his daughters receive the same level of education as their brothers, supported Ida's friendship with Richman and her subsequent fund-raising for local public schools.

In one of his letters to Ida, he gently urged her to 'Be a little selfish; don't always think only of others.'[73] They were one of New York's most prolifically generous couples when it came to charitable donations. The Strauses had helped fund the foundation of the Recreation Rooms and Settlement to alleviate the impact of poverty in Brooklyn; Isidor sat on the board of the Montefiore Home for Chronic Invalids and the Manhattan Hospital. He aided organisations that provided low-income loans to working-class applicants. He and his brothers supported the Hebrew Orphans Society; he advised the Federation of Jewish Farmers of America, funded Jewish cultural organisations, joined a fund-raising committee to erect a memorial to New York fire fighters who lost their lives in the line of duty, and he served as treasurer of the Clara de Hirsch Home for Working Girls in Manhattan.[74] The *New York Times* estimated their wealth in 1912 at around $3.5 million, although a later article in the *Atlanta Constitution* put it at $4,565,106.[75] Isidor had set a significant sum of money aside in his will for Ida and the children, as well as earmarking which charities various sums should be distributed to. Of those latter bequests, by far the most substantial went to the Educational Alliance, which Isidor had co-founded in 1889.[76] The Alliance sought to provide shelter, education and English-language lessons for Jewish immigrants to America and its work quickly became a passion of Ida's, as well as fuelling a mounting sense of anger at the injustice she witnessed. The intensification of Ida's political awareness, and an eventual sea-change in contemporary American attitudes towards both mass immigration and Jews, lay with the assassination of Tsar Alexander II of Russia in 1881. Like Captain Smith's supposed last voyage, a story sprang up that the Tsar had been en route to grant Russia its first democratic constitution when he was killed. In reality, he had been returning from a military revue.[77]

The anti-monarchist bomb thrown at the feet of the 'Tsar-Liberator' ushered him off the political stage and, instead of inspiring the revolution hoped for by the assassins, replaced him with his ultra-conservative son, Alexander III. Much was made later of the Grand Guignol of Alexander II's final moments as an explanation for the ensuing reaction. Carried dying into his study at the Winter Palace, the Tsar had been surrounded by relatives jolted from their everyday routines – his wife appeared in her negligee; his eldest daughter-in-law arrived carrying a pair of ice skates. Convinced that the assault on the Emperor presaged a wave of similar attacks against other members of the Imperial Family, the grand duchesses refused to be separated from their children, with the result that they too were ushered to his deathbed, remembering for the rest of their lives how 'large spots of black blood showed us the way up the marble steps' to the Study where they were left clutching each other in terror.[78] The future Nicholas II, then the thirteen-year-old Grand Duke Nicholas, stood shaking in his schoolroom sailor suit, watching his grandfather haemorrhage to death in front of him. The family's chaplain performed the last rites, while the soon to be Tsar knelt down to hold his father's hand until he passed.[79] It was a wretched scene that permanently hardened the attitudes of several of the Romanovs towards revolutionaries, and even liberals, as 'mindless malefactors who . . . won't be satisfied by more concessions, they'll become crueller'.[80] However, any attempts to identify Alexander II's death as either reason or justification for Alexander III's policies towards his Jewish subjects is a hopelessly naive, or equally disingenuous, piece of revisionism. Long before the assassination, the man who became Alexander III had been the acknowledged head of the reactionary clique at the Russian court and he had vehemently opposed his father's tentative steps towards constitutionalism. One courtier attempted to square the circle of how Alexander III, 'an excellent husband, a loving father, an economical and conscientious master of his house', could simultaneously be 'almost impervious to counsel and opinions of other people', as well as callously indifferent to the suffering of those he deemed unworthy of sympathy.[81] He was not impervious to the counsel of his former tutor, Constantine Pobedonostsev, a devout Orthodox Christian, 'so honourable and pious that he makes no secret of his bigotry', who distrusted Protestants, disliked Catholics, hated democracy and loathed Jews.[82] Dry, petty and dour enough to have allegedly provided inspiration for Tolstoy's Alexei Karenin, Pobedonostsev had an impact on Russian life that was uniformly negative, as was Alexander III's decision to entrust to him the management of both the Russian Orthodox Church and his eldest son's education. From Pobedonostsev, Alexander III had learned to be a ferocious anti-Semite and, as a fish rots from its head, anti-Semitism, already energetic in Imperial Russia, took on a new vigour thanks to the Tsar's undisguised attitudes. Within a year of Alexander III's accession, 225 Jewish communities in the Russian Empire had been targeted in pogroms. Twenty years later, Jewish leaders admitted they could no longer keep count.[83] In the margins of government reports detailing the violence of the pogroms, Alexander III scribbled, 'Yes, but we must remember that people are entitled to feel anger to those who crucified Our Lord and spilled His precious blood.'[84] The new reign was marked by economic rejuvenation, massive foreign investment in Russian industries and resurgent nationalism that limited the rights, language and culture of the empire's Finns, Ukrainians, Poles, Letts, Lithuanians and Estonians and brutalised most of its Jews.[85] A particularly horrifying policy was enacted after the Tsar appointed one of his younger brothers, the Grand Duke Sergei, as Governor-General of Moscow, who ordered the city's Jewish residents to label themselves in preparation for deportation. Jewish women who had married Muscovite Christians and begged for permission to stay with their husbands were told they could do so only if they legally re-registered themselves under the classification of prostitutes. Rewards were offered for those who betrayed any Jews in hiding. The Grand Duke temporarily halted the expulsions when stories circulated of hundreds of Jews collapsing in the December snows as they waited for the chartered trains to take them out of Moscow. The deportations resumed in the spring. There were spikes in anti-Semitism elsewhere in the Old World, most prominently with the resurrection of the Blood Libel by Christian and Islamic communities in Syria, but nothing influenced the wave of emigration to the United States as heavily as the policies of Alexander III, most of which survived his death from kidney failure in 1894.[86]

Many of the eastern European Jews arrived in New York poverty-stricken, uneducated and traumatised. Isidor, who during his career as a senator had campaigned for English to be recognised as the official language of the United States, was a champion of assimilation and he prioritised funding educational programmes for the new arrivals. Ida shared her husband's beliefs, as well as focusing on establishing and funding orphanages and women's shelters. The stories told of the pogroms, particularly by those who escaped the Ukrainian cities of Kiev and Odessa, were chilling and they took a toll on both Ida's physical health and her mental well-being. She was incensed by Tsar Nicholas II's failure to protect his Jewish subjects, and in the summer of 1910 she wrote an open letter to him in the form of a poem, 'To the Tsar: A Prophecy', which was first published anonymously in the *New York Times* on 11 September:

How canst thou face thy Maker, how canst thou even
    dare
With all the guilt upon thy head to turn to Him in
    prayer?
Thou rearest thy religion to cloak thy evil deeds,
The tortures thou inflicted on those of other creeds,
The exilings, the pogroms, the persecutions all,
Thou plannest with thy minions, within thy palace wall.

To thy corrupt officialdom, thou givest a free rein
To murder, pillage, harass thy subjects for its gain.
With olden-time barbarity, with cruelty unsurpassed,
Thou rulest o'er an Empire, so wonderful, so vast,
Whose boundless wealth lies buried for ages, 'neath the
    soil,
Whose undeveloped resources wait but for honest toil,
While sore distress and famine go stalking in the land
All enterprise, initiative, stayed by a tyrant's hand.

Bright shines the torch of progress in every land but
    thine,
Illuming every pathway that leads to Freedom's shrine,
In thy realm superstition and ignorance hold sway,
Grim allies of oppression that darken every way;
That foster crime and vices of all the vilest sort
And make of human beings a beastly dangerous horde,
Thou art a shame, a byword among the nations all,
Thy subjects' executions hang o'er thee like a pall!
. . . [87]

The influx of these immigrants did not excite sympathy in
everyone. Anti-Semitism increased in America, alongside nativist
opposition to mass immigration.[88] For some American Jews,
including Isidor's brother Nathan, this was a sign that the historical dangers they had escaped in Europe were slowly following

them to the United States and thus proof that only the creation of a specifically Jewish homeland could offer permanent safety. When he visited Isidor and Ida at their hotel on the Riviera a few weeks before they boarded the *Titanic*, Nathan had been on his way to Jerusalem to view both the progress of various charities he had established to help the local poor during previous visits and to research Zionism, accompanied by Dr Judah Magnes, whose zeal had recently resulted in him being ousted from Temple Emanu-El on the Upper East Side to take over as rabbi for the more conservative congregation at B'nai Jeshurun.[89] Nathan and Dr Magnes tried but failed to convert Ida and Isidor to their way of thinking. A few months earlier, Isidor had explained their opposition on the grounds that:

I look upon Zionism as a dangerous dogma for us in this country. If the new immigrants who arrive here by the hundreds of thousands during the course of a few years, and of whom the Educational Alliance is trying to make good American citizens, are met with the dogma that this country is only a tarrying ground for an ultimate home in Palestine, it places in the hands of anti Semites, as well as those who are opposed to immigration, a weapon which can be used . . . Zionism is incompatible with patriotism . . . If Zionism means a home for the Jews, I am radically opposed to it. If it simply means a spiritual hope for the oppressed and persecuted people of Russia, Roumania, and Galata, then it is a different proposition. But political Zionism, or Zionism in shape, manner or form, as propaganda in this country, I have no patience with, and I am utterly and irrevocably opposed to it.[90]

Unlike Nathan, Isidor was not particularly religious. Comments made towards the end of his life, in which he expressed support for a guiding spiritual morality over the strictures of organised religion, suggest that his beliefs may have lain closer to deism than Judaism, and unlike Ida, who had noted that their London hotel did not offer matzoh for Passover, Isidor had not kept to a religiously based diet since he left Germany as a child.[91] More important, however, in explaining their hostility towards Zionism was the phrase that appears frequently in Isidor's correspondence in the 1890s with President Cleveland: 'the American people are good people'.[92] The Strauses believed, passionately, in America, and their lives are fascinating windows into episodes that nurtured, divided, brutalised, traumatised and revitalised their adopted country. They trusted in America's capacity to renew itself and to offer safety from the extremism they had seen damage so many lives in Europe. In a letter to their children, Isidor mentioned Nathan's support for Zionism, while insisting that a difference in opinion should not lead to a rupture among friends or family: 'None of us is perfect and we can always detect little shortcomings in others more quickly than we will recognise greater ones in ourselves. Difference of opinion will arise between thinking persons. Whoever may have been right should not exalt [sic] and taunt the other for having been wrong.'[93]

Above all, there is no doubt that Ida and Isidor loved one another. Before they left for their vacation in Europe, a friend had noticed that Ida still darned Isidor's socks, despite their wealth. 'If you had a husband like mine,' she had apparently replied, 'you would do far more than this for him.'[94] Colonel Gracie, whose marriage had suffered since his eldest daughter was killed when lift cables snapped in 1903, envied and admired the Strauses for the happiness they still took in each other and their children. When he saw them later in the afternoon of Sunday 14 April, a few hours after their earlier rendezvous in the Lounge, Ida told him that they had sent their telegram to their son, daughter-in-law and granddaughter on the *Amerika*. Telegrams were generally encouraged to be kept short, so the Strauses had opted for 'FINE VOYAGE FINE SHIP FEELING FINE WHAT NEWS', to which they received a cheering reply.[95] Jesse's message to his parents was the first of two telegrams sent from the *Amerika* to the *Titanic* that day. The second, between the respective captains,

Ida (far left) and Isidor (far right) celebrating their silver wedding anniversary in 1896, with their children. Isidor's father, Lazarus, is seated in the centre.

informed the *Titanic* that, like the ship that had carried Isidor to the United States in 1854, the *Amerika* had passed 'two large icebergs'. The *Titanic*'s wireless operators dutifully relayed the warning to other ships in the vicinity and transcribed one from the *Baltic*, which they delivered to the Bridge.[96]

Two More Boilers

Do not suppose that every man understands the sea.

Pirî Reis, *Kitab-ı bahriye* (1521)

B Y SUNDAY AFTERNOON, TOMMY ANDREWS WAS FAIRLY
certain that the next day would see the *Titanic's* full running
speed tested for the first time.[1] All twenty-four of her principal boilers were to be operational that evening, with the five
auxiliary boilers due to be fired up the next day or, failing that,
Tuesday.[2] Around lunchtime on the previous day, Andrews had
received news that the fire burning too intensely in one of the
coal bunkers in Boiler Room 5 since the sea trials in Belfast had
been extinguished. To enable a damage inspection by the ship's
Leading Firemen, the Boiler Room had been emptied of coal,
which produced a list to port so slight that the only passenger who
seems to have noticed it was a Cambridge-educated science teacher
taking lunch in the second-class Dining Saloon.[3] One of the
inspectors, Fred Barrett, reported that in several spots the 'bottom
of the watertight compartment was dinged'. His colleague Charles
Hendrickson agreed and added that 'all the paint and everything
was off'.[4] Decades later, this mild mutilation would be blamed, at
least in part, for the loss of the *Titanic*, with proponents believing

that the fire had weakened the bulkhead between Boiler Rooms 5 and 6, thus speeding or, in some schools of thought, securing the sinking after the collision with the iceberg had created 'a perfect storm of extraordinary factors coming together'.[5] In 2017, this theory was the focus of renewed speculation, when it was somewhat misleadingly presented as a new theory. In fact, it had previously been articulated at length in a television documentary first broadcast twenty years earlier, then re-examined in a 2004 report by the Geological Society of America in partnership with Ohio State University and scrutinised again in 2008 in a series of articles in the *Independent*.[6] During the 2017 revival of the bunker fire theory, footage of the wreck was marshalled to show where the *Titanic*'s hull had fatally exploded outwards upon collision, thereby opening Boiler Room 5 to the sea. The underwater footage in question showed the exterior of the *Titanic*'s Mail Room on G-Deck, not one of its boiler rooms, and it had almost certainly buckled out due to the impact generated when the *Titanic* ploughed into the seafloor after she sank, not when she hit the iceberg. Contemporary newsreels of the *Titanic* preparing to leave Belfast also allegedly show a discolouration of the hull, cited as evidence of how dangerous the bunker fire had been. The discolouration is more probably a consequence of deterioration in the century-old film and the highlighted area again corresponds with the Mail Room, not the boilers. Unless the mail clerks had taken to torching every letter on the *Titanic* and holding their epistolary inferno up against the hull for ten days, it is hard to see how any of the film footage corroborates the suggestion that the fire, which was without doubt a nuisance, played a role in the eventual tragedy.

The coal fire in Boiler Room 5 is a constituent part in a series of arguments that attribute the loss of the *Titanic* to a mistake in design or construction. Variations include the quality of the steel or rivets used during construction by Harland and Wolff, the failure to extend the watertight compartments higher than E-Deck and too small a rudder. It is true that, as with many things used in the industries of 1912, the steel hammered together to create the *Titanic* might not pass inspection today, but it has survived at the bottom of the inhospitable Atlantic for over a century and at no point did any contemporaries, many of whom were desperate to shift the blame from the *Titanic*'s operators, suggest that the fault lay with her builders. Tests carried out on small pieces of the *Titanic*'s hull that have been raised to the surface since her discovery in 1985 have all shown strength, rather than weakness, to the extent that a report commissioned by the US National Institute of Statistics and Technology in 1997 concluded that 'no apparent metallurgical mistakes were made in the construction of the RMS *Titanic*'.[7] As for the rudder, it was only fractionally smaller than a modern ship's would need to be to obtain certification to commence trading.[8]

At the time of her launch, the *Shipbuilder* magazine had described the *Titanic* and her sisters as 'practically unsinkable'. After the disaster, popular culture seized on the adjective, while defenders of the ship and her owners pointed to the qualifying adverb. The White Star Line never advertised the *Titanic* as an unsinkable ship, which is not to say that she was never described as such by those who might reasonably have been expected to show more restraint. During post-dinner drinks in the Reception Room on Saturday evening, a passenger was close enough to hear 'Captain Smith tell his party that the ship could be cut crosswise in three places and each piece would float'.[*][9] Interestingly, this was, almost verbatim, a quote remembered independently by another passenger, who heard it from Thomas Andrews when he allegedly told her 'that the *Titanic* was absolutely unsinkable. He said that she could break in three separate and distinct parts and that each part would stay afloat indefinitely.'[10] It is hard to credit that a captain and a naval architect sincerely believed that a trifurcated ship could remain afloat, yet as reassuring hyperbole the 'cut in three' imagery seems to have become something of a

---

* Smith did not hold much interest in the possibilities of a shipwreck, having told a journalist three years earlier that 'modern shipbuilding has gone beyond all that'.

stock phrase during the voyage. The two passengers who heard
it from Smith and Andrews did so independently of one another,
on different days of the voyage, and they published their accounts
without any perceptible opportunity to be influenced by the other's
testimony. The unsinkable claim related to the watertight compartments being impacted by a force capable of piercing the *Titanic*
beneath the waterline. A fire or a devastating freak weather occur-
rence was still understood as having the power to destroy anything
on the sea, whereas collisions were increasingly regarded as incon-
veniences. Three years before, the public's confidence in modern
ships had been strengthened by the sinking of the White Star's
Republic when, on a voyage from New York to Gibraltar, she had
been hit in heavy fog by an Italian immigrant ship, the *Florida*.
By the time the *Republic* foundered nine hours later, all passengers and crew, barring six unfortunates who had been asleep in
their cabins at the point where the *Florida* struck, had been
transferred to rescue ships which had been summoned by her
wireless transmissions. The sinking seemed to prove that, even
in the worst possible scenario, liners could remain afloat for long
enough to allow help to arrive in time for a full evacuation.[11]

As historical ironies go, few are more temptingly didactic than
a serious flaw in a ship labelled 'unsinkable'. Yet there is scant
evidence to suggest that there was any significant dereliction in
the *Titanic*'s design or construction which contributed to her
demise. Considering the extent of the damage inflicted by the
iceberg, the most remarkable feature of the *Titanic*'s final hours
is that she stayed afloat for as long as she did. The various attempts
to explain the sinking as the result of human error, either by
Harland and Wolff or by the White Star Line, ring in some way
like a distorted continuation of the contemporary mind-set that
trusted in the *Titanic* as 'practically unsinkable'. If the *Titanic*
had been of 'the highest skill and perfection in marine construction', a product of the greatest level of craftsmanship and
expertise available between 1909 and 1912 then the disaster that
overtook her would not have happened.[12] If her rivets had been

of better quality. If her steel had been stronger. If the boiler-room bunker fire had been extinguished in Belfast rather than halfway across the Atlantic. If her rudder had been larger. If she had been worthy of the confidence placed in her, human endeavour might still have triumphed over Nature. On closer examination, however, there was only one truly egregious error in how the *Titanic* was handled and that was with her speed.

Proof of the ship's incrementally increasing speed had been displayed for passengers in daily postings at noon showing the distance covered in the previous twenty-four hours. A sweepstake was typically organised on transatlantic crossings to guess the next day's run, with passengers good-naturedly trying to tease out hints from officers and stewards.[13] Those who had bet on a superior performance from Saturday to Sunday were rewarded when 546 miles was announced, an increase of twenty-seven compared to the previous day.[14] After Sunday lunch, John and Jack Thayer ran into Bruce Ismay, who showed them a telegraphed ice warning from a nearby White Star liner, the *Baltic*, and told them that in preparation for a full-speed run, weather permitting, the next day, 'Two more boilers were opened up today.'*[15] Ismay also remarked that he did not think the *Titanic* would reach ice until about nine o'clock that evening. When father and son took a walk on deck, the conversation with Ismay made sense to Jack, who had thought before breakfast that they were 'in for another very pleasant day', but now realised that it was 'noticeably colder'.[16] It was not the first time the two men had spoken to Ismay or to Thomas Andrews, whom they also bumped into that afternoon during their stroll.[17] Andrews, Ismay and the ship's Chief Engineer Archibald Frost had had several 'short chats . . . all observing the performance of the ship' with the Thayers earlier in the voyage.[18]

In contrast to his son, John Thayer was more interested in the

---

* This telegram had been passed on to Ismay by Captain Smith to whom it was returned that evening for posting in the Officers' Mess. It was the only ice warning to the *Titanic* that was shown to Ismay and it may have been given to him as a courtesy because it came from another White Star ship.

ship's performance than in the weather. He was a sincere believer in progress's symbiotic relationship with capitalism as he had shown in his career at the Pennsylvania Railroad, where he campaigned to limit government involvement in industry, testifying before the Pennsylvania Senate Railroad Committee in February 1907 that any attempt by the state legislature to impose a cap on the price of a train ticket would result in increases for commuting fares, the curtailment of services or the use of freight revenues to cross-subsidise passenger traffic, thereby ending 'the tremendous volume of business thrown upon us by the increased prosperity' of the previous decade.[19] There had been a crisis of faith for Thayer in 1910 when, immediately before the financial crisis of that year, he had assured the railroad's investors that 'the outlook is splendid for a continuation of these [favourable] conditions'.[20] How much his work aggravated the depression with which Thayer struggled all his adult life is unclear, although in the aftermath of the 1910 upset he had visited 'nerve doctors' in Switzerland. Marian accompanied him and she may have been the first to suggest the retreats to help her husband. They had spent time in Switzerland in the winter of 1911–12, before their visit to Berlin and then the *Titanic*, and it is probable though unprovable that a sojourn in a clinic was the reason behind the Swiss leg of their trip.

Despite the economic setbacks and the bouts of mental anguish, Thayer remained hopeful about the future and advances in transportation. It was a worldview that kept Thayer in step with Ismay and other plutocrats on board, including Colonel Astor and, to a lesser extent, Isidor Straus. It was not a universally shared optimism. Ida Straus had attributed the unpleasantness with the *New York* to the dangers inherent in ships the size of the *Titanic*, and during an evening conversation with John Thayer in the Smoking Room the Canadian railway tycoon Charles Hays gloomily warned that 'The White Star, the Cunard and the Hamburg-American lines are now devoting their attention to a struggle for supremacy in obtaining the most luxurious appointments for their ships, but the time will soon come when the greatest and most appalling of all disasters at sea will be the result.'[21] To some, the pursuit of greater man-made glory smacked of the Tower of Babel, producing a superstitious foreboding that cautionary vengeance would be inflicted to temper such arrogance.[22] For those with more terrestrial neuroses, it seemed lunatic for companies to be led primarily by the pursuit of breaking a record.

Fourteen years before the *Titanic*'s maiden voyage, an American novelist, Morgan Robertson, published a novella, *Futility*, which described the maiden voyage of a British luxury liner called the *Titan*:

> She was the largest craft afloat and the greatest of the works of men. In her construction and maintenance were involved every science, profession, and trade known to civilization. On her bridge were officers, who, besides being the pick of the Royal Navy, had passed rigid examinations in all studies that pertained to the winds, tides, currents, and geography of the sea; they were not only seamen, but scientists. The same professional standard applied to the personnel of the engine-room, and the stewards' department was equal to that of a first-class hotel.
>
> From her lofty bridge ran hidden telegraph lines to the bow, stern engine-room, crow's nest on the foremast, and to all parts of the ship where work was done . . . From the bridge, engine-room, and a dozen places on her deck the ninety-two doors of nineteen water-tight compartments could be closed in half a minute by turning a lever. These doors would also close automatically in the presence of water. With nine compartments flooded the ship would still float, and as no known accident of the sea could possibly fill this many, the steamship *Titan* was considered practically unsinkable.
>
> . . . In short, she was a floating city – containing within her steel walls all that tends to minimalize the dangers and discomforts of the Atlantic voyage – all that makes life enjoyable.[23]

On the fourth night of the fictional trip, the *Titan* is running at too high a speed through a dense fog, causing her to hit an iceberg and sink with the loss of thousands of lives due to insufficient provision of lifeboats. *Futility* was not a particularly successful novella at the time of first publication in 1898, which explains why the White Star Line were unaware in 1911 that they had christened their flagship with a name unsettlingly similar to a fictional leviathan that had capsized in the North Atlantic. *Futility* had articulated fears of the moment – at the time of writing, the *Kaiser Wilhelm der Große* had just taken the Blue Riband for the fastest crossing of the Atlantic, the first of her larger running mates had been commissioned from a shipyard in Germany, and White Star were celebrating the launch of the *Oceanic*. Boundless confidence in the future of societies often jostles alongside fear at the impact of irrevocable change, and the evolution of the ocean liners between 1898 and 1912 had intensified both sets of feelings. The near doubling in size between the *Kaiser*-class and the Cunard sisters and then the riposte from the *Olympic*-class struck some observers as hubristic mania.

Contrary to the oft-repeated assertion that the *Titanic* was intent on snatching the Blue Riband from the *Mauretania*, she was not attempting to break the record for the fastest crossing to New York. Her creators and her owners knew that her engines were incapable of matching the speeds reached by the *Mauretania* or *Lusitania*. They had designed her that way. The White Star Line had ostentatiously dropped out of the Blue Riband frenzy thirteen years earlier, when they announced their intention to focus on comfort, size and safety in lieu of speed and their tactic had paid dividends with increased passenger revenue and an enviable reputation with all three classes of travel.[24] Even the way in which the losses of their *Republic* and *Suevic* had been handled had augmented White Star's prestige.[25] Holding the speed record was not even necessarily advantageous, beyond the first flurry of favourable publicity. It had ruined the career of the *Deutschland*, the winner in 1900 subsequently notorious for the discomfort she created with vibrations when she ran at full speed; she suffered a steep decrease in reservations to the point that she was retired, renamed, fitted with new engines and deployed as a cruise ship.[26] Furthermore, although shorter voyages meant reduced catering and accommodation costs for the ship's operators, those savings were often erased by the cost of the extra fuel consumption needed to maintain the liner's record.[27]

In contrast, the *Olympic* was widely praised for her displays of 'excellent, though not excessive, speed and of great comfort'; some second-class passengers who had previously sailed on the *Lusitania* remarked over Sunday lunch on the *Titanic* that this crossing was more comfortable because the latter was a smoother ship; and, as with every White Star commander at the start of a voyage, when he boarded the *Titanic* at Southampton Captain Smith had received a letter from his employers reiterating, 'You are to dismiss all idea of competitive passages with other vessels, and to concentrate your attention upon a cautious, prudent and ever watchful system of navigation which will lose time or suffer any other temporary inconvenience rather than incur the slightest risk which can be avoided.'[28]

That the *Titanic* lacked both the intention and the capability of taking the Riband from the *Mauretania* did not, however, mean that she proceeded at a leisurely pace. In the testing of her engines, her speed had been increased progressively since leaving Queenstown. Even after warnings of ice ahead had been received from other ships, seven of which arrived on Sunday the 14th, Captain Smith's approach was still in keeping with received professional wisdom at the time which held that thanks to the advances in technology 'speed makes for safety under practically all conditions except that of fog'.[29] If ice was ahead, the easiest course of action for a ship as large and as safe as the *Titanic* was to get through it quickly, a view Captain Smith had expressed earlier in his career when, discussing ice with a colleague, he remarked, 'I go as fast as I can for by so doing I shorten the time of danger.'[30]

The temperature had dropped further by the time John Thayer took his next walk on deck at about five o'clock with his bereaved friend, Arthur Ryerson, a lawyer by profession, with family money from a Chicago-based steel distributor, who had spent most of the voyage sequestered in his suite with his wife and children, mourning his eldest son's death in a car crash. The funeral was planned for Friday afternoon at St Mark's Episcopal Church in Philadelphia, two days after the *Titanic* was due to reach New York.[31] John and Marian had called on the Ryersons and persuaded them to take advantage of decks rendered quiet as most other passengers trooped indoors 'restlessly searching for a warm place'.[32] The wind had picked up, whipping around the decks and cancelling in the name of safety any vague plans to conduct a lifeboat drill that afternoon.[33] Two days earlier, the *Yale Daily News* had printed a resolution that would be forwarded to the Ryersons when they reached America: 'Whereas Almighty God in His incomprehensible wisdom has taken from among us our beloved classmate and friend Arthur Larned Ryerson, who died bravely far from the comforting presence of those nearest and dearest to him, be it Resolved, That we, the Class of 1914, express to his family our most sincere sympathy for their terrible loss, and be it further Resolved, That these resolutions be printed in the News and that a copy be sent to his family.'[34]

'I absolutely hate myself': J. Bruce Ismay, Managing Director of the White Star Line.

The *Titanic* was sailing westward, with the sun setting ahead of her in the course of Thayer and Ryerson's hour-long promenade and the sky was 'quite pink' when they saw Bruce Ismay, in a blue lounge suit, talking to their wives. As the men approached, Ismay got up from his deckchair, bid all four a good afternoon and beetled through the nearby entrance leading to the aft Grand Staircase. Ismay's own marriage had long ago atrophied as his wife struggled to find happiness with an impatient perfectionist and, after Florence Ismay passed the menopause, sexual relations between the couple had ceased.[35] She had done her duty as first lady of the Line by joining Ismay for the maiden voyage of the *Olympic* and she saw no reason to burden herself with a repeat appearance for the *Titanic*'s. Her husband had, in the days since meeting them at Cherbourg, developed an infatuation with Marian Thayer, which Marian herself was either blithely unaware of or tactfully oblivious to. The two women told their husbands that, on what Emily Ryerson called a 'very cold but perfectly beautiful' afternoon, Ismay had joined them to check if the extra staff and rooms he had arranged for the Ryerson party had made them more comfortable. Whatever his good intentions, no one could ever accuse Bruce Ismay of getting ahead on charm. Failing to recognise that Mrs Ryerson was still too fragile to conduct willingly a conversation about anything other than the depth of her own grief, and perhaps not even then, Ismay had launched into a spiel about the ship's speed and the ice warnings he had been shown by Captain Smith. There was a German tanker near by 'wanting a tow', which Ismay reasonably felt was not the responsibility of a passenger carrier of the *Titanic*'s size. Regarding the ice, Emily Ryerson had apparently asked, 'Of course you are going to slow down?' To which Ismay, parroting the line taken by Smith and most other captains he had known, answered, 'Certainly not, we are going to put on more steam and run away from them.' He also predicted that if the *Titanic* performed as well as was expected during the full-speed test the next day, they might reach Manhattan late on Tuesday evening, rather than at sunrise on Wednesday, as timetabled. As they descended to their respective cabins and the bugle sounded in advance of dinner, the two couples wondered what they would do if they reached New York early. The Thayers had access to a private railway car, which they might need to send a telegram for it to be dispatched to wait for them on Tuesday evening. In his rambling, awkwardness-addled braggadocio, Ismay had forgotten to mention that if a White Star vessel arrived at its pier after 8 p.m. it was company policy to permit passengers to stay on board and disembark after breakfast.[36]

A Thousand Uneasy
Sparks of Light

To liken a modern liner to a floating hotel is hackneyed enough.
But that is only half the story. The colossal hotel, capable of accom-
modating two to three thousand guests, with its social gaiety and
an acme of luxury, is rushing across half the globe, through the
sunshine of day and the darkness of night, through calm and blizzard,
relentlessly driven by an enormous energy generated within her . . .

Gerald Aylmer, R.M.S. 'Mauretania':
The Ship and her Record (1935)

THE THAYERS HAD BEEN INVITED TO A SUNDAY-EVENING
dinner party in honour of Captain Smith and hosted by
their fellow Philadelphians Eleanor and George Widener.
At home, they socialised in the same circles, including attending
Philadelphia's annual First Assembly Ball, where in 1911 Marian
Thayer's high-waisted white satin gown 'spangled with gold' won
an admiring write-up in the *Women's Wear Daily*.[1] The Wideners
had since spent six months in England and France from which
they were returning to arrange their daughter's wedding. As he
was only seventeen, Jack, who arrived back at their suite to
change for dinner at about half-past six, had not been asked to

join the party, which meant he would be eating alone in the Saloon that evening while all three of his usual companions – his parents and the Captain – joined the Wideners.[2] Once Marian Thayer had been dressed with the help of her maid Margaret, the couple went upstairs to the B-Deck Restaurant, managed by a London-based Italian restaurateur with his own hand-selected staff of waiters, who were technically classed as his employees rather than White Star's. Restaurants that charged a fee independently of one's ticket price to offer an à la carte service had first been introduced on German transatlantic liners, a fact that at least partially explained the chilly reception they received from several British commentators, who regarded the restaurants as poor taste, a temptation to advertise one's wealth in a vulgar fashion even in relation to other first-class passengers, and an unnecessary erosion of the camaraderie supposedly engendered by eating at the same time as one's fellow travellers in a saloon.*

Most passengers and travel journals were more enthusiastic about the restaurants' 'great convenience to those whose appetites are not equal to sampling all the courses which constitute a dinner on an ocean liner, who do not like to sit and wait and do nothing until the next course they want arrives . . . if a passenger does not want anything between the *hors d'oeuvre* and the dessert he can skip from one extreme to the other and lose no time in watching other people attend to the numerous intermediate courses.'[3] Panelled in walnut with its supporting pillars wrapped in gilt ribbons, the Restaurant's fawn chairs in the Louis XVI style ringed circular tables on rose-coloured carpets. Matching lampshades cast a soft glow on each table, reflected in the circular mirrors lining the walls.[4] Louis Seize was also one of the more popular styles deployed in decorating the *Titanic*'s first-class cabins, although at least one of her Edwardian compatriots had voiced patriotic pique complaining that the aesthetic in which

---

* Several of the *Titanic*'s passengers referred to the Restaurant as 'the Ritz Restaurant', a confusion that likely originated with the subcontracting of the first restaurants on Hamburg-Amerika liners to the Ritz hotels.

'all was done with a light, delicate, and reserved touch . . . is as wrongfully termed "Louis Seize" as America has been christened after Amerigo Vespucci. We ought, rather, to speak of the "Marie-Antoinette style", for it is she whom these subtle and charming characteristics recall. They have nothing in common with the stout and massive Louis XVI . . . '[5] It might have pleased this Austrian critic to know that a journalist who had been invited to see the *Titanic*'s accommodation before she left Southampton had informed his readers of the ship's 'Marie Antoinette bedrooms' and restaurant.[6]

A contemporary advertisement showing the *Titanic*'s Restaurant in use.

A smaller band, a trio, played string music by Puccini and Tchaikovsky from the Restaurant's foyer as the guests ordered off the menu. Ismay had chosen to eat in the Restaurant that evening as well, reserving a table in the middle of the room and inviting Dr O'Loughlin as his guest.[7] The Duff Gordons were also dining, joined by Lady Duff Gordon's secretary, Laura Francatelli. Leila Meyer, dressed in mourning, took a small table in one of the alcoves to dine with her husband; her father, Andrew Saks, founder of the Manhattan department store that bore his name, had passed away five days earlier and throughout the journey home for his funeral Leila had preferred to dine in the more intimate Restaurant. A round of applause went up from other diners at the entrance of Irene Harris, a Broadway producer's wife with her broken collarbone nestling in a sling, courtesy of Dr O'Loughlin's expertise, after she had slipped on the Grand Staircase the previous afternoon.[8] News of her fall had made the rounds, prompting the delivery to the Harrises' C-Deck stateroom of notes from many well-wishers.[9] Their companions at table, the novelist Jacques Futrelle and his wife May, were impressed by the Restaurant's 'brilliant crowd'. May Futrelle continued:

> Jewels flashed from the gowns of the women. And oh, the dear women, how fondly they wore their latest Parisian gowns . . . The sweet odors of rare flowers pervaded the atmosphere . . . It was a buoyant, oh, such a jolly crowd. It was a rare gathering of beautiful women and splendid men. There was that atmosphere of fellowship and delightful sociability which made the Sabbath dinner on board ship such a delightful occasion . . . We were all filled with the joy of living.[10]

Her sentiments did not extend to a solo diner, identified by the crew as a professional gambler, who booked passage on ships guaranteed to attract a wealthy clientele suitable for fleecing. The stewards had discreetly passed this information on to habitués of the Smoking Room.[11]

The Thayers most likely dined at a table of eight, possibly of nine. The exact guest list has not survived and, in the years since, reconstructing it has been complicated by others in the Restaurant that evening who subsequently described themselves as 'of that party', or by genuine lapses in memory, such as Lady Duff Gordon, who wrote in her memoirs two decades later that Ida Straus, her husband and the Astors were also guests of the Wideners.[12] The Strauses and the Astors took their Sunday dinner in the Saloon and it may be that Lady Duff Gordon had seen them in the Restaurant on one of the previous evenings which, at the distance of twenty years, she conflated with the Sunday-night dinner party.[13] Harry Anderson, a stockbroker from New York, ate in the Restaurant on Sunday, although accounts vary as to his presence at the Wideners' table. Whether the Wideners' son, Harry, was present is likewise unclear. At twenty-seven, he was old enough to merit an invitation, but since Jack Thayer was too young, as was the twelve-year-old son of another couple, it seems that the Wideners had erred on the side of manners in keeping all children, regardless of age, off the guest list.[14] To toast the Captain, the Wideners had sent invitations to a third Old Money Pennsylvanian, William Carter, and his wife Lucile, 'a beauty of a pronounced type' and descendant of American President James Polk.[15] Conversation at the table flitted between what was happening on Wall Street, the impending US presidential election, the forthcoming nuptials of the Wideners' eldest daughter and the *Titanic*'s speed.

The November election was shaping up to be both vicious and important for the country and specifically for most of the guests at the Wideners' table. Four candidates were expected to stand, including the incumbent President, William Taft, who would almost certainly secure the Republican nomination, prompting his predecessor, Theodore Roosevelt, to make good on his threat to desert the Grand Old Party to run as a Progressive. By April, the Democrats' contenders had narrowed to a choice between Senator Champ Clark of Missouri, Speaker of the House of

Representatives, and Woodrow Wilson, Governor of New Jersey, who clinched the nomination at the Democratic National Convention in June. The Socialists had already proffered Eugene Debs, who had scored only 2.8 per cent of the popular vote during his previous reach for the White House in 1908. However, he was expected to, and did, poll better in 1912.[16] A series of recessions in the previous decade, mounting inflation after 1909 and a financial crisis in 1907 had hardened many Americans' attitudes towards the 'East Coast elite', perceived as a selfish class, wholly and wilfully out of touch with the American heartlands, themselves categorised with each westward expansion as the centre of the country rather than the founding states to the east. The dissatisfied mood in America had drifted left, something capitalised on by the Democrats, who would have Woodrow Wilson running on a platform of increased diplomatic isolationism, the removal of protectionist tariffs, the creation of a national banking system, reform of American industrial practices and the introduction of legislation to improve the working classes' access to healthcare.[17] Wilson's anti-trust pronouncements like 'The flower does not bear the root, but the root the flower' and 'The amount of money on Wall Street is no indication of the energy of the American people' struck a chord with millions of voters.[18]

Shock, and then resentment, concerning the amount of money possessed by the plutocracy had been building since the actions during the Panic of 1907 of the *Titanic*'s owner, J. P. Morgan, who was missing the ship's maiden voyage as his health had fatally collapsed during his holiday to Europe.[19] Known variably as the 1907 Bankers' Crisis or the Knickerbocker Crisis, after the Trust whose collapse triggered a panic on Wall Street that spread through the country, bouncing dozens of smaller banks and trusts into declaring bankruptcy, it had been the most serious financial fright in American history thus far. Over the course of three purgatorial weeks in October, there was a real fear that the crisis would tear down the American economy, wiping out the savings and future prospects of millions of families, until

Morgan gathered a coalition of bankers who stepped into the breach to stabilise and then end the Panic. After the danger had passed, conspiracy theories evolved from whisper to shout that Morgan had engineered the whole debacle solely to enrich himself. That was incorrect, unfounded and wholly irrelevant to the main point unintentionally highlighted by Morgan's intervention. Even many who applauded Morgan's patriotism and indefatigability in working to halt the crash were appalled at what it revealed about the clout of big business in America. A cabal of private citizens had sufficient funds to decide the future of a country's economy; by 1907, Morgan and his partners disposed of 40 per cent of the liquid industrial, commercial and financial capital of the United States, by far the largest single pool of money in the world.[20] In the case of Morgan in 1907, they had utilised this for the national good. There was nothing to prevent them one day doing the opposite, a point vigorously stressed by the Democrats and the Socialists in their 1908 presidential campaigns. Although the contest was won by the Republicans, on 12 July 1909 Congress approved a resolution to add a sixteenth amendment to the Constitution allowing for the federal government to 'lay and collect taxes on income, from whatever source derived, without apportionment among the several States, and without regard to any census or enumeration'.[21]

Due to be enacted in February 1913, the Sixteenth Amendment would do to people like John Thayer what the House of Lords Act had done to Lord Rothes. It dealt a blow, if not quite a fatal one, that would irrevocably alter the existence of their class. No federal income tax had been levelled in the United States since 1872, when a policy enacted to help pay for the Civil War had been rescinded. The astronomical wealth gathered by the plutocracy in the succeeding Gilded Age had, at least in part, been rendered possible by the fact that they did not have to pay income tax, or death duties, which were not imposed until 1916. The Democrats were harnessing the momentum generated by the impending implementation of the Sixteenth Amendment along with wider concerns about the perceived injustices and instability of the American economy to make the abolition of protectionist tariffs a vote-winning plank of their campaign. Critics of the tariffs pointed out that the United Kingdom did not impose them, having remained since 1865 'perhaps history's purest example of a free-trade nation', refusing to levy them even against imports in competition with those from its vast empire.[22] American protectionism in 1912 favoured the wealthy and industry over agriculture, making the Democratic stump against it, and for income tax, hugely popular with Southern, mid-Western and Californian voters, particularly after tariffs had been repeatedly identified by various newspapers as a contributory cause of recent inflation. All of the presidential candidates, bar President Taft, had committed themselves to supporting the implementation of the new Amendment in February and even in Taft's own party various Republican congressmen and senators, and former President Roosevelt, had been won over, seeing the future revenue generated by the new tax as necessary to fund a significant, sustained expansion of the US military. Fortunes like the Thayers', the Wideners', the Astors' and the Guggenheims' would be created in the American future, but it would not be until the arrival of the internet billionaires of the early twenty-first century that they would reach comparable heights and never again have they been accumulated with so few restrictions.

Eleanor Widener's *placement* on Sunday evening had put Major Archibald Butt, an early casualty of the 1912 presidential campaign, next to Marian Thayer. Butt, forty-six years old, tall, urbane and a talented writer with a wide circle of friends, had been an adviser first to Theodore Roosevelt and, after he left office, to his successor, Taft. Their feud over the 1912 Republican nomination had caught Butt in its crosshairs, compounding the fatigue building as President Taft's reliance on him evolved into dependence. By the new year, Butt had been hovering close to a nervous breakdown, but such was his respect, bordering on veneration, for the office of the President that he refused to mention his deteriorating health to

Taft.* Taft was only made aware of his confidant's misery through the intervention of Butt's companion, the architect and art historian Francis 'Frank' Millet, who begged the President to authorise a leave of absence, permitting Butt to spend ten weeks recuperating in Rome with Millet, who had been tasked with early designs and recommendations for the Lincoln Memorial and during his winter abroad planned to visit for research the Italian capital's *Il Vittoriano* monument to King Victor Emmanuel II.[23] Millet promised to have Butt back in good time to accompany the President to the Republican National Convention in Chicago in the third week of June.

Marian Thayer.

Marian Thayer had a gift for friendship, a talent for making her partners in conversation feel fascinating, and she was delighted with Major Butt whom she had not met, despite having several

---

* During several visits to the Mid-West, Major Butt had been deeply distressed to hear groups of children mocking the presidential embonpoint with the nick-names 'Tum-Tum' and 'Taft the Tubby', shouted at the presidential train as it pulled into the station.

friends in common, until they were both guests of the Wideners. As she told President Taft in a letter a week later, 'From the moment we met we never moved from each other for the rest of the evening. Never before have I come in such close contact immediately with anyone. He felt the same & we both marvelled at the time of the strangeness of such a thing for we both realised it while actually opening our innermost thoughts to each other. He told me much about his mother and their letters, his sister-in-law, you, and someone else he loved but that I do not,' an oblique reference to Theodore Roosevelt, whose support for income and inheritance taxes had rendered him *persona non grata* to Marian.[24]

Butt's stay in Italy had been devoted to recuperation, except for a sightseeing trip to the Quirinal Palace where he had witnessed the attempted assassination of King Victor Emmanuel III and his wife, Elena of Montenegro, by an anarchist, who fired several shots as the royals were driven to a memorial Mass for the King's late father. A crowd attempted to lynch the young gunman before he was rescued through arrest by the police.[25] Butt, still suffering from nervous exhaustion, had dutifully telephoned the US embassy to inform them of the news and then joined the procession of 350,000 well-wishers who marched to the Palace, where the King, the Queen and their four children appeared on the balcony to acknowledge the cheers.[26] Particular admiration was reserved for Queen Elena who, when she heard the first shot, had thrown herself in front of her husband.[27] Armed with a letter of introduction from Taft, Butt had seen the King of Italy in happier and more relaxed circumstances two weeks later when, accompanied by the American Ambassador, he was granted an audience at the Quirinal to convey President Taft's good wishes following the King's narrow escape from the assassin.[28]

The failed regicide in Rome summoned up ghosts of the recent past – the royal couple had been on their way to mark the anniversary of the birth of the King's late father, who had himself been assassinated by a gun-wielding anarchist twelve years earlier.[29] Umberto I's murder had been cited by the American anarchist

Leon Czolgosz as inspiration for his own assassination of the US President, William McKinley, a year later. In the same week as the King and Queen of Italy had dodged the near murder witnessed by Butt, the Governor-Prince of the Ottoman province of Samos was killed by a nationalist gunman.[30] A list of the politically motivated assassinations of high-ranking individuals in the twenty years before the *Titanic* set sail makes for sobering reading. With the benefit of hindsight, it is hard not to see them as the first splutters of a death rattle, although they might more accurately serve as examples of unheeded warnings of avoidable danger. On holiday in Switzerland in the autumn of 1898, the Empress of Austria had been stabbed through the heart by an anarchist whose diary recorded that he 'wanted to kill someone famous enough to get in the newspapers'. At his subsequent trial, he turned the jury decisively against him by declaring that 'human suffering *was* the motive for my attack'.[31] Along with the Empress, King Umberto I and President McKinley, assassins had also wiped out the King and Queen of Serbia, a Russian grand duke, prime ministers of Russia, Bulgaria, Greece and Spain, two Russian ministers of the interior, a president of France, the Governor-General of Finland and two kings of Portugal.[32] The King and Queen of Spain had arrived at their wedding breakfast with rubble and blood on their outfits after a republican bomb bounced off their carriage.[33] There had been diplomatic disasters concerning French and German interventions in Morocco and, as a moribund Ottoman Empire crumbled, wars had almost broken out over Austria-Hungary's annexation of the former Ottoman provinces of Bosnia and Herzegovina and then over the Italian conquest of Libya. The Tsar of Russia and the Ottoman Sultan had been forced to accept seismic political change after popular protest shook their empires from within, and in 1910 centuries of Braganza rule collapsed as Portugal declared itself a republic for the first time in its history.

Butt, in service to a non-isolationist presidency and a sympathiser with European culture, watched these near misses with laconic unhappiness, continuing to advise President Taft while worrying sincerely about the future. During his visit to Rome, he was also accorded audiences first with the Vatican Secretary of State, who Butt described as 'one of the handsomest men I have ever seen', and, two days afterwards, with Pope Pius X, an unusual honour for a Protestant dignitary and one which excited the prejudices and pens of the anti-Catholic sections of the American press.[34] After Rome, Butt made quick trips to the same spots as the Thayers, missing his future friend by a few days in each place, first in Switzerland and then as a guest of the American Ambassador in Berlin. He visited his niece in Paris, and they crossed the Channel together to spend Easter in Chester with his brother, followed by a weekend in London.[35] His cousin and hostess in London, Baroness Rebecca Rosenkrantz, thought that Butt seemed 'in a distressed and sad state of mind', something perceived almost immediately by Marian Thayer over dinner and confirmed when Butt told her 'he was very nervous & did not know how he was going to stand the rushing life he was returning to'.[36] She offered to teach him some of the techniques her husband had learned at the Swiss clinic to tackle his depression.

He made an engagement for the next afternoon as I was going to teach him a method of control of the nerves through which I had just been with a noted Swiss doctor knowing it would be a wonderful thing for him if he could get a hold of it . . . we were going to work so hard over it the rest of the time on board. He said I was just like his mother and opened his heart to me & it was as though we had known each other well for years. It was the strangest sensation and felt as tho' a veil was blown aside for those few hours eliminating distance between two who had known each other always *well* long, long before and had just found each other again – I believe it.[37]

Marian Thayer's interest in spiritualism and homeopathy, as well as the strident tone she adopted in her letters and affidavits in the months after the *Titanic*'s sinking, have earned her an unjustified reputation as a loquacious eccentric, but many of her contemporaries, including Archibald Butt, shared her views and he agreed that it felt as if he and Marian 'had just found each other again'.[38]

Marian's dinner party companion, Major Archibald Butt (right), walking with President Taft (centre) in 1911.

Their immediate intimacy does not seem to have riled Thayer any more than Bruce Ismay's ungainly infatuation had earlier that afternoon. Archibald Butt had been timidly heterosexual for most of his adult life, professing unrequited passion for a series of Society women who were, for a variety of reasons, unquestionably beyond his romantic reach. George Behe in his moving recent account of Butt's career in 1911 and 1912 has described Butt's relationship with the architect Frank Millet as that of close friends who had shared a house and living expenses, which may explain their shared residency of a townhouse in Washington, DC.[39] There is, however, much to support the suggestions of Richard Davenport-Hines and Hugh Brewster in their respective studies of the *Titanic*'s passengers that Millet and Butt may have been romantically involved with one another and perhaps had been for years.[40]

Millet, the father of three and amiably married since 1879 to a woman who shared both his artistic interests and his wit, but who spent most of her time living in a refurbished manor house in the Cotswolds, was bisexual, and passionate letters survive between him and American author Charles Warren Stoddard, with whom he shared a home in Venice in the five years preceding his marriage.[41] Mark Twain had stood as best man at Millet's wedding and he so admired Millet's geniality that he coined the phrase 'a Millet' to mean 'a warm and likeable fellow'; Butt was even more struck by Millet's virtues when the two met in Washington in the 1890s.[42] First Lady Nellie Taft seems to have believed that Millet and Butt were a couple, while her husband tacitly ignored the evidence in front of him, something made easier by Butt's necessary discretion as 'too canny an individual for that, too conscious of the risk in military and political ranks, where such an idea would have put a quick end to any hopes of advancement'.[43] Millet's protective concern for Butt and his intercession with President Taft as Butt's weight plummeted due to stress could, of course, be platonic, as could, perhaps at more of a stretch, their living together in Washington, recuperating in the same Italian villa and travelling home on the same ship. Against that, there is a letter Millet wrote on the first morning of the *Titanic*'s voyage and posted at Queenstown. Sent in reply to his friend the British artist Alfred Parsons, its description of Millet's cabin is perhaps the most relevant to a discussion of the relationship between Millet and Archibald Butt:

Dear Alfred,
    I got yours this morning and was glad to hear from you. I thought I told you my ship was the *Titanic*. She has everything but taxicabs and theatres. Table d'hôte, restaurant à la carte, gymnasium, Turkish bath, squash court, palm gardens, smoking rooms for 'ladies and gents',* intended I

---

* A possible confusion of the Writing Room as a Smoking Room 'for ladies'.

fancy to keep the women out of the men's smoking room which they infest in the German and French steamers. The fittings are in the order of Haddon Hall and are exceedingly agreeable in design and colour. As for the rooms they are larger than the ordinary hotel room and much more luxurious with wooden bedsteads, dressing tables, hot and cold water, etc. etc., electric fans, electric heater and all. The suites with their damask hangings and mahogany oak furniture are really sumptuous and tasteful. I have the best room I ever had in a ship and it isn't one of the best either, a great long corridor in which to hang my clothes and a square window as big as the one in the studio alongside the large light. No end of furniture cupboards, wardrobe, dressing table, couch etc. etc. Not a bit like going to sea. You can have no idea of the spaciousness of this ship and the extent and size of the decks . . .

Yours always,

Frank[44]

Millet was booked into cabin E-38, on the same corridor as Dorothy Gibson in one of the cheapest parts of First Class. Admittedly, he does identify his accommodation as 'not one of the best' on board, yet it is hard to square his description of 'suites with their damask hangings . . . and a great long corridor in which to hang my clothes' with surviving photographs or deck plans of any of the E-Deck bedrooms, and impossible to do so when it comes to mention of 'a square window as big as the one in the studio'.[45] The only staterooms on the *Titanic* to have windows were outside cabins on A- and B-Deck; any located below that had circular portholes. Archibald Butt had reserved B-38, which had all the features mentioned in Millet's letter – a large bed, tables, large wardrobe space, a couch, a dressing table and a rectangular window.[46] While the exact extent of the men's involvement with one another is unknowable, the logical solution to the inconsistencies between Butt's cabin, Millet's ticket and his letter is that for propriety's sake they had booked two separate cabins, three decks apart, picked the cheapest cabin possible for the one least used and spent most of their time in Butt's stateroom, from where Millet penned his reply to Alfred Parsons on the morning of the 11th.

Apart from her burgeoning friendship with Butt, the only other details Marian recalled of that dinner were how quickly their food arrived and that Captain Smith 'refused to drink' any alcohol. The latter claim is backed up by other survivors who dined with Marian that evening, with one deviating testimony that Smith 'sipped once' at a glass of port to halt the jovial hectoring of a friend. In light of subsequent newspaper claims that Smith had been drunk as a result of the Wideners' hospitality, surviving guests were willing to go on record, either before the Senate inquiry or in newspaper interviews, that Smith had not imbibed anything stronger than one sip of port. In this, they are corroborated by statements from other passengers in the Restaurant who, since they had not been in that party, had no discernible reason to exculpate themselves from the charge of having plied a captain with wine.[47] Where Marian may have been overzealous in her defence of Captain Smith was in her insistence that their plates had been cleared and coffee served by about 8.25 p.m., which means ordering, preparation, serving, eating and clearing was managed in about fifty minutes, leaving Smith time to make it back to the Bridge to talk with one of his officers by 8.45. The probability of this timeline is undercut further by a statement made to the Senate inquiry into the events of that night. Daisy Minahan, who ate with her family at a table near by on Sunday the 14th, swore that 'Capt. Smith was continuously with his party from the time we entered [about 7.15] until between 9:25 and 9:45, when he bid the women good night and left. I know this time positively, for at 9:25 my brother suggested my going to bed. We waited for one more piece of the orchestra, and it was between 9:25 and 9:45 (the time we departed), that Capt. Smith left . . . I had read testimony before your committee stating that Capt.

Smith had talked to an officer on the bridge from 8:45 to 9:25. This is positively untrue, as he was having coffee with these people during this time. I was seated so close to them that I could hear bits of their conversation.'[48] A fully sober Smith talked later in the evening with two of his officers and Marian Thayer's recollection of an unfeasibly swift dinner was either a mistake or a well-intentioned lie to exonerate a man she had sincerely liked from charges she felt to be unwarranted.

At one point, Dr O'Loughlin allegedly stood at his table in the centre of his restaurant and proposed a toast with his glass of champagne – 'Let us drink to the mighty *Titanic*' – which was returned along with some applause and cheers.[49] Two decks below, Lady Rothes, Tommy Andrews, Ida Straus, Dorothy Gibson and Jack Thayer dined in the Saloon. The Stewardess Mary Sloan saw Andrews arrive and thought he looked 'splendid', in far better spirits than when she had spoken to him on the Friday.[50] Two of Andrews' dining companions, Dr O'Loughlin and the stockbroker Harry Anderson, were in the Restaurant that evening, but everyone else was present in the Saloon, including two Canadian newly-weds, the Purser Hugh McElroy, William Stead, an American lawyer called Frederic Seward and a thirty-six-year-old New Yorker, Eleanor Cassebeer, who was sailing home to initiate divorce proceedings after years of living apart from her husband in Paris. It was down to the Purser that Mrs Cassebeer was at their table. After boarding, she had gone to his office to make sure she got a good table in the Saloon. While standing in the queue, she had been irritated by the delay caused by the requests of a man she decided must be Jewish and turned to the gentleman behind her to explain, 'I hope I don't get put next to that Jew.' The man to whom she made the comment, Benjamin Foreman, was a thirty-year-old Jewish embroidery merchant from upstate New York, who perhaps showed more magnanimity than Mrs Cassebeer deserved when she saw him two days later and asked if he would like to join her for a walk on the Promenade Deck. 'You don't want to walk with me,' he laughed. 'You said you didn't like Jews and I'm one too.'[51] He joined her for coffee in the Lounge, where he apparently managed to undo most of her prejudices. She had also been the subject of some teasing from her companions for her refusal to change out of her afternoon suits for dinner. On Sunday, as the hors d'oeuvres and oysters made way for a Consommé Olga or a Cream of Barley, Cassebeer arrived at table in a white lace gown, with an ermine stole and jewels, inspiring Tommy Andrews to joke as she took her seat, 'Now that's the way a lady should look!'[52] Andrews did not apparently talk shop too much at meals since, although the newlyweds heard him refer to the ship affectionately as 'his baby', after five days and fourteen meals together Eleanor Cassebeer understood him as 'someone who it was said had something to do with building the *Titanic*'.[53] Instead, 'upon every occasion, and especially at dinner on Sunday evening, he talked almost constantly about his wife, little girl, mother and family, as well as of his home'.[54] During dinner, a young couple from Montreal brought their daughter Loraine, who at two years old was the same age as Andrews' child Elizabeth, into the Saloon to introduce her to some fellow Canadians at their table.[55]

At the Countess of Rothes' table, poached salmon in a mousseline sauce for the fish course was cleared away for a choice between filet mignon, chicken Lyonnaise and a marrow farci, before Steward Ewart Burr moved around behind the Countess and her companions with offerings of green peas, creamed carrots, boiled rice and two types of potatoes – Parmentier, flavoured with rosemary, and new – as possible complements to the lamb, duck or sirloin. A punch romaine palate cleanser served as interlude before pigeon accompanied by cress, followed by an asparagus vinaigrette salad, then pâté de foie gras and dessert options of peaches in chartreuse jelly, chocolate and vanilla éclairs and French ice cream. There was also a Waldorf pudding on the menu, for which no precise recipe survives. A vanilla pudding containing diced apples, sultanas and a dash of nutmeg was offered on the *Olympic* in 1914 and it may be that it was a company recipe.[56]

On the Sabbath, there were performances by the band but no

dancing on board British liners, so Lady Rothes and Gladys Cherry listened to music in the Reception Room after pudding. The Steward bringing them their coffee told the two ladies that icebergs were responsible for it having become 'very, very cold' on deck, which did not seem to lessen how 'very gay we felt that night'.[57] The last tune they stayed to hear was the Barcarolle from Offenbach's *The Tales of Hoffmann*, after which they returned to their stateroom where they were in bed for about ten o'clock.[58] Tommy Andrews went to thank one of the ship's bakers, another Ulsterman, who had as a favour to Andrews baked a speciality bread, almost certainly either potato or soda bread.[59] Andrews had planned to take coffee in the Café Parisian or Reception Room, with two of his dinner companions but they lingered so long over dessert that Andrews retired to his cabin 'full of charts . . . making calculations and drawings for future use'.[60] Dorothy Gibson and her mother went to the Lounge in search of some bridge partners, which they found in the New York-based lawyer Frederic Seward and a twenty-eight-year-old stockbroker from New Britain, Connecticut, William Sloper.[61] Also in the Lounge, two middle-aged sisters, Martha Stephenson and Elizabeth Eustis, were looking at photographs of icebergs in Sir Ernest Shackleton's *Heart of the Antarctic*. They returned the book to the Lounge's lending library and walked down to their shared cabin on D-Deck. On their way, the sisters paused to say hello to John and Marian Thayer. They were neighbours in Haverford, Pennsylvania, and a quick greeting turned into a forty-five-minute conversation about the voyage thus far. Martha and Elizabeth were enjoying their time so much that they joked about their mild distress at news of the ship's speed, since they wanted to spend as much time as possible at sea.[62]

Later, stories circulated, one originating in the *New York World* and the other in the *New York Telegraph*, that Ida Straus and Dorothy Gibson took separate strolls on the deck that night, with Dorothy walking out of the Lounge at about 11.50 on to a deck lit by the moon 'shining brilliantly'.[63] There was no moon that night and Dorothy and her companions had been gently ushered from the Lounge by the stewards at its 11.30 closing time; Ida's maid had helped her prepare for bed after dinner.[64] Jack Thayer did walk on deck late that evening. After his dinner, he had gone to enjoy a cup of coffee and listen to the live music in the Reception Room. Seeing him alone, a twenty-nine-year-old man with light-brown hair, grey-blue eyes and a prominent nose approached and asked if he would like some company.[65] Milton Long was a legal clerk and judge's son from Massachusetts, travelling alone and profoundly bored. They chatted over coffee for an hour or so, before Long called it a night to head to his cabin on the same deck and Thayer popped up to his to grab an overcoat for 'a few turns around the deck'.[66]

On the Boat Deck, with its white-painted and covered lifeboats,

This suite on the *Olympic* was almost identical to the one occupied by John and Marian Thayer on the *Titanic*, with the door leading through to Jack's cabin.

Jack thought it was 'deserted and lonely. The wind whistled through the stays, and blackish smoke poured out of the three forward funnels.'[67] The natural breeze from earlier had died and the wind around Jack Thayer was generated solely by the *Titanic's* forward motion. It was darker on deck, since First Officer William Murdoch, then on duty on the Bridge, had ordered several hatches closed to reduce the light from below deck and facilitate the spotting of the icebergs they had been warned about.[68] Jack noticed,

It had become very much colder. It was a brilliant, starry night. There was no moon and I have never seen the stars shine brighter; they appeared to stand right out of the sky, sparkling like cut diamonds. A very light haze, hardly notice-able, hung low over the water. I have spent much time on the ocean, yet I have never seen the sea smoother than it was that night; it was like a mill-pond, and just as innocent looking, as the great ship rippled through it.[69]

At about eleven, he returned indoors and chatted with his parents in their suite.[70] He then went into his bedroom and about ten or fifteen minutes later called 'Good night' through the closed door, which was answered by his mother since his father had already dozed off.[71] The electric heaters in the Thayers' bedrooms were temperamental and, despite the frigid weather, Jack decided to prop open his porthole slightly, before changing for bed. His mother evidently had the same idea but, assuming her son was asleep and reluctant to wake her husband, rang for a steward to help her with the window. Next door, Jack was awake but 'sleepy' and standing next to his bed, adjusting his wristwatch to keep in line with the ship's clocks when the *Titanic* grazed an iceberg in trying to swerve to avoid it. He swayed slightly on his feet and felt the 'ship had veered to port as though she had been gently pushed. If I had had a brimful glass of water in my hand not a drop would have spilled, the shock was so slight.'[72]

12

Going Up to See the Fun

Why is it that all the main work of breaking down human souls
went on at night?

Aleksandr Solzhenitsyn, *August 1914* (1971)

T HE *Titanic'*S LOOKOUTS HAD RUNG THE WARNING BELL
three times and then telephoned the Bridge from the
Crow's Nest to inform them that they had spotted an
iceberg in the ship's path. The senior presiding officer on duty,
William Murdoch, ordered evasive action to be taken by the
Quartermaster Robert Hitchens, who took the ten or so seconds
expected to slam the wheel counter-clockwise, supervised by
Murdoch's accompanying junior colleague for that shift, James
Moody. The manoeuvre almost worked, as predicted by the posi-
tive indicators of the *Titanic'*s stopping and turning capabilities
recorded during her trials in Belfast. One of the lookouts thought
'it seemed almost as if she might clear it' until part of the iceberg
made contact with the ship's starboard, at which point Murdoch
ordered the closing of the watertight doors.[1] In certain parts of
the ship, the tremor of the impact was so slight that hundreds
of passengers slept through it.[2] Those who were, like Jack, awake
and in one of the A-, B- or C-Deck cabins noticed 'a funny

203

rumbling noise', 'a grating sound' or 'a slight lift of the bed'.[3] Stewards preparing the Saloon for the next morning's breakfast unknowingly concurred with a school teacher reading in bed in his second-class cabin when they attributed the jolt to the *Titanic* throwing one of her nine propeller blades, an occupational irritant that had already happened to her sister a few months earlier and would require a few days in Belfast to right once they made it back from New York.[4] Another passenger wondered if the sea, so calm as to be compared to 'a lake' earlier that evening, had dramatically changed and the *Titanic* had been hit by a wave.[5]

In C-77, the Countess of Rothes was awoken by 'a slight grating sound – a slight shock'.[6] However, she then almost certainly went back to sleep for ten or fifteen minutes. The *Titanic*'s engines halted briefly to enable a cursory inspection about five minutes after the impact. Jack Thayer was one of the few passengers to notice when 'the engines started up again – slowly – not with the bright vibration to which we were accustomed, but as though they were tired'.[7] The engines carried the *Titanic* forward at half-speed for about twelve minutes more, until Captain Smith ordered them stopped.[8] It was the 'terrible silence' that settled over their cabin that prompted Lady Rothes to get out of bed, wake Gladys and ring for the Steward, who told them they had struck an iceberg – news which, in Gladys's words, 'rather excited us and we put on our dressing gowns and fur coats'.[9] Far above them, the two women heard 'the awful noise of steam being let off' through the ship's funnels, but neither they nor their Steward 'in the least realised there was any danger'.[10]

They were beaten to the deck by Jack Thayer, who had grabbed his slippers and a heavy overcoat while calling through to his parents' bedroom that he 'was going up on deck to see the fun'. John Thayer, roused from his sleep either by the cut of the engines or by Jack's excitement, dressed more thoroughly than his son, who was one of the first two or three passengers to brave the cold.[11] His parents joined him on the Promenade, where they heard from a crew member that they had hit an iceberg, bits of which were still visible on the Well Deck. Marian mentioned to her son and husband that she felt a 'very slight list to starboard' beneath their feet. They agreed with her, after which Marian went back inside since it was 2 degrees below freezing on deck and her overzealous radiator thus no longer seemed so inconvenient.[12]

The publicity surrounding Dorothy Gibson's experiences on the *Titanic* produced a sufficient number of contradictory newspaper articles in the weeks immediately after the sinking to make it difficult to pinpoint where she was at the moment of the collision. It has already been mentioned that she cannot have felt 'a slight jar' while playing bridge in the Lounge, as the room had been closed and she politely asked to leave ten minutes before the *Titanic* struck the berg.[13] Considering that she was still wearing only her evening gown with no wrap or shawl, one can also dismiss the story that she left the Lounge to stroll on the Promenade, where through the windows she allegedly saw her fellow passengers playing cards 'and other forms of divertissement' as the *Titanic* sailed with 'icebergs around us and the water filled with the shattered remains of others'.[14] William Sloper, who had first met Dorothy that Sunday when she and her party 'asked me if I would make a fourth at bridge', wrote down his account of the sinking three days after it happened, in which he confirms that he, Dorothy, her mother Pauline and their friend Frederic Seward played bridge in the Lounge until 11.30, when 'the steward asked us to finish our game as everyone else had gone to bed and the lights were going to be put out in the room. We finished the game, and at 11:40 I said good-night to the ladies and was on the stairway going down to my own cabin. Suddenly there was a lurch and a creaking . . .'[15]

Sloper's version of events renders more credible the particular story that Dorothy was, like him, on her way to bed when she felt the corridor around her shake. On E-Deck, the force of the impact was considerably more noticeable and when 'the boat seemed to shiver' Dorothy was left badly frightened. She and her mother returned to the Grand Staircase on A-Deck, where Sloper had tracked down a few stewards who 'assured everyone who asked them that the water tight bulkheads were closed and that while there was a hole in her, she could not possibly sink, and many who had got out of bed to ascertain the trouble returned satisfied. All this time the steam from the boilers was blowing off furiously over-head, and the noise on the deck was deafening.' Dorothy was not completely convinced by the reassurances of the stewards or Sloper, who said she suffered 'an attack of nervous prostration, and [she] was greatly alarmed and excited, stopped everyone as they came out from the lower deck and asked them if there was any danger'.[16]

One person Dorothy tried to ask for more information was Thomas Andrews, when she saw him rush up the stairs from B-Deck.[17] He was uncharacteristically brusque, not specifically to Dorothy, to whom he had not been introduced by the Sunday evening, but to most of the passengers attempting to stop him, although he stopped for longer when he saw Albert and Vera Dick, a couple who ate at his Saloon table and with whom he had planned to have coffee earlier that evening. He told them, 'There is no cause for any excitement. All of you get what you can in the way of clothes and come on deck as soon as you can. She is torn to bits below, but she will not sink if her after bulkheads hold.'[18] Dorothy thought Andrews had a 'face of greenish paleness' as he went up the Grand Staircase to the Boat Deck.[19] It was about forty minutes since the collision and he was on his way to make his report to the Captain, informing him that the *Titanic* would not survive the damage inflicted by the iceberg. Andrews had been working in his cabin when the Captain sent for him and asked him to make an inspection of the boiler rooms. The ship's Fourth Officer, Joseph Boxhall, had already carried out a cursory exami-nation, but Smith was not satisfied. After the engines had stopped for the second and final time, Ismay, sporting a coat thrown over his pyjamas, visited the Bridge to ask if Smith thought the *Titanic* was seriously damaged. Even though he had not yet heard from Andrews, Smith told Ismay that he 'thought it was'.[20]

On his way below after receiving his commission from Smith, Andrews was hailed by Eleanor Cassebeer, wearing an evening kimono and slippers. She was sitting near the Grand Staircase with another of their Saloon set, stockbroker Harry Anderson, who had seen a 75–100-foot iceberg pass by the windows of the Smoking Room, the only first-class public room still open at 11.40 p.m.[21] It was at this stage, in response to Eleanor's numerous questions, that Andrews said the *Titanic* 'could break in three separate and distinct parts and that each part would stay afloat indefinitely'.[22] He initially expressed similar jocular confidence to the Dicks, likewise congregated near the Staircase's torch-clutching cherub, when he told them 'that he was going below to investigate. We begged him not to go, but he insisted, saying that he knew the ship as no one else did and that he might be able to allay the fears of the passengers. He went.'[23]

When he reached G-Deck a few minutes later, Andrews saw clerks struggling to move the sacks of correspondence as freezing water seeped into the two-storey Mail Room, as well as one of the nearby storage compartments for first-class luggage.[24] If he had begun to suspect the seriousness of the danger they were in, he received confirmation in the boiler rooms. Despite the gruesome insinuations of several cinematic adaptations of the sinking, no stokers were trapped or maimed as the doors had slid into place after the collision. After the doors had shut, the crew were able to make their way up ladders to escape exits that opened onto Scotland Road on E Deck. Now they were back at their posts trying to get the fires down and to shut off the boilers. Those not needed had been assigned to help work the pumps deployed to tackle the water, but with five of the forward watertight compartments now open to the Atlantic, Andrews understood it was a question of when, rather than if, the ship would sink. He hypothesised that either a gash of about 300 feet or a series of tears had been made below the waterline and the latter suggestion was proved right by a sonar survey of the *Titanic*'s wreck eighty-four years later. All bar one of the actual points of impact are now buried in sediment but the exploration, conducted by sonar specialist Paul Matthias, determined that there were six slits of various sizes, extending at intervals across the first 230 feet of the *Titanic*.* There was a small trace wound near the prow, followed by punctures of about 5 feet, then 6, then 16, then further aft and slightly lower of 33 and finally, the only one visible to submersibles today, a gash of 45 feet.[25] The width of the respective tears has never been determined, either by Thomas Andrews in 1912 or by Paul Matthias in 1996, and given that each hole is likely to have buckled or distended further when the ship settled on the seafloor, it now most likely never will be.

Captain Smith joined him just as the horror of the situation revealed itself to Andrews. Referring to the flooding of the watertight compartments, Andrews told the commander, 'Well, three have gone [fully flooded] already, Captain.'[26] Smith left Andrews to complete his observations, which took another ten minutes before he was certain.[27] Three years earlier, the *Republic* had taken nine hours to founder when another ship had slammed into her side, but the *Titanic* was dealing with an extraordinary amount of damage, with Andrews guessing that nearly one-third of her total length had been intermittently opened to the sea. The ship's second, third and fourth compartments were flooding uncontrollably – the first had largely been spared by Officer Murdoch's attempts to turn the ship away from the iceberg. The *Titanic*'s Forepeak Tank with a capacity of 190 tons had already filled, adding critical forward weight and helping slowly yet inexorably to drag the bow lower in the water. It was in Boiler Room 6, where Andrews saw such swift flooding that he concluded that the ship had become a lost cause, even with the pumps working at full capacity. He ran up from the depths through the E-Deck corridors and the empty Reception Room, dodging the queries of passengers who had emerged from their cabins to find out why the *Titanic*'s engines had stopped. It was then that he brushed aside Dorothy Gibson's questions and tried

---

* Andrews' guess that they extended for approximately 300 feet might explain why he misdiagnosed by thirty minutes to an hour the time it would take for the *Titanic* to founder.

to avoid panicking the Dicks, while still admitting that the *Titanic* was 'torn to bits' below.

Where he delivered the news to Smith is unknown, although the most likely place was either on the Bridge or in the Captain's quarters. It was a grim mathematical certainty that, having been designed to float with four, but not five, of her compartments flooded, the gathering water would pull the bow down until the seawater spilled over into the next bulkhead, and so on, until the *Titanic* settled by the head and sank. To Smith's question of 'time of death', Andrews calculated somewhere between one hour and ninety minutes, depending on how long the bulkheads held.[28] It was a devastating prognosis, not least because of the brevity predicted by Andrews, and Smith immediately gave the order for the lifeboats to be filled and lowered.

Merriment continued on the Promenade Deck, where the Countess joined a small group of those likewise seeking information and spotted on the forecastle below third-class passengers 'walking about laughing and picking up pieces of ice off the Deck'.[29] She spotted chunks of ice all over the ship's bow, 'but we could not see the berg', which had retreated back into the darkness when the *Titanic* had briefly restarted her engines. The Countess and Gladys 'watched a bit on deck and talked and then wondered if we should go back to bed or not'. Their deliberations were interrupted by the arrival of Captain Smith, who spoke to Lady Rothes in a low voice, 'I don't want to frighten anyone, but will you go quietly and put on your life belts and go up on the top deck?'[30]

Only a moment or so after she had asked Tommy Andrews if the *Titanic* had been badly damaged, Dorothy questioned another crew member passing by the Grand Staircase. He 'said that the water was rushing in through the squash court wall, and that she was filling rapidly'.[31] As stewards circulated with the Captain's request for passengers to dress warmly and put on their lifejackets, Dorothy was one of the few in First Class who knew at this early stage that one of their public rooms, the Squash Court located on the deck below her cabin, had started to flood.

The stewards and stewardesses began to move from door to door, reviving those who had gone back to sleep trusting in earlier assurances, or waking those who had so far slept through the whole incident. None of the crew members assigned to look after the passengers had yet been told that the wound inflicted by the iceberg was fatal. Ida Straus, asleep on the starboard side of the ship when the engines fell silent, put on her dressing gown before venturing into the corridor in search of answers.[32] Her maid, Ellen, one of those who had slept through the collision, believed that her employer had come across one of the ship's officers who told her that they had struck an iceberg. None of the *Titanic*'s officers ventured down to the passenger corridors at this stage in the evening and Ida instead probably heard the news from one of the stewards dispatched to rouse the passengers. Ida walked down the corridor populated by an increasing number of the curious, passing twenty doors on her left until she reached her maid's, whom she asked to fetch Isidor's valet from the next cabin 'to assist him in dressing'.[33]

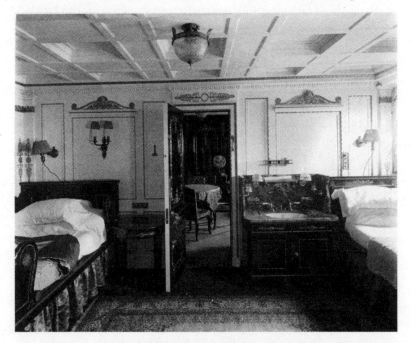

The Strauses were asleep in their suite at the time of the collision.

The Strauses' two servants dressed themselves before reporting to C-55, where Ida decided against wearing any other rings barring her wedding and engagement bands, donned two coats, one woollen under fur, and filled a little jewellery pouch with a golden purse, decorated with diamonds and emeralds, that Isidor had bought for her as a surprise during their stay in Paris two weeks earlier.[34] Once Farthing had helped Isidor, Ida put on a pair of tight-fitting leather gloves and the party moved up to A-Deck, eschewing the warmth indoors in favour of the enclosed Promenade Deck, from where rumour had it the lifeboats, if deployed, might be filled. They 'mingled with other passengers and discussed the danger in a perfectly calm and collected manner. No one seemed to believe that there was any great danger of the ship sinking.'[35] They sat on two of the unused steamer chairs and waited.[36]

13

Music in the First-Class Lounge

Things are desperate, but not serious.

Viennese proverb

L ADY ROTHES RETURNED TO HER STATEROOM WITH Gladys, where they were relieved to find that her maid had already been woken by the activity and come up to find them. Less fortunately, a lack of printed notices on the stateroom doors meant that they could not find where their lifebelts were stored and in the end they walked out into the corridor and flagged down 'an awfully nice man' who unsuccessfully helped in the hunt until Noëlle gave up by ringing for the Steward who, when they explained what they were looking for, said, 'I did not even know the order for life belts had been given.'[1] After the lifejackets had been located underneath their beds, they dressed quickly, tying the cork-filled lifebelts in place over the top of their fur coats, but left behind most of their jewellery, except for the string of pearls that had been with the countesses of Rothes since the sixteenth century, which Noëlle decided to wear. Some nervous urge jolted Gladys into picking up a photograph of her sweetheart, whose name unfortunately is missing from her surviving letters.

It was the only personal memento she considered taking from the cabin until she thought, 'How silly, we shall soon be back here.' She put the photograph back and 'calmly and quietly went to the top boat-deck; you see by this the perfect confidence the people had in that great boat, no one could believe there was danger.'[2] Exiting their corridor, they met the Purser, who told them of several passengers who had contacted his office to request the return of their jewels. The same twinge of foreboding that had prompted Gladys to consider carrying a photograph with her from their stateroom apparently briefly unsettled the Countess, who turned back to shake the Purser's hand as they said goodbye, although she did not want to bother him by also requesting the rest of her jewels back from his safe. She thought she had heard him call her 'Little lady', although in the crush of the C-Deck atrium it is equally possible that she had misheard the more proper 'milady' or 'my lady'.[3]

As the Captain's commands roused the ship, Andrews moved through her corridors, where to his relief he saw stewards and stewardesses opening the unoccupied first-class cabins to gather spare lifejackets and blankets – even if they remained dangerously oblivious of the severity of the situation, the victualling staff were all aware of how cold it would be for passengers put into the lifeboats. Andrews was keen for the crew to set an example and told Stewardess Annie Robinson, working on the empty A-Deck staterooms, 'Put your lifebelt on and walk about and let the passengers see you.' Robinson's response, 'It looks rather mean,' earned her the order, 'No, put it on.' Then a pause, followed by Andrews turning back to say quietly to her, 'Well, if you value your life put your belt on.'[4] It was the first time he articulated to anyone bar the Captain and officers that the ship was in a mortal condition.

Andrews was struggling against his own panic as he moved from the A-Deck corridors to their B-Deck counterparts, where another Stewardess, his admirer Mary Sloan, 'read in his face all I wanted to know'.[5] He encountered his own cabin Steward,

forty-six-year-old Harry Etches, also performing errands of useful-
ness on B-Deck, and, once they were certain they had woken up
the more determined sleepers and had hurried stragglers to the
Lounge or boats, Andrews asked Etches to help him do the same
on C-Deck. A few days earlier, Andrews had agreed with Eleanor
Cassebeer when she remarked over lunch that the *Titanic* did
not have the typical information notices attached to the back of
the cabin doors, the same point that frustrated Lady Rothes'
search for her lifejacket. The frames were there, but in the rush
to prepare for the maiden voyage the notices had been left behind
in Southampton. Their absence now worried Andrews and he
stressed to Etches that the passengers needed to be told that
their lifebelts were either under their beds or on top of their
wardrobes.[6]

*

The *Olympic* and *Titanic's* identical Lounges were described by a trade journal
as 'the finest room ever built on a ship'.

The *Titanic*'s Lounge achieved apotheosis *in extremis*. It finally, if briefly, fulfilled its intended purpose to serve as a hub for first-class passengers. With the funnels still screaming like industrialised banshees, the lifeboats in the process of being uncovered and the temperature outside below freezing, the Lounge was reopened on the Purser's orders. It filled with light, with people and then with music as the ship's orchestra turned up to perform a concert. Ragtime and waltzes were played as the electric fire and the chandelier sparked back to life. Coffee, cocoa and brandies were served to passengers, some of whom were still in their dinner wear. Others had changed into the kind of warm clothes they might wear for stalking, hiking or hunting. Some carried their lifejackets; others wore them over furs or overcoats. Publishing heir Henry Harper arrived in the Lounge in flamboyant bad form, clutching his Pekingese Sun Yat-sen and still weak from a bout of tonsillitis that had bothered him since his holiday in Egypt. To him, the scene in the Lounge 'was rather like a stupid picnic where you don't know anybody and wonder how soon you can get away from such a boresome place'.[7] The author Helen Churchill Candee had a different impression of the scene. With the same benefit of hindsight as Harper but greater intelligence, she thought the unscheduled soiree on A-Deck had resembled 'a fancy dress ball in Dante's Hell'.[8]

The Thayers hovered around this exquisite Inferno as a party of six. Marian, dressed and accompanied by her redoubtably loyal lady's maid, Margaret Fleming, had sent her husband to offer their companionship to Martha Stephenson and Elizabeth Eustis, their neighbours from Haverford and conversation partners on the stairwell a few hours earlier. He found the sisters nearly dressed 'as if for breakfast', with sensible boots and woollen suits. From their wardrobe, they had also brought out fur coats into the pockets of which, for safety's sake, they had placed their letters of credit and some rolls of money. Jack Thayer had exchanged his pyjamas for a 'warm greenish tweed suit and vest with another mohair vest underneath [his] coat'. They were all wearing lifejackets, 'which were really large thick cork vests'. In Jack's case, it went on between his mohair sweater and the heavy coat his mother had gone back to their suite to fetch and insisted he wear. They arrived in the Lounge 'which was now crowded with people', including Milton Long, Jack's erstwhile companion from after-dinner coffee. Still alone and a little overwhelmed, Long asked if he could join the Thayers, which they agreed to, with Jack arranging introductions amid 'a great deal of noise. The band was playing lively tunes.'[9]

The group regretted their decision to quit the Lounge for the deck, where they discovered 'the noise was terrific. The deep vibrating roar of the exhaust steam blowing off through the safety valves was deafening, in addition to which they had started sending up rockets. There was more and more action. After standing there for some minutes talking above the din, trying to determine what we should do next, we finally decided to go back into the crowded hallway where it was warm.'[10] From there, they heard stewards delivering the order, 'All women to the port side.' Marian, her maid, and the two sisters from Haverford said a quick goodbye at the top of the staircase, beneath the famous clock, before they 'went out onto the port side of that deck, supposedly to get into a lifeboat'. The three men went to the starboard side to watch the activity there, where 'it seemed we were always waiting for orders and no orders ever came. The men had not yet commenced to lower any of the forward starboard lifeboats, of which there were four.' Jack noticed crew, including stokers, pooling on to the deck, also 'waiting for orders'.[11] From behind him, the band were still playing in the Lounge as passengers milled about in various moods of piqued curiosity.

*

The *Titanic* had twenty lifeboats, all located on the Boat Deck, bar four collapsibles – emergency craft tied to the roof of the Officers' Quarters, near the base of the ship's first two funnels. Those collapsible boats were designated by letters running from

A to D, while the lifeboats proper were numbered. These were wooden, white and suspended from davits with the exception of Lifeboats 1 and 2, both of which had been swung out at Southampton in case a passenger fell overboard and there needed to be a swift rescue dip to the sea below. The odd numbers, running from 1 to 15, were located on the starboard side of the deck; the even-numbered on the port. They were not stacked atop one another, but arranged in horizontal groups of four, with a gap for railings, around which was a low fence marking where the first-class section of the deck gave way to the second.* Since they were to be swung out to sit alongside the deck for loading, there was some confusion as to whether or not they would be filled from the Boat Deck or the Promenade below, from where passengers might be helped in more easily. Captain Smith apparently considered this idea at first, a hangover from his days commanding the *Olympic* with her unshuttered Promenade. Officers and sailors sent to prepare the Promenade as a loading point for the lifeboats apparently had to report back to the Bridge with the reminder that half the *Titanic*'s Promenade was enclosed with glass, which would have to be opened or popped out of its frame entirely.[12]

The lifeboats were not lowered in numerical order and the first to leave was the starboard side's 7, uncovered around the same time as her forward neighbours 3 and 5. These were the lifeboats watched by Thayer, Jack and Milton Long, before they again retreated to the warmth.[13] Officer William Murdoch was assigned to oversee the boats' loading and lowering, with two juniors to help him. Having accompanied them during the bridge game, William Sloper and Frederic Seward felt honour-bound to escort the Gibson women throughout the subsequent drama. Sloper explained later, 'As a man, I was bound to cheer up the ladies and act as calm as I could, but to say that I felt that underneath

---

* The davits could have accommodated a second vertical row of lifeboats, which were added to the *Olympic* after the *Titanic*'s sinking. Prior to the disaster, it was felt too many lifeboats would clutter the Boat Deck.

would be untrue. All this time there was no sign of panic or distress among passengers or crew. Everyone behaved wonderfully calm and cheerful.' What set Dorothy Gibson's impromptu clique apart from most of the other passengers was that they had over-heard the report about the flooding of the Squash Court, news that fuelled Dorothy's nerves, which in their turn made that small group one of the very few keen to leave the *Titanic* in the hour after the collision. They later overheard passengers discussing the sinking of the *Republic* as a likely blueprint for what might happen in the worst-case scenario – with the watertight compartments keeping the *Titanic* afloat long enough for rescue ships to arrive and safely evacuate all the passengers and crew.[14]

To Sloper's suggestion that she and Pauline return to their room to find warmer clothes, Dorothy had bolted down five decks, grabbed a cardigan to wear over her evening gown, and returned to the Grand Staircase with her mother. Although he did not always approve of how visible she made it, Sloper shared Dorothy's fright:

I felt as certain as anyone could feel that we had come to the end, and that many, if not all, would soon be gone. All of the people who were there in this companionway at this time, passed out quietly onto the deck where the lifeboats were. I remember distinctly that there was no crowding through the doorway – everyone was over polite. The covers had been taken off the lifeboats and they were quickly swung off the davits and lowered to the level of the deck. From this deck, we were, if I remember correctly, somewhere about eighty feet above the water, and to leave a well-lighted ship that at the time seemed to have listed slightly, and step into a small boat that might plunge down into the darkness below, or, if it reached the sea safely, be capsized by the water, was a question which made some people hold back. Miss [Gibson], who was now in a state of high nervous excitement, made for the first boat, and for fear that she might misstep or jump, I kept hold of her arm, and I remember [I] tried to keep her quiet by saying, 'Keep a stiff upper lip.' When the officers in charge of the first boat motioned for us to step in she stepped forward with her mother and the gentleman that had been playing cards with us, and I helped them into the boat and followed after them. People sort of hung back at this time.[15]

What Sloper did not mention was that Dorothy grabbed his arm as she reached Lifeboat 7 and either gestured or asked for him to follow her. She provided this detail in an interview she gave a few days later in New York, although her insistence that her companion be allowed to accompany them into the boat was not, at this stage of the night, a controversial request.[16] The famous rule of 'women and children first' into the boats was inconsistently enforced on the *Titanic*, tightening or slackening depending on time and location. Officer Murdoch, for instance, the senior officer on the starboard side, was far less stringent than his immediate inferior, Second Officer Charles Lightoller, placed in charge of the port-side boats and inclined to enforce 'women and children first' to such an extent that in certain instances it almost became 'women and children only', with the exception of crew members ordered in to steer and row.

Murdoch in fact asked if anyone else wanted to board Lifeboat 7 before it was lowered with twenty-eight occupants despite having a capacity of sixty-five. He allowed Frederic Seward to climb in with Dorothy, Pauline and Sloper. Also in the boat were a French aviator, Pierre Maréchal, and the Dutch car salesman travelling under the pseudonym of a German baron; the young Manhattan socialite Margaret Hays got in carrying her Pomeranian, Bébé, and Dickinson Bishop, a businessman from Michigan, was permitted to accompany his pregnant wife. According to Sloper a similar offer was made to J. J. Astor, who had been standing immediately behind the Gibson party 'with Mrs Astor, and he suddenly drew back and pulled his wife with him. Someone spoke to him, but I did not overhear what was said. At any rate they did not follow us into the boat. When twenty-nine people [*sic*], including three of the crew, were in the boat, and as nobody else seemed ready to follow, the officer on the deck gave word to "lower away" . . . As we left the deck somebody had thrown in a number of steamer rugs which were wrapped around the women.'[17] Dorothy had need of their warmth; after being slowly lowered down the side of the *Titanic*, during which Sloper 'expected one end of the boat would drop faster than the other and that we should be thrown out in the sea', Lifeboat 7 settled gently into the Atlantic, still 'as smooth as a mill pond'. William Sloper 'was glad to take up an oar and help row', while Dorothy screamed as she felt freezing water slosh around her ankles.[18] To prevent rainwater gathering during the voyage and rotting the wood, a drainage hole was left unplugged at the bottom of the lifeboats. Unfortunately, in this case it had accidentally remained unplugged as number 7 was filled and lowered. Her passengers and crew handed over what articles they could to help stop the leak, including Dorothy who gamely tore off her own stockings. When he saw that she was shivering, Sloper offered Dorothy his coat and she kissed him on the cheek as she accepted it.[19]

On deck, Andrews and Ismay had arrived to help with the loading of the second craft, Lifeboat 5. Both men were torn between their desire to get as many passengers into the boats as possible and their fear of inspiring a panic. The profound trust in the *Titanic*'s safety which both of them, particularly Andrews, had encouraged over the past five days had been transformed into a liability. Some passengers and crew were joking that they would need their tickets to reboard and 'you'll be back in the morning for breakfast'.[20] What William Sloper had noticed in J. J. Astor as he stood behind the Gibsons and then backed away from the offer to join their lifeboat was anxiety about what the trauma of being put to sea in a rowing boat might do to his pregnant wife. He refused to board either Lifeboat 7 or 5 in the belief that 'We are safer on board the ship than in that little boat.'[21] He then retreated to the warmth of the adjacent first-class Gymnasium, where he entertained Madeleine by using his penknife to cut open a lifejacket and show her the cork that gave them their buoyancy.[22] Faith in the *Titanic* had mingled with a feeling of bonhomie engendered by the collective cosiness offered in the Lounge to suffocate all sense of urgency. The Astors' friend Margaret Brown later told the *New York Times*, 'The whole thing was so formal that it was difficult for anyone to realize it was a tragedy. Men and women stood in little groups and talked. Some laughed as the boats went over the side. All the time the band was playing . . . I can see the men up on deck tucking in the women and smiling. It was a strange night. It all seemed like a play, like a dream that was being executed for entertainment. It did not seem real. Men would say "After you" as they made some woman comfortable and stepped back.'[23]

Tommy Andrews offered his arm to the quasi-reformed anti-Semite Eleanor Cassebeer, steadying her when she caught her foot on one of the ropes now snaking across the starboard deck. To her suggestion that he accompany her in the boat, Andrews demurred, 'No, women and children first', a rule he chose to impose upon himself although the tennis star Karl Behr and the New York-based surgeon Dr Henry Frauenthal were among the men allowed to cross by the officers.[24] Andrews was, at least at this stage, still masking his terror, an exercise in self-control at which Ismay with the finest intentions failed. The liner's Third Officer, Herbert Pitman, had been ordered to help with the loading of the first three lifeboats and to command one after it had been lowered. As he admired the efficient operation of the Welin davits that managed to swing the three empty boats over the side of the ship with minimum effort from the seamen, Pitman was surprised and irritated to be approached by Ismay, who told him he needed to fill the boats with as many women and children as quickly as possible. Chairman of the Line notwithstanding, the at-sea chain of command clearly relegated Ismay to the role of a passenger, prompting Pitman to snap, 'I await the *commander's* orders.' Pitman claimed later that he had not recognised Ismay when he rebuked him, although this rings untrue in light of his brisk walk to the Bridge where he informed Captain Smith of Ismay's nervousness about getting the boats away, to which Smith replied, 'Go ahead; carry on.'[25] Ismay also riled another of the officers stationed at the first three lifeboats, Harold Lowe, who, when he saw Ismay trying to encourage the sailors to lower quickly, screamed at him, 'If you'll get the hell out of the way, I'll be able to do something! You want me to lower away quickly? You'll have me drown the lot of them!'[26] Ismay, so eager to help that he had simply thrown trousers on over his pyjamas and then rushed back on deck, beat a tactical retreat, perhaps appreciating that he was doing more harm than good. It was the sight of the pyjama legs poking out from the trousers of the usually fastidious Ismay that gave Eleanor Cassebeer her first suspicion that this might not simply be a temporary manoeuvre to fulfil some pedantic British seafaring guide about proper procedure in the aftermath of collision with an iceberg.[27]

14

Vox faucibus haesit

Entreat me not to leave thee, or to turn from following after thee; for whither thou goest, I will go . . .

Ruth 1:16

THE COUNTESS, HER MAID AND GLADYS CHERRY DID NOT go into the Lounge and obeyed the Captain's earlier request to them that they congregate on the Boat Deck, where they again heard the din created by the ferocious screams from the forward three funnels as the safety valves attached to the *Titanic*'s boilers continued to release steam from below.[1] 'The noise when we got up was *appalling*,' Noëlle wrote, an assessment supported by one of the *Titanic*'s officers who compared the roar from the funnels to 'a thousand railway engines thundering through a culvert'.[2] From where they stood, the Countess, like Jack Thayer on the opposite side of the deck, saw white distress rockets streak hundreds of feet into the sky above her.[3] The bellowing of the funnels finally stopped as her party were marshalled into lines by Second Officer Charles Lightoller in preparation for loading Lifeboats 6 and 8.[4] By this point, it is possible that the Countess, at least, had begun to appreciate something of the seriousness of the situation, since Cissy had apparently also heard and repeated the rumour about the flooding in the Squash Court.[5]

The *Titanic's* Lifeboat 8 is in the foreground. It was here that Ida Straus and the Countess of Rothes gathered for the lowering of lifeboats 8 and 6, which was behind 8 but out of shot.

Lightoller's stringent application of 'the rule of the Sea' to evacuate women and children inspired panic in the couples standing near the Countess, including a pair she recognised as the honeymooning Spanish pair, Victor and María-Josefa de Peñasco, whose cabin had been on the same corridor as Noëlle's. Realising 'they could not speak any English & were terrified', Noëlle stepped out of line for the lifeboat to talk to them, correctly guessing that they might have a mutual language in French, which Peñasco used to beg Noëlle to 'take his wife with me'. María-Josefa clung to her husband, her terror morphing into a hysteria she could not control. Perhaps it was the sight of the distress rockets that explained the shift in mood, a perceptible shaking of certainty, prompting another woman, next to the Countess but unknown by her, to turn away from the boats at the last minute saying, 'I've forgotten Jack's photograph and must get it.'[6] Whoever she was, Noëlle did not see her again and her attention was soon taken by the Captain, who she thought 'looked to be under a terrible strain'.[7] As they were loading the lifeboat, Smith told the occupants to 'row to the steamer whose lights we could see & leave our passengers & return for more'.[8] Both Lady Rothes and, later from a different vantage point, Marian Thayer saw the mastheads of a much smaller vessel on the horizon. It turned out to be a British cargo ship, the *Californian*, which had turned off her wireless for the evening and whose crew had embraced permanent timidity in dealing with their draconian commander, Captain Stanley Lord. Either missing or misinterpreting the *Titanic*'s rockets from a distance, they decided there was no point in waking Lord from his slumber, and the scale of their 'reprehensible' mistake did not become clear until the next morning when they turned their wireless back on for the day.[9]

As she got into the lifeboat, Lady Rothes heard Ida Straus say from the deck, 'I am not going without my husband.'[10] Her account makes no mention of the anecdote recounted in the *New York World* five days later that Ida's foot was already in Lifeboat 8 when she turned to ask, 'Aren't you coming, Isidor?'[11] The Countess, who was only feet away from Ida, wrote that 'tho' we all begged her to get into the Boat, she refused & went back to join her husband'.[12] The Strauses' friend Colonel Gracie was one of those who tried to persuade Ida to join the ladies in the boat, but 'she promptly and emphatically exclaimed: "No! I will not be separated from my husband; as we lived, so will we die together"; and when he, too, declined the assistance proffered on my earnest solicitation that, because of his age and helplessness, exception should be made and he be allowed to accompany his wife in the boat. "No!" he said, "I do not wish any distinction in my favor which is not granted to others."'[13] There are several variations on Ida and her husband's responses, none of which deviate from her refusal to leave him and his refusal to violate his honour by stepping into a boat ahead of other male passengers.[14] Several survivors heard her say to Isidor, 'We have lived together for many years. Where you go, I go.'[15] It may be that Ida's heart problems and Isidor's poor health helped influence their decision not to take a place in the lifeboats. Then again, it seems obtuse to miss the most obvious point and the one articulated by Ida: they did not want to live without one another.

First-class passenger May Futrelle, standing near by and likewise refusing to part from her husband, reported that on other occasions that night, when husbands had begged their wives to go, crew members had physically wrestled the women into the lifeboats: 'It appears the officers let the husbands decide that point. Straus was the only one who chose to let his wife stay. We had watched them on the boat and noticed what a sweetly affection[ate] old couple they were. He did the highest thing he knew to let her die in his arms, and it was sweet and beautiful according to his lights.'[16]

Lady Duff Gordon, who survived the sinking, was openly contemptuous of the rules obeyed by the Strauses and others that night. When her husband Sir Cosmo was denied entry to the lifeboats on Lightoller's watch, she refused to leave the *Titanic* without him and so they crossed to the other side of the ship, where Murdoch allowed them to get into Lifeboat 1. In her memoirs, written twenty years later, Lady Duff Gordon claimed that she remained 'filled with wonder at nearly all the American wives who were leaving their husbands without a word of protest or regret, scarce of farewell. They had brought the cult of chivalry to such a pitch in the States that it comes as second nature to their men to sacrifice themselves and to their women to let them do it.'[17] It was a markedly unkind assessment of the *Titanic* widows, especially since many of the wives who stepped into the majority of lifeboats trusted in the reassurances of the crew and their fellow passengers that this was a temporary rather than a permanent farewell. Lady Duff Gordon also had an axe to grind in rubbishing the concepts of honour adhered to by Isidor Straus, principally because her husband's life had been haunted by accusations that he ought to have drowned on the *Titanic*.[18] This was a charge that plagued many male survivors, several of whom were accused of dressing as women in order to facilitate their escape.[19] Even today, the Toronto home of Major Arthur Peuchen, who left the *Titanic* at the request of an officer by scaling down a 65-foot rope to help an under-manned lifeboat, is still frequently referred to as the house of the 'man who should have drowned on the *Titanic*', along with colourful stories that he donned women's clothes to get into a boat.[20] There is only one recorded incident of a man cross-dressing, or something akin to it, while leaving the *Titanic* – Daniel Buckley, a young third-class passenger who had boarded at Queenstown and who jumped into a lifeboat during the later stages of the sinking. At that point, a first-class lady gave him her shawl to wear and told him, 'Lay down, lad, you are somebody's child.'[21]

In the aftermath of the sinking, the playwright George Bernard Shaw entered into a war of words with Sir Arthur Conan Doyle, via printed letters to one another in a national newspaper, about the nobility of the *Titanic*'s evacuation procedure. Shaw poured scorn on what he saw as the mawkish celebration of a policy that had resulted in the needless deaths of dozens, if not hundreds, of men:

What is the first demand of Romance in a shipwreck? It is the cry of Women and Children First. No male creature is to step into a boat as long as there is a woman or child on the doomed ship. How the boat is to be navigated and rowed by babies and women occupied in holding the babies is not mentioned. The likelihood that no sensible woman would trust either herself or her child into a boat unless there was a considerable percentage of men on board is not considered. Women and Children First: that is the romantic formula. And never did the chorus of solemn delight at the strict observance of this formula by the British heroes on board the *Titanic* rise to more sublime strains than in the papers containing the first account of the wreck by surviving eye-witness, Lady Duff Gordon. She described how she escaped in the captain's boat [*sic*]. There was one other woman in it, and ten men: twelve all told. One woman for every five. Chorus: 'Not once or twice in our rough island history,' etc. etc.[22]

For Shaw, it was the apogee of a lethal idiocy that compelled the male passengers to stand back while boats left half empty, when no other women or children were present on that part of the deck. All subsequent praise for the men's actions was, to Shaw, hagiography to hide futility. For Conan Doyle, Shaw's rubbishing of the sacrifices was proof that 'his many brilliant gifts do not include the power of weighing evidence; nor has he that quality – call it good taste, humanity, or what you will – which prevents a man from needlessly hurting the feelings of others'.[23]

Finally accepting that Ida Straus would not go without Isidor and that Isidor would not go, 'several male passengers lifted Miss Bird into the boat'.[24] Ida removed her lifebelt to take off her fur coat, which she handed to her maid with the words, 'I won't need this anymore. You take it.'[25] Ellen Bird was helped into the lifeboat, 'which was lowered with all haste'.[26] As it prepared to go, a gentleman handed his address over to the Countess and asked her to contact his family in Torquay if he did not make it and Victor de Peñasco dragged his sobbing wife to where Gladys Cherry and Lady Rothes were sitting and 'threw her in our arms', repeating his request that they take care of her.[27] Two days afterwards, Gladys wrote that 'the lowering of that boat 75 feet into the darkness seemed too awful, [and] when we reached the water I felt we had done a foolish thing to leave that big safe boat, but when we had rowed out a few yards, we saw that great ship with her bow right down in the water'.[28] The settling forward as the *Titanic* was slowly dragged under was far more obvious when seen from the lifeboats than it was to those still on board. Gazing back at the *Titanic* as their lifeboat rowed away in the direction of the apparent light of another ship's masthead, the occupants could see that the water had risen far enough to cover up the *Titanic*'s name on her bow.[29]

*

Over the course of the next hour, there were several further attempts to get Ida Straus into a lifeboat. At some point between 1 and 1.30 a.m., May Futrelle 'saw Mrs Straus clinging to her husband Isidor, the New York banker [*sic*]. I heard her say to an officer who was trying to induce her to get into a boat: "No, we are too old, we will die together."'[30] The disgraced British investment banker Hugh Woolner, who helped escort women to the lifeboats until just after 2 a.m., remembered 'a very handsome old gentleman, Mr Isidor Straus, and his wife were there and declined to be separated and when we suggested that so old a man was justified in going into the boat that was waiting, Mr Straus said: "Not before the other men." His wife tightened her grasp on his arm and patted it and smiled up at him and then smiled at us.'[31]

One anecdote about the Strauses, in keeping with their character yet suspect nonetheless, comes from second-class passenger Imanita Shelley, who had spent most of the voyage complaining of how cold her cabin was and of how her health had been damaged in consequence. Imanita Shelley was a voracious social climber, widely disliked and so dense that after she had been rescued from the *Titanic*'s lifeboats she 'took pains to inquire of steerage passengers as to whether or not they had heat in the steerage of the *Titanic*'.[32] Mrs Shelley claimed that as she and her mother were being escorted to the boats with the other second-class passengers, the Strauses, who had heard of her illness, 'met them on the way and helped them down to the upper deck, where they found a chair for [Mrs Shelley] and made her sit down'. A sailor ran up to their deckchairs and implored them to leave because 'it was the last boat on the ship'.[33] Isidor and Ida allegedly accompanied the two ladies to a boat on the port side, number 12, and Ida waited to wave goodbye to them as it was lowered.[34]

The flaws in Imanita Shelley's account of Ida's solicitousness are numerous, beginning with provable falsehoods, such as the fact that there were still nearly a dozen lifeboats left to launch from the *Titanic* when number 12 was lowered at about half-past one, which means no sailor was running up and down the Promenade proclaiming it 'the last boat on the ship'. She lied, prolifically, about the sinking later, including glibly responding to a letter from the grieving relative of a lost passenger, 'You ask if he wore a life-belt. Alas! no, they were too scarce.'[35] It was an appallingly insensitive lie, considering that the *Titanic* in fact had thousands of lifebelts, far more than her capacity for passengers and crew. However, Mrs Shelley pursued a publicity feud against the White Star Line in the weeks after the sinking, constantly returning to the apparent outrage that they had not upgraded her gratis from a cabin 'that could only be called a cell', an assessment she saw fit to stress even when called to testify at the Senate inquiry, which sought to understand how so many lives had been lost rather than investigate the woes of Imanita's malfunctioning radiator.[36] It is also doubtful that the Strauses, of whom there is no record of any previous friendship with Imanita Shelley or her family, could have heard that a passenger in Second Class was claiming to have tonsillitis and then, during the evacuation, known where to find her. Ida and her husband had spent about thirty minutes 'mingling with the other passengers' near the Grand Staircase and first-class Promenade Deck after the initial call to the boats, without expressing any worry about, or knowledge of, Imanita Shelley.[37] Keen to link her name to that of some of the *Titanic*'s most prestigious casualties, Imanita also dubiously claimed to have been the last person to see the journalist William Stead alive, 'alone, at the edge of the deck, near the stern, in silence and what seemed to me a prayerful attitude, or one of profound meditation'.[38]

*

One of Tommy Andrews' preoccupations was the need to start moving the third-class passengers up to the Boat Deck as quickly and as efficiently as possible.[39] After stewards had passed over more blankets and Lifeboat 5 had left, Andrews went back inside to continue his mission to move passengers to the Boat Deck. As he had with Annie Robinson, he told Mary Sloan, still knocking on passengers' doors, to put on her lifebelt 'and go on deck'.[40] Retracing Andrews' movements with precision after this point in the sinking is unfortunately not always possible. However, given that he had gone through every corridor of accommodation in First Class before journeying to Scotland Road where he allegedly urged stewards to shepherd Third Class 'up on deck', it seems unlikely that he did not also use Scotland Road to visit Second Class.

Unlike the aesthetic kaleidoscope in First Class, the *Titanic*'s Second Class was decorated with sombre, wood-heavy similarity. All three of its main public rooms – its Smoking Room, Library and Dining Saloon – were panelled in mahogany or 'handsomely carried out in oak' – as was its staircase, up which its 284 passengers were ushered from their cabins and out on to the Boat Deck with relative ease.[41] Of all the classes on the *Titanic*, it was Second who had the clearest path to the lifeboats – unlike First, with its numerous exits on to different parts of the Boat and Promenade spaces, and unlike Third, which was split into two sections, one in the bow and the other in the stern, and kept from easily accessible distance of the other two classes in order for the *Titanic* to conform with US quarantine laws.

Andrews' instructions to the stewards concerning Third Class speak to one of the most distressing and horrible parts of the *Titanic*'s legend, in which those travelling in Third Class were deliberately locked below until the other passengers were safely in the lifeboats. Cited in support of this wretched scenario are testimonies from two survivors. The first, and most frequently referenced in passing if not in specifics, is from the twenty-one-year-old Anglo-Irish immigrant, Daniel Buckley.[42] When looked at in detail, Buckley's statement to the American inquiry mentions only one locked gate, not inside Third Class but at the top of a short stairwell of about nine or ten steps, leading from a third-class promenade space to that of Second Class.[43] He mistakenly, though understandably, assumed it led to First. This gate, low enough for a man to step over comfortably, was unlocked at the time of the collision, although a crew member, one of hundreds who did not realise the *Titanic* was sinking until it was too late, locked it when he saw dozens of passengers walking through in what he assumed was a contravention of the US immigration laws that the crew were under strict instructions to uphold. After he had bolted it, some passengers continued to clamber over it until one third-class gentleman decided that it being locked was discouraging the more conservative or nervous travellers from going up to the boats, at which point he kicked the lock open.[44] This was the only incident of obstruction that Buckley recalled. To the question, 'Was there any effort made on the part of the officers or crew to hold the steerage passengers in the steerage?' Buckley answered, 'I do not think so.'[45] When asked, specifically, what he thought a third-class passenger's chances of survival had been, Buckley told the querying Senator, 'I think they had as much chance as the first and second class passengers.'[46] Single men travelling on a third-class ticket were housed in cabins in the bow, separated by a long corridor from families and unmarried ladies, who were accommodated in the stern. It was thus in these cabins that the first passenger sightings of flooding occurred and Buckley recalled that, as soon as that became clear, far from discouraging them from going to the lifeboats, stewards rushed through the single males' corridors shouting, 'Get up on deck, unless you want to get drowned!'[47]

The second eyewitness testimony to recall locked gates on the night of the sinking comes from Norwegian farmer Olaus Jørgensen Abelseth, who in a letter written to his father four days after the sinking, made no mention of being trapped, but who later remembered that while on his way from cabin G-63 to find his unmarried sister, Karen, he encountered barriers between various corridors, which he had to ask the crew to open.[48] These were the gates locked every night between the two sections of Third Class, used as a selling point to convince female travellers that they would be safe from harassment on White Star ships.

There is thus no account from any survivor mentioning iron grilles being bolted into place to keep the classes separate after Captain Smith gave the order to fill the lifeboats, much less of staff physically beating the passengers to keep them below deck. When pressed about unhelpful crew members, Daniel Buckley mentioned only one sailor, who became irate after he saw the promenade gate's lock being kicked open.[49] Furthermore, at no point during the hundreds of exploratory dives to the *Titanic's* wreck conducted since its discovery in 1985 have the gates to and from Third Class been found in their locked position, whereas many have been photographed or filmed unlocked and open.

While there is no evidence whatsoever that crew members actively conspired to hold them below, and much to the contrary, Daniel Buckley was nonetheless profoundly incorrect when he told the Senator that those in Third Class 'had as much chance as the first and second class passengers' of surviving. Basic mathematics disproves him when one considers that 62.5 per cent of those in First Class were saved, against 41.2 per cent in Second and 25.3 per cent in Third. It should, for fairness' sake, be pointed out that not all historians or statisticians would accept that these figures are as damning as they appear on first inspection, instead arguing that the defining contributory factor to survival from the *Titanic* disaster was gender rather than class – with 68 per cent of female passengers saved, against 31.9 per cent of the men, while 44 per cent of those in First Class were women, compared to only 23 per cent in Third.[50] Gender was a major component in explaining the comparative loss of life in each of the *Titanic's* three classes of accommodation. Nearly half of third-class women were saved, compared to only 16.2 per cent of the men; yet 97.2 per cent of first-class women lived, which leaves room for three further explanations for why Third Class suffered a higher casualty rate than the others.

The first is the crew's ignorance of the situation. The recollections of Daniel Buckley and Olaus Jørgensen Abelseth refer to crew members, posted to the bloc of third-class cabins for single men, hurrying their passengers on deck. Those cabins were located close to the site of the ship's impact with the iceberg, while the rest of Third Class, including its two public social spaces, the General Room and Smoking Room, were positioned in the stern, the last point on the *Titanic* that night where it became obvious that something was physically wrong with the ship. To describe Captain Smith's handling of this particular aspect of the sinking as a dereliction of duty seems charitable for, while he had found time to personally encourage the Countess of Rothes and Gladys Cherry to return to their stateroom and dress warmly for the impending drama, he had somehow failed to muster the crew to inform them that the ship, according to her designer, had around ninety minutes left to live. The Countess of Rothes again proves a useful point of reference, when one bears in mind that after she rang for her Steward to help her find a lifebelt, he professed ignorant surprise that the call to the lifeboats had been issued. This Steward's attitude was replicated hundreds of times across the *Titanic*, with many of his colleagues hearing garbled accounts of what had gone wrong and only realising around the same time as their passengers that the ship was genuinely in danger. In light of their failure to be furnished with the facts, some sailors panicked at the sight of third-class passengers coming up to, or over, the small dividing gate between the stern and the second-class promenade. They also failed to nurture any sense of urgency among the families or unmarried women who congregated in the General Room, awaiting instructions and not noticing a marked tilt in the deck until the last hour or forty-five minutes of the sinking.

Secondly, unlike First and Second Class, most third-class passengers did not have English as their first language. About nine out of every ten first-class passengers and eight out of ten in Second Class were native English-speakers, while the same was true of only two-fifths in Third.[51] The overwhelming majority of the *Titanic*'s crew, and all of its internal signs, had English as their only language. Third Class's labyrinthine corridors frustrated the evacuation even more when crew struggled to impart directions to the German, Magyar, Arabic, French, Dutch, Bulgarian, Chinese, Danish, Finnish, Greek, Italian, Norwegian, Portuguese, Russian, Swedish and Turkish speakers in Third Class. The Countess of Rothes had noticed how 'terrified' and confused the Peñascos were while waiting to board the lifeboats; she was able to offer help and information to them only thanks to their having French as a shared language. María-Josefa de Peñasco's paralysed bewilderment played out in hundreds of third-class passengers, without the fortuitous coincidence of standing next to someone who could communicate properly with them.

Finally, there were the problems posed by the geography of Third Class. No one can reasonably fault the White Star Line for designing the respective classes of accommodation to conform with the laws put in place by the US government concerning immigration. The alternative to compliance was to eradicate Third Class as an option on board their ships. However, that is not to say that there were not grave errors in other decisions regarding its design. While Third Class could not be granted access in ordinary circumstances to the adjoining promenades provided for First and Second Class, there was no reason not to install a set of davits on the Poop Deck, to which they did have easy and frequent access as their designated on-deck space. That this was a wretched mistake was evidenced by subsequent alterations made to the *Titanic*'s younger sister, the *Britannic*, which had davits positioned on her third-class outdoor decks. The failure to envisage any collision damaging enough to require the evacuation of everyone on board in a relatively short period of time meant that third-class passengers, speaking over a dozen languages between them, needed to be guided to a part of the ship of which they had no prior experience since it was constructed to discourage their interaction with it, by crew members who struggled both to communicate with them and fully to appreciate the danger until it was too late. It was thus egregious if commonplace incompetence, in design and command, rather than malevolent snobbery that helps explain the heavier loss of life among third-class passengers. Without lessening its tragedy, it at least serves to make the final figures less gut-wrenchingly, intentionally monstrous.

*

A rumour later circulated that the Thayer men had attempted to use their position as first-class ticket holders to board the lifeboats ahead of other passengers. However, it seems that during the early stages of the evacuation, they, along with most passengers, assumed that there were sufficient lifeboat spaces for everyone on board and that their questions to the crew were to establish which of the lifeboats on the Boat Deck had been set aside to evacuate passengers from different parts of the ship. Each crew member they asked seemed to be sufficiently unsure to send them to enquire from another officer at a different lifeboat.[52] An unpleasant appreciation that there was no such organisation at play began to dawn when Thayer, his son and Milton Long, having briefly returned to the warmth of the Grand Staircase, were approached by one of the stewards, who had waited on their table in the Dining Saloon since Wednesday, and gave them the unwelcome news that Marian was still on the *Titanic*.[53] They had found her on the port side, in a towering bad temper, still accompanied by Fleming her maid, Elizabeth Eustis and Martha Stephenson. In the course of the previous fifteen or twenty minutes, they had been moved between the Boat and Promenade decks as orders arose in contradiction of one another about their lifeboat's point of loading. Marian had snapped at one of the crew, 'Tell us where to go and we will follow you. You ordered us up here and now you are taking us back.'[54] Thayer decided to stay with them until he could see all the ladies safely into a boat, so he escorted the party indoors, cutting through a Lounge still 'filled with a milling crowd' to reach some of the forward port-side boats.[55] In that milieu, their group became separated and, theorising that Jack had a companion in Milton, Thayer pressed ahead with the four women. His failure to go back immediately to locate his son need not be judged an act of paternal neglect since, by all accounts, the two Thayers shared a close and loving relationship. Rather, by the time Thayer and the four women rushed through the Lounge the situation on the *Titanic* had deteriorated significantly.

Most passengers had a moment in which complacency was replaced by concern or justified fear. For Marian Thayer, it had been as 'rockets were going up beside us, and the Morse signal light had begun' and she turned to see stokers standing next to her, bedraggled and some soaked in their sleeveless white work shirts, then third-class passengers coming up on to the first-class decks, carrying their uninsured luggage with which they hoped to start their new lives in the United States. No suitcases were permitted in any of the *Titanic*'s lifeboats, leading to anguished scenes of begging, 'struggling and fighting, deliriously' between the officers and some of the third-class passengers. A few second-class passengers were overheard laughing at the sight of the suitcases, until another second-class traveller told them to shut up.[56]

Elsewhere, there were signs of collective unravelling. The band had quit the Lounge and relocated to one of the entrance halls between the Boat Deck and the Grand Staircase.[57] Although the ship's secondary post-collision list, to starboard, had gently been righted when Boiler Room 5 flooded to capacity, the *Titanic* had since, in addition to the gradually more perceptible dip forward, taken on a noticeable list to port due to the renewed unevenness of the below-deck deluge. In the thirty or so minutes since the Countess of Rothes' lifeboat had left, eight more had departed at closer intervals than that between hers and Dorothy Gibson's.[58] Fifth Officer Lowe had fired shots into the air to discourage pushing at Lifeboat 14, pleading with a male passenger who climbed in to 'get out and be a man – we have women and children to save'.[59] When that did not work, Lowe turned to the crowd and shouted, 'Stand back! I say, stand back! The next man who puts his foot in this boat, I will shoot him down like a dog.'

A second-class passenger, helping his wife and sobbing seven-year-old daughter over the gap between the deck and the boat, assured Lowe, 'I'm not going in, but for God's sake look after my wife and child.'[60] When it was finally lowered, number 14 caught in its ropes, which had to be cut to allow it to drop the final 5 or 6 feet into the water.[61] Thayer, who helped some passengers into the neighbouring Lifeboat 10, almost certainly saw these scenes and they may explain why he decided to move his wife, her maid and their friends through the Lounge to the forward-positioned boats. During the boarding of number 10, they saw a woman fall through the gap between the deck and the lifeboat. She was caught, mercifully, by an eagle-eyed passenger on the Promenade Deck below, who dragged her on board and escorted her back to the Boat Deck, where she successfully made it to the safety of the lifeboat.[62] Worse screams were heard from further below when Lifeboat 13 was hit by water pouring out from one of the *Titanic*'s condenser exhausts and pushed into the path of the descending Lifeboat 15, which nearly crushed everyone in 13, before the latter's occupants managed to shove their craft away from the *Titanic*'s hull with their oars.

Thayer's decision to relocate his party paid dividends when they were directed down, once again, to the Promenade Deck, where Officer Lightoller had successfully had some of the windows prised away. There was another brief delay on account of the *Titanic*'s deepening list to port which had opened up a gap between the deck and the boats. 'Ladders were called for,' according to Marian, 'but there being none, it was necessary to lash two steamer chairs to serve as a sort of gang plank to enable the women to get into the boat.' Marian's maid, Elizabeth and Martha were helped over this improvised walkway, held together by rope and faith, before Thayer told Marian he would go back to look for their son and gave her his arm as she stumbled into the boat. Several of the Thayers' acquaintances had gathered to help the crew with the lifeboats, including Marian's new friend, Major Archibald Butt, and his companion Frank Millet. The Ryersons,

Based on the accounts of eyewitnesses, this sketch depicts the moment when Lifeboat 13 was nearly crushed by the lowering of number 15.

the Thayers' friends who had lost their son to a car crash earlier that week, were among those boarding Lifeboat 4. Mrs Ryerson prepared to follow Marian, with her thirteen-year-old son, also called Jack, attempting to join her until Officer Lightoller put out his arm and declared, 'That boy can't go.' Arthur Ryerson, on deck with Thayer, stepped forward and said, 'Of course, that boy goes with his mother; he's only thirteen.' Lightoller backed down and Jack Ryerson was passed to a sailor in the boat, joining his two sisters, his mother's lady's maid and his governess. If Emily Ryerson had been asked to leave her only surviving son on the *Titanic*, she almost certainly would have refused. Instead, as she recalled later, 'I turned and kissed my husband, as we left he and the other men I knew – Mr Thayer, Mr Widener, and others – were all standing there together very quietly.' They were soon joined by two colonels, Gracie and Astor, the latter of whom had changed his mind about the dangers posed by the lifeboats. He passed his pregnant wife to Gracie, who helped her into Marian Thayer's lifeboat, while Astor spoke quietly to Lightoller, asking if he could accompany Madeleine in light of her condition. According to Gracie, Lightoller replied, 'No, sir, no men are allowed in these boats until the women are loaded first.' Astor 'did not demur, but bore the refusal bravely and resignedly, simply asking the number of the boat to help find his wife later in case he also was rescued'. Kornelia Andrews, another occupant of number 4, was deeply and patriotically moved by the sight of:

> that unbroken line of splendid Americans, not allowed to get into the boats before the women and children were off. It would make you proud of your countrymen. There was Mr Thayer, [vice-]president of the Pennsylvania Railroad; Col. Astor waving a farewell to his beautiful young wife; Major Archibald Butt, Taft's first aide; Mr Case, president of the Vacuum Oil Co., all multi-millionaires, and hundreds of other men, standing without complaint or murmur, not making one attempt to save themselves, but happy to think wives and relatives were in the boat. Was that not chivalry for you?

Astor lingered with the other husbands for a few moments until the lifeboat was lowered and then he walked away. There are no firmly corroborated sightings of him after that.[63]

The continuing evacuation, with the shouting of the frightened and the commands of the officers, was now illuminated only by the ship's electric lights, still burning thanks to the engineers from Ireland and England who had chosen to stay below to keep the power running as long as possible. The last distress rocket was fired around the time Marian Thayer left the *Titanic*. Thayer stayed on the Promenade with George Widener, Colonel Gracie's friend James Smith and, for a brief time until they wandered off, Astor, Butt, Millet and Gracie. Realising that nearly all the lifeboats had gone and that in any case there were not enough for everyone still left on board, Gracie wrote that their group 'experienced a feeling which others may recall when holding the breath in the face of some frightful emergency and when "vox faucibus haesit," as frequently happened to the old Trojan hero of our school days'.*[64]

Looking at the *Titanic* from her place in the lifeboat where she had been for forty-five or fifty minutes, Lady Rothes had kept her word to look after María-Josefa de Peñasco, 'trying to soothe her & keep her spirits up by saying I was sure her husband would follow in the next boat, tho' I knew by this time there was no chance of that & very little hope for anyone'.[65]

---

* From Virgil's *Aeneid*, referring to the moment when Aeneas's voice catches in his throat.

Be British

The river of death has brimmed his banks,
And England's far, and Honour a name,
But the voice of a schoolboy rallies the ranks:
'Play up! Play up! And play the game!'

This is the word that year by year,
While in her place the school is set,
Every one of her sons must hear,
And none that hears it dare forget.

Sir Henry Newbolt, 'Vitaï Lampada' (1897)

AFTER NINETY MINUTES OF WATCHING THE RUIN OF HIS creation, Tommy Andrews retreated to the first-class Smoking Room, where he stood brooding by its fireplace, the only passengers' grate to use coal and wood instead of electric bars. Above the mantelpiece was the Norman Wilkinson painting *Plymouth Harbour*.[1] There, amid the Smoking Room's stained-glass windows, mahogany walls accented with gold and mother of pearl, Andrews had halted, his arms folded, staring sightlessly.[2] A passing steward, John Stewart, whose normal duties had been in the adjacent Verandah Cafés, interrupted Andrews' reverie with the question, 'Aren't you going to try for it, Mr Andrews?' Andrews, 'like one stunned', did not seem to hear him. In any case, he gave no response and Stewart left to see if he could be of help with the lifeboats.[3]

The Smoking Room, where Thomas Andrews was briefly spotted in silent despair.

It is an unforgettable vignette of a mind buckling under a sorrow and shame that few can imagine. It has been presented in several cinematic takes on the *Titanic*'s demise, as well as dozens of non-fiction accounts of the sinking, as the last known sighting of Tommy Andrews, often placed at about five or ten minutes past two o'clock.[4] This particular detail is unsustainable in light of the fact that Stewart left the *Titanic* in Lifeboat 15, one of the aft lifeboats positioned close to the Smoking Room and lowered away at about 1.40 a.m.[5] Stewart's was the most memorable sighting of Andrews that night. It was not, however, the last and it was definitively disproven as such as early as the autumn of 1912 when a writer commissioned by the Andrews family and the unionist politician Sir Horace Plunkett tracked

243

down three survivors' accounts mentioning Andrews' behaviour after his temporary stasis at about 1.30 a.m.[6] Twelve days after the sinking, Stewardess Mary Sloan wrote in a letter to her sister, 'Last time I saw and heard him was about an hour later [after he had told her to put on her lifebelt at about 12.45 a.m.] helping to get women and children into the boats, imploring them not to hesitate, but to go when asked as there was no time to be lost, so Mr Andrews met his fate like a true hero realising his great danger, and gave up his life to save the women and children of the *Titanic*.'[7] After the last lifeboat had left, Andrews was spotted throwing deckchairs overboard to provide those jumping with something to cling to.[8] A bellboy saw him on deck, carrying his lifejacket and encouraging the Captain to don one, just before the final plunge.[9] Of later relevance is a fourth account, not discovered by Andrews' friends or family in 1912, which goes into more detail about where Andrews was for the final moments of the *Titanic*.[10]

During his childhood in County Down, Tommy Andrews had been allowed by his parents to keep bees. One day he told his father that he could not go hunting, his favourite pastime, because he had noticed that his hive was in trouble. For the rest of the afternoon and evening, the family's servants watched him repeatedly carrying small trays of half-famished bees from the hive to the kitchen to feed them and keep them warm.[11] Thomas Andrews was a man of vital compassion. His goodness was useful, rather than simply comforting. After a few moments of mental anguish in the Smoking Room, he returned on deck to continue helping with the lifeboats and, when that was no longer possible, he tossed into the ocean anything that might help those jumping from his ship.

After the last lifeboat had been safely lowered from the *Titanic* at 2.05 a.m., the number on board included Ida Straus, John Thayer and his son Jack, along with about 1,500 other people. A mission, led by Officers Murdoch and Lightoller, to free the two remaining collapsibles from the deck roof of the Officers' Quarters failed for lack of time and those last two lifeboats were washed off the *Titanic*, overturned. Of all the negligence attributed to the management of the *Titanic*, none appears more criminally idiotic than the White Star Line's decision to provide twenty lifeboats with a combined capacity of 1,178 on a ship with room for 3,327 and which sailed in April 1912 with about 2,208. Their provision of lifeboats was in fact in excess of the legal stipulations laid down by the British Board of Trade, which gauged lifeboat requirements on the size of ships, rather than the number of cabins. Woefully outdated when it came to the leviathans produced by Cunard and White Star after 1907, the Board of Trade regulations stated that any ship over 10,000 tons must carry a minimum sixteen lifeboats.

If a law did not compel a company, one might query why basic sense did not. No major passenger liner carried sufficient lifeboats before 1912. Since then, they all have. However, not every industry expert was swayed even by the casualty figures of the *Titanic*. Twenty years later, a former captain in the Royal Navy argued,

> The case of the *Titanic* itself is one of the very few in which boats for all could have been useful; as a general rule a disaster at sea means it is quite impossible to launch all the boats which any ship carries, while the space might be far more advantageously used for life rafts and other buoyant apparatuses. Also the heavy weights placed as high up as possible carry their own disadvantages, as was proved many times during the war when the boats for all slogan resulted in many ships capsizing long before they would have otherwise gone down, drowning many who would have had at least a chance of safety.[12]

Most memorably, his point had been at least partly proved by the attack by a German submarine on the *Lusitania* in 1915, when dozens were killed while attempting to escape by lifeboats tumbling from their davits on to those below them.[13]

In the case of the *Titanic*, more lifeboats almost certainly would have made no substantial difference to the overall loss of life. It took forty minutes from the collision for a sufficiently thorough examination to justify the decision that the lifeboats should be filled and another fifteen to twenty minutes before the first boats were ready. The first craft was not lowered until an hour after the *Titanic* had struck the iceberg and it was another forty or so minutes before most passengers were keen to get into them. Given that senior officers, helped by passengers and sailors, were still fighting to free two lifeboats when the ship went under, the depressing conclusion must be that even if there had been double the number of lifeboats on the *Titanic* there still would not have been enough time to fill them before the ship sank. The death toll was of course augmented by the initial reluctance of many passengers to leave the apparently secure *Titanic*, which arose from the failure to impress upon them, or many crew members, the gravity of the situation.

One of the only photographs of Captain Smith on the *Titanic*'s Bridge, from which he was swept or jumped into the ocean.

It was allegedly in reaction to the diminishing number of life-boats that Captain Smith spoke to a group of stewards gathered near the Bridge, telling them, 'Well, boys, do your best for the women and children, and look out for yourselves.'[14] Not long before he had shared a glass of water in his cabin with first-class passenger Frederick Hoyt, who knew from Smith's demeanour that there was not much longer left.[15] Either after seeing Hoyt or warning the small group of stewards, Smith then used his megaphone to give the order to abandon ship, some time shortly after two o'clock. His precise choice of words is contested, with two phrases each having its own proponents. It is entirely possible that both are correct, with the Captain delivering the respective cries through the megaphone on either side of his Bridge. The first claim is that he shouted, 'Abandon ship! Every man for himself!' The other reports that Smith encouraged those still trapped on the *Titanic*, 'Be British!', by which he meant that they should remain calm while they fled, to avoid undue panic, and should maintain the proverbial stiff upper lip. In the years after the sinking, however, that latter phrase took on a totemic value that far exceeded what Smith meant when, or if, he said it.

At the time of the *Titanic*'s launch in 1911, a White Star magazine had predicted that with her British construction and American ownership the ship would come to 'stand for the pre-eminence of the Anglo-Saxon race on the Ocean'.[16] As with any good prophecy delivered by an oracle, this came to fruition in a jarringly different way to the one imagined. Within weeks of the disaster, Captain Smith's alleged promotion *in extremis* of British values had been commemorated in thousands of postcards and dozens of songs. Lyrics praised the Belfast-born engineers, all of whom drowned at their posts, for remaining 'in obedience to the instinct of their race and the grand old Captain's exhortations: "Be British!"'[17] Others lauded all the crew members who had 'worked like Britons, side by side, all faithful to the last'.[18] Newspapers carried the story to the public of how 'before [Smith] was literally washed from his post of duty he called through his megaphone, "Be British!" to the mass below'.[19] One of the owners of the Hodder and Stoughton publishing house wrote an open letter arguing that Smith's alleged last quote 'was what we would have expected and wanted him to say. He belonged to the race of the old British sea-dogs. He believed with all his heart and soul in the British Empire. He had added that to his creed. I am glad he recited it at the end.'[20] By the time an Admiral of the Fleet, Lord Charles Beresford, was invited to unveil a memorial statue to Smith in the winter of 1912, the phrase had become so inextricably linked to the late Captain that, with the approval of Smith's widow, it was carved on the plinth of the monument.[21] When questioned later about the bravery of the Strauses, with their American citizenship, Lord Charles considered that Smith's command instead spoke more broadly to the 'true spirit of manly duty of the English-speaking races'.[22]

Captain Smith and Thomas Andrews were both incorporated into pieces of didactic patriotism. Supplementary to Smith's extolment of British values was the belief that he had done so moments before he was swept overboard. In reality, Smith did his duty by remaining with the *Titanic* until he was of no further perceptible use, which is not to say he intended to go down with her. De facto suicide was not required of him, even by the most extreme defenders of maritime tradition, and a steward, whose testimony of course may have been addled by the trauma suffered when he himself jumped overboard, specifically stated that Smith had leaped from the Bridge rather than be caught by a rush of water. That claim was forgotten or roundly ignored as inconvenient to a narrative that preferred Smith to die at his post. Likewise, it helped solidify the adjustment of chronology in the press and popular history to have Tommy Andrews standing in the Smoking Room with bereft stoicism at 2.05 a.m., by no coincidence immediately after the last lifeboat had been safely lowered from a davit. These edited stories unconsciously if potently mirrored the myths of ancient Greece, in which heroes like Achilles choose to embrace glorious death, rejecting the allure of home in favour of immortality and continued service.[23]

Once again, it was George Bernard Shaw who dipped his pen in acid before critiquing the lionisation of Smith and what it said about British attitudes to other nations. While he had no quarrel with the tributes paid to Thomas Andrews, Shaw was revolted by the panegyric heaped on Captain Smith, regarding it as a vulgar attempt to excuse posthumously Smith's multiple errors in command. He joked that by the summer of 1912 British journalists were writing about Smith with praise that they would hesitate to bestow on Nelson. He thought the press coverage of the *Titanic* had descended into 'ghastly, blasphemous, unhuman, braggartly lying' as newspapers eagerly embraced any anecdote that confirmed their prejudices, even though 'the one thing positively known was that Captain Smith had lost his ship by deliberately and knowingly steaming into an icefield at the highest speed he had coal for. He paid the penalty; so did most of those for whose lives he was responsible. Had he brought the ship safely to land, nobody would have taken the smallest notice of him.' Shaw was also incensed by the symbiotic link established between Smith's alleged final words and the racial judgements that peppered subsequent accounts of the disaster. He did not blame the press for creating these attitudes, confining himself to remarking that they had simply articulated ad nauseam the public's pre-established sympathies, with accounts that sought 'to assure the world that only Englishmen could have behaved so heroically, and to compare their conduct with the hypothetic dastardliness [of] Italians or foreigners'.[24]

Edwardian attitudes to race and nationality had followed the *Titanic* throughout her career and Shaw was correct when he characterised the press as a mirror rather than the person in front of it. To read dozens of survivors' accounts of the sinking is to be struck by how often behaviour, usually negative, was attributed to a person's race. The Countess of Rothes was by far the mildest in her assumption when she heard shouting on deck and assumed it must have come from Italians.[25] When Marian Thayer stated later that she had seen only one man panicking, she specified that he 'looked like a foreigner'.[26] A steward referred to passengers causing trouble at one of the lifeboats as 'dagoes', a catch-all slur for Spaniards, Italians and Portuguese.[27] Despite the fact that the man who disguised himself as a woman to escape the ship was a young Anglo-Irish farmer, Fifth Officer Harold Lowe told an American journalist he had been an Italian and then, in his subsequent testimony at the Senate inquiry, used 'Italian' to describe unruly behaviour from passengers 'all glaring and ready to spring' without permission into the lifeboats.[28] Lowe's pronouncements reached such a wide audience that the Marquis of Cusani Confalonieri, the Italian Ambassador to the United States, petitioned White Star for a public retraction, which Lowe was ordered to give via a published letter to the Ambassador. It was heavy on qualifying justification and jarringly low on contrition:

This is to testify that I, Harold Godfrey Lowe, of Penrallt Barmouth, fifth officer of the late steamship 'Titanic', in my testimony at the Senate of the United States stated that I fired shots to prevent Italian immigrants from jumping into my lifeboat.

I do thereby cancel the word 'Italian' and substitute the words 'immigrants belonging to Latin races'. In fact, I did not mean to infer that they were especially Italians, because I could only judge from their general appearance and complexion, and therefore I only meant to imply that they were of the types of the Latin races. In any case, I did not intend to cast any reflection on the Italian nation.

This is the real truth, and therefore I feel honoured to give out the present statement.

H. G. LOWE,
Fifth Officer, late steamship 'Titanic'

Shortly after 2 a.m., as Edward Smith prepared to issue one, both or neither of his alleged final commands as Captain of the *Titanic*, as Tommy Andrews was throwing wooden deckchairs overboard and as Harold Lowe was threatening to shoot men who almost certainly were not Italian, the *Titanic*'s band played their last set. The seven musicians had taken up their third position that night, wearing thick coats to perform outside one of the deck's entrance doors to the Grand Staircase. This placed them on the Boat Deck somewhere between the first and second funnels, near where Thayer, Jack and the Strauses had also congregated.[29] Thayer was with George Widener, near the second stack, both possessed of the misapprehension that their respective sons must have escaped in one of the starboard-side lifeboats. Jack, too, after returning to the Lounge and whipping round the Promenade Deck, concluded that his father must have been allowed to accompany Marian when she left.[30] Scrambling up on to the officers' roof to help Lightoller in his attempt to disengage one of the collapsibles, Colonel Gracie spotted his friends the Strauses standing together near the Bridge. He was too busy with his task to call out to them, but he and others helping Lightoller remembered seeing Ida 'clasped in her husband's arms'.[31]

Every now and then in history a popular myth can be restored to its place, rather than dismissed to make way for a less poetic truth. This seems to be the case with 'Nearer, My God, to Thee', the Methodist hymn indelibly associated with the *Titanic*'s final moments as the last piece of music played by the ship's orchestra before the deck tilted so far beneath them that they had to abandon their instruments. 'Nearer, My God, to Thee' has been roundly dismissed as a part of the *Titanic*'s denouement by many specialists, who see it as pious nonsense, attempting to do for Christianity what Captain Smith's exhortation of 'Be British' did for national pride. In its place, a slow waltz, 'Songe d'Automne', was identified as one of the last pieces of music, or the very last, performed that night. However, there is persuasive evidence that 'Nearer, My God, to Thee' formed the logical conclusion to a progression of music that evolved from jolly to patriotic and finally to religious. Earlier in the evening, there are accounts of the band playing 'Land of Hope and Glory' and 'Jerusalem' while they were stationed at the Staircase, abandoning the waltzes and ragtime they had offered in the Lounge. There are numerous quotations from survivors, including some made on their rescue ship, about hymns being played just before the ship sank and numerous extant testimonies from survivors specifically identifying 'Nearer, My God, to Thee' as a tune they heard from the Boat Deck.* As those recollections originated with several survivors before they even reached New York, it is not possible to sustain the argument that the band chose to play only secular music because they wanted to calm rather than frighten the passengers and that the playing of 'Nearer, My God, to Thee' was thus invented by the newspapers. Although it is not conclusive evidence that he followed through on his intention, an interview in an English newspaper conducted with the band's leader, Wallace Hartley, three weeks before he joined the *Titanic*, posed the question of what he would play if he ever found himself in a shipwreck. To which Hartley answered, 'I don't think I could do better than play "O God Our Help in Ages Past" or "Nearer My God to Thee".'[32] The *Titanic*'s most junior officer, James Moody, told his family, 'When I read the statement in the papers that he had gone to his death leading the band in *Nearer My God to Thee*, I believed it. If it had been some other hymn I might not have done so, but as it is I can quite believe it. It is just what he would do.'[33] In his recent analysis of the veracity of claims concerning 'Nearer, My God, to Thee', George Behe may be correct in arguing that the hymn may not have been the very last one heard on deck, but 'it is hard to envision *all* of the literally dozens of witnesses being wrong, or having fabricated the stories. The proof is not conclusive, but is strongly suggestive.'[34]

A hymn was certainly in keeping with the mood on board around 2 a.m. Water had spilled over the forecastle and the liner's forward tilt, while still allowing people to stay upright, was now

---

* In Lifeboat 8, Lady Rothes heard music from the ship until nearly the end, but she could never swear to the tunes floating over the water.

obvious both from the lifeboats and on the deck. The ship's lights dipped in strength but then rose again, though not to their previous brightness. Power to the Wireless Room, where the two operators were still frantically trying to reach ships close enough to save them, vanished. A second-class passenger, Father Thomas Byles, who fourteen hours earlier had celebrated Mass in the second-class Library and then in the third-class General Room, led prayers with his colleague, Father Joseph Peruschitz. The British priest and the German priest had gone down into Third Class earlier in the night to encourage people to come up to the deck.[35] Now, they stood together on deck, offering absolution, praying and 'whispering words of comfort and encouragement' to the seventy-five or so passengers who approached them, most of them Irish.[36] A century later, the two priests have been proposed as candidates for canonisation, but although they refused a place in the lifeboats and welcomed those Protestants and Jews on deck who also asked for their help, calling them 'my good people', not all were won over by the priests' 'absolute self-control'.[37] As Father Byles led a recitation of the Rosary, with those around him responding to the Hail Mary with 'Holy Mary, Mother of God, pray for us sinners now and at the hour of our death', August Wennerström, a socialist journalist who had decided to emigrate after the hostile reception given to his article calling for the abolition of the Swedish monarchy, was revolted by the sight of seventy-five people 'in a circle with a preacher in their middle, praying, crying, asking God and Mary to help them . . . They just prayed and yelled, and never lifted a hand to help themselves. They had lost their own will power and were expecting God to do all the work.'[38] He had, however, misunderstood the purpose of their prayers. Byles and Peruschitz were telling their impromptu flock to 'prepare them-selves to meet the face of God'.[39] They were under no illusions about the chances of physical survival. In that regard, whether one jumped or took the time to pray before doing so would make very little difference.

Over the Top Together

One by one her port lights, that still burnt row above row in dreadful sloping lines, sank slowly into darkness. Soon the lights would tilt upright, then flash out and flash bright again; then, as the engines crashed down through the bulkheads, go out once more, and leave that awful form standing up against the sky, motionless, black, preparing for the final plunge. But that time was not yet. Some fifteen minutes were left . . .

Shan Bullock, *Thomas Andrews:
Shipbuilder* (1912)

G EORGE HOGG HAD BEEN DUE TO START HIS NEXT shift as one of the *Titanic*'s lookouts twenty minutes after she struck the iceberg. The shift would have lasted, as did all the lookouts', for two hours.[1] At about 2 a.m. on Monday the 15th, instead of climbing down the interior stairs from the Crow's Nest, Hogg was ordering the lifeboat he had been put in charge of by Officer Murdoch to row energetically from the *Titanic*'s vicinity. Since leaving the liner eighty minutes earlier, Dorothy Gibson and the other occupants of Hogg's Lifeboat 7 had watched the unfolding drama from the distance of about twenty yards, from where Hogg was waiting for

Murdoch or another officer to order them to return once the damage had been repaired.[2] By 2 a.m., he had surrendered that as a false hope and now wanted to get the lifeboat safely away from any suction that might catch them when the *Titanic* went under.

William Sloper, rowing in obedience to Hogg's commands, had found himself becoming progressively more irritated by Dorothy's behaviour since he had escorted her into the lifeboat. Sloper wrote later that, as it became clear that the *Titanic* would sink, 'every passenger seemed to have taken a firm grip on his nerves. [Except] Dorothy Gibson . . . who had become quite hysterical.' In the course of their affair, Jules Brulatour had given Dorothy a small grey motor car with a pastel chintz interior.[3] Watching the *Titanic* settle into the sea, Dorothy 'kept repeating over and over again', loudly and frequently enough for others in the boat to hear clearly what she was saying, 'I'll never ride in my little gray car again.' Sloper was mortified that people might think he was related to Dorothy or sympathetic to her self-absorbed jeremiad.[4] She was also in pain from the icy water that had spilled up to her ankles when the lifeboat was first lowered and, as did several survivors, Dorothy remembered the suffocating weight of that chill for the rest of her life: 'I never knew one could be so cold and live. I ached from head to foot.'[5]

The band was still playing as Tommy Andrews made his way through the crowds to the Bridge, where he talked with Captain Smith.[6] Near by, Jack Thayer and Milton Long stood by one of the deck rails and discussed whether or not they should jump. Jack, an experienced swimmer, changed his mind three or four times. He was afraid of being stunned when he hit the water and Long intermittently convinced him that 'she might possibly stay afloat'.[7] While they considered what to do next, Long sat down and Jack continued to stand, staring at a nearby empty davit, where he 'got a sight on a rope between the davits and a star and noticed that she was gradually sinking'.[8]

256

The ship's boilers; for scale, a man can be seen halfway down
the photograph on the right.

A trainee steward, Cecil Fitzpatrick, twenty-one years old and
from Kilkenny in Ireland, decided to cut across the Bridge to reach
the other side of the deck. He heard the Captain tell Andrews to
save himself, as the time had come for the last of those in command
to abandon ship. Fitzpatrick could not remember Smith's precise
choice of words to Andrews, although it was something to the effect
of 'We cannot stay any longer, she is going!'⁹ He was right. One of
the most memorably horrifying things about the *Titanic*'s sinking
was not just that she lasted over an hour longer than her designer
expected, but that the end, when it came, came with terrifying
speed. Two hours and forty minutes, considerably longer than
Andrews' original prediction, elapsed between the collision with the
iceberg and the *Titanic*'s disappearance. Two and a half hours after
the impact, her bow had settled forward by 8 degrees and the water
had still not reached the Bridge or the base of her first funnel. She
had held up remarkably well in the wake of a blow from which few
ships, then or now, could survive. Then, at about 2.10 a.m., those
in the lifeboats heard several roars from within the hull, which

sounded like the boilers exploding but which were in fact the bulk-heads finally giving way. Cecil Fitzpatrick, standing near to Andrews and Smith, felt the 'ship suddenly dipping, and the waves rushing up and engulfing me'.[10] The young Steward saved himself by grabbing on to the empty lifeboat davit and dragging himself to a still dry part of the Boat Deck, from where he scrambled to help Colonel Gracie, Officer Lightoller and those still attempting to free the collapsible. The lurch had knocked one of the collapsibles off the roof, on to the deck below, upside down. As the ship slid under, water again covered Fitzpatrick, floating the lifeboat away from him and taking Gracie, Lightoller and their companions off the *Titanic*. The same 'slight but definite plunge' caught Tommy Andrews and Captain Smith, either carrying them from the Bridge or compelling them to jump.[11] It also hit Ida and Isidor Straus, washing them overboard.[12] The band members were caught in that wave or fled, like Jack and Milton Long, who ran out of its way and only stopped 'by the rail about even with the second funnel'.[13]

Water filled the Bridge and the abandoned Wireless Room. It swept over the roof of the Officers' Quarters and up to the Grand Staircase, spilling in through the open doors leading from the deck and then shattering its glass dome, from where it reached the Writing Room and Tommy Andrews' cabin.[14] Survivors recalled hearing 'a sickening roar like hundreds of lions' as four of the *Titanic*'s 91-ton boilers broke free and crashed through the ship.[15] As the bow disappeared, the stern rose. The ship's propellers edged out of the water and more people began to leap overboard. Others used the hanging lifeboat ropes to lower themselves into the ocean, where they tried to swim in the direction of the lifeboats. Still debating if it was safe to jump, Jack Thayer and Milton Long were nearly toppled over by a man who lurched past them, swigging from a bottle of Gordon's gin.* Surrounded by 'a mass of hopeless,

---

* This man was probably one of the ship's bakers. His blood alcohol level was so high that he insulated himself to the point that he survived in the waters far longer than any of the others who jumped from the *Titanic*. He died in New Jersey in 1956.

dazed humanity', Jack did not want to be knocked into the darkness and he tried to impress upon Milton the need to jump before they were sucked under or accidentally pushed.[16] Milton, who unlike Jack did not know how to swim, kept trying to find an alternative, but the awful groans coming from the bowels of the ship and the terror seizing the people 'pushing, towards the floating stern and keeping in from the rail as far as they could' persuaded him that Jack was correct and they needed to go.[17] The two friends had agreed to stick together throughout the ordeal and Jack promised they would jump together, too. In case only one of them should make it, they 'sent message through each other to our families'.[18] The two young men climbed on to the rail, shook hands, wished one another good luck and swung their legs out. Milton nervously asked, 'You are coming, old boy, aren't you?' 'Of course,' Jack replied. Hoping to avoid becoming entangled or landing on Milton, he then said, 'Go ahead. I'll be with you in a minute.'[19]

Milton jumped and then, a second after him, Jack hurled himself from the side of the *Titanic*. It is hard, with hindsight, not to see in this leap some horrible pre-echo of the millions of young men who would go over the top of the trenches, side by side, most of them unprepared for what they were about to face. Jack swam to the surface and came up 'facing the ship', from where he heard a 'rumbling roar, mixed with more muffled explosions. It was like standing under a railway bridge while an express train passes overhead, mingled with the noise of a pressed steel factory and wholesale breakage of china.'[20] He looked around for Milton for a few seconds until the *Titanic*'s first funnel collapsed 'with a mass of sparks and steam' into the sea full of people who had just been swept, or had jumped, overboard.[21] The wave created by the funnel's collapse, 'right amongst the struggling mass of humanity already in the water', most likely killed Milton Long, who did not resurface.[22] Jack, caught but not submerged in the wash from the funnel, was struggling to breathe. Despite its temperature, he trod water, fixated by the sight of the *Titanic*:

The ship seemed to be surrounded with a glare, and stood out of the night as though she were on fire. I watched her. I don't know why I didn't keep swimming away. Fascinated, I seemed tied to the spot. Already I was tired out with the cold and struggling, although the life preserver held me head and shoulders above the water. She continued to make the same forward progress as when I left her. The water was over the base of the first funnel. The mass of people on board were surging back, always back toward the floating stern. The rumble and roar continued, with even louder distinct wrenchings and tearings of boilers and engines from their beds.[23]

The second funnel likewise shattered, pulverising more swimmers and then disappearing. Its wake sucked Jack under, twice. He tried to cover his head to shield himself from the 'great deal of small wreckage' spilling from the *Titanic* and as he did so, 'my hand touched the cork fender of an overturned life boat. I looked up and saw some men on top and asked them to give me a hand. One of them, a stoker, helped me up.'[24] From there, with the four or five other men who had made it to the flipped collapsible Jack, 'holding on for dear life' and sitting on his haunches, again turned to face the *Titanic*.

It seemed as though hours had passed since I left the ship; yet it was probably no more than four minutes, if that long. There was the gigantic mass, about fifty or sixty yards away . . . Her stern was gradually rising into the air, seemingly in no hurry, just slowly and deliberately . . . Her deck was turned slightly towards us. We could see groups of the almost fifteen hundred people still aboard, clinging in clusters or bunches, like swarming bees . . . [25]

The Awful Spectacle

Watchman, what is left of the night?

Isaiah 21:11

WHILE HIS SON HUDDLED ON AN OVERTURNED LIFE-
boat, shivering and nearly losing consciousness, John
Thayer moved with hundreds of others towards the
stern.[1] A passenger who had made it to the lifeboats told his
mother three days later, 'It was a terrible sight. It would make
stones cry to hear those on board shrieking.'[2] The *Titanic* added
her own screams to those of her passengers and crew, as nearly
everything movable within her came free, sliding and shattering,
'partly a roar, partly a groan, partly a rattle and partly a smash . . .
It was stupefying, stupendous . . . It was as if all the heavy things
one could think of had been thrown downstairs from the top of
a house, smashing over each other, and the stairs and everything
in the way.'[3]

She rose until her stern was completely clear of the water
and pointing into the night at a 30 degree angle. Those scrambling to the Poop Deck struggled to maintain their footing. A
second-class passenger in one of the nearby lifeboats was, as
Jack Thayer had been in the water, transfixed by 'the terrible

beauty of the *Titanic* at that moment . . . To me she looked like an enormous glow worm, for she was alight from the rising water line to the stern – electric lights blazing in every cabin on all the decks and lights at her mast heads.'[4] Two minutes before she disappeared, the *Titanic*'s lights flickered, then went out for the last time, plunging those on board into darkness. A few seconds later, the liner buckled and ruptured from her super-structure to her keel. Either at that point or shortly before, John Thayer jumped into water with a temperature of just under minus 2 degrees.[5]

That the *Titanic* shattered as she sank was confirmed only by the discovery of her wreck. Between 1912 and 1985, the standard account of her final moments, agreed on at both the American and British inquiries into the disaster, had the *Titanic* sinking intact, with no greater damage to her superstructure than the two collapsed forward funnels and none to the hull beyond the punc-tures inflicted by the iceberg. This version of events was stated by the ship's three most senior surviving officers – Charles Lightoller, Herbert Pitman and Joseph Boxhall – and in Lightoller's case forcefully so. In answer to a question from Lord Mersey, head of the British inquiry, whether the *Titanic* had broken in two as she sank, Lightoller answered: 'That is not true, my lord. I was watching her the whole time.'[6] Another crew member, a sailor called Thomas Dillon, and a surviving passenger Hugh Woolner likewise testified to the respective inquiries that they had seen the ship disappear in one piece. Newspaper interviews given by two American survivors, Elisabeth Allen and Caroline Bonnell, expressed the same belief, which received widespread, and enduring, corroboration from two of the most thorough and eloquent accounts published by survivors – *The Loss of the S.S. Titanic: Its Story and its Lessons* (1912), a memoir by Lawrence Beesley, a British school teacher who travelled in Second Class and left in Lifeboat 13, and Colonel Gracie's *The Truth about the Titanic* (1913), both of which argued 'that the *Titanic*'s decks were intact at the time she sank'.[7]

This was thus understandably the version presented to millions of viewers in the numerous dramatisations of the disaster filmed between 1912 and 1985, including *Titanic* (1953) and *A Night to Remember* (1958), both of which were watched by various survivors who praised the painful authenticity of the sinking scenes and, in the latter's case, received the endorsement and advice of the *Titanic's* by then two most senior surviving officers, Herbert Pitman and Joseph Boxhall, the latter of whom served as a consultant for the filmmakers.[8] This orthodoxy was overturned by the discovery that the *Titanic's* bow and stern lie nearly 2,000 feet away from each other on the ocean floor, with a debris field scattered between them like some horrible trail, extensive enough to contain the rotting, rusted form of five of the boilers. In 1997, the celluloid imagining of James Cameron's *Titanic*, one of the most commercially successful movies on record, offered the world a new finale for the *Titanic* that saw the on-screen liner tear between her third and her fourth funnel, down from the Boat Deck to the double bottom, which temporarily survived to link the two sections, enabling the bow to drag the stern into a vertical position before they fully detached from one another.[9]

In the years since his film's release, James Cameron has retained his fascination with the *Titanic* and he was part of several subsequent dives to the wreck site, which eventually led to his participation with marine forensic experts in a new computer simulation of the sinking, which posited that the break had originated further forward, between the second and third funnels. In a macabre way, extensive analysis of the wreck site and, crucially, the debris field has confirmed that Tommy Andrews' and Captain Smith's quip to passengers about the *Titanic* breaking into three did, in some way, transpire at about 2.18 a.m. on Monday the 15th. The ship seems to have snapped twice, more or less simultaneously, on either side of her third funnel. The section immediately impacted by that tear fell separately to the seabed, itself rebreaking into multiple pieces around and over the debris field. Its subsequent absence from either of the largest remaining pieces of the bow or stern explains the difficulty until recently of pinpointing where the *Titanic* fell apart.

With no moon and the ship in darkness as her electricity failed, passengers struggled to see what happened. Yet remarkably, of the 149 extant survivors' testimonies that specifically mention the final plunge, only seven stated categorically that the ship did not shatter. It was because those seven included three of her officers and two astute, meticulous authors that their version acquired its longevity and influence. Nine of the 149 said that due to the darkness they could not be sure what happened, twenty-four, including Dorothy Gibson, mentioned terrifying if non-specific sounds, fifty-one did not specify whether it did or did not tear, while fifty-three stated that they saw the *Titanic* when she 'broke in two pieces'.[10] A second-class passenger, Nellie Becker, was subsequently proved to have been one of the most eagle-eyed eyewitnesses when she told a colonial newspaper how the *Titanic* 'seemed to break right down the middle, and the middle to fall in. It was terrible beyond words.'[11] From their vantage point in Lifeboat 8, Lady Rothes was convinced she saw the *Titanic* snap in two with a roar that Gladys compared to 'an earthquake or a distant battle'.[12]

Identifying where the tears started and finished enables us to see which rooms they shredded as the *Titanic* fell apart. They cut through the Smoking Room and the Lounge on A-Deck, the ruins of which jut out from the brutalised bow. The Lounge's mantelpiece statue of Artemis settled into the silt of the debris field. It then shattered some of the B-Deck suites before rupturing the C-Deck first-class cabins, including the Countess of Rothes', where Gladys had left her photograph in the mistaken belief that they would be back before breakfast in the Dining Saloon, itself breaking at its final section, while its Pantry where first- and second-class meals were prepared was destroyed entirely. It then hit Scotland Road and a section of the E-Deck cabins, before completing its journey in the third-class Dining Saloon, store rooms, crew quarters and one of the boiler rooms.

Although his account of the split was rubbished for years, one of the most accurate interpretations by a survivor was Jack Thayer's. He had jumped from the ship only a few moments beforehand and saw the shattering of the *Titanic* from the close quarters of an upended lifeboat. Five days after the sinking, he gave a statement describing how 'it seemed to me that she broke in two just in front of the third funnel . . . The stern seemed to rise in the air and stopped at an angle of about 60 degrees. It seemed to hold there for a time and then with a hissing sound it shot right down out of sight with people jumping from the stern. The stern either pivoted around towards our boat, or we were sucked toward it, and as we only had one oar we could not keep away.'[13]

The 'hissing sound' he heard were pockets of air expelled by the advancing seawater. The last of the first-class public rooms to go under was the Verandah Café, its roof apparently exploding from the force of the air that tried to escape during the plunge and the descent to the seafloor. The last room to fill with water was the General Room, a lounge and meeting space for third-class passengers, located below the Poop Deck, on to which the majority of those trapped on board after the lifeboats had been lowered and from where they continued to jump until the stern disappeared. Last to sink was the *Titanic*'s name, inscribed on the hull above the word 'Liverpool' denoting the home of White Star's headquarters and thus their vessels' port of registry. The sea's seemingly preternatural calmness and the smooth yacht-like lines given to the *Olympic*-class liners worked together to dissipate the drag feared by so many in the nearby boats. Apart from Jack Thayer's collapsible being briefly pulled in towards the vanishing ship, there 'did not seem to be very much suction'.[14] Then came 'the anguished cries of many hundreds of people'.[15]

*

On his overturned raft, which within minutes of the sinking physically did not have any more room if it wanted to avoid capsizing, Jack Thayer thought, incongruously, that the noise of so many voices in the darkness reminded him of locusts at home in Pennsylvania.[16] Shivering in her lifeboat, her feet still in agony in her soaked pumps, Dorothy Gibson temporarily forgot her own discomfort as the *Titanic* vanished. She later told a New York newspaper, 'I will never forget that terrible cry that rang out from people who were thrown into the sea and others who were afraid for their loved ones.'[17] At one point, Dorothy saw a green silk cushion floating past their lifeboat. It was from the Lounge where she had played bridge three hours earlier and which had spilled its contents into the ocean as it ripped apart with the *Titanic*.[18] But her terror and heartache did not induce her, or hundreds of people like her, to go back to help the survivors. Dorothy, when pressed later for the reason why her lifeboat did not return to rescue people from the water, could not explain it adequately. She told the *Morning Telegraph* that the *Titanic* 'disappeared, leaving nothing behind her on the face of the sea but a swirl of water, bobbing heads and lifeboats that were threatened by the suction of the waters. After the vessel had disappeared, the officer [sic] in charge of our boat wanted to return, saying that there was room for several more passengers and pointing out the possibility of being able to rescue some of those who might be swimming. But immediately behind us was another lifeboat carrying forty people and as no one could be seen in the water some of the passengers in the other boat were transferred to ours.'[19]

It is an incomplete timeline, light on detail and portraying events separated by hours as happening side by side. Dorothy's lifeboat did not take on more passengers from a fuller companion craft until at least an hour after the sinking and George Hogg, a lookout rather than an officer in charge of number 7, said afterwards that almost no one supported him in going back. Dorothy seems to have carried a sincere sense of guilt with her for their failure to go back, even though it was an action mimicked by nearly every other lifeboat in the vicinity. While in her interviews with journalists she appears deliberately to have exaggerated the pull of the *Titanic's* almost non-existent suction as she vanished, Dorothy nonetheless conveyed how much that suction had been dreaded before the event itself, which gave way to the fear of being swamped by panicked swimmers. Something of the tortured mentality of those in the lifeboats was caught at the subsequent British inquiry when survivor Sir Cosmo Duff Gordon mentioned that, assailed by the 'noise', some survivors had objected to rowing back to help, in case they were swamped. The Attorney-General, Sir Rufus Isaacs, representing the Board of Trade, asked him, 'We do not want unnecessarily to prolong the discussion of it, but they were the cries of people who were drowning?' There was a momentary pause before Sir Cosmo's answer, 'Yes.'[20]

18

Grip Fast

There is sorrow on the sea . . .

Jeremiah 49:23

ALTHOUGH CAPTAIN SMITH HAD ORDERED THEM TO ROW in the direction of the *Californian*, Lifeboat 8 had long since given up trying to row to that 'awful light that never got nearer'.[1] The cargo ship, her name as yet unknown to them, was too far from them and Lady Rothes wanted to go back to retrieve some of the survivors screaming near by. She appreciated that 'the cold of the water was so *awful* that very few could bear it alive for more than a few minutes,' but her suggestion that they row back to help was supported only by Thomas Jones, the sailor in charge of the boat, Gladys Cherry and an American lady whose name she did not quite catch.[2] According to Gladys, they were the only four who 'wanted to go back and get more people into our boat, but the other women and the two stewards would have killed us rather than go back'. Eventually, the majority had its way, to the visible distress of the commanding sailor who made a point of telling them, 'Ladies, if any of us are saved, remember I wanted to go back. I would rather drown with them than leave them.'[3] When they reached New York, he was so pained by guilt at the memory of the way 'the fearful screams and shrieks' had dwindled into a thunderously loud silence that he wrote to Noëlle and Gladys asking them to provide written testimony that he had wanted to do the decent thing by rowing back, which they did. Gladys tried to comfort Jones by pointing out, 'if you remember, there was only an American lady, my cousin, self, and you who wanted to return. I could not hear the discussion very clearly, as I was at the tiller, but everyone forward and the three men refused . . . You did all you could, and being my own countryman I wanted to tell you this.'[4] She understood his anguish, however, referring to their failure to answer the cries for help as 'the dreadful regret I shall always have'.[5]

Those in the lifeboats felt more than craven self-preservation. The 'heartrending, never-to-be-forgotten sounds' which 'seemed to go through you like a knife' inspired fear, futility and remorse.[6] For some, including those in Lifeboat 10 which had been launched with John Thayer's help, the screams were quite literally unbearable; they tried to sing 'saying it would help us keep our bearings, but we all knew it was only a kindly ruse to try and drown out that awful moaning cry, and we were unable to utter a sound. God grant that I never hear such a sound again. No words, just an awful despairing moan, and all of them seemed to moan in the same key, regardless of what their voices may have been.'[7] A 'thin light-gray smoky vapour' briefly marked the spot where the *Titanic* had vanished; it reminded one passenger of the River Charon. After a minute or so, it faded away.[8] Survival time in water of minus 2 Celsius is, at the very most, thirty minutes, with consciousness lost around fifteen and most deaths following within the next five. Initial symptoms from being submerged into such waters include panic, shock and confusion, such as the kind mentioned by Jack Thayer when he resurfaced after his leap. In those with pre-existing heart conditions, like Ida Straus, it can cause instantaneous cardiac arrest. Breath is commonly driven from the body by shock at contact with water so cold, forcing an involuntary breath to be taken which can significantly increase the chances of drowning. For those who survive this, disorientation is the immediate sequel, typically lasting for about thirty seconds, and roughly correlating with Jack Thayer's stupefied amazement when he failed to swim away from the hull. His limbs had begun to numb to the point of uselessness when he reached the collapsible, which is why he required the help of the stoker to pull him up. For those caught in the sea for longer, severe pain would have clouded rational thought before hypothermia set in as the prelude to unconsciousness and then death.[9] By about 2.30, the site had fallen quiet. 'Afterwards,' Dorothy Gibson remembered, 'for the next two hours, the passengers in our boat just sat in the darkness and tried to keep warm. No one said a word. There was nothing to say and nothing we could do.'[10] Gladys Cherry wrote to her mother of how it had become 'the stillest night possible, not a ripple on the water and the stars wonderful; that icy air and the stars I never want to see or feel again'.[11]

*

During the hours that fell between the *Titanic's* sinking and their rescue, some of her survivors faced character tests that they failed to pass. The Countess of Rothes was not one of them. While one of her lifeboat's occupants, Mrs Ella White, deployed both frequency and volume to express her conviction that it was poor form for the sailors to smoke at such a distressing time, Lady Rothes turned to Able Seaman Jones and asked if there was anything she could do to help 'as I know a little about small Boats from a small racing yacht [Lord] Rothes had in Devonshire'.[12] Almost exactly the same age as Lady Rothes, Jones came from a family of Welsh fishermen and miners. He had been put in charge of the boat by Captain Smith, but he warmed to the Countess in his own gruff way. Seaman Jones and his colleagues in Lifeboat 8 later nicknamed Noëlle 'the plucky little Countess'. He entrusted her with the tiller, since 'she had a lot to say, so I put her in charge of steering the boat'.[13]

Of the five hours that followed, during which 'one began to feel rather hopeless', the Countess's lifeboat fell almost as silent as

Dorothy's, full of what the Countess called 'the ghostliness of our feelings'.[14] Here too, 'no one talked much,' except sailors who occasionally shouted to lifeboats near by in futile pursuit of more information about any possible rescue.[15] The motto of the Rothes earldom has been, since the thirteenth century, 'Grip Fast', inspired by the legend of an ancestor escorting Margaret of Wessex (later St Margaret, Queen of Scots) on horseback through a storm, urging her to ride pillion and hold on to his belt. The Countess displayed a comparable sense of tenacity in that, having no idea if they were going to be rescued, she nonetheless strove to hide the fact that she was now 'really frightened. The *fearful* cold made it all much worse, tho' after a few hours one felt very sleepy. The water was so black & very calm.'[16] No one else in Lifeboat 8 noticed that Lady Rothes was feeling haunted and exhausted; instead they remembered how she had steered and then volunteered to row, which she did for five hours. She and Gladys took turns steering and comforting the often sobbing María-Josefa de Peñasco and Noëlle helped calm things down when Mrs White again complained about people smoking, at which point one of the sailors had snapped, 'If you don't stop talking through that hole in your face, there will be one less in the boat.'[17] For the rest of her life when asked about the sinking of the *Titanic*, Noëlle made a point of complimenting the 'magnificent' crew and she never mentioned their contretemps with Mrs White, who was also keen to point out that the ankle she had sprained when boarding at Cherbourg was still a source of pain.[18]

Dawn cast light on the grotesque beauty of the ice field the *Titanic* had been steaming into. Lifeboats rowed past cathedrals of ice, the sight of which broke the spirits of many survivors, as did the wind that began to lacerate the lifeboats. Lady Rothes told an historian years later how 'at dawn the weather turned . . . [and] one felt an awful loneliness & exhaustion'. Her maid Cissy, having behaved 'wonderfully' all evening, was also trying to hide signs of distress – in her case, severe seasickness noticed only by Gladys.[19] The Countess was still rowing at about 7.30 when the sailor next to her whispered, 'Can you see any light? Look on the next wave we top, but don't say anything in case I am wrong.'[20] She tried to look surreptitiously at the horizon where, eventually, she saw a plume rising from a single smokestack with the red and black livery of the Cunard Line. The 13,500-ton *Carpathia* had been crossing from New York to Fiume, via Gibraltar when she received the *Titanic*'s distress call. Noëlle confirmed that she could see a ship ahead, which reassured the sailor that he could safely announce the news to the rest of their boat.[21] Helping to row towards safety, the Countess suggested they pray and sing hymns until they reached the *Carpathia*. Lifeboat 8 began renditions of 'Pull for the Shore' and 'Lead, Kindly Light':

> Lead, kindly light, amid the encircling gloom
> Lead thou me on!
> The night is dark, and I'm far from home
> Lead thou me on!

Similar reactions to the appearance of the *Carpathia* were expressed in the other boats. In Colonel Gracie's, a crew member asked, 'Don't you think we ought to pray?' A quick survey established that the boat carried Catholics, Methodists and Presbyterians, making the Lord's Prayer the most obvious choice for ad hoc ecumenicalism.[22] Later, some of the Catholics on the lifeboat joined in their own quiet offering of the Hail Mary to supplement the Lord's Prayer, as it does in the recitation of the Rosary.[23]

In number 8, there was a final drama when they crested a wave that nearly dashed them against the *Carpathia*'s side, but Seaman Jones managed to get the lifeboat under control as a Cunard sailor jumped down to help those who, like Noëlle, struggled to grip on to the rope ladder leading up to the *Carpathia*.[24] She let go of her oar and found her hands were too stiff to bend, which meant that she was one of those who was put into a kind of swing made from wood and canvas bags that was then winched up the black-painted hull of the ship. Earlier they had been used only for babies in the lifeboats, but more were cobbled together as it became clear that there were dozens of adults so damaged by exposure they would be unable to climb.[25] Gladys wrote to her mother that Lady Rothes had fainted the moment her feet touched the *Carpathia*'s deck.[26]

19

Where's Daddy?

Straight away all the extraordinary things of yesterdays and all that incredible, wild night, with its almost impossible adventures, at once, suddenly, in all their terrifying fullness, appeared to his imagination and memory.

Fyodor Dostoevsky, *The Double* (1846)

Jack Thayer's lifeboat, a different one from the overturned craft on which he had been pulled from the water by a stoker, was the last to reach the *Carpathia*, pulling up alongside her at about 8.15 a.m. In the small hours, everyone on Collapsible B had been transferred to one of the less full boats from which they eventually boarded the *Carpathia*. Her battered contingent included an Irish immigrant who had lost consciousness, one of the ship's wireless operators suffering from hypothermia and a crew member whose feet were so swollen he climbed up the rope ladder to the *Carpathia* on his knees.[1] When Jack, with the hands of his watch stopped at 2.22 a.m., reached the top of the ladder he saw his dishevelled mother, who had joined many other survivors in gathering to greet the arriving lifeboats. Glancing over her son's shoulder, the 'overjoyed' Marian asked, 'Where's Daddy?'[2] To which Jack replied, 'I don't know, Mother.'[3] Marian had apparently assumed, until that moment, that her husband and their son had reunited after she was evacuated.[4] For at least a few more hours she, along with many on the *Carpathia*, nurtured the comforting chimera that there could be another rescue ship near by, which might have picked up more survivors. Shipboard rumour had it that White Star's *Baltic* might be in the vicinity. The *Titanic*'s senior surviving officer, Charles Lightoller, who had been saved in the same lifeboats as Jack, found himself fielding questions about these other liners. 'After serious consideration it seemed the kindest way to be perfectly frank and give the one reply possible,' Lightoller explained later, when justifying why he told survivors that if someone had not made it to the *Carpathia* then there was no hope. 'What kindness was there in holding out a hope, knowing full well that there was not even the *shadow* of hope. Cold comfort, and possibly cruel, but I could see no help for it.'[5]

Since picking up the *Titanic*'s distress call and rushing to the disaster site, the *Carpathia*'s passengers and crew had organised themselves to help the influx of émigrés as best they could. As Jack and his mother talked,

> somebody gave me a coffee cup full of brandy. It was the first drink of an alcoholic beverage I had ever had. It warmed as though I had put hot coals in my stomach, and did more too. A man kindly loaned me his pajamas and his bunk, then my wet clothes were taken to be dried, and with the help of the brandy I went to sleep till almost noon. I got up feeling fit and well, just as though nothing bad had happened. After putting on my clothes, which were entirely dry, I hurried out to look for Mother. We were then passing to the south of a solid ice field, which I was told was over twenty miles long and four miles wide. I found that Captain Arthur H. Rostron, Commander of the "CARPATHIA", of the Cunard Line, had given up his cabin to my Mother, Mrs. George D. Widener, and Mrs. John Jacob Astor. I slept on the floor of the cabin every night until we reached New York . . . [6]

One account claimed later that when he first woke up on the *Carpathia*, Jack pitifully assured his mother as she hovered over him that he had endeavoured to be brave, or, as he allegedly put it, 'I tried to play the man.'[7] What Jack had seen and endured in the hours between escape and rescue had been horrific enough to haunt him for the rest of his life. As his overturned lifeboat had reached capacity, he had seen men beaten away with oars and Officer Lightoller pleading with those seeking to climb on, 'It's thirty-one lives against yours. You can't come aboard. There's not room.'[8] Collapsible B had been so close to the site of the *Titanic*'s final plunge that she was also at the heart of the anguish that followed: it took the only other lifeboat that eventually returned to try to rescue those in the water nearly half an hour to row twenty yards, so thick had the field of bodies become – a sight 'enough to break the stoutest heart' according to one of the sailors.[9] On his boat, Jack had cradled Harold Bride, the *Titanic*'s only surviving wireless operator, and had tried to keep Bride's feet out of the water when he realised they had already started to succumb to frostbite. It is possible that Bride's colleague Jack Phillips, who had also stayed at his post until the power failed, was one of those who died on their lifeboat and then slid into the sea.[10] Jack Thayer saw John Collins, a crew member from Belfast who had helped prepare meals for the first-class Dining Saloon and, at seventeen, Jack's contemporary, shivering meekly in the water, waiting for somebody to die so he could take their place on the boat.[11] One of those who, like Jack, had made it to the overturned boat before it became too crowded was the Strauses' shipboard friend Colonel Gracie, who witnessed 'one transcendent piece of heroism that will remain fixed in my memory as the most sublime and coolest exhibition of courage and cheerful resignation to fate and fearless-ness of death'. It came from a man who swam to their lifeboat and asked to be helped up but, when told he might capsize them, Gracie and other eyewitnesses remembered the 'deep manly voice of a powerful man, who, in his extremity, replied: "All right, boys; good luck and God bless you."' The man swam off without further comment to his death, and a rumour arose later that it had been Captain Smith, although Gracie, who knew the Captain, was emphatic that it had not been: 'He was not an acquaintance of mine, for the tones of his voice would have enabled me to recognize him.'[12] 'During all this time,' Jack wrote in his memoirs, 'nobody dared to move, for we did not know at what moment our perilous support might overturn, throwing us all into the sea.'[13]

From where he was clutched by a kneeling, terrified Jack, Harold Bride gave them some good news – that, of all the ships they had managed to contact by wireless after the collision, one of them, the Cunard Line's *Carpathia*, was close enough to reach them by about

Lifeboat 6, which Ida had refused to enter, carries her maid Ellen to the *Carpathia*.

four o'clock that morning.[14] Another moment of comfort arrived when the group, in Colonel Gracie's words, elected to say the Lord's Prayer and 'our voices with one accord burst forth in repeating that great appeal to the Creator and Preserver of all mankind, and the only prayer that everyone of us knew and could unite in, thereby manifesting that we were all sons of God and brothers to each other whatever our sphere in life or creed might be.'[15]

In the succeeding hours, Jack had narrowly missed an earlier reunion with his mother. As the weather shed its previous calm, the upturned collapsible pitched in the revived waves, allowing air to leak out from under the boat, which thus settled further into the water. Officer Lightoller organised the men into two rows and subsequently called out orders for them to lean in different directions to help steady the craft, which they all obeyed. Two lifeboats, numbers 4 and 12, later came by in time to help empty Collapsible B and in the dark neither Marian, who was in Lifeboat 4, nor Jack, who was helped into 12, realised they had been so close to one another.[16] Also moved into boat 12 were the ailing operator Harold Bride, Colonel Gracie and another first-class passenger, the Yorkshire landowner Algernon Barkworth, who sat next to Gracie in their new boat with a blanket, gifted by a female survivor, over their knees and a corpse, another victim of hypothermia, next to them.[17] Gracie was moved by Barkworth's kindness and thought his 'tender heart is creditable to his character'.[18] For his part, Barkworth was impressed by Jack, describing him in an interview given later that year as a 'clear-cut chap'.[19] Jack had initially been intimidated by the stokers and sailors on the now abandoned boat B, a view which he had discarded in the course of the morning, explaining later that 'they surely were a grimy, wiry, dishevelled hard looking lot. Under the surface they were brave human beings, with generous and charitable hearts.'[20] Along with his first sip of alcohol, that night was also Jack's first time of prolonged contact with anyone outside his own class, with the exception of his family's servants.[21]

By the time Jack emerged from his first sleep in twenty-four hours, a short service of thanksgiving and prayer had been led by one of the *Carpathia's* passengers, an Anglican clergyman.[22] It had temporarily soothed some of the passengers and, while they were thus occupied below deck, it enabled the *Carpathia's* Captain Rostron to conduct one last search of the vicinity, after which he slowly navigated his ship away from the ice field and turned her back towards New York.[23] It was to the credit of Rostron's passengers that none apparently objected to their trip being postponed by this return to their point of origin. The *Carpathia's* passengers behaved as beautifully as possible to the *Titanic's* survivors, offering up cabins and clothes. They were soon aided by some of the *Titanic's* surviving stewards who, although they were no longer technically employed, began 'looking after the passengers as though on our own ship'.[24] Public rooms were cleared to become dormitories. Over forty years later, Bertha Watt, then a twelve-year-old survivor from the *Titanic's* Second Class, told the historian and novelist Walter Lord that it was on the *Carpathia* that 'I learned a great deal of the fundamentals I have built a happy life on, such as faith, hope, and charity.'[25]

At about four o'clock that afternoon, the bodies of several of those who had died in the lifeboats or shortly after boarding the *Carpathia* were buried at sea.[26] Among them was first-class passenger William Hoyt, a businessman from Ohio, who had been one of the few victims heavy enough to survive in the waters for any length of time.[27] He had been hauled from the ocean almost an hour after the *Titanic* disappeared. Even then, he had been retrieved bleeding from his mouth and nose and died within a few moments of being rescued.[28] Two of those buried in the same ceremony as Hoyt were almost certainly the swimmers who had made it, 'raving and delirious', into Marian Thayer's lifeboat, where they had expired next to an unconscious crew member who, when he came to, understandably began screaming.[29] From the *Carpathia's* rails, the bodies in their canvas shrouds were committed to the sea with the traditional words:

> For as much as it hath pleased Almighty God to take unto
> Himself the soul of our dear brother departed, we therefore

commit his body to the deep, to be turned to corruption, looking for the resurrection of the body (when the sea shall give up her dead) and the life of the world to come, through our Lord Jesus Christ; who at His coming shall change our vile body, that it may be like unto His glorious body, according to the mighty working, whereby He is able to subdue all things to himself.[30]

Between the service of thanksgiving and the first of the *Titanic* funerals, a roll call was taken of the survivors. The Stewardess Violet Jessop, who had greeted the Strauses on their first day on board, realised at the name-gathering that 'dear Tommy Andrews' was not on the list of survivors, neither were the Strauses, nor 'the good doctor', O'Loughlin. She called the roll call 'the saddest search it has ever been my lot to witness'.[31] For Jack and his mother, it confirmed too that his father was dead. It confirmed that their family friend Emily Ryerson had lost her husband as they had sailed home for the funeral of their eldest son. The other two Society women with whom Jack and Marian now shared a cabin had also been bereaved – Eleanor Widener, the Thayers' host at the dinner party held the night before in the *Titanic*'s Restaurant, had lost her husband and her son; Madeleine Astor, only a year older than Jack, had become a pregnant widow with her arm badly hurt from boarding the lifeboats.

The scenes of distress throughout the *Carpathia* are painful enough to read about; to have lived through them borders on the unimaginable. Tennis champion Karl Behr considered that although 'the sinking of the *Titanic* was dreadful, to my mind the four days among the sufferers on the *Carpathia* was much worse and more difficult to try and forget'.[32] During his time in the lifeboats, when Behr had struggled to warm the feet of the woman he subsequently married, another passenger sitting next to them nudged him and showed him a gun from his coat, then whispered, 'Should the worst come to the worst, you can use this revolver for your wife, after my wife and I have finished with it.'[33] The man speaking to Behr was calm and his offer reflects the despair rampant in most of the lifeboats between the sinking and the first sighting of the *Carpathia*. Yet even the rescue that spared them from dying adrift offered horrible scenes to the survivors. An acquaintance of Jack Thayer, Richard Norris Williams, who was preparing to start his first semester at Harvard that autumn, was begging the *Carpathia*'s doctors not to amputate his legs. He had felt fine when he climbed on board, but within a day his frostbite was so bad that the physicians told him that both of his legs needed to be removed. They eventually yielded to the patient's wishes and, in time, Williams made a full recovery, offering one of the few happiness-tinged epilogues from the *Carpathia*.[34] Elsewhere on board, an Irish passenger from Third Class, with strands of her hair still frozen together, lay on the deck, eschewing the offer of a cabin since the hard floor was the only way to ease the pain in her back.[35] Some women had emerged from hours in the lifeboats with their lips cracked and bleeding from the cold and the ocean spray.[36] At least two widowed passengers threatened to commit suicide; another, a young Swedish woman, who had been travelling in Second Class with her fiancé and her brother, realised she had lost them both, and wrote to her uncle, 'I would have been glad if I had been permitted to die, because life no longer has any value for me since I lost my beloved.'[37] An Italian child from Third Class was taken to the *Carpathia*'s hot press to try to warm him up, prompting panic in his confused mother, who thought she had lost him.[38]

A British survivor, Charlotte Collyer, had a chunk of hair pulled from her head so violently it had left her scalp bleeding; she had caught her hair on one of the lifeboat's oar locks, yet did not feel the pain until she reached the *Carpathia*.[39] Like many widowed mothers, she was struggling to deal with her own sudden grief while explaining to their children what had happened. Another former second-class passenger, Sylvia Caldwell, had already witnessed Charlotte Collyer's attempts in the lifeboat to explain to her seven-year-old daughter, Marjorie:

[The child] leaned over to her mother and said, 'Mother, do you think daddy is alright? Do you think he is safe in a boat?' And the mother answered, 'I don't know, darling, but I hope so.' 'Mother,' said Marjorie, 'do you think if I pray to Jesus it would help daddy?' And the trembling lips of the mother said, 'Yes, dear, I am sure it would.' She put up her dear little hands and asked God to save her daddy. Her prayer was not answered on earth, but I feel sure that she will find her father saved in that bright Beyond.[40]

Not everyone was comforted by their religion. Irene Harris, the Broadway producer's wife who still had her arm in a sling from her Saturday-afternoon fall on the *Titanic*'s Grand Staircase, remembered that, as her lifeboat left the liner, the Strauses had called out to her 'God go with you,' but once on the *Carpathia*, widowed and in shock, she thought, 'No, God is not with me. He is with you and my beloved . . . He too went down on the *Titanic*.'[41] Whether she meant God or her husband is unclear.

One of the *Carpathia*'s passengers, en route to a holiday in the Mediterranean, was John A. Badenoch, a buyer for Macy's, who received a telegram from one of Ida's sons, Percy, asking him to find out what he could about Percy's parents, and Badenoch's employers. Badenoch had first approached the *Titanic*'s Third Officer, Herbert Pitman, to confirm that the lifeboats picked up by the *Carpathia* were indeed the only ones that had made it from the *Titanic*:

when I stated my reason for knowing and insisted on an answer, he told me that all the boats had been accounted for and that in his judgement there was almost no hope for those who were not already rescued. Thinking possibly that your father and mother had been taken aboard and I had missed them, I covered the entire ship from bow to stern, and searched the saloon, second and steerage. Also looked in every state-room, irrespective of its occupants so that I could satisfy myself beyond doubt whether or not they were aboard.[42]

Badenoch then circulated among the survivors, attempting to find out what had happened to the Strauses, and eventually he located Ida's maid, Ellen Bird, still wearing the fur coat Ida had given her just before she left. She was the only one of their party of four who had survived; Isidor's valet, John Farthing, had also perished, although information about his final few hours alive was scanty.

Upon waking from her faint, the Countess of Rothes had taken some broth and sent her maid to order two telegrams, which could be sent once the congestion in sending had cleared – one to request an update on the health of her son Malcolm and another to her parents in France, informing them that she had survived.[43] After that, she worked with the other survivors. The Countess had kept her promise to the bridegroom on deck who had asked her to look after his wife and she kept a traumatised María-Josefa de Peñasco close to her throughout the voyage.[44] Watching the grief of María-Josefa and others unfold around them, Lady Rothes and Gladys Cherry felt deep gratitude that they had not been travelling with any male relatives.[45] The Countess volunteered her services as a nurse, utilising the training she had received a few months earlier from the Red Cross, and Gladys admitted that the Countess was relieved to be busy over the next three days:

> I think we all feel a little better this morning. We, that are so fortunate, having lost no one; but all the poor women's faces are piteous to see; yesterday morning I was very busy with a Ship's Bosun, cutting out garments for the Steerage and Second Class children, some of whom had no [day] clothes at all, we made little coats and leggings out of the blankets.
>
> Then I went round the Steerage and Hospitals with the Doctor, who is a charming man, and he said a cheery face and word did so much for them, our *Titanic* men most of them with legs and feet frozen are wonderful when you think what they have been through . . . If only you could imagine

how we long for land – This water all round is terrible, and one's nerves now seem worse than on that dreadful night. The Doctor gave me a little Bromide last night and I slept a little better, but one wakens terrified, which is very silly, as we have nothing to grumble at in comparison with the poor widows. Oh it is too dreadful to see them. Noëlle and I have helped in seeing after these poor distressed souls, and it has helped us, so much . . .

Gladys added:

I dread the voyage back [to England] again . . . all the crew, Captain, passengers, and stewards are perfectly sweet to us; there are two little French children 3 years and 20 months old, who have lost their father and I take one of them every day for a bit while the mother rests.

I love to do something, as it stops one thinking. I hope we shan't have another accident in this fog – Noëlle's poor maid is very sick, she was sick all the way from Cherbourg but she behaved splendidly in the boat that night.[46]

The third-class section for survivors on the *Carpathia*. It is almost certain that the lady seated and sewing in the centre is the Countess of Rothes.

Many passengers had left the *Titanic* in their evening attire or pyjamas and soon, despite the generosity of the *Carpathia*'s contingent, there was a clothes shortage for survivors.[47] Gladys, along with several other women, including Daisy Spedden, a Tuxedo Park resident, attempted to tackle that want.[48] Wrote Spedden, 'Yesterday was spent in cutting up blankets and making garments for the women and children and loads of clothes have been ordered by wireless from the N.Y. Stores. I feel so sorry for the five officers rescued from our ship, for people are questioning them to death and criticising everything that was done, but the more sane passengers are going to do their utmost to contradict any statements derogatory to officers and crew, for they are a noble lot and did their very best.' She also recorded the most viciously amoral comments overheard by 'the more sane passengers': 'We spend our time sitting on people who are cruel enough to say that no steerage should have been saved, as if they weren't human beings!'[49] In deference to US immigration laws, the *Carpathia*'s crew attempted to separate the third-class survivors from the others, a policy at which Lady Rothes seems to have taken umbrage and which she disregarded, since most of her time during that voyage was spent helping third-class passengers.[50] Officer Charles Lightoller was particularly impressed by her actions, remembering the Countess as 'one of the foremost amongst those trying to carry comfort to others'.[51]

Of all the hideous tragedies encountered by Lady Rothes between 15 and 18 April, few were more obviously painful than that of third-class passenger Rhoda Abbott, a thirty-nine-year-old Salvation Army member from Buckinghamshire, who had left an abusive marriage with her two teenage sons, sixteen-year-old Rossmore and eleven-year-old Eugene.[52] When she reached the *Carpathia*, Rhoda had been taken to the ship's hospital where she had been treated for hypothermia, leg contusions, burns, frostbite and shock.[53] She had stayed on board after her elder son, because of his strength and maturity, was judged a man by the *Titanic*'s crew and refused entry to the lifeboats.[54] The family had been swept overboard and Rhoda had felt her youngest son's hand slip from her own.[55] Both boys had perished. Even decades later, one of the Countess's grandsons told the historian Randy Bryan Bigham that the memory of what had happened to the Abbott family had pained his grandmother, who also became worried that since Rhoda was 'very poor' and their tickets had apparently been paid for by their church congregation, there might be no one to greet her or care for her when they reached New York.[56]

That arrival was postponed by the weather, which deteriorated further after Monday the 15th. On the night of Tuesday the 16th, they encountered a 'most awful thunder storm' and the sound made one passenger scream that distress rockets were being released.[57] Gladys Cherry was not the only survivor to request a sedative to help her sleep. As the storm gave way to 'a dense fog' on the 17th, the *Carpathia* slowed again and fear of a second accident settled over many survivors.[58] During the purgatorial wait, rumours, often contradictory, spread among the survivors, one of whom admitted later that, initially, 'I did not think for a moment that any passengers had remained on the ship' when it sank.[59] Some had initially believed the sounds of the screams they heard in the minutes afterwards had been crew members. Now that the truth dawned that 'there has probably never been a bigger disaster at sea', some claimed that nearly 2,000 had been lost; others that 'not more than 100 out of the 3,000' had lived.[60] The Countess and Gladys heard a rumour that Captain Smith had been trying to take the Blue Riband; they also heard that he had shot himself moments before the *Titanic* disappeared.[61] Both were untrue. Stories circulated that there had been more lifeboats, some of which had capsized, drowning everybody on board.[62] The news that many had died since being rescued was running alongside gossip that Colonel Astor, Major Butt and George Widener had entered into a murder–suicide pact during the ship's final moments, that Captain Smith had jumped only to swim back to die at his post, that one of the senior officers, Wilde or Murdoch, had committed suicide on deck.[63] It was the reports of ice warnings received and a speed unreduced that began to turn the mood from wounded credulity to anger at 'such reckless waste of lives'.[64] On the 16th, a committee of survivors, consisting mainly of second-class passengers, was formed. A member reported: 'Yesterday we stated our case before a committee of ladies and gentlemen, who intend to get as much as possible from the White Star Company.'[65]

Feelings also hardened against many of the male survivors. Margaret Brown told a journalist later that 'the attitude of the men who were rescued was indeed pathetic. Each and all seemed as though they were trying to efface themselves when they were encountered passing to and fro. It was noticed how they all tried to explain how it came about like a miracle that their lives were saved, with an expression of apology as though it were a blight on their manhood.'[66] A yachtsman who had been asked by Lightoller to help with one of the lifeboats, and whose life was subsequently ruined by accusations that he had disguised himself as a woman in order to escape, approached Lightoller on the *Carpathia* and asked for an affidavit, which the officer provided, stating, 'Major Arthur Peuchen was ordered into the boat by me, owing to the fact that I required a seaman, which he proved himself to be, as well as a brave man. C. H. Lightoller, Second Officer late S.S. *Titanic*.'[67] When Dr Henry Frauenthal, a New York-based surgeon, came to check on Irene Harris' arm – he had helped the late Dr O'Loughlin set it after her fall on Saturday – he began to discuss how he had escaped the *Titanic*, at which point Irene brutally told him, 'I wouldn't have my husband back at the cost of a woman's life.'[68] Other male survivors, admittedly, did nothing to endear themselves to the freshly bereaved widows. Alfred Nourney, the Dutch citizen travelling under the pseudonym of a German nobleman, went to the *Carpathia*'s Smoking Room where he lay down on a pile of blankets, using them as a comfortable bed for himself. When a woman asked him to move so that she could wrap herself in some of the blankets, he refused and she shouted at him, 'To think of it: the like of you saved and women left to drown; shame on you.' She then yanked a blanket from beneath Nourney, causing him to roll on the floor and bystanders to cheer so loudly that he retreated from the room.[69]

Men like Colonel Gracie, Algernon Barkworth and Jack Thayer, those who had jumped and survived rather than leaving in one of the lifeboats, were generally spared the opprobrium gathering around the others. In Jack's case, the story of his escape had already been heard and repeated by other survivors. Margaret Brown described him as 'one of the heroes on board . . . While swimming, he was drawn twice under the keel by the suction.' Brown also noticed how Marian Thayer juxtaposed grief at losing her husband with joy at her son's survival, and 'in her great thankfulness in having one spared her, for the rest of the voyage not more than a few minutes at a time would she permit him to be separate from her'.[70] Marian did, however, allow, and perhaps even encourage, a temporary separation when Jack went to check on the mental well-being of Bruce Ismay. They were nearing New York when the *Carpathia*'s doctor called on the Thayers, expressing his worry about Ismay, who had described the Thayers as his friends. In the years ahead, no figure was to suffer more from the resentment against male survivors than Bruce Ismay; even Maggie Brown, who expressed sympathy for the other gentlemen who had lived, was revolted by Ismay, referring to his cabin on the *Carpathia* as 'the quarters of the secluded plutocrat'.[71] Having helped with loading the earlier lifeboats, Ismay had escaped in one of the last and arrived on the *Carpathia* in a state that bordered on the catatonic. The ship's doctor, Dr Frank McGee, had approached him at that point and asked him, 'Will you not go into the saloon and get some soup, or something to drink?' Ismay answered, 'No, I really do not want anything at all.' 'Do go and get something.' Ismay again refused: 'If you will leave me alone I will be very much happier here. If you will get me some room where I can be quiet, I wish you would.' The doctor found a cabin for him, where he stayed until they reached New York, eating nothing but soup, repeating over and over again to Charles Lightoller 'that he ought to have gone down with the ship because he found that women had gone down'.[72]

This was the state, 'the terribly nervous condition', in which Ismay was found by Jack on Thursday the 18th:

as there was no answer to my knock, I went right in. He was seated, in his pajamas, on his bunk, staring straight ahead, shaking all over like a leaf. My entrance apparently did not dawn on his consciousness. Even when I spoke to him and tried to engage him in conversation, telling him that he had a perfect right to take the last boat, he paid absolutely no attention and continued to look ahead with his fixed stare . . . I have never seen a man so completely wrecked. Nothing I could do or say brought any response. As I closed the door, he was still looking fixedly ahead.[73]

*

Lady Rothes found relief in being useful, both in Lifeboat 8 and on the *Carpathia*. Four decades later, in her correspondence with an historian, she remembered, 'All on board the *Carpathia* were wonderful to us & there was a lot to do for the orphaned children . . . Of course I made various friends on the *Carpathia*. Capt. Rostron was a wonderful man. Also the ship's Dr.'[74] For others, like Dorothy Gibson, the voyage from the disaster site to New York was spent more quietly. After their lifeboat had reached the *Carpathia*, Dorothy was standing on the deck, still wearing the evening gown she had worn to her last dinner on the *Titanic*, when a couple approached her to offer their cabin for her use and her mother's. There, as Dorothy remembered it, 'I was so tired I slept twenty six hours.'[75] She emerged in time to see her former lifeboat companion Alfred Nourney unceremoniously hurled from his monopolisation of the blankets and to listen to the stories of other survivors.[76] Generally, however, she concentrated on trying to get a telegram through to her lover, Jules Brulatour. The *Carpathia*'s operator was under so much pressure that Harold Bride had hauled himself from the hospital to assist him with the flow of outbound and inbound telegrams. One of the few incoming messages that was directly answered was from President Taft, seeking information about Major Butt, to which the *Carpathia*'s Chief Purser authorised the terse reply, 'Not on board.'[77] Eventually, a telegram arrived for Dorothy, which Brulatour signed off with their shared nickname for him: 'Will be worried to death till I hear from you, what awful agony, Julie.' On the last day of the trip, Dorothy's reply got through: of 'Safe, picked up by *Carpathia*, don't worry, Dorothy' was received by Brulatour.[78]

With the approach to New York, some of those who had been emigrating on the *Titanic* tried to adjust to the horrible fact that most of their earthly possessions had been lost. Huddled on the floor of one of the dining saloons, an American passenger over-heard one immigrant say, 'I have nothing in the world and I have no place to go since my husband is lost. But I am not afraid. I have always heard that the Americans were the kindest people in the world.' Another suggested, 'Never mind, I never saw an American who didn't have a big heart. I am sure they will take good care of us.' In a letter penned a few days later, the lady listening to them wrote, 'I think I was never so proud that I was an American as then.'[79] Their faith seemed to be justified by a telegram received by the *Carpathia* stating that the requirement to disembark immigrants at Ellis Island had been waived for the *Titanic*'s survivors. The United States Commissioner for Immigration had also sent a handwritten note to the Secretary of Commerce and Labor announcing his intention to 'supervise the work of caring for them . . . This is likely to be a terrible night.'[80]

They arrived late on Thursday the 18th, in a torrential down-pour.[81] As the *Carpathia* approached the harbour, strange flares went off from the impromptu flotilla of small boats that had sped out to meet her; the flares were lit to help newspaper photogra-phers get snaps of the survivors lining the decks. One journalist even made it on board the *Carpathia*, using the rope ladder dropped for the harbour pilot, but he was apprehended and detained on the Bridge before he could question any of the survi-vors. Nearly 10,000 people stared in confusion as the *Carpathia* passed her designated pier 54 and steamed to the White Star

Line's pier 59, where she slowly, eerily unloaded the thirteen empty white lifeboats, returning them to their owners.* The *Carpathia* then returned to 54, where the crowd was swelling to 30,000. The Mayor of New York and the city's Police Commissioner had authorised a heavy police presence to control the curious. Mrs Virginia Fair Vanderbilt had persuaded her socialite friends to donate their cars to help transport survivors to wherever they needed to go in New York. The Municipal Lodging House, the Red Cross and the Salvation Army had already offered lodgings. Donations were pouring in to relief funds to help the immigrant survivors. The White Star had promised to pay for railway tickets for any third-class passenger to reach their final US destination or tickets on White Star ships back to Europe, if they preferred. Thirty-five ambulances had lined up near by, sent gratis from every hospital in Manhattan.[82]

The survivors were disembarked in order of class.[83] A weeping Dorothy and her mother Pauline flung themselves into the arms of Dorothy's stepfather, Leonard, who had joined the throng of worried relatives at the Cunard docks. Pauline's sister, Dorothy's agent, an actress colleague called Muriel Ostriche and several of Pauline's friends from Hoboken First Baptist had accompanied Leonard to the dock and witnessed the reunion. When a young porter approached offering to help them with their luggage, Pauline told him they had saved nothing, which prompted Leonard to give the boy a tip anyway, saying 'But they are saved, my child. Praise God!' He immediately took them away to a nearby hotel restaurant, to reunite with other friends. Muriel had brought a change of clothes for them.[84] Jack joined his mother, her maid and any surviving friends from their home county who had been offered a place on their private railway carriage, which took them home to Pennsylvania. In a telegram she had sent to make the arrangements, Marian had issued the instruction, 'Let anybody

---

* Damaged lifeboats and the collapsibles had been set adrift after their passengers were rescued by the *Carpathia*.

meet us but not children. My hope [is] gone.'[85] She still could not face breaking the news to her other children – fifteen-year-old Frederick, thirteen-year-old Margaret and eleven-year-old Pauline. Lady Rothes did not disembark with the other first-class passengers, instead opting to stay with Rhoda Abbott until the Salvation Army came to provide help and a home for her.[86] She then left with Gladys, Cissy and María-Josefa de Peñasco. They seem to have spent at least a night at the Great Northern Hotel, but within a day or two they had relocated to the Ritz, where they were reunited with Lord Rothes, who had travelled to New York upon reading of the *Titanic*'s sinking, and with Gladys's brother, Charles.[87] Their walk along the pier, away from the *Carpathia*, was an unpleasant one, through anxious relations and volunteer medical staff. For many, the worst part had been the journalists, who had even swarmed around the pregnant Madeleine Astor, trying to get her to confirm whether her husband was alive or not, despite the fact she was so overwhelmed she had to be helped into the car on her sister's arm.[88] The fashion correspondent Edith Rosenbaum, who disembarked with the other survivors, remembered for the rest of her life how 'the cannonade of flashes from photographers' lamps as we went into the street seemed a cruelly inappropriate thing'.[89]

20

Extend Heartfelt Sympathy to All

A lurking instinct in me says that they are right; all the bridges are broken between today, yesterday and the day before yesterday.

Stefan Zweig, *The World of Yesterday:*
Memoirs of a European (1942)

IN THE SUMMER OF 1914, JACK THAYER BOARDED A WHITE Star Line ship for the first time since jumping from the *Titanic*. The *Oceanic* had been one of the ships docked in Southampton on the day the *Titanic* set sail, moored alongside the *New York*, which nearly scuppered the voyage. Boarding in New York Thomas Andrews' first great project for the White Star Line, Jack discovered that one of the senior officers on board was Charles Lightoller, the officer who had helped lead his lifeboat to safety two years earlier. The two men had an opportunity to talk during the voyage and 'again went over our experiences and checked our ideas of just what had happened. We agreed on almost everything, with the exception of the splitting or bending of the ship. He did not think it broke at all.'[1]

It was a more tranquil crossing than some which had taken place in the immediate aftermath of the *Titanic* disaster. Five days after the sinking, first-class passengers on the German liner *Bremen* had been horrified when, from their promenade, they:

> could make out small dots floating around in the sea, a feeling of awe and sadness crept over everyone on the ship . . . looking down over the rail we distinctly saw a number of bodies so clearly that we could make out what they were wearing and whether they were men or women. We saw one woman in her night dress, with a baby clasped closely to her breast. Several women passengers screamed and left the rail in a fainting condition. There was another woman, fully dressed, with her arms tight around the body of a shaggy dog. The bodies of three men in a group, all clinging to one steamship chair, floated near by, and just beyond them were a dozen bodies of men, all of them encased in life-preservers, clinging together as though in a last desperate struggle for life . . . Those were the only bodies we passed near enough to distinguish, but we could see the white life-preservers of many more dotting the sea.[2]

Their captain rejected passenger requests to stop to retrieve the bodies on the grounds that the White Star Line had already chartered trawlers staffed by sailors, clergymen and undertakers to recover as many of the *Titanic* dead as possible. A day after the *Bremen*'s upsetting discovery, the first of those trawlers, the *Mackay-Bennett*, arrived from Newfoundland and retrieved 306 corpses over the next five days, 116 of which were in such a state of decomposition that they had to be buried at sea.[3]* She was then replaced by the *Minia*, which salvaged fifteen and buried two at the site, between 26 April and 1 May. The *Montgamny* found four and the last, the *Algerine*, found only one on 16 May. The *Oceanic* later discovered one of the abandoned, leaking

---

* There is no truth in the urban legend that the bodies of third-class passengers were simply thrown back in the sea. Bodies were buried at sea only if they were in a state of decomposition.

collapsibles – Collapsible A – with the bodies of two crew members and a passenger, a wedding ring and a fur coat. The three corpses had been people who had died shortly after fleeing the *Titanic* and had been left in the damaged boat when the living occupants were moved to another lifeboat before reaching the *Carpathia*. The bodies of two other victims, both stewards, were picked up by two other ships on 6 and 8 May. All five of those accidentally discovered bodies were buried at sea. A total of 209 bodies were brought back to the trawlers' native Canada, fifty-nine of which were claimed by relatives, include Isidor Straus's. Ida's body either had not been discovered or had been one of those that were never properly identified. If that was the case, then her remains lie in one of the anonymous graves in the Mount Olivet, Fairview or Baron von Hirsch cemeteries, the three Canadian sites that house the 150 unclaimed bodies. The south-drifting current also carried many of the bodies away from the original site and in total 1,159 of the *Titanic* dead were never accounted for.[4]

Perhaps fortunately for Jack's state of mind, in 1914 the *Oceanic* did not sail through the area where the *Titanic* had foundered. After the respective American and British inquiries, the recommended shipping routes had shifted south. The US Senate inquiry had opened at the Waldorf-Astoria Hotel in New York, the day after the *Carpathia* deposited the survivors. The fine impression created by this 'startling display of bureaucratic efficiency' in organising an inquiry so swiftly did not last, particularly among the *Titanic*'s crew who were called as some of the eighty-two witnesses.[5] Charles Lightoller and the other surviving officers had been increasingly contemptuous of the 'complete farce' of the American inquiry, reserving particular scorn for the admittedly curious decision to entrust it to Senator William Alden Smith, a representative for Michigan, a state which borders lakes but not the sea, and who asked a few nautical questions which the officers evidently felt were so staggeringly obvious that they were hard pressed to deliver polite answers.[6] One of Senator Smith's questions seemed to suggest that he did not know what a watertight bulkhead was, leading to certain sections of the British press nicknaming the Senator 'Watertight Smith' and mocking him for questions through which he 'betrays once more the amazing ignorance'.[7] However, although Lightoller painted the American inquiry as representing 'such a contrast to the dignity and decorum of the Court held by Lord Mersey in London', in reality both sets of inquiries reached broadly similar conclusions.*[8] Both were subsequently accused of whitewash for failing to indict any one responsible guilty party, both recommended twenty-four-hour wireless operation so that no ship could be so close to a disaster, as the *Californian* had been, and miss the radioed requests for assistance. They both demanded sufficient lifeboat provisions for all passengers, mandatory lifeboat drills at the start of a voyage so that there would never again be a disaster in which passengers, unsure of what to do, congregated for an impromptu concert in the first-class Lounge or waited to be given directions to the Boat Deck from the third-class General Room. The American inquiry recommended that rockets should never be fired at sea except for distress, largely to undercut the problematic claim by the *Californian*'s crew that they had not been aware of what the *Titanic*'s rockets signified. The internal height of watertight bulkheads should be raised because, although it was unlikely that higher bulkheads would have saved the *Titanic*, it might have marginally slowed the sinking; and in 1914, acting on the inquiries' findings, the International Ice Patrol was established as an arm of the United States Coast Guard, with funding from thirteen nations.[9]

Both the British press and the surviving officers were arguably too harsh in their criticisms of Senator Smith, except in their unease at what the *Daily Mail* had called his 'inflated rhetoric'. Nowhere had this been more apparent than in the Senator's treatment of Bruce Ismay. A lifetime of thinly veiled hostility towards the media and an unfortunate run-in with press baron William

---

* The British inquiry, chaired by John Bigham, 1st Viscount Mersey, met in London from 1 May to 3 July 1912 and published its findings on 30 July of the same year.

296

Randolph Hearst at a dinner party years earlier had left Ismay as an easy, desirable target for many American newspapers; those under Hearst's control took to printing Ismay's photograph with captions that changed 'Bruce' to 'Brute'. There were suggestions that the company's logo should be changed from a white star to a yellow liver; the *New York American* called Ismay's survival when so many had perished the act of a man who had crawled 'through unspeakable disgrace to his own safety'. Contemporary opinion in America was disinclined to feel sympathy for plutocrat or aristocrat, and Ismay seemed a lugubrious combination of both; that he had inherited his position from his father made him a perfect embodiment of the effete, entitled European, a curious mingling of the useless and the malign.[10] He had also made an error, although seemingly from honest intention rather than malice, in booking passage home on White Star's *Cedric* for the day after he reached New York, which he apparently did in the mistaken belief that since the *Titanic* had flown the British flag the only inquiry into the loss would be held in London.[11] To his growing number of critics, it looked as if Ismay had been attempting to flee.

He was helped neither by his own mistakes nor by others' mendacity. Some of the lies about him, like the claim from first-class passenger Mahala Douglas that Ismay had fled in the first lifeboat, seem to have been genuine errors. No such charity can be extended to the outrageous spite that motivated Mrs Charlotte Drake Cardeza's claim that she had personally witnessed Ismay depart in the first lifeboat, after hand-selecting the crew members to row him to safety.[12] There were stories of Ismay parading on the *Carpathia* and immediately shouting, 'I'm Ismay, for God's sake give me something to eat,' or 'I'm Ismay! I'm Ismay! Get me a stateroom!', which bear no relation to the behaviour reported by eyewitnesses on deck at the time. Initially, it seemed that his British compatriots would treat Ismay more kindly. There had been unease and then anger at how he had been handled by the Senate inquiry and revulsion at the tone adopted by the Hearst newspapers. Ismay was greeted with cheers from the dockside crowd who gathered to see him when he returned to England, Thomas Andrews' aunt Lady Pirrie had written in Ismay's defence, and at the subsequent Board of Trade inquiry Lord Mersey concluded that 'Mr Ismay [had], after rending assistance to many passengers, found "C" collapsible, the last boat on the starboard side, actually being lowered. No other people were there at the time. There was room for him and he jumped in. Had he not jumped in he would merely have added one more life, namely his own, to the number of those lost.' This conclusion was borne out by the most reliable accounts of Ismay's final moments on board the *Titanic*; there were, admittedly, discrepancies between various testimonies about whether it had been Captain Smith or Chief Officer Wilde, but several survivors recalled hearing someone order Ismay into the boat. What was almost universally agreed upon was that when Ismay stepped into the lifeboat, either of his own volition or on the orders of the Captain or an officer, there had been repeated calls for more women or children and since that particular stretch of deck had been relatively empty, there had been none near by, hence Lord Mersey's conclusion that if Ismay had stayed on the *Titanic* no other lives would have been spared in lieu of his own. Several female passengers and crew credited Ismay with saving their lives by urging them into the boats. One stewardess recalled a horrible incident where some officers and crew had ordered female crew members, who subsequently lost their lives, out of the boats in the final hour of the evacuation, while in contrast Ismay dismissed the protestation of 'We are only stewardesses, sir' and urged them into the lifeboats.[13]

However, the charitable attitude in Britain towards Ismay was neither universal nor enduring. His wife banned the *Daily Mail* from their homes after it offered a criticism of his conduct that was mild in comparison to the opinion expressed in the periodical *John Bull*, which called for Ismay to be executed for cowardice. A former friend closed the door in Ismay's face when he called on them and he was blackballed from his club. There were times when he would wake up his whole household with his screams from some nightmare, yet this private anguish was hidden by his public rigidity. There were tone-deaf statements, like the one issued to reporters upon leaving the *Carpathia*: 'The *Titanic* was the last word in shipbuilding. Every regulation prescribed by the British Board of Trade had been strictly complied with, the master, officers and crew were the most experienced and skilful in British service.' Whether that was true or not was beside the point. In the context of unprecedented losses at sea, it rang in the public's ears like a callous boast. Two of Ismay's servants, his valet Richard Fry and his secretary William Harrison, had drowned on the *Titanic*. It made Ismay's survival seem somehow more suspicious, while his insistence that he had done nothing wrong sounded heartless.

Ismay's wife also banned all discussion of the *Titanic*, hoping it would soothe the pain her husband felt. Despite the strained state of their marriage before the sinking, Florence had felt such a rush of relief at the news that Ismay had not been lost that she emerged determined to fix their relationship. Ismay, however, retreated from her and struck up an epistolary relationship with Marian Thayer. The crush he had developed for Marian on the *Titanic* seemingly blossomed after the tragedy into an infatuation. For her part, Marian had done her best to defend Ismay in America. It has been suggested here that in order to protect Captain Smith's posthumous reputation Marian fudged the timeline of his attendance at the Wideners' dinner party a few hours before the collision. Even those who had also been in the Restaurant and corrected her narrative, in letters to the Senate or in letters to, or interviews with, the press, did not suggest that Smith had drunk anything or dallied too long after coffee. It seemed in her zeal to correct the more outrageous charges against the departed, such as the tale that Smith had drunkenly steered the *Titanic* into the iceberg, Marian was quite prepared to massage the facts, often unnecessarily. In her biography of Ismay, Frances Wilson has persuasively argued that Marian may have mounted a similar campaign for Ismay by persuading her friend Emily Ryerson to omit from her affidavit to the Senate inquiry the information that, during their conversation with Ismay on the afternoon of Sunday 14 April, he had mentioned that more boilers were being lit over the next few hours to increase the *Titanic*'s speed. Judging, almost certainly correctly, that Ismay had been the recipient of that news, rather than the instigator, Marian felt the senators and the wider public would not properly understand the information and thus worked to have it withheld.

Marian's sympathy for the White Star Line's Managing Director was not shared or understood by many in her circle. Eleanor Widener may have disliked Ismay even before the disaster – it is interesting that when arranging a dinner in the Captain's honour she had not issued an invitation to Ismay, despite the fact that he also frequently dined in the Restaurant – but her attitude towards him lacked any ambiguity afterwards. When comparing Ismay to Marian's dead husband, Eleanor said, 'Better a thousand times a dead John B. Thayer than a living Ismay.' A distant relative of the Thayers, US Rear Admiral Alfred Thayer Mahan, was unmoved by the argument that the empty deck and half-filled lifeboat exonerated Ismay, since 'so long as there was a soul that could be saved, the obligation lay upon Mr Ismay that that one person and not he should have been on the boat'.

Yet in the weeks after returning to Pennsylvania, Marian suffered terribly and she felt that Ismay was one of the few people who understood her. Before he left New York on 5 May 1912, she had a telephone conversation with him in which she expressed the wish that she had drowned alongside her husband. She tried to fill her days – at the end of the month she journeyed to New York to attend a luncheon thrown by Madeleine Astor to honour the *Carpathia*'s Captain Rostron and Dr McGee. She gave both men golden cigarette cases and hosted a similarly themed dinner in Philadelphia. It did nothing to detract from the fact that she found herself a widow with four children in the most unexpected of circumstances and she poured those feelings out in her letters to Ismay, who was as entranced by Marian's gift for friendship, her capacity for sympathy, as the dead Major Butt had been on the *Titanic*. While she expressed her heartbreak in their letters, Ismay gave vent to the depths of his self-disgust: 'Of course one cannot hurt people without hurting oneself. Very often a word would make things right, one's horrid pride slips in and this causes unhappiness. I wonder if you know all I mean. I can hear you saying what a horrible character and I agree. I absolutely hate myself. Tell me what I can do to cure myself.'

Ismay had a masochistic streak, nurtured by his late father, who had habitually humiliated him in front of White Star colleagues. After the *Titanic*, he seemed to yearn for punishment. His letters to Marian shifted into agonising self-reproach, which she soon found uncomfortable and even unsettling. When she suggested that he should not isolate himself further but rather attempt to socialise more frequently, his response was, 'What do you mean by saying "don't lock yourself tight up?" When did you notice this was another of my failings? Do you know that I always put my worst side forward and very very few people ever get under the surface? I cannot help it, can you help me to change my horrid nature?' His half of the correspondence also took on an unambiguously romantic tone: 'My wife has gone to church and I am sitting writing to you by the open window, looking over the garden. Oh, how I wish you were here.'

His love, however, was never strong enough to trump his punctilious commitment to due process. When Marian began the process of filling in life insurance forms concerning her late husband, she decided to utilise her friendship with Ismay by asking him to use his influence at the White Star Line on her behalf. Like many socialites, Marian lived in a world of mutual favours, something which Ismay found objectionable. While he may have been comfortable with such attitudes when it came to offering the grieving Ryersons extra cabins on the *Titanic*, he drew the line at interfering in a legal matter:

I would do a great deal for you, and you know it, what you ask is impossible . . . I am deeply sorry for the loss you have sustained and of course I know any claim you put in would be absolutely right, but you must agree with me that all claims must be dealt with on the same basis now don't you?. . . You must not think me unkind or inconsiderate and I am satisfied that if you will think this matter over you will agree that I am acting rightly. Don't let us say anything more about this please.

It is tempting to suggest that, once he proved of no use to her, Marian discarded Ismay, yet the truth is that even before this she had felt uneasy about his reliance on her. In her letter of 18 June 1912, she had begged him not to confuse her hyperbolic expressions of friendship with a declaration of love. Falling back on the power of etiquette to convey the point subtly if firmly, Marian sent a letter of Christmas good wishes to Ismay's wife, followed by several polite letters addressed to Florence, while the frequency of her correspondence to Ismay decreased. 'Please,' he wrote to her with a mixture of patronising demand and despair, 'do not think a cable message is satisfying, you owe me at least two letters and they can't be cables.' When Marian returned to Europe in 1914 on the *Lusitania*, she did not visit Ismay and she deliberately allowed their friendship to wither. Even before the *Titanic*, he had been planning to retire from both the White Star Line and her parent organisation, the International Mercantile Marine, in 1913 and, when he briefly hesitated, it was made politely clear to him that his retirement was now required, rather than simply allowed. He donated $50,000 to aid the widows of the *Titanic*'s crew and in 1924 he founded the National Mercantile Marine Fund with a personal donation of $125,000. He lost part of his right leg to diabetes in 1936 and, following a stroke, died in October the following year. During his last Christmas, his wife's ban on discussing the *Titanic* was innocently broken by one of their grandchildren who asked if Ismay had ever been in a shipwreck. Apparently, he replied, 'Yes, I was once in a ship which was believed to be unsinkable.'[14]

After he reached Southampton in 1914, it does not seem that

Jack called on Ismay either. He had come 'to play cricket in and around London, on a Marion Cricket Club team', just as his father had when he was a young man.[15] Honouring the late John Thayer had shaped a significant number of Jack's decisions after April 1912 – he had abandoned his plans to apply to Princeton to enrol at the University of Pennsylvania, his father's former college, where he joined junior societies, social clubs and athletic associations and pledged the Delta Psi fraternity. In 1913, he started a courtship of Lois Buchanan Cassatt, whose grandfather had served as President of the Pennsylvania Railroad and moved in the same circles as the Thayers. The weather for his 1914 sojourn in England was perfect for cricket – a hot and dry summer. His games in London coincided with the Season, unofficially commencing with the Royal Academy Private View and the Chelsea Flower Show, at its new home at the Royal Hospital, Chelsea, where it had first met for the 1912 show, the one which Lady Rothes had missed for her trip to America. She and her husband did not miss the 1914 round of merrymaking, unknowingly the last of the Edwardian era, as they moved through concerts from the military bands in Hyde Park and St James's Park, nights at the Royal Opera House, tennis at Wimbledon, rowing at the Henley Royal Regatta, horses at Ascot and balls held in the great townhouses of the aristocracy, including the Royal Caledonian, co-organised by Lady Rothes, who was once again singled out for her beauty and the 'superb jewels' she wore when greeting guests alongside her fellow organisers, the duchesses of Sutherland and Roxburghe and the Countess of Strathmore and Kinghorne.* The 1914 Royal Caledonian was the largest it had ever been, with 2,000 guests; Lady Rothes returned to dancing the reels after sitting them out the previous year, for the first time since her marriage.[16] The Rotheses hosted garden parties for the Archbishop of Canterbury, with invitations extended to Lord Curzon, former Viceroy of India, and a former Liberal Prime Minister, the Earl of Rosebery.[17]

---

* The latter's youngest daughter was later Duchess of York, Queen Consort and then Queen Elizabeth the Queen Mother (1900–2002).

There was no repeat of the unpleasant incident that had occurred the previous Season when Lady Rothes had been at the Ritz in London 'dining out with some friends & not thinking or talking of the *Titanic* when I suddenly felt the awful feeling of intense cold & Horror that I associated with it all & I then realised the Orchestra was playing the *Tales of Hoffmann* which was the last music I heard played after dinner on the *Titanic* tho' until that moment I had quite forgotten this'.[18] In 1914, young daughters of privilege flocked to Vacani's School of Dancing in Knightsbridge to master the deep curtsey they were expected to give to Their Majesties at the formal presentation at Buckingham Palace, along with lessons in how to carry a court train while managing a bouquet and fan, to do it all gracefully, followed by memorising diagrams of the Palace's relevant rooms and which members of the Royal Family would be standing or sitting, and where.[19] The Season's polo at Hurlingham, Roehampton and Ranelagh had brought the Duke of Peñaranda over from Spain to show off his equestrian and sporting prowess.[20]

Some socialites kept busy, like the Marchioness of Londonderry, who was busy dispensing funds, patronage and, in her own words, 'beautifully packed bundles' of guns to hard-line unionist organisations in the north of Ireland, and the Duchess of Portland, who with less controversy yet no corresponding diminution of zeal threw herself into her work for the Royal Society for the Protection of Birds.[21] In southern Ireland, county Society in Kilkenny prepared to celebrate the marriage of two young members of the Ascendancy – Marguerite Connellan to her soldier fiancé, Richard Solly-Flood. Wedding gifts from local families, like the diamond and fire opal pendant from the Earl and Countess of Bessborough or the diamonds from Lord and Lady Donoughmore, had arrived, as had the bride's £200 wedding trousseau from London in time for the service at the Protestant cathedral in Kilkenny, with the Archbishop of Armagh presiding.[22] In the north, the turreted Thomas Andrews Memorial Hall in his home town of Comber was nearing completion, facing the same route a horse and cart driven by a Harland and Wolff employee had travelled two years earlier with a telegram to inform Thomas Andrews' parents that their son had been lost at sea.[23] It had been the first in an avalanche of correspondence received by Andrews' grieving parents and by his widow, who had agreed to open the Memorial Hall. Some of the condolences arrived from strangers who, having read of Andrews' fate in the newspapers, felt moved to tell his parents, as did one correspondent, 'I would be a proud and thankful woman if, when the day arrives for my son to face the portals of his life, I might have the joy of feeling he left behind him the unstained noble record of your dear son.'[24] Others arrived from relatives, including one bearing the heartbreaking conclusion, 'There is not a better boy in heaven.'[25] Members of the Ascendancy, including the Duke of Abercorn, wrote to the Andrews family to express their sorrow at the news and one in particular, the unionist politician Sir Horace Plunkett, persuaded the family to approve the writing of a short commemorative biography of Andrews by Ulster-born writer Shan Bullock. Plunkett himself would write the foreword. While there is no suggestion that Plunkett was not distressed by Andrews' death – his letter to Andrews' father four days after the sinking began with the words, 'No act of friendship is so difficult as the letter of condolence upon the loss of one who is near and dear' – his desire to memorialise Andrews sat alongside a political agenda. In his foreword, he attributed the biography's creation to a committee of men 'deeply interested in the great achievements of Ulster industry' and tied that cause to the life of Thomas Andrews who 'notwithstanding his noble end, [has] been represented as the plain, hard-working Ulster boy, growing into exemplary and finally the heroic Ulster man that we knew'.[26] Perhaps keener to paint a picture of the man, in the course of his research its author Shan Bullock visited the Harland and Wolff shipyards where he personally witnessed the grief of many of its employees. When news broke in Belfast of the *Titanic's* loss, men from the yard were seen weeping in the streets. During their ensuing shifts on Queen's Island, they composed songs about it – one of which ran, 'I lost the best friend that ever I had when the great ship *Titanic* went down,' and another, specifically about Andrews, which Bullock heard and transcribed:

> A Queen's Island Trojan, he worked to the last;
> Very proud we all feel of him here in Belfast;
> Our working-men knew him as one of the best –
> He stuck to his duty, and God gave him rest.[27]

These same men continued to work on Andrews' last creation, the *Britannic*, throughout the spring and summer of 1914, in time for her projected maiden voyage the following year. The *Aquitania* sailed from Liverpool as the new Cunard flagship, earning the nickname 'the Ship Beautiful' for her first-class interiors, and the *Vaterland* left on her maiden voyage from Hamburg to New York as the world's largest liner. In Russia, the Tsar's second daughter, the Grand Duchess Tatiana, made her Society debut at a ball thrown in her honour at the Anichkov Palace by her paternal grandmother, the Dowager Empress. Chaperoned by her father and free from the frivolity-aversion of her mother, who left early due to a combined attack of sciatica and antipathy towards her mother-in-law, the young Grand Duchess danced until 4.30 in the morning. The hostess was one of the most popular members of the Imperial Family and the guest of honour generally considered one of the most beautiful. In later years, the ball was judged the highlight of the St Petersburg Season.[28] Much as many survivors of the *Titanic* seemed to remember the final night of the voyage as the most splendid or contented of the trip, despite the fact that it was a Sunday, which meant it was in fact one of the quietest days of the trip, the European Seasons of 1914 acquired a reputation for unparalleled majesty that may perhaps have been endowed with hindsight by the fact that they were the last of the line.

The Vienna Bank Employees' Club gave a costume ball – the year before, ladies came dressed as balance sheets, thin men were encouraged to come as deposits, and the heavier male guests good-naturedly turned up as withdrawals – and on 25 June the Duchess of Hohenberg arrived at the spa town of Ilidža.[29] Two days later she was joined there by her husband, the Archduke Franz Ferdinand of Austria-Este, heir to the Austro-Hungarian thrones, and they used the town as their base for a series of official visits into the neighbouring city of Sarajevo.[30] A Belfast of the Balkans, Sarajevo was divided between two communities, those who wished to remain under Habsburg rule and those who hoped to unite with the independent kingdom of Serbia. On 28 June, while returning in their car from a civic luncheon, the Archduke and his wife were shot and killed by a Serbian nationalist. As soon as doctors had confirmed the couple's deaths, the empire's telegraph wires were shut down to ensure their three children did not hear the news from anyone except their aunt, who told them after dinner that evening.[31] The Hohenberg children had the unhappy distinction of becoming the first orphans of the First World War.

The Austrian government suspected, correctly, that the gunman had not acted independently, but had received backing from the highest levels of the Serbian government. The step from what is correct to what is sensible was taken with catastrophic ease when this allowed the hawks in Vienna to deliver an ultimatum, to the Serbian government and which they could not possibly agree to in its entirety without a de facto abdication of their country's independence. Apparently surprised that funding and facilitating the murder of Austria's next emperor could rebound upon them with negative consequences, Serbia appealed in a spirit of Slavic brotherhood to Imperial Russia, where public opinion generally remained sympathetic towards 'little Serbia'. Austria-Hungary asked for, and received, a promise of full support from its German ally, which prompted Russia to request the same from France, which Germany then decided to attack by marching through Belgium; in turn, Belgium's independence and right to neutrality had been guaranteed by the Treaty of London, which the United Kingdom felt called upon to honour. Following Germany's failure to leave Belgian territory, Britain declared war on 4 August. The assassinations at Sarajevo had tripped the wire of long-festering tensions between the Great Powers and to the surprise of millions of Europeans, including a worrying number of people involved in the highest levels of their governments, caused a continent-wide war.

The *Britannic* in service as a hospital ship during the First World War.

There was a general feeling that one should 'do one's part' for the war effort, which extended to the *Titanic*'s former operators who, despite their American ownership, proved their sincerity when they had promised a decade earlier that they would remain under British sovereignty. The *Olympic*'s fittings went into storage and she served as a troop transport for the next four years, while the *Britannic* became a hospital ship before she had ever completed a commercial voyage. As part of the Middle Eastern and then Mediterranean campaigns, the latter was on a return trip and thus mercifully sailing with comparatively empty wards when she struck a German mine on the morning of 21 November 1916 and sank near the Greek island of Kea with the loss of thirty lives. The largest ship built on British soil for the next twenty years remains, at the time of writing, the largest-known passenger ship on the seafloor. There was a hideous poetry in the fact that the first ship to sink on service in the First World War was the *Kaiser Wilhelm der Große*, the ship whose creation had inaugurated the race of the great liners and who ended her career by being scuttled by her own crew after a tussle with the Royal Navy off the coast of Africa. By the time the *Britannic* went down, the *Lusitania*, one of the last to remain in passenger service, had been torpedoed on a return trip from New York to widespread international condemnation. Another Cunard casualty, inflicted in the war's dying days, was the *Carpathia*, also struck by a German torpedo while off the southern Irish coast. Five lives were lost. She was no longer commanded by Captain Arthur Rostron, who had been promoted after 1912, and was then serving as commander of the *Mauretania*, which had also been reconfigured as a troop transport for the Royal Navy.

Just as she had on the *Carpathia*, the Countess of Rothes volunteered to serve as a nurse during the Great War and her husband went off to the Front. The happiness of their marriage had not diminished. In 1912, Lord Rothes had escorted her from the *Carpathia* to a suite he had reserved at the Ritz-Carlton, where he 'had every room banked with flowers' and they quietly observed their twelfth wedding anniversary the following day. A doctor had been summoned to treat the Countess for exhaustion and she had declined requests for press interviews, until she took the bait when a spiteful story ran that 'The Countess of Rothes is at the Ritz-Carlton under the care of a physician. It is not so much the exposure and the shock that ails her as the effects of her hard labor in pulling at the oars of her lifeboat.' She was as irritated by that poor reflection on her character as she was embarrassed by subsequent stories from survivors which described her as a heroine. She invited journalists to a series of interviews over the course of 22 April in a private lounge at the Ritz. She kept her composure throughout and made frequent reference to her maid's bravery. She confirmed that, in her opinion, the

Californian had been close enough to mount a rescue operation, turning to her husband during the interview to ask, 'I am a fair judge of distance, am I not?' To which Lord Rothes replied, 'Yes, you are.' At the end, when asked about the crew, several journalists heard the Countess's voice catch in her throat before she answered, 'Brave men all that stood back so that women should have at least a chance, their memories should be held sacred in the mind of the world forever.'[32] Her father later funded the establishment and staffing of a lifeboat, the *Lady Rothes*, based in the east Scottish town of Fraserburgh in 'thanks to Almighty God for the safety of his only child from the wreck of the *Titanic*'.[33] Back in Leslie, the local chapter of the Women's Unionist Association, of which Lady Rothes served as chairperson, organised an open-air celebration of her survival and by the time Lady Rothes returned to Britain in the summer of 1912 she hoped that the interest in her by both public and press had been satisfied. Her father's decision to fund the lifeboat rescue station bearing her name allegedly helped soothe the guilt she felt at failing to persuade other people in Lifeboat 8 to return to rescue those who had jumped from the *Titanic* in April 1912.[34] When the war came, she converted parts of Leslie House into wards and opened up the grounds to raise money for French and Belgian refugees, and military medical supplies. The 21st Earl of Rothes, her grandson, wrote later, 'My grandmother presided over a lot of garden party bazaars in the interest of the war. That sort of thing was at the centre of life in villages then, and held more importance than it does today. I remember meeting people, even years after her death, who said they recalled my grandmother's charming way with guests, her laugh and her knack for getting money for her charities out of the hardest-heart cases! "More tea?" she would ask, quickly followed by, "And you know you have got to pay for it!"'[35]

She was still serving as a nurse and fund-raiser when she received the news that her husband had sustained what *The Times* called 'a bad shrapnel wound to the leg' on the Western Front.

She helped care for Norman, who then returned to military service, from which he was released in 1917 after sustaining another wound, which cost him one of his eyes. While nursing her husband in London, Lady Rothes sent a message to her eldest son at Eton asking him to take the train back to Scotland to stand in for her at the opening of a fund-raiser for the Soldiers and Sailors Fund. In 1918, she also loaned to a jewellery exhibit some of the pearls she had worn when she escaped the *Titanic*. The ticket-generated proceeds of the event benefited the Red Cross, with the Rothes pearls displayed along with several pieces on loan from the Queen Mother Alexandra. It was to be the last grand public display of Rothes splendour. To meet rising wages, the cost of living and taxes, Lord Rothes had been selling off pieces of the family estates in Scotland since 1904, and by the time the First World War ended in 1918 he was no longer able to cope. When news leaked in the village that the Earl of Rothes planned to sell his patrimony, a delegation was formed to beg the family to stay, but the management of the estate and the realities of a changing world had gone well past the point where they could be ameliorated by good intentions. Leslie House and the adjoining lands were sold to Captain Alexander Crundall, who himself sold it several years later to a buyer who gifted it to the Church of Scotland who later sold it to a property developer.*[36] At their farewell supper in the Town Hall, which was followed by a parade, Lord Rothes told his former tenants that it had been 'a heavy blow to him to sever his connection to a property which had been in his family for many generations, and which has been his chief interest in life for the last fourteen years. The estate of Leslie, he regretted to say, was the last of the many properties which had been owned by his family in Scotland.' The family relocated permanently to

---

* In 2009, Leslie House was gutted by a fire which inflicted even greater damage than the inferno of 1763, almost completely destroying the interiors and leaving only the façade intact. However, at the time of writing, planning permission has been granted for the restoration of the house for its development into a residence with several private apartments.

smaller homes in England, where in the post-war world Lady Rothes kept up many of her former charitable activities and half hid her discomfort when her father's long-standing interest in Catholicism culminated with his conversion in 1924.[37]

The horrors of the First World War help explain, in part, the relative dwindling of interest in the *Titanic* after 1914. While the sinking retained the record as the worst single maritime disaster until 1945, the *Titanic*'s casualty list of just under 1,500 had been matched and then exceeded by the deaths caused in the first two hours of the Battle of the Somme.[38] All the memorial services held and the monuments erected for the *Titanic* dead in the days immediately after the disaster – the Requiem Masses ordered in every church in the archdiocese by the Archbishop of New York, Cardinal John Farley, the commemoration at St Paul's Cathedral in London, where a crowd of 10,000 had gathered outside and where Thomas Andrews' predecessor at Harland and Wolff, Alexander Carlisle, became so moved that he fainted, or the 6,000 New Yorkers who gathered outside Carnegie Hall for a service in memory of Ida and Isidor Straus – as beautiful as they had been, paled in comparison to the collective grief and trauma engendered by the Great War.

For families of those lost on the *Titanic*, private mourning continued while public interest dissipated. Thomas Andrews' widow, Helen, continued to live at their home for several years after her husband's death until she remarried in 1917 to Henry Pierson Harland, who also worked at the shipyard which bore his family's name. With Harland, Helen had four more children and she passed away at their Malone home in Adelaide Park in 1966.[39] Her daughter with Andrews, Elizabeth, nicknamed Elba in the family, outlived her mother by seven years, dying in a car crash just outside Dublin in 1973. She never married and became the first Northern Irish woman to gain her pilot's licence, which she put to use when she volunteered for service in the Second World War.[40] Her paternal uncles had also been active in the public life of Northern Ireland after it was partitioned from the south in

1921 – Tommy's brother James was created a baronet by George VI in 1942 and served as Lord Chief Justice of Northern Ireland from 1937 until his death in 1951. Their eldest brother, John, became leader of the Ulster Unionist Party and then Prime Minister of Northern Ireland from 1940 to 1943. It is from Pathé newsreels of John Andrews as Prime Minister that we can gain an idea of what Tommy Andrews' accent sounded like, which seems to have been relatively clipped in its consonants and with anglicised vowels, not too dissimilar to what was then common in most members of the upper and middle classes in south Belfast, county Society, and the northern parts of County Down.[41]

Ida and Isidor Straus's children and grandchildren encountered stories of their loved ones' generosity at unexpected intervals over the years, which was by turns painful and comforting for them. Ida's maid Ellen Bird had sought out their daughter Sara to return the fur coat Ida had given to her as she left the *Titanic*, an offer which Sara refused on the grounds that it had been a gift to Ellen from their mother.[42] In 1934, the family received a letter from a British clergyman, the Rev. H. H. Redgrave, who had been in communication with Isidor during his final stay in London. On 9 April 1912, the day before he and Ida boarded the *Titanic*, Isidor had been reading the *Daily Telegraph* over breakfast at Claridge's and was inspired to write to the Rev. Redgrave, 'I learn from the *Daily Telegraph* . . . of the dire distress you are attempting in aid in relieving in the Pottery Districts, with which my firm has been in business for almost half a Century. I ask you to accept enclosed order in the Manchester & Liverpool District Bank for Fifty Pounds to assist in the worthy work.'[43] It was a legacy that Isidor and Ida's family did their best to preserve. Donors from across New York had contributed to the foundation of a memorial park to Ida and Isidor Straus on the Upper West Side and their sons built a mausoleum at Woodlawn cemetery in the Bronx. Although Ida's body had never been recovered, Isidor's remains were moved to the Woodlawn after the mausoleum's completion in 1929. Both memorials to

Ida and her husband contained biblical verses – in the case of the Straus Park, from the lives of King David and Prince Jonathan, 'Lovely and Pleasant Were They in Their Lives, and in Their Death They Were Not Divided'.[44] At Woodlawn, Ida and Isidor were commemorated with a verse from the Song of Solomon: 'Many waters cannot quench love – neither can the floods drown it.'[45]

The Spinner of the Years

Over the lives borne from under the shadow of death there seems
to fall the shadow of madness.

Joseph Conrad, *Lord Jim* (1900)

The travel back and forth between Europe and America that had
formed such a part of their parents' year was again possible for the
Strauses' children and grandchildren once peace returned. To
compensate the shipping lines for their vessels lost in military
service, the Allied governments stripped the defeated Germans of
theirs. The *Imperator* became Cunard's *Berengaria*, the *Vaterland*
became the United States Line's *Leviathan* and the just completed
Bismarck was reborn as the White Star's surrogate *Britannic*, a new
Majestic. As American and British society continued to change and
diversify, those ships were spitefully nicknamed the *Bargain-Area*,
the *Levi-Nathan* and the *Ma-Jew-Stick* because of the number of
American Jews who, in the 1920s, had been able to rise quickly
from the poverty of immigration to the kind of prosperity once
enjoyed by the Strauses, and who now often travelled in First
Class.[1] In 1933, Ida's eldest son, Jesse, with whom she and her
husband had exchanged telegrams on the *Titanic's* last day afloat,
crossed the Atlantic again after his appointment as US Ambassador

to France, from where he was well placed to watch Europe's drift towards fascism. Like his father, Jesse Straus remained opposed to Zionism and he even initially remained uncomfortable with German Jewish organised opposition to the new Nazi government in Berlin, fearing that it would only lead to more trouble. Already weakened by cancer, he died of pneumonia in October 1936, before seeing where the ascent of fascism in his parents' homeland would lead.

Dorothy Gibson did not share the Strauses' worries about European fascism. Indeed, by the mid-1930s, she regarded it with approval. Her career was, of her own volition, long since over. After the reunion dinner organised by her stepfather when he escorted her and Pauline from the Cunard docks, Dorothy had picked up the little grey car she had spent so much time worrying about while the *Titanic* sank in front of her and drove it to a New York hotel where Jules Brulatour was waiting for her. The fright of nearly losing Dorothy had apparently spurred him genuinely to consider initiating divorce proceedings against his wife Clara, and at their reunion on 18 April 1912 he presented Dorothy with a diamond engagement ring worth, she estimated, about $1,000. His joy at her safe return had not, however, completely sedated Brulatour's business acumen. His company had been one of those benefiting from the cameras filming the *Titanic*'s survivors as they disembarked; he spliced the footage together with some of the *Olympic* and Captain Smith on the latter's Bridge, released it with *Animated Weekly*, an early American equivalent of the Pathé news-reels and owned by Brulatour, and even hired a *Titanic* survivor, third-class passenger Olaus Jørgensen Abelseth, to attend several showings, regaling audiences with his memories of the disaster. It may have been during this stint of employment that Abelseth, one of the alleged sources for the legend that third-class passengers had been deliberately locked below during the sinking, began to change his story, since he made no such claims in correspondence with his family in the days immediately after reaching America.

Dorothy was disseminating her own curious cocktail of half-truths, as she granted interviews to *Variety*, *Moving Picture News*, *Billboard*, the *New York Dramatic Mirror*, the *New York Sun* and the *New York Morning Telegraph*. Although she had left the *Titanic* in the first boat to be lowered away, Dorothy strongly implied that she had stayed on board for longer and witnessed more. In her interview with the *New York Dramatic Mirror*, she described how 'a panic broke out on the *Titanic* after the first boats left, and men had been shot to keep them from filling the remaining boats. The steerage had broken loose and swept things before them. The women who were saved after that owe their lives to the sublime heroism of the men among the passengers.' She dismissed the *Titanic*'s crew as 'wretched' and elsewhere waxed loquacious about their 'deplorable lack of discipline'. She fudged the details of her own behaviour immediately after the sinking, as much from concern for her reputation as from seemingly heartfelt guilt at how many lives had been lost by the lifeboats' refusal to return to those crying for help in the water. Sensing the tingling anti-Europeanism, the leaning among many American citizens towards cultural as well as political isolationism, Dorothy insisted that 'Europe offers no inducements now that can drag me away from the Western shore of the Atlantic.' She charmed some of the journalists who interviewed her, at least one of whom was impressed by her chutzpah when she announced at the beginning of their meeting, 'These aren't my clothes at all. I was fortunate enough to have a chum just my size who fitted me out as soon as I landed in New York. A white silk evening dress will do to escape in from a sinking liner, but it would look rather queer in the street in the afternoon.' The journalist who thought Dorothy was 'pretty and cheerful beyond the average lot' was amused when she then corrected her focus by announcing, 'But that is the wrong end of the story. Suppose we begin at the beginning.'[2]

Although Dorothy concluded one of her post-disaster interviews with the observation that 'the whole adventure was so unreal that it seems more like a story I have read, but I don't care to read any more like it', Abelseth was not the only *Titanic* survivor recruited by Jules Brulatour. He also wanted to utilise Dorothy's experiences for Éclair's benefit. Years later, Dorothy claimed that the idea to produce a movie based on the disaster, with herself as the star, had been hers. It is impossible to verify or dismiss that particular detail. What is undeniable was that production of *Saved from the Titanic* began only a few days after Dorothy left the *Carpathia*. The studio entrusted the task of directing the picture to Frenchman Étienne Arnaud, who had directed one of Dorothy's previous projects, *The White Aprons*; her boss Harry Raver served as producer, with Brulatour as a silent partner, and the storyline was allegedly provided by Dorothy, who preferred to insert a fictional romantic storyline, which had her falling in love with a handsome naval officer who, to increase the patriotic appeal of the movie, was presented as one of those who first heard the *Titanic*'s distress call, rather than the civilian wireless operator on the *Carpathia*.

Filming *Saved from the Titanic* was taxing for Dorothy. The studio had bought a decommissioned cargo ferry in upstate New

A promotional still for *Saved from the Titanic*, with Dorothy posing in the actual outfit she wore when she boarded her lifeboat.

York to stand in for the sinking *Titanic* and Dorothy, despite being unsettled when she first saw the set, offered to wear the exact same clothes she had worn on the night of the sinking. Several times she could be seen on set in her black pumps, white evening dress and long cardigan, shaking and crying. Her studio pumped a huge amount of money into the production which, as they had all predicted, was a runaway success. It hit cinemas just as the Senate inquiry into the loss of the *Titanic* was closing and Britain's was gathering momentum. Cinemas began to re-release Dorothy's earlier movies as part of double- or triple-ticket events. Initially, many movie-review magazines buzzed with accounts of the tragic quasi-autobiographical flick from 'a heroine of the shipwreck'. The *Moving Picture News* praised the movie's 'wonderful mechanical and lighting effects, realistic scenes, perfect reproduction of the true history of the fateful trip' and described it as 'magnificently acted. A heart-stirring tale of the sea's greatest tragedy, depicted by an eyewitness.' It was also a great commercial success upon its release later that summer in France and the United Kingdom.

Inevitably, *Saved from the Titanic* did not impress everybody. There had already been moral qualms over silent movies based on recent real-life traumas – the assassination of the Tsar's uncle in a Moscow bomb attack had inspired 1905's *Assassination of the Grand Duke Sergius* – but discomfort at the Romanov movie paled in comparison to the opprobrium generated in some circles by *Saved from the Titanic*.[3] In Britain, the *Spectator* thundered,

> The bare idea of undertaking to reproduce in a studio, no matter how well equipped, or re-enacted, sea scenes of an event of the appalling character of the *Titanic* disaster, with its 1,600 victims [sic], is revolting, especially at this time when the horrors of the event are so fresh in the mind. And that a young woman who came so lately, with her good mother, safely through the distressing scenes can now bring herself to commercialize her good fortune, is past under-standing.

As *Saved from the Titanic* delighted and divided, Dorothy ended her own moribund marriage with her Southern pharmacist husband, George Battier, while Jules once again began to drag his feet over his own divorce. Now, at the height of her career, Dorothy's ennui returned. Neither her holiday to Europe nor the success of *Saved from the Titanic* could restimulate her love for the movie industry and the *Titanic* film, which unfortunately for historians of cinema has since become one of the Silent Era's 'lost movies', was her last because she resigned from the Éclair studios later in 1912.[4] That summer, despite her assurances to the press that nothing could entice her back to decadent Europe, Dorothy sailed on the French liner *La Provence* for an extended, discreet vacation with Brulatour. Upon their return to the United States, she embraced her earlier love of singing, with Brulatour funding her professional singing lessons, which culminated with her moderately well-received debut at the New York Metropolitan Opera in 1915. Given how her short career in opera was to be traduced later, it is worth noting that the chorus, in which she first appeared, was singled out for its excellence by a reviewer from *Vogue*.

Less amenable press coverage had made Dorothy's affair with Brulatour a matter of public knowledge following her appearance in a New York court, where she was charged with a hit and run. She had been driving her grey car out of the city for a weekend in the Hamptons when her concentration lapsed, causing her car to mount the pavement where it struck a young married couple, killing the husband and seriously injuring the wife. The car she had been driving was a gift from Brulatour and had been purchased in his name. In one particularly painful exchange, a lawyer for the prosecution asked Dorothy, on the stand, if she was acquainted with Mrs Brulatour. Mortified, she eventually replied, 'No.' The ensuing scandal persuaded Clara Brulatour to initiate divorce proceedings herself. When these were finalised, Dorothy became the second Mrs Brulatour in a union that lasted until 1919, when it was dissolved on the grounds that Jules' first divorce had been applied for in Kentucky but never approved in New York. In reality, a wedding ring had staled Brulatour's passion for Dorothy. Anxious to limit the fall-out at a time when he was considering trading the movies for a career in politics, he offered Dorothy an extremely generous alimony payment, which she accepted before escaping yet more uncomfortable media attention by moving to Paris. She was joined, as ever, by her mother. There was an extended trip back to America in 1928 and a shorter visit, Dorothy's last, in 1933. Neither she nor her mother returned for her stepfather's final illness or funeral in 1938.

Dorothy Gibson, photographed in 1930.

Wealthy and still in love with what she had once called 'the pleasures of this lovely world', Dorothy divided her time between Paris and Italy, particularly Florence, where she took a villa. She enthused to a journalist about 'what a time I am having! I never cared much for motion pictures, you see, and I am too glad to be free of that work. I tell you it was an immense burden. I have had my share of troubles, as you know, but since coming to France, I have recovered from that and feel happy at last. Who could not be deliriously happy in this country? I have such fun.' In 1930, a Society columnist praised Dorothy as 'one of the smartest women arriving in the capital for the summer season'. Among her new friends were members of the Italian aristocracy and she attended parties where guests included another *Titanic* survivor, the couturier Lucy, Lady Duff Gordon, American expatriate socialites, Grand Duke Boris Vladimirovich, one of millions of Russians who had fled after the Revolution, and another exiled royal in the form of a Spanish prince. Five years after the deposition of King Alfonso XIII in 1931, Spain had slid into a civil war from which the ultra-conservative General Francisco Franco emerged victorious, inaugurating a crypto-fascist regime that endured until his death and the ensuing restoration of the monarchy in 1975. Dorothy's longest romantic relationship after Brulatour was with Emilio Antonio Ramos, an attaché at the Spanish embassy in Paris and a prominent Francoist. Ramos accompanied General Franco's brother to the 1937 Nazi Party rally at Nuremberg. Whether Dorothy went with Ramos on that trip to Germany is unknown and, although Ramos was privately unimpressed and unconvinced by Adolf Hitler, Dorothy's mother was enraptured. In her conversations, Pauline frequently embarked on 'a tirade of laudatory comments regarding Nazi concepts and actions . . . She expounded on her hatred of Jews and sympathy with Hitler's goal of a "permanent solution".'

Dorothy's modern biographer, Randy Bryan Bigham, has suggested that subsequent allegations made against Dorothy and her mother concerning their spying activities for fascist governments may be more plausible than slanderous. It seems unlikely that either woman ever passed on particularly useful information, but Bigham's theory is lent further credence by the research of the late Philip Gowan into the extremity of Pauline Gibson's political views and the contemporary suspicions of the British secret service, which closely watched the Gibsons' circle of acquaintances in Florence, where they were living when Italy entered the Second World War in June 1940. The following year, Dorothy was horrified to learn that the character of the talentless opera singer Susan Alexander, propelled on to the stage by her wealthy lover in the new Orson Welles movie *Citizen Kane*, was partly inspired by her, partly by Jules Brulatour's third wife and partly by William Randolph Hearst's long-term mistress, Marion Davies. Welles only ever denied the Davies comparison and the Hollywood gossip columnist Louella Parsons recalled him telling her that Susan Alexander was 'not so much about Hearst at it was old Brulatour and his sad gals'.

More pressing concerns arrived following the attack on Pearl Harbor and America's entry into the war against the Axis powers. Dorothy missed the train evacuating Americans from Florence because her mother's health collapsed. Unlike Pauline, Dorothy had come to regret her previous sympathy for fascism and befriended an anti-Mussolini journalist, Indro Montanelli, in 1943. In her days as an actress, Dorothy had gamely admitted to allowing her mother to organise her life. During the Second World War, she began to understand what a mistake that had been when she remarked, 'I have brought myself nothing but unhappiness and have perhaps completely ruined my life to do the best – as I thought – for my mother.' Yet, as Germany became the clear dominant partner in the alliance with Italy and as the Gestapo's presence in Florence increased, Dorothy once again passed on an opportunity for escape – this time to Switzerland – in order to stay with the ailing Pauline. In April 1944, her friendship with Montanelli and her changing political views caught up with her, when she received a tip that she was about to be arrested and transported to the Fossoli internment camp, from where thousands of Italian Jews were sent north to the German extermination camps. It was a system her mother had long applauded, and in 1944 it threatened to seize her daughter. Faced with the possibility of dying in a concentration camp, Dorothy fled, but German soldiers identified and detained her before she made it to the

Italian border with Switzerland. She was sent to the San Vittore political prison in Milan, where her friend Montanelli was also held. She described it as 'a living death. You can speak to no one – and if you try and are caught the punishment is awful.'

Cardinal Ildefonso Schuster, Archbishop of Milan, paid public lip-service to fascism while providing aid to the Resistance and it was thanks in no small part to him that Dorothy escaped San Vittore. A young priest, Father Giovanni Barbareschi, was assigned by the Cardinal to the mission which had Dorothy, Montanelli and another prisoner driven out of San Vittore with paperwork implying they were on their way to interrogation by SS officers, when in reality they were driven north to Switzerland. They walked the last leg of the journey, over what Montanelli called 'the blessed little hill that separated oppression and liberation', where Dorothy, sobbing, told Father Barbareschi, 'God has saved my soul and you have saved my life.' When interviewed decades later about his actions, Barbareschi was self-effacing: 'Consider that I was 22 years old at the time and what everyone calls heroic deeds were normal actions for young people. Although the risk was really great, I felt a deep need to help prosecuted politicians and my Jewish brothers, and to continue on the path to spread the values of liberty and democracy.' Father Barbareschi died, aged ninety-six, in October 2018, a recipient of honours from the Israeli and Milanese municipal governments and a few years after sharing his recollections of rescuing Dorothy from San Vittore with her biographer, Randy Bryan Bigham. Barbareschi was also a survivor of San Vittore since, a few months after helping her, he had been imprisoned there himself for helping a local Jewish family evade capture by the Gestapo. Apparently, in her determination to save herself, Dorothy had once again been economical with the truth. For decades, Father Barbareschi believed Dorothy had been related to President Franklin D. Roosevelt, a lie which apparently explains why the Cardinal and the Resistance believed her removal from Milan should be a priority before her prominence could be exploited by the Axis.

Father Giovanni Barbareschi, the priest who rescued Dorothy
from the San Vittore prison.

Away from Italy, Dorothy was exonerated from the suspicion
of espionage for the fascist powers by the US consulate in Zurich,
whose staff concluded that 'the accused hardly seems bright
enough to be useful in such capacity'. Her health deteriorated
and she was still unwell when she returned to Paris after the
end of the war in 1945. There, she took a suite at the Ritz and
was reunited with her lover, Emilio Antonio Ramos. There were
visits with her mother, who chose to stay in Florence, but Dorothy
admitted to Montanelli that she now found her mother's views
and prejudices difficult to understand. She did not, however,
update her will which had Pauline and Ramos as the chief beneficiaries, as they discovered when a long holiday to Lake Geneva
with Ramos to ease her cardiac problems failed and Dorothy
died of a heart attack in her suite at the Ritz in Paris on

17 February 1946, at the age of fifty-six. When asked years later about her, her friend Montanelli delivered eloquent evidence that affection need not always trump brutal conversational vigour, when he described Dorothy as 'stupid as a goat', 'very gullible' but with a 'big heart'. It was Montanelli who provided Dorothy with her last silver-screen appearance, of sorts, when his best-selling novel *Il generale Della Rovere*, based on his experiences at San Vittore, was adapted for the screen in 1959. Directed by Roberto Rossellini, the movie *Il generale Della Rovere* features a character named Clara Fassio, played by French actress Anne Vernon and allegedly inspired by Dorothy Gibson. Dorothy's mother, Pauline, died two years after its release and was buried next to her daughter at the Saint-Germain-en-Laye cemetery in Paris.[5]

Through her experiences in the San Vittore prison, the Second World War had indirectly killed Dorothy Gibson and the conflict arguably did the same to Jack Thayer. He had volunteered after American entry into the First World War in 1917, serving in the 79th Infantry Division on the Western Front. Speaking of her father's military carer, Jack's daughter Julie remembered, 'I don't think he talked much about it. Like he never talked about the *Titanic*. In those days, a man did not talk about his feelings. In fact, nobody really talked about emotions at all.' After marrying Lois Buchanan Cassatt, Jack became a banker, as he and his father had planned for him before the *Titanic*, and in 1937 he stepped down to become Treasurer and then Financial Vice-President of their alma mater, the University of Pennsylvania. He and Lois had six children together – Edward, John Thayer IV, Lois, Julie and Pauline (their son Alexander tragically died shortly after his birth in 1920). Jack's love for athletics did not diminish – he was apparently an excellent ice skater, became president of the local racquet club and joined the Rose Tree Fox Hunt. On the surface, this was a life of achievement and privilege broadly similar to his father's. Yet if Jack Thayer seldom spoke about the *Titanic*, it does not seem to have been far from his mind. His conversation with Charles Lightoller on the *Oceanic* in 1914 witnessed the two men rehashing, in detail, their memories of the sinking and in 1932, for the twentieth anniversary of the sinking, Jack wrote a short piece narrating his experiences on board for the *Philadelphia Evening Bulletin*.[6]

As he grew older, Jack increasingly came to feel that the modern world of terrifying changes and rapidly eroding certainties was somehow ineluctably tied to the tragedy he had witnessed with the *Titanic*. In 1940, he penned a short memoir, *The Sinking of the S.S. Titanic*, which was printed privately and distributed to family friends and interested acquaintances. It has since become one of the most beloved and trusted survivors' accounts of the disaster. It was Jack's fourth *Titanic* testimony – along with the 1932 article, he had made statements to some of his father's colleagues in 1912 and then, briefly, at a 1915 insurance hearing – and it is only by comparing all four that one is able to piece together the story of his escape. Those familiar with the 1940 account may notice that no mention has hitherto been made here of Thayer's recounting of a conversation, by turns chilling and moving, between his father and Thomas Andrews during the stage of the evacuation when passengers were congregating near the Grand Staircase and the first-class Lounge:

> It was now shortly after midnight. My father and I came in from the cold deck to the hallway or lounge. There were quite a few people standing around questioning each other in a dazed kind of way. No one seemed to know what next to do. We saw, as they passed, Mr. Ismay, Mr. Andrews, and some of the ship's officers. Mr. Andrews told us that he did not give the ship much over an hour to live. We could hardly believe it, and yet if he said so, it must be true. No one was better qualified to know.[7]

Not only is this report difficult to square with what multiple other eyewitnesses remembered of Thomas Andrews' movements that night – he had, for instance, not yet delivered the news to Captain Smith at the time Jack recalled him imparting it to the Thayers – but in his 1932 account Jack attributed the same conversation to Bruce Ismay rather than Andrews, after Jack had gone to the Swimming Pool and Mail Room, where he witnessed water 'coming in very rapidly', a dramatic claim which he did not repeat in the 1940 memoir. More glaringly, in the 1940 testament Jack described in detail his memories of boarding the *Titanic* with his family at Southampton and then of witnessing the near-collision with the *New York*, the name of which he misremembered as the *St Paul*. This was despite the fact that the Thayer party had boarded at Cherbourg and thus it was impossible for Jack to remember the moment the *New York* 'almost hit us'.[8]

In trying to explain this particularly baffling mistake, mention should be made of how preoccupied Jack had remained with the *Titanic*, despite seldom mentioning it in his conversations. His memoir contains a lengthy list of facts about the *Titanic*'s constructions, dimensions and passenger capacity, which would require a level of research beyond what a passenger might remember at the distance of a quarter of a century. Five years earlier, Charles Lightoller had, on his wife's advice, written his own autobiography, *Titanic and Other Ships*, in which he described the *New York* incident and also incorrectly gave her name as the *St Paul*.[9] It seems unlikely almost to the point of impossible that Jack Thayer's account of the *Titanic*'s departure from Southampton, which contains the same error of referring to the *New York* as the *St Paul*, was not influenced by his reading of the former officer's account. Elsewhere in *The Sinking of the S.S. Titanic*, it is clear that Jack had, over the years, been impressed and moved, and had his memories changed, by testimonies of other survivors and accounts of the sinking by historians. It speaks to years of sustained, inescapable and ultimately deeply damaging fascination with the night he lost his father.

He remained close to his widowed mother, although his children were less enamoured with their grandmother, whose grief at her husband's death conspired to push her interest in spiritualism into an obsession. Jack's daughter Julie later referred to Marian as 'a spooky old lady' and as a child she remembered that her grandmother 'kept all these books full of handwriting, mirror writing, which she believed came from her late husband's spirit. She thought she was in touch with him.'[10] To Marian, it would have seemed no coincidence that she died on 14 April 1944, the thirty-second anniversary of the *Titanic*'s collision with the iceberg. To Jack, it was simply devastating. Writing and recalling his time on the *Titanic* for his memoir had given voice to extremely painful memories and his mother died only a few months after Jack's son, Second Lieutenant Edward Thayer, was shot down and killed while on active service in the Pacific. The impact of that terrible event decimated Jack's already fragile mental health.

Ten of the *Titanic*'s survivors are known to have committed suicide. The first had been the Stewardess Annie Robinson, one of those whom Thomas Andrews spoke with during the loading of the lifeboats. A year after the sinking, she had been presented to King George V and Queen Mary during a royal visit to Liverpool where, on finding she had survived the *Titanic*, the 'very interested' King asked Robinson so many questions that she eventually had to violate etiquette by politely telling him that she found it too painful a topic to discuss for long.[11] A few months after that, Robinson was emigrating to Massachusetts to live with her daughter when her ship, the *Devonian*, entered a thick fog. The sound of the ship's whistle seemed to trigger something in Robinson, who walked up on to the deck and threw herself over-board.[12] On 18 September 1945, in Philadelphia, Jack Thayer became another of the *Titanic*'s suicides when he left his office at the University of Pennsylvania, drove to 48th Street and Parkside Avenue, smoked a cigar, removed a razor, slashed both his wrists and then slit his throat. His body was found in his car a few days later, with its hat still on. The depression which had taken their father to Switzerland in 1911 may have been hereditary, because in 1962 one of Jack's sisters, Margaret Talbott, also took her own life by leaping from her twelfth-storey apartment on New York's Fifth Avenue.

Within a few years of Jack Thayer's death, interest in the *Titanic* revived and expanded. 20th Century Fox produced a 1953 romance, *Titanic*, with Barbara Stanwyck as a millionaire's estranged wife returning to raise her children in America, away from European decadence. At the same time, a young author from Baltimore, Walter Lord, conducted impeccable research for his forthcoming novel, *A Night to Remember*. As a child in the 1920s, Lord had travelled to Europe on board the *Titanic's* only surviving sister, the *Olympic*. Back in commercial service after the war, the *Olympic* had continued her glittering career as one of the most successful transatlantic liners, until the Great Depression knocked the bottom out of the industry and the *Olympic* herself was among many older ships that were retired and scrapped, in her case in 1935. The British government had encouraged the two old rivals to merge as the Cunard-White Star, presenting a united front to the challenges of the Depression. As a compromise, they abandoned their respective traditions of naming their ships with names ending in *-ia* or *-ic*, which is how the *Queen Mary* came into being in 1936. There was, however, no question of who was the dominant partner, given the Cunard red used to paint the new flagship's funnels. The suffixed White Star was quietly dropped by the company in 1949. With White Star gone and the survivor roster dwindling with the passing years, Lord's desire to write an accurate account of the sinking led him to contact many of the remaining survivors, including the Dowager Countess of Rothes.

Lord Rothes had died in March 1927.* The wounds he received in the war contributed to his early death a few months before his fiftieth birthday. Having lost Leslie House, the Dowager Countess also lost the expected inheritance of her childhood home at

---

* Despite her remarriage, Lady Rothes continued like many aristocratic widows to use her title from her first marriage.

Prinknash Park when her father, following his conversion to Catholicism, willed the entire estate to the Benedictines, hoping to right the historical wrong he felt had been inflicted when Henry VIII confiscated the monastery from the order in the 1530s. Lady Rothes and her mother had attempted to halt Thomas Dyer-Edwardes' bequest, yet both the Countess's husband and her eldest son felt it would be wrong to go against Thomas's final wishes and the Order took control of Prinknash again in 1928. A relic followed with them in the form of the bones of Richard Whiting, the beatified abbot who had been martyred in 1539 for his refusal to surrender his monastery to Henry VIII's commissioners. Whiting's bones and the Benedictine brothers are still at Prinknash, now Prinknash Abbey.

Only a few months after Lord Rothes' death, his widow married a long-standing family friend, Colonel Claud Macfie, and the couple spent much of their time at Fayre Court, his country house in her home county of Gloucestershire. If it lacked the passion of her first marriage, it had all of the friendship. It was a comfortable and apparently happy union that lasted for the next thirty years. The Dowager Countess was close to her two sons and remained active with the Red Cross. When Walter Lord contacted her, asking if she would mind answering some of his questions about the *Titanic*, she was in her seventies and suffering from heart trouble. Her reply to Lord began with an apology for her tardy response, explaining that she had been in hospital. As with Jack Thayer, the Dowager Countess's account contained one or two errors, mainly in her brief confusion over a conversation with the Captain and the words used to her by Purser McElroy.* Apart from that, her correspondence with Walter Lord is to the point and only occasionally interrupted by apologies for anything she considered potentially irrelevant or dull. She told him of how she had kept

---

* Admittedly, this was nothing compared to Cissy Maioni's lapses in memory. In 1926, she had won an essay-writing competition for the *Daily Express* with an account of her time as a first-class passenger on the *Titanic* and omitted to reveal that she had been travelling as a lady's maid.

María-Josefa de Peñasco in her care in America until her relatives could make the journey from Spain to collect her, and in gratitude María-Josefa's 'father sent me a most wonderful letter later & a lovely sapphire ring, which I always wear'. Unlike her husband's cousin and her friend, Gladys, who had detested the media's intrusiveness after the *Titanic*, Lady Rothes had kinder memories of the press, after her meeting with them at the Ritz to answer their questions about the sinking. She revealed that she had maintained her friendship with Able Seaman Thomas Jones since 1912; she had sent him a silver pocket watch and he had removed the number-plate from their lifeboat to give to her as a token of his admiration for her bravery that night. He had framed it for her and sent it with the accompanying note:

My Lady,

I beg to ask your acceptance of the number of my boat from which you were taken on board SS Carpathia.

This number is the original taken from the boat by myself. In asking you to accept the same I do so in respect for your courage under so terrifying circumstances.

Trusting you are now fully recovered to health, I am,

Your obedient servant,

Tom Jones AB Late SS Titanic

Despite answering Lord's questions, the Dowager Countess was unsure of how useful her recollections would be or why interest in the *Titanic* was reviving: 'I am afraid this is a terribly long & discursive letter & may not be at all what you want. I have of course many newspaper accounts, some not very accurate, but the Press were very kind to us & I much appreciated their consideration. Can you tell me anything more about yr. book & the reason you are interested in the *Titanic* disaster?' She signed it off with 'every good wish' and a brief postscript praising the *Carpathia's* captain and doctor. She died at her country house at Hove in Sussex, aged seventy-seven, on 12 September 1956, a few months after publication of *A Night to Remember* but before the acclaimed film adaptation of the same title. It was assumed by journalists and historians, although unconfirmed publicly by the family, that the Countess's body was taken north to rest at the Leslie family mausoleum near their former home, while her second husband erected a memorial plaque to her in the church of St Mary, Fairford, the pretty fifteenth-century parish church where Noëlle had been an active member of the congregation since moving to the village; it commemorated her as 'the Widow of the 19th Earl of Rothes, and Beloved Wife of Col. Claud Macfie D.S.O. of Fayre Court, Fairford, At Rest 12 Sept. 1956. Holiness is an infinite compassion for others. Greatness is to take the common things of life and walk truly among them. Happiness is a great love and much serving.' Her grandson, the 21st Earl, remembered her for her wit, strength of character, devout Christian faith and 'warm understanding of humanity'.[13] It was, however, the Countess's association with the *Titanic* that kept her name alive. *A Night to Remember* was one in a long series of dramatisations of the disaster and interest surged again upon the discovery of the shattered wreck in 1985. Submariners who braced themselves for hundreds of bodies were, however, relieved if confused to find none. Conditions on the Atlantic floor had preserved some of the *Titanic*'s material, its half-shattered chandeliers, the Turkish Bath's tiles, unopened bottles of champagne, even the hat of a first-class passenger still resting on its bedpost, but the same conditions had rotted away the bones of its victims entirely. It was only when one observer spotted many matching pairs of shoes in the debris field, some with their laces still tied, that they realised they had found where some of the *Titanic*'s dead had come to rest.[14]

*

In the immediate aftermath of the *Titanic*'s sinking, Christian homilies, sermons and reflections on the disaster frequently pointed both to the heroism or piety of many on board and to the moral issues which, they felt, were highlighted by the catastrophe. For some, the latter clearly pointed to the sins of materialism – a sermon, delivered in New York by Rev. Dr Charles Pankhurst, warned, 'Grand men, charming women, beautiful babies, all became horrible in the midst of the glittering splendor of a ten million dollar casket!' More, however, saw the *Titanic* as illustrative of human arrogance and several secularly minded observers felt the same way, for whether one viewed nature as an independent, powerful, impersonal agent or as the strong arm of God, it seemed clear that in the *Titanic* man's confidence, to the point of arrogance, had hurled itself against nature and, as always in a contest between the two, the former had lost spectacularly. Preaching in Southampton in the aftermath of the disaster, Edward Talbot, the newly appointed Bishop of Winchester, reflected, '*Titanic*, name and thing, will stand as a monument and warning to human presumption.'[15]

It has been argued here that of the many myths which have attached themselves to the *Titanic*, and the new ones yet to be conjured, which seek to explain why she sank – inferior steel, subpar rivets, malign capitalist conspiracy, dire boiler-room conflagrations – all, in their way, are inadequate, incorrect or in some cases utterly divorced from reality. At every stage of her construction and her voyage, the *Titanic* marched in step with her age. The disaster was the fault of everybody and thus, potentially, of nobody. She was one of the best-built ships of the era; she actually exceeded the (ludicrously low) lifeboat requirement for ships of her size and, even if she had carried enough for her passengers and crew, they likely would have made no difference to the death toll. Officers, crew and volunteering passengers were still struggling to free collapsibles when the *Titanic* began her final plunge.[16] There was insufficient time to launch the few lifeboats the *Titanic* had. The only aspect of her management that contributed shamefully and disastrously to her fate was the speed with which she ran, despite the number of ice warnings she had received. Although some contemporary observers pointed out that it was standard practice to run liners at speed through any obstacle save fog, there were plenty who were stunned by Captain Smith's failure to slow down on Sunday 14 April. The American Rear Admiral French Ensor Chadwick, who wrote in to the *New York Evening Post*, was almost completely correct when he concluded that 'the *Titanic* was lost by unwise navigation, by running at full speed'.[17] It is hard to disagree with the pained, confused queries of Gladys Cherry in the letter she wrote to her mother from the *Carpathia*: 'Isn't it awful? Why did we go at that pace when they knew we were near ice bergs?'[18]

In the eleventh century, Harald Hardrada, King of Norway, hoped to prove the seafaring might of his country, to which end he allegedly commissioned a fleet of ships to explore 'the expanse of the Northern Ocean'. This fleet set sail in 1040 and soon passed, in a chronicler's words, 'beyond the limits of the land'. It sailed north, until staring out over pack ice, some of it up to 10 feet thick, the King and his expedition halted. At the sight of the field ice, the story had Harald writing, 'There lay before our eyes, at length, the darksome bounds of a failing world,' and he gave the order to abandon the mission on the grounds that no man could overcome such obstacles put in their way by nature and he must bow to forces he could not defeat.[19] For those inclined to pillage the *Titanic* for lessons, one of the most frequently cited is modernity's failure to heed warnings of the power of nature. For others, like Jack Thayer, the disaster had been the harbinger of a collective shattering, a horrible prologue to an ensuing age of instability. Undoubtedly, Jack's memories of the Edwardian age were shaped in part by his privileged position within that society, by his youthfulness in 1912 and by the horrors that had followed in the decades after it:

I want to emphasize some of the everyday conditions under which we were then living, to show how much humanity was shocked by the approaching disaster.

These were ordinary days, and into them had crept only

gradually the telephone, the talking machine, the automobile. The airplane due to have so soon such a stimulating yet devastating effect on civilization, was only a few years old, and the radio as known today, was still in the scientific laboratory . . . The safety razor had just been invented, and its use was gradually spreading. Upon rising in the morning, we looked forward to a normal day of customary business progress. The conservative morning paper seldom had headlines larger than half an inch in height. Upon reaching the breakfast table, our perusal of the morning paper was slow and deliberate. We did not nervously clutch at it, and rapidly scan the glaring headlines, as we are inclined to do today . . . These days were peaceful and ruled by economic theory and practice built up over years of slow and hardly perceptible changes. There was peace, and the world had an even tenor to its ways.

He continued:

True enough, from time to time there were events – catastrophes – like the Johnstown Flood, the San Francisco Earthquake, or floods in China – which stirred the sleeping world, but not enough to keep it from resuming its slumber. It seems to me that the disaster about to occur was the event, which not only made the world rub its eyes and awake, but woke it with a start, keeping it moving at a rapidly accelerating pace ever since, with less and less peace, satisfaction, and happiness.

Today the individual has to be contented with rapidity, of motion, nervous emotion, and economic insecurity. To my mind the world of today awoke April 15th, 1912.[20]

Jack Thayer's assessment can of course fairly be accused of gross exaggeration, in seeing the *Titanic* as a cause rather than simply a reflection of the changes that would end the Edwardian era.

His was the most moving of such exaggerations, yet it was by no means the last. One of the most palpably absurd distortions of the disaster's historical importance was the claim made by one maritime historian that it was 'so shattering, so demoralizing that it was looked upon as the beginning of the end of the British Empire'.[21] Truthfully, the *Titanic* disaster had no real political impact, beyond perhaps mildly exacerbating resentment in certain left-wing circles against the wealthy. The story that the steerage passengers were deliberately prevented from having a fair chance at escape fuelled, but did not create, a conspiracy-heavy view of social relations on the eve of the First World War. In 1912, the recently formed British Seafarers' trade union had seen in the *Titanic* proof that 'The ruling class rob and plunder the people all the time, and the Inquiry has shown that they have no scruples in taking advantage of death and disaster. Who needs sharks?'[22] Yet socialist criticism of societal inequality and tensions between conservatism and radicalism had existed for decades before 1912.

Its true significance was what the *Titanic*'s survivors and contemporaries endowed it with and which we continue to bestow upon it. Its Edwardian sobriquet of 'the ship of dreams' has become true, if transmogrified, by her century-long fame. The *Titanic* remains a story from which we can extract lessons on hubris, folly, greed, love, class, magnificent courage and pitiable weakness. The iceberg that pierced her gave her an immortality that no other ship, no matter how large or luxurious, can ever hope to emulate. It does not matter that the *Titanic* is now rotting away 2½ miles beneath the Atlantic swell, consumed by rare marine bacteria that feed on the iron ore in her hull. She is one of the greatest examples in history of the convergence of the twin forces of fate and free will, of circumstance and human decisions.

GLOSSARY

Able Seaman   A crew member with more than two years' experience, who is considered well acquainted with his duties

Aft   Towards the stern

Amidships   The middle section of a ship

Bosun   A crew member who oversees equipment and other crew members

Bow   The forward section of a ship

Breakwater   A barrier built to protect a harbour or stretch of coast from strong waves

Bridge   A forward-facing platform, typically enclosed, which houses most of a ship's navigation instruments

Bulkhead   A partition wall in a ship's interior

Crow's Nest   A ship's lookout post, usually positioned near the top of the forward mast

Davit   A curved on-deck crane used for the raising and lowering of lifeboats. This was manually operated on the *Titanic*

Double Bottom   Two complete layers of watertight hull surface

Ensign   A national flag, as it is flown at sea. Some countries, like the United Kingdom, have a variant of their usual flag that serves as their ensign

Fireman	On board, a crew member attached to the Engine Department tasked with monitoring the boiler fires and their steam pressure
Forecastle	Sometimes pronounced 'foke-sil' by crew members, it is the section of deck ahead of the forward mast
Foremast	The forward mast
Galley	A ship's kitchen
Morse Light	An electric light on open deck used for the transmission of Morse Code to other ships
Poop Deck	Exterior deck at the stern
Port	Facing forward, the left side of a ship
Quartermaster	A petty officer who steers the ship
Rivet	An iron or steel pin used to hold together plates of metal in the ship's hull
Rudder	A device at the stern used for steering
Starboard	Facing forward, the right side of a ship
Stern	Towards the back end of a ship
Surgeon	On ship, the equivalent to a doctor
Well Deck	A space of open deck lying on a lower level between the Forecastle and Poop decks

ACKNOWLEDGEMENTS

My friend and agent, Brettne Bloom, has been a tireless champion of this project since we first discussed it in 2015. It would not have been possible without her, nor my wonderful editors, Arabella Pike and Trish Todd, who have my sincere gratitude, as does everyone who worked on *The Darksome Bounds of a Failing World* in London and New York.

My thanks to the staff at Claridge's Hotel, London; the Belfast *Titanic* Society; the Bodleian Library, Oxford; the Hotel Savoy, Florence; the Linen Hall Library, Belfast; the New Jersey State Archives; the Mariners' Museum and Park, Newport News, Virginia; the McClay Library, Belfast; the Public Record Office of Northern Ireland; the *Queen Mary* Hotel, Long Beach, California; the Straus Historical Society; the Varsity Hotel, Cambridge; the Victoria and Albert Museum, London; the Titanic Hotel, Belfast; and the *Yale Daily News*.

The *Titanic*, her victims and her sister ships have inspired a rich world of interest and research from which I have benefited and been inspired. Colleagues, professionals and academics who graciously lent their time were Joan Adler, Executive Director of the Straus Historical Society, Gavin Bell, Mark Chirnside, Fiona Fisher, Charles A. Haas, President of the *Titanic* International Society, Iain Hunt, Daniel Klistorner, Raymond Lepien, the Hon. Alexander Leslie, Fiona Leslie and the Clan Leslie Charitable Trust, Don Lynch, Tom Lynskey, Samantha McCombe, John McDonald,

ACKNOWLEDGEMENTS

Dr Aidan McMichael, Chairman of the Belfast *Titanic* Society, Rich Turnwald, Jeanne Willoz-Egnor and Angela Young. Adrienne Dillard, my first reader, is an indefatigable *Titanic* enthusiast and equally well informed. The same is true of Randy Bryan Bigham and Mike Poirier, whose friendship and time were provided in equal measure as we discussed the *Titanic* and theories surrounding her into the small hours. The world is finer for the likes of all three.

It was from my family that I first heard stories of the *Titanic* and although the great-grandparents who saw and remembered the ship have passed, my parents, my grandparents Iris and Richard, my sisters, my great-uncle Ivan and my cousin June have all helped with queries, memories and encouragement. My love and thanks to them and to friends who helped in different ways along the road to this book's completion – Olivia, Jessika and Jonathan Auerbach, Kelly and Evan Branfman, Cailum Carragher, Charles C. W. Cooke, Mimi Cossitt, Scott De Buitléir, Jake Douglas, Mary Flanigan, Claire Handley, Theodore Harvey, Rafe Heydel-Mankoo, Debra Hill, Sarah Houghton, Janice and the Rev. James Hyndman, Dan Kelly, Rebecca Lenaghan, Dr Hannah and Dr David McCormick, Ashley Montgomery, Olivia Moore and Scott Naismith, the current Headmaster of Methodist College, Belfast, who fielded questions about the school's Edwardian-era uniform colours and crests, Ryan Nees and Eric Spies, Coco, Deonne, Jeff and Mary Tate Pannell – and Deonne's impromptu Book Club in Columbia, Tennessee, who were the first to be kind enough to listen to a section of this book read aloud and then took me out for lashings of the best of Southern hospitality afterwards – David Paulin, Patrick Quinn, Will Reid, Kerry Rogan, Lady Susie Sainsbury, Davi Santos, Antonia Sebag-Montefiore, Alexa Reid Smith, David Storrs, Paul Storrs and Laura and Tom Woodward, as always. Lastly to Emerald Fennell, who was the first to suggest I write a book about the *Titanic* provided it contained a character called Jack.

Gareth Russell,
Belfast,
Christmas 2018

NOTES

Abbreviations

B – A document number for primary sources reproduced in George Behe, *On Board RMS Titanic: Memories of the Maiden Voyage* (Stroud: The History Press, 2017).

LMQ – From the Lord-Macquitty Collection at the National Maritime Museum, Greenwich.

PRONI – The Public Record Office of Northern Ireland.

SHS – The archives of the Straus Historical Society.

TRNISM – Transcripts of letters, newspaper extracts and reports regarding the *Titanic* from the collections of Thomas Henry Ismay and Joseph Bruce Ismay at the National Maritime Museum, Greenwich.

The Inquiries

Both inquiries into the *Titanic* disaster have been digitised and can be found at Titanicinquiry.org.

For the printed version of the American inquiry, see *Report of the Committee on Commerce, United States Senate, Pursuant to S. Res. 283, Directing the Committee on Commerce to Investigate the Causes leading to the Wreck of the White Star Liner 'Titanic'*, Report No. 86 (Washington DC: Government Printing Office, 1912).

For the printed version of the British inquiry, see *British Wreck Commissioner's Inquiry: Report on the Loss of the 'Titanic' (s.s.)* (London: His Majesty's Stationery Office, 1912).

Author's Note

1 Tad Fitch, J. Kent Layton and Bill Wormstedt, *On a Sea of Glass: The Life and Loss of the RMS Titanic*, 3rd edn (Stroud: Amberley, 2015), p. 269.

2 John Roach, 'Titanic Was Found During Secret Cold War Navy Mission', *National Geographic*, 21 November 2017.

3 This was the Hamburg-Amerika Line's *Imperator* which, after the First World War, was requisitioned by the British government who gave it to the Cunard Line, where she was renamed *Berengaria*.

4 Second-class passenger Imanita Shelley in the *Anaconda Standard*, 6 May 1912 (Courtesy of the Mike Poirier Collection).

5 Mark Chirnside, *RMS Olympic: Titanic's Sister*, 2nd edn (Stroud: The History Press, 2015), pp. 65–8.

6 John Malcolm Brinnin, *The Sway of the Grand Saloon: A Social History of the North Atlantic*, 2nd edn (New York: Barnes & Noble Books, 2000), pp. 398–9.

7 Diana Preston, *Wilful Murder: The Sinking of the Lusitania* (London: Corgi Books, 2003), pp. 381–2.

8 Jeffrey Richards, *A Night to Remember: The Definitive Titanic Film* (London: I. B. Tauris, 2003), pp. 11–12.

9 *The Independent Exhibitors Film Bulletin*, 16 July 1938; Professor Charles Barr, 'Hitchcock's *Titanic* Project', filmed lecture for the British Film Institute, 11 April 2012; Mark Glancy, 'The Titanic: Three Films', *History Extra*, 12 April 2012. *Atlantic* was shot with an English and then German-speaking cast, by the same director, a standard movie-making procedure until the advent of dubbing.

10 David Welch, *Propaganda and the German Cinema, 1933–1945* (Oxford: Oxford University Press, 1983), p. 325.

11 Brian Hawkins, 'Titanic's Last Victim', *National Post*, 14 April 2012.

12 Welch, *Propaganda and the German Cinema*, p. 270; *CQD Titanic* magazine, no. 54 (Glengormley: The Belfast Titanic Society, 2016).

13 Welch, *Propaganda and the German Cinema*, p. 279.

14 Robert P. Watson, *The Nazi Titanic: The Incredible Untold Story of a Doomed Ship in World War II* (Cambridge, MA: Da Capo Press, 2017), Appendix I, 'Why Did the Nazis Load Prisoners on the Ship?', pp. 239–44.

15 Violet Jessop, *Titanic Survivor: The Memoirs of Violet Jessop, Stewardess*, ed. John Maxtone-Graham (Stroud: The History Press, 2010), pp. xxix–xxx.

16 Logan Marshall, *The Sinking of the Titanic and Great Disasters* (New York: L. T. Meyer, 1912), pp. 221–2.

17 Depending on the allocation of a bloc of cabins interchangeable between First and Second Class, her elder sister ship, the *Olympic*, sometimes had marginally more of her 1911–12 capacity set aside, as a percentage, for her first-class passengers.

Chapter 1: *The Lords Act*

1 It is now generally accepted that James V, King of Scots, was not the author of the poem. However, in 1910 the story that he was, and that he had written about Leslie, was still current.

2 Randy Bryan Bigham, 'A Matter of Course', *Encyclopedia Titanica* (April 2006).

3 *Sketch*, 25 April 1900; the British Census of 1911 gives the future Countess's date of birth as 25 December 1878.

4 Bigham, 'A Matter of Course'.

5 The Hon. Lilah Wingfield, daughter of the 7th Viscount Powerscourt, quoted in Jessica Douglas-Home, *A Glimpse of Empire* (Norwich: Michael Russell Publishing, 2011), p. 6.

6 *The Sketch* cited in Bigham, 'A Matter of Course'.

7 Bigham, 'A Matter of Course'.

8 Jerome Blum, *The End of the Old Order in Rural Europe* (Princeton, NJ: Princeton University Press, 1978), p. 420.

9 *Washington Post*, 16 May 1900.

10 *Bystander*, 27 November 1907.

11 *Scotsman*, 31 March 1927.

12 Lucinda Gosling, *Debutantes and the London Season* (Oxford: Shire Publications, 2013), pp. 49–50.

13 Bigham, 'A Matter of Course'; *The Times*, 10 April 1919.

14 Her younger sister, Princess Victoria (1868–1935), had never married and their youngest, Maud (1869–1938), married the future King Haakon VII of Norway.

15 George Plumptre, *Edward VII* (London: Pavilion Books, 1995), p. 257.

16 Giles MacDonogh, *The Last Kaiser: William the Impetuous* (London: Weidenfeld & Nicolson, 2000), p. 321; Kenneth Rose, *King George V* (London: Weidenfeld & Nicolson, 1983), p. 76.

17 Rose, *George V*, p. 76.

18 Jane Ridley, *Bertie: A Life of Edward VII* (London: Chatto & Windus, 2012), p. 467. Alexandra of Denmark was the first British dowager queen to be styled Queen Mother since Henrietta Maria of France, Charles I's widow, in the seventeenth century. The suggestion that the title be revived in 1910 was put forward by the Archbishop of Canterbury, who had the title used instead of 'Queen Dowager' in the section of the Prayer Book dealing with prayers for the Royal Family – see G. K. A. Bell, Bishop of Chichester, *Randall Davison, Archbishop of Canterbury* (Oxford: Oxford University Press, 1935), vol. I, pp. 609–10. Outside of the prayer books, Mary of Teck did not use it during her own widowhood from 1936 to 1953, but it was famously revived for Elizabeth Bowes-Lyon from 1952 to 2002.

19 Rose, *George V*, pp. 76–7.

20 PRONI D/4091/A/6/1, Sir Schomberg McDonnell's journal, 'Edward VII', May 1910, pp. 42–3.

21 Ridley, *Bertie*, p. 469.

22 Ibid., p. 463.

23 Ibid.

24 Piers Brendon and Philip Whitehead, *The Windsors: A Dynasty Revealed* (London: Pimlico, 2000), pp. 5–6; E. Digby Blatzell, *The Protestant Establishment: Aristocracy and Caste in America* (New Haven and London: Yale University Press, 1964), pp. vii–viii, doubted that Roosevelt regarded the pecking order with his professed equanimity.

25 Rose, *George V*, p. 77.

26 Ibid., p. 139.

27 Edward Gregg, *Queen Anne* (London: Routledge & Kegan Paul, 1980), p. 144. The Queen used the veto for the Militia of Scotland Bill in March 1708.

28 David Cannadine, *The Decline and Fall of the British Aristocracy*, 2nd edn (London: Picador, 1992), p. 524.

29 Ibid.

30 Rose, *George V*, pp. 121–31.

31 Mary of Teck was born at Kensington Palace on 26 May 1867. Between Queen Mary and Katherine Parr, there had been Lady Anne Hyde, born at Windsor in 1637, who married the future King James II in 1660, but she died before her husband succeeded to the throne.

32 Rose, *George V*, p. 103.

33 Stephen Cameron, *Titanic: Belfast's Own* (Dublin: Wolfhound Press, 1998), p. 24. In total, eight men died during the ship's construction, six of those before the launch. The first victim was Samuel Scott, a fifteen-year-old catch-boy. Unlike James Dobbin, most died as the result of falls.

34 Richard Clarke, *The Royal Victoria Hospital, Belfast: A History, 1797–1997* (Belfast: The Blackstaff Press, 1997), pp. 71–2. The hospital, with its current site and name, was the descendant of various hospitals dating back to the eighteenth century. It had been opened by King Edward VII in 1903.

35 For the size of the crowd, see Fitch, Layton and Wormstedt, *On a Sea of Glass*, p. 26. The 1911 census for Ireland gives the population of Belfast at 386,947.

36 Cameron, *Belfast's Own*, p. 45.

37 Michael Ross and John R. Hume, *Shipbuilders to the World: 125 Years of Harland and Wolff, Belfast, 1861–1986* (Dundonald: The Blackstaff Press, 1986), p. 144.

38 Cameron, *Belfast's Own*, p. 24; permanent exhibition at *Titanic Belfast*, author's visit, 9 June 2018.

39 *Belfast News-Letter*, 1 June 1911; Pauline Matarasso, *A Voyage Closed and Done* (Norwich: Michael Russell, 2005), p. 17; Frances Wilson, *How to Survive the Titanic, or, The Sinking of J. Bruce Ismay* (London: Bloomsbury, 2012), pp. 88–9; Hugh Brewster, *Gilded Lives, Fatal Voyage: The 'Titanic's' First-Class Passengers and their World* (New York: Broadway Paperbacks, 2012), p. 12.

40 Charles R. Morris, *The Tycoons: How Andrew Carnegie, John D. Rockefeller, Jay Gould, and J. P. Morgan Invented the American Supereconomy* (New York: Henry Holt, 2005), p. 268.

41 The *Olympic's* maiden voyage began in Southampton on 14 June 1911 and ended in New York on the 21st.

42 *Belfast News-Letter*, 1 June 1911.

43 Ibid.

44 Ibid.

45 Ibid.

46 Chirnside, *RMS Olympic*, p. 41.

47 An earlier White Star liner, the *Adriatic*, which entered service in 1906, was the first to have a 'plunge bath', but the *Olympic* was the first to offer a practically sized swimming pool, see ibid., p. 57.

48 Ibid., pp. 78–9.

49 Douglas-Home, *Glimpse of Empire*, p. 50.

50 Sir Robert Sanders, diary entry for Thursday 23 March 1911, cit. John Ramsden, (ed.), *Real Old Tory Politics: The Political Diaries of Sir Robert Sanders, Lord Bayford, 1910–35* (London: The Historians' Press, 1984), pp. 25–6.

51 Helen Rappaport, *Four Sisters: The Lost Lives of the Romanov Grand Duchesses* (London: Macmillan, 2014), pp. 157–8.

52 Frederic Morton, *Thunder at Twilight: Vienna, 1913–1914* (Boston: Da Capo Press, 2014), p. 79; Alan Palmer, *Twilight of the Habsburgs: The Life and Times of the Emperor Francis Joseph* (London: Weidenfeld & Nicolson, 1994), p. 311; *The Times*, 23 October 1911.

53 Gordon Brook-Shepherd, *The Last Empress: The Life and Times of Zita of Austria-Hungary, 1892–1989* (London: HarperCollins, 1991), pp. 18–20; James and Joanna Bogle, *A Heart for Europe: The Lives of Emperor Charles and Empress Zita of Austria-Hungary* (Leominster: Gracewing, 2000), pp. 35–6.

54 Princess Zita's relation to the former French ruling house was through her father Roberto I, Duke of Parma (1848–1907), son of Louise-Marie-Thérèse of Artois, Duchess of Parma and Piacenza (1819–44), daughter of the Duke of Berry who was assassinated in 1820, younger son of Charles X, King of France, whose reign ended in the July Revolution of 1830. Her late sister, Princess Marie-Louise of Bourbon-Parma (1870–99), had been the first wife of the future Tsar Ferdinand of Bulgaria (1861–1948) and mother of Tsar Boris III (1894–1943). Her mother, Maria-Antonia of Portugal, Duchess of Parma (1862–1959), was a daughter of Miguel I, King of Portugal (1802–66), who had also been deposed in the 1830s as a result of his absolutist policies. He was also the father of Maria-Josepha of Portugal, Duchess in Bavaria (1857–1943), mother of Elisabeth of Bavaria, Queen of the Belgians (1876–1965).

55 R. W. B. Lewis, *Edith Wharton: A Biography* (London: Constable, 1975), pp. 314–15; Hermione Lee, *Edith Wharton* (New York: Alfred A. Knopf, 2007), p. 391.

56 Hugo Vickers, *Gladys, Duchess of Marlborough* (New York: Holt, Reinhart & Winston, 1979), pp. 129–30.

57 Bigham, 'A Matter of Course'.

58 Simon Thurley, *Hampton Court: A Social and Architectural History* (New Haven and London: Yale University Press, 2003), pp. 166, 182–4.

59 Unless otherwise stated, these descriptions of Leslie House and the chapter's earlier description of the parish of Leslie come from compiling information in William Blackwood (ed.), *The New Statistical Account of Scotland* (Edinburgh: William Blackwood & Sons, 1836), pp. 111–16; John M. Leighton, *History of the County of Fife*, illus. Joseph Swan (Glasgow: George Brookman, 1840), pp. 188–90; Sir James Balfour Paul (ed.), *The Scots Peerage: Founded on Wood's Edition of Sir Robert Douglas's Peerage of Scotland* (Edinburgh: David Douglas, 1910), pp. 305–6; and James Macaulay, *The Classical Country House in Scotland, 1660–1800* (London: Faber & Faber, 1987), pp. 3–5, 51.

60 There remains some debate about the life of Bartholomew (sometimes referred to as Bartolf) Leslie, who was allegedly Malcolm Leslie's father. If Bartholomew died in 1121, as tradition states, it would have made Malcolm extremely old by twelfth-century standards when he was knighted and then endowed with land by King William. *The Scots Peerage* did not doubt Bartholomew's existence, but questioned on chronological grounds his paternity of Malcolm Leslie and in regards the legends of Bartholomew's early career in Scotland noted 'nothing of all this is authenticated', see Paul, *Scots Peerage*, pp. 264–6.

61 It is possible, although perhaps unlikely, that the portrait was of Queen Mary's mother Laura Martinozzi, Duchess of Modena (1639–87).

62 For the history of the earldom of Rothes see Leighton, *History of the County of Fife*, p. 189; Paul, *Scots Peerage*, pp. 264–309; *Lodge's Peerage, Baronetage, Knightage & Companionage of the British Empire for 1912, with which is incorporated Foster's Peerage, Baronetage and Knightage*, 81st edn (London: Kelly's Directories, 1912), p. 1654; Caroline Bingham, *James V: King of Scots* (London: William Collins, 1971), pp. 74, 190; Norman MacDougall, *James III: A Political Study* (Edinburgh: John Donald, 1982), p. 39; Horace Walpole, *Memoirs of King George II*, ed. John Brooke (New Haven and London: Yale University Press, 1985), ii, p. 47; Macaulay, *The Classical Country House in Scotland*, pp. 3–5; Christine McGladdery, *James II* (Edinburgh: John Donald, 1990), p. 104; Gordon Donaldson, *All the Queen's Men: Power and Politics in Mary Stewart's Scotland* (London: Batsford Academic and Educational, 1983), pp. 20, 40–1, 51, 95, 123, 135, and Jenny Uglow, *A Gambling Man: Charles II and the Restoration, 1660–1670* (London: Faber & Faber, 2009), pp. 193, 482–4.

Chapter 2: *The Sash My Father Wore*

1 Norman Weatherall and George E. Templeton, *South Belfast* (Dublin: Nonsuch Publishing, 2008), pp. 41–3; Fitch, Layton and Wormstedt, *On a Sea of Glass*, p. 23.

2 As of 2018, the older name of Stockman's Lane survives in the former top half of the road.

3 The peer in question was Thomas Bateson, 1st Baron Deramore of Belvoir (1819–90), who briefly served as Lord of the Treasury in the Cabinet of the Earl of Derby. The embankment-honoured countess was Anne Wellesley (née Hill-Trevor), Countess of Mornington (1742–1831), daughter of the 1st Viscount Dungannon and mother of the 1st Duke of Wellington. In the eighteenth century, many Irish members of Lady Mornington's family spelled the family's surname 'Wesley'.

4 Wellington College was created after the merging of the Annadale and Carolan grammar schools.

5 Weatherall and Templeton, *South Belfast*, pp. 9–11.

6 In 1912, Dunallon House was 12 Windsor Avenue; it is now 20 Windsor Avenue.

7 Shan F. Bullock, *Thomas Andrews: Shipbuilder* (Dublin and London: Maunsel, 1912), p. 63.

8 According to the 1911 census for Ireland, Elizabeth's nurse was forty-four-year-old Bessie Abernethy, who lived with the Andrews family.

9 Cameron, *Belfast's Own*, p. 92.

10 Ronald Marshall, *Methodist College Belfast: The First Hundred Years* (Belfast: Methodist College Belfast, 1968), p. 49.

11 *Belfast News Letter*, 19 March 1912; Paul Fry (ed.), *Methodist College Belfast 1st XV: 1875–76 to 1993–94* (Belfast: Methodist College Belfast, 1994). The 1912 match was played in Malone, in the grounds of the Royal Ulster Agricultural Society; the Schools' Cup Final was given its current established venue elsewhere in south Belfast, at the Ravenhill Road, in 1924.

12 Bullock, *Thomas Andrews*, p. 5; John Jamieson, *The History of the Royal Belfast Academical Institution, 1810–1960* (Belfast: William Mullan and Son, 1959), p. 165.

13 Victoria College, Belfast, is now spread over two campuses, both of them in Malone, only a few streets over from Thomas Andrews' former home. However, in 1912 the school was located in the University Quarter, in a building which is, as of 2018, serving as the Crescent Arts Centre; see Paul Larmour, *Belfast: An Illustrated Architectural Guide* (Belfast: Friar's Bush Press, 1987), p. 12.

14 Keith Haines, *Campbell College* (Stroud: Tempus, 2004), pp. 8–20; 1 Peter 2:17.

15 Information courtesy of North Down Cricket Club.

16 Bullock, *Thomas Andrews*, p. 3.

17 Ibid., pp. 1–2.

18 Ibid., p. 1.

19 William Pirrie was created a baron in 1906 and raised to a viscountcy in 1921, which became extinct upon his death in 1924.

20 W. H. Crawford (intro.), *The Industries of Ireland: Part I – Belfast and the Towns of the North* (Belfast: Friar's Bush, reprint, 1986), p. 40.

21 C. E. B. Brett, 'The Edwardian City: Belfast around 1900', in J. C. Beckett and R. E. Glasscock (eds), *Belfast: The Origin and Growth of an Industrial City* (London: British Broadcasting Corporation, 1967), p. 120; C. E. B. Brett, *Buildings of Belfast, 1700–1914*, 2nd edn (Belfast: Friar's Bush Press, 1985), p. 64.

22 Sean J. Connolly, 'Belfast: The Rise and Fall of a Civic Culture', in Olwen

Purdue (ed.), *Belfast: The Emerging City, 1850–1914* (Dublin and Portland, OR: Irish Academic Press, 2013), p. 26.

23 Brett, 'The Edwardian City', pp. 120–1.

24 Lyn Gallagher, *The Grand Opera House Belfast* (Dundonald: The Blackstaff Press, 1995), p. 5; Brett, *Buildings of Belfast*, p. 58.

25 Brett, 'The Edwardian City', p. 130; *Pictorial World*, 14 February 1889.

26 The 1901 census for Ireland gives the name of the head of the house as Jane Scott, a fifty-year-old dressmaker, living with her forty-three-year-old sister, Hannah Scott. Like Andrews, both listed their religion as 'Unitarian', a confessional label then generally denoting non-subscribing Presbyterians.

27 Brett, 'The Edwardian City', p. 126.

28 Ibid., pp. 125–6. The original sources describing the busts at Robinson and Cleaver's state that one of them was of the Duchess of Marlborough; it is this author's view that it must have been of the 8th Duke of Marlborough's second wife, Lily, who was duchess at the time the busts were installed. After the Duke's death, Lily had remarried into the Ascendancy with her wedding to Lord William Leslie de la Poer Beresford VC, a younger son of the 4th Marquess of Waterford.

29 Brett, 'The Edwardian City', p. 126.

30 The *Britannic*'s keel was laid on 30 November 1911.

31 The *Britannic* was not, however, the largest ship to fly the British flag in the same period. After her sinking in 1916, that accolade reverted to the *Olympic* and from 1922 to 1934 to the White Star flagship and *Britannic*'s replacement, the *Majestic*, which had been constructed at the Blohm and Voss shipyards in Hamburg and requisitioned as part of the terms of the Treaty of Versailles. The *Britannic*'s record as the largest British-built liner was broken with the launch of the 81,000-ton *Queen Mary* at the John Brown shipyards in Scotland in 1934.

32 Bullock, *Thomas Andrews*, pp. 51–2.

33 Connolly, 'Belfast: The Rise and Fall of a Civic Culture', p. 44.

34 Ibid., pp. 46–7; Jonathan Bardon, *A History of Ulster* (Dundonald: The Blackstaff Press, 1992), p. 387.

35 Bardon, *History of Ulster*, p. 387. Much of Ireland's early twentieth-century anti-Semitism seems to have originated from the sermons of local Catholic priests, particularly the 1904 boycott in Limerick of local Jewish businesses, which was largely the result of sermons by the Redemptorist priest Father John Creagh; see Eugenio F. Biagini and Mary E. Daly (eds), *The Cambridge Social History of Modern Ireland* (Cambridge: Cambridge University Press, 2017), p. 445.

36 Connolly, 'Belfast: The Rise and Fall of a Civic Culture', p. 48.

37 Bullock, *Thomas Andrews*, pp. 52–3.

38 Ibid.

39 John Gray, *City in Revolt: James Larkin and the Belfast Dock Strike of 1907* (Dundonald: The Blackstaff Press, 1985), p. 205.

40 Ibid., pp. 206–9.

41 Ibid., p. 212.

42 Ibid.

43 Gillian McIntosh, *Belfast City Hall: One Hundred Years* (Belfast: The Blackstaff Press, 2006), pp. 10–11.

44 For the construction and the Victorian building craze's impact in west Belfast, see Caroline M. McGee, 'A Most Noble Church in the Most Catholic Quarter of a Bitterly Protestant and Presbyterian City: The Church of the Most Holy Redeemer, Clonard, West Belfast', in Purdue, *Belfast: The Emerging City*, pp. 157–80.

45 Andrew R. Holmes and Eugenio F. Biagini, 'Protestants', in Biagini and Daly (eds), *The Cambridge Social History of Ireland*, p. 95.

46 Bardon, *History of Ulster*, pp. 419–22.

47 Eugenio F. Biagini, 'Minorities', in Biagini and Daly (eds), *The Cambridge Social History of Ireland*, p. 439.

48 Bardon, *History of Ulster*, pp. 400–2.

49 Bullock, *Thomas Andrews*, p. 50.

50 Article 44.1.2 of the Bunreacht na hÉireann, enacted on 27 December 1937, declared, 'The State recognises the special position of the Holy Catholic Apostolic and Roman Church as the guardian of the Faith professed by the great majority of the citizens. The State also recognises the Church of Ireland, the Presbyterian Church in Ireland, the Methodist Church in Ireland, the Religious Society of Friends in Ireland, as well as the Jewish Congregations and the other religious denominations existing in Ireland at the date of the coming into operation of this Constitution.' The stipulation of a 'special position' for Catholicism fell short of the granting of the status of state religion, as lobbied for by many Irish nationalists, but in practice it facilitated an enormous amount of cooperation between the Irish state and local Catholic hierarchy. Article 44 was removed as the fifth amendment to the Irish Constitution, which passed by plebiscite with a vote of 84.38 per cent in favour of repeal, on 7 December 1972.

51 *Morning News from Belfast*, 2 June 1886.

52 Pope Pius VI issued the rescript on St Joseph's Day, 1785; Raymond M. Lee, 'Intermarriage, Conflict and Social Control in Ireland: The Decree "Ne Temere"', *Economic and Social Review* (October 1985), p. 16.

53 Marianne Elliott, *When God Took Sides: Religion and Identity in Ireland: Unfinished History* (Oxford: Oxford University Press, 2009), pp. 138–9.

54 Lee, 'Intermarriage, Conflict and Social Control in Ireland', p. 17.

55 Ibid., p. 19.

56 For the technical logistics of the *Titanic*'s sea trials, see Fitch, Layton and Wormstedt, *On a Sea of Glass*, pp. 50–2.

57 Bullock, *Thomas Andrews*, pp. 54–5.

58 Its existence had not been continuous, however. The Order had gone into abeyance for eleven years before it was reconstituted in August 1847.

59 David Fitzpatrick, *Descendancy: Irish Protestant Histories since 1795* (Cambridge: Cambridge University Press, 2014), pp. 83–4.

60 Andrew R. Holmes and Eugenio F. Biagini, 'Protestants', in Biagini and Daly (eds), *The Cambridge Social History of Modern Ireland*, p. 94.

61 Feargal Cochrane, *Unionist Politics and the Politics of Unionism Since the Anglo-Irish Agreement* (Cork: Cork University Press, 1997), p. 76.

62 Thomas Andrews' eldest brother, John, later served as Grand Master of the Orange Institution of Ireland from 1948 to 1954.

63 Letter from Matthew Banks Hogg of Keady, Co. Armagh, to the *Belfast News-Letter*, 2 April 1912.

64 John Frederick MacNeice, *Carrickfergus and its Contacts: Some Chapters in the History of Ulster* (London: Simpkin Marshall, 1928), p. 76.

65 Denis Gwynn, *The Life of John Redmond* (London: George G. Harrap, 1932), p. 201.

66 Fitzpatrick, *Descendancy*, p. 110.

67 Andrews' father and two brothers all signed the Covenant – Thomas Sr at the local Orange Hall, his sons inside or in the grounds of the local Presbyterian church. There was a separate Declaration for women, which was signed at the Comber 1st Presbyterian Church by Andrews' mother, Eliza.

68 Geoffrey Lewis, *Carson: The Man Who Divided Ireland* (London and New York: Hambledon & London, 2005), p. 143.

69 Joseph Valente, *The Myth of Manliness in Irish National Culture, 1880–1922* (Champaign, IL: University of Illinois Press, 2011), p. 103.

70 Lewis, *Carson*, p. 113.

71 Fitch, Layton and Wormstedt, *On a Sea of Glass*, p. 53.

Chapter 3: *Southampton*

1 Fitch, Layton and Wormstedt, *On a Sea of Glass*, p. 53. The White Star Line's original name was the Oceanic Steam Navigation Company and, although

never formally changed, the popular nickname was eventually used on company literature, nameplates and buildings.

2 Bruce Beveridge et al., *Titanic: The Ship Magnificent*, 2 vols, 5th edn (Stroud: The History Press, 2016), vol. II: *Interior Design & Fitting Out*, p. 15; Grace Evans, *Titanic Style: Dress and Fashions on the Voyage* (Ludlow: Moonrise Press, 2011), pp. 15–48.

3 Andrews boarded at about six o'clock that morning. Using data provided by the National Oceanic and Atmospheric Association, Fitch, Layton and Wormstedt, *On a Sea of Glass*, p. 384, estimate the time of sunrise in Southampton on 10 April 1912 to have been approximately 5.23 a.m.

4 Chirnside, *Olympic*, pp. 91–7.

5 Bullock, *Thomas Andrews*, p. 58; Fitch, Layton and Wormstedt, *On a Sea of Glass*, p. 60.

6 Bullock, *Thomas Andrews*, p. 59; Fitch, Layton and Wormstedt, *On a Sea of Glass*, p. 56.

7 Bullock, *Thomas Andrews*, pp. 58–9.

8 Fitch, Layton and Wormstedt, *On a Sea of Glass*, p. 90.

9 Bullock, *Thomas Andrews*, pp. 59–60.

10 Ibid., p. 60.

11 The 1912 British miners' strike began on 29 February 1912, with industrial action initially beginning over the issue of a standardised minimum wage. In its opening few weeks, it attracted nearly one million participants. Wages were paid during the protest by the industry's trade unions; however, between 2 and 4 April nearly 40,000 miners went back to work and a union vote by the Miners' Federation to end the strike passed by 440 to 125 on 6 April. In the five weeks of the strike, an estimated 28 million tons of coal had been lost to British industry.

12 C. R. Vernon Gibbs, *Passenger Liners of the Western Ocean: A Record of the North Atlantic Steam and Motor Passenger Vessels from 1838 to the Present Day* (New York: P. Staples, 1952), pp. 122–4.

13 Laurence Dunn, *Famous Liners of the Past: Belfast Built* (London: Adlard Coles, 1964), p. 196.

14 Beveridge et al., *Ship Magnificent*, II, p. 23.

15 Ibid., p. 9.

16 R. A. Fletcher, *Travelling Palaces: Luxury in Passenger Steamships* (London: Sir Isaac Pitman & Sons, 1913), pp. 275–6.

17 Frank C. Bowen, *A Century of Atlantic Travel, 1830–1930* (London: Sampson Low, Marston, 1932), pp. 207–8; letter from third-class passenger Marion Meanwell to her cousin, posted from the *Titanic* at Queenstown on 11 April 1912 (B71); Ernest Townley, *Daily Express*, 16 April 1912; letter from third-

class passenger Daniel Buckley to his mother, 18 April 1912; *Whitehaven News*, 2 May 1912.

18 Beveridge et al., *Ship Magnificent*, II, p. 15.

19 Bowen, *Century of Atlantic Travel*, p. 197.

20 'The Cholera of 1892 in Hamburg', *British Medical Journal* (1893), vol. I, no. 1677, pp. 373–5; Paul S. B. Jackson, 'Fearing Future Epidemics: The Cholera Crisis of 1892', *Cultural Geographies* (2013), vol. XX, no. 1, pp. 43–65; Tara Zahra, *The Great Departure: Mass Migration from Eastern Europe and the Making of the Free World* (New York: W. W. Norton, 2016), pp. 35–6.

21 Fletcher, *Travelling Palaces*, pp. 164–5.

22 Ibid., p. 140.

23 Bigham, 'A Matter of Course'.

24 United States District Court, Southern District of New York, *In the Matter of the Petition of the Oceanic Steam Navigation Company, Limited, for Limitation of its Liability as Owner of the Steamship 'TITANIC' – the Claim of The Rt. Hon. Lucy-Noel Dyer Martha, Countess of Rothes*, 13 January 1913 (The National Archives at New York).

25 Fitch, Layton and Wormstedt, *On a Sea of Glass*, p. 65.

26 There has been some confusion over why the train did not arrive at the *Titanic* until 11.30. There were two boat trains in operation that day from London, one for first-class passengers and another for second and third, in separate classes of carriages. Almost unanimously, passengers on the first-class train remembered leaving Waterloo at eight o'clock in the morning, meaning that they took nearly three times longer than expected to reach Southampton. A dissenting recollection is that of a trainee Jesuit priest, Francis Browne, who wrote later that the first-class train had pulled out of the station at quarter to ten. The train carrying the second- and third-class passengers left at eight o'clock, while First Class set off an hour and forty-five minutes later, something that would fit with the policy of trying to embark third-class travellers before those in First, although it remains difficult to find any other first-hand accounts, barring Browne's, that square the respective arrival times in Southampton with the approximate journey duration. A possible explanation can be found in the account of Sidney Clarence Stuart Collett, another travelling clergyman, this time an ordained Baptist pastor whose vocation was taking him to Missouri via *Titanic*'s second-class quarters. In an interview on 23 April 1912 with the *Auburn Citizen* (Courtesy of the Mike Poirier Collection), he stated that the first of the boat trains set off at eight in the morning, as timetabled, but 'at the very start there was trouble. The train stopped because somebody had interfered with the brake valve' – a version of events corroborated by Elizabeth Dowdell, a third-class ticket holder, who worried that the interruption might

cause them to miss the sailing. That delay may, in its turn, have caused the first-class train's departure to be pushed back until quarter to ten, the time recalled by Browne, which fits within an estimated travel time that got them to Southampton just before half-past eleven. It also helps explain the relatively short embarkation window eventually experienced by first-class passengers taking the train, who arrived in Southampton at half-past eleven in time for the ship's noon departure.

27 Ibid., p. 67.

28 For the design of the White Star shed, see fig. 1-1 in Beveridge et al., *Ship Magnificent*, II, p. 10.

29 Brewster, *Gilded Lives*, p. 29.

30 Fletcher, *Travelling Palaces*, p. 144.

31 *Titanic* ticket number 110152.

32 Later, in their testimonies or memories, a few of the *Titanic's* passengers and crew referred to the decks by name rather than letter.

33 There has been some confusion over where Maioni slept during her time on the *Titanic*. I am extremely grateful to Daniel Klistorner for sharing his research on cabin allocation with me, which proves that Maioni was not lodged next door to Lady Rothes, but was most probably allocated cabin E-11.

34 *Paris Herald*, 11 April 1912, which was then reprinted in the *New York Herald*; Bigham, 'A Matter of Course'.

35 For the deck plans consulted, please see figs 8-1 and 8-9 in Beveridge et al., *Ship Magnificent*, II, pp. 306–13.

36 Captain E. G. Diggle, *The Romance of a Modern Liner* (London: Sampson Low, Marston, 1930), p. 172.

37 Fig. 8-1 in Beveridge et al., *Ship Magnificent*, II, pp. 306–7.

38 There was a Scottish baronet in the person of Sir Cosmo Duff Gordon and a man in Second Class, demanding to be upgraded to First Class, calling himself 'Baron Alfred von Drachstedt', but the name on his Dutch birth certificate identified him as Alfred Nourney.

39 For Edward VIII's rejection of the suite, see Chirnside, *Olympic*, p. 201.

40 June Hall McCash, *A Titanic Love Story: Ida and Isidor Straus* (Macon, GA: Mercer University Press, 2012), pp. 159, 181.

41 Ibid., p. 179.

42 Jessop, *Titanic Survivor*, p. 134.

43 Shelby Foote, *The Civil War, a Narrative: Red River to Appomattox* (New York: Vintage Books, 1986), p. 640.

44 McCash, *Titanic Love Story*, p. 156.

45 Colonel Archibald Gracie, *Titanic: A Survivor's Story* (Stroud: The History Press, 2011), p. 6; McCash, *Titanic Love Story*, p. 9.

46 McCash, *Titanic Love Story*, p. 170.

47 Ibid., pp. 167–9.

48 Ibid.

49 That is why a decommissioned ocean liner, like the former Cunard-White Star's *Queen Mary*, which has served as a floating hotel at Long Beach, CA, since her retirement in 1967, contains signs advising patrons of increased noise in certain parts of the ship thanks to the silence of the retired engines. Author's visit, 30–31 August 2017.

50 John P. Eaton and Charles A. Haas, *Titanic: A Journey through Time* (Yeovil: Patrick Stephens, 1999), pp. 46–8; Fitch, Layton and Wormstedt, *On a Sea of Glass*, p. 75.

51 Gracie, *Titanic*, p. 6.

52 Interview with passenger May Futrelle, given to the *Philadelphia Evening Bulletin*, 29 April 1912.

53 For an excellent analysis of the logistics of the *New York–Titanic* incident, see Fitch, Layton and Wormstedt, *On a Sea of Glass*, pp. 80–2.

54 Letter from second-class passenger Amelia Brown to her mother, 17 April 1912 (B109); Roberta Maioni, 'My Maiden Voyage', *Daily Express* (1926), accessible on *Encyclopedia Titanica*, 2 October 2008.

55 Letter from Ida Straus to Lilian Burbidge, 10 April 1912 (LMQ/7/2/30). Ida's handwriting has faded quite badly on the second page of the letter and elsewhere it has been transcribed as 'in the pleasant anticipation of seeing you with us next Sunday'. On inspection, the words are 'next summer'. The original is kept at the National Maritime Museum, with a copy owned by the Straus Historical Society.

Chapter 4: *A Contest of Sea Giants*

1 Brewster, *Gilded Lives*, p. 5. As regards this chapter's epigraph, the author of the original piece in the *Standard* made a mistake when he identified the *Imperator* and the *Kronprinzessin Cecilie* as ships of the Hamburg-Amerika Line. The former was, but the *Cecilie* was operated by the Norddeutscher Lloyd.

2 Fitch, Layton and Wormstedt, *On a Sea of Glass*, pp. 91–5.

3 Passenger Margaret Brown in the *Newport Herald*, 28 May 1912 (B149).

4 Passenger R. Norris Williams II, cit. Brewster, *Gilded Lives*, p. 18.

5 Morris, *Tycoons*, p. 272.

6 Charles Emmerson, *1913: The World before the Great War* (London: The Bodley Head, 2013), pp. 145–6.

7 *New York Herald Tribune*, 7 October 1893; for the archducal letters from the

United States, see Greg King and Sue Woolmans, *The Assassination of the Archduke: Sarajevo 1914 and the Murder that Changed the World* (London: Macmillan, 2013), pp. 24–6.

8 Zahra, *Great Departure*, p. 3; Morris, *Tycoons*, p. 277.

9 A notorious article actually naming the Four Hundred was published in the *New York Times* on 16 February 1892. See also Virginia Cowles, *The Astors: The Story of a Transatlantic Family* (London: Weidenfeld & Nicolson, 1979), p. 96; Derek Wilson, *The Astors: The Life and Times of the Astor Dynasty, 1763–1992* (London: Weidenfeld & Nicolson, 1993), pp. 105–6; Lloyd R. Morris, *Incredible New York: High Life and Low Life from 1850 to 1950* (New York: Syracuse University Press, 1996), p. 145. For the relevant allusions and descriptions of the Virgin, scriptural and artistic, see Revelation 12:1 and Dante's *Paradiso*, Canto XXII.

10 Fitch, Layton and Wormstedt, *On a Sea of Glass*, p. 94.

11 John B. Thayer III, *The Sinking of the S.S. Titanic: April 14–15, 1912* (Chicago: Academy Chicago Publishers, 2010), p. 329.

12 Chirnside, *Olympic*, p. 43.

13 Bullock, *Thomas Andrews*, p. 61.

14 Fitch, Layton and Wormstedt, *On a Sea of Glass*, p. 92.

15 For the *Titanic*'s specifications, see *The Shipbuilder: White Star Line Royal Mail Triple-Screw Steamers, 'Olympic' and 'Titanic'*, facsimile of the 1911 edition (Holywood, Co. Down: Ulster Folk and Transport Museum, 1987), p. 5, and Fitch, Layton and Wormstedt, *On a Sea of Glass*, Appendix A, '*Titanic*'s Technical Specifications & Some Common Misconceptions', pp. 283–5.

16 *The Shipbuilder*, p. 71.

17 Don Lynch and Ken Marschall, *Titanic: An Illustrated History* (London: Hodder & Stoughton, 1992), p. 20.

18 Emmerson, *1913*, p. 68.

19 This was not the first time that the Archduchess had waged unsuccessful war on a *mésalliance*. Two decades earlier, she had regularly invited the Archduke Franz Ferdinand to her home in the hope of securing an engagement between him and one of her daughters. Instead, Franz Ferdinand fell in love with Isabella's lady-in-waiting, Countess Sophie Chotek. Upon discovering this, Isabella summoned her entire household staff to berate and then dismiss Sophie, before launching herself headlong into a campaign of spreading wholly false and equally unkind rumours about Sophie's morals. This seemed only to stiffen Franz Ferdinand's resolve and the couple married in 1900, although their three subsequent children were barred from the line of succession.

20 *New York Times*, 25 October 1913; *New York Times*, 28 March 1924, John Leishman's obituary.

21 The First Reich had been the Holy Roman Empire, a millennium-old political construct covering most of modern-day Germany with an elected emperor who had decreasing influence as the centuries passed. The emperors were often chosen from the Habsburg family, who retained their hereditary authority in their central European provinces after the dissolution of the Holy Roman Empire in 1806.

22 Brinnin, *Sway of the Grand Saloon,* p. 306.

23 Ibid., p. 316.

24 Ibid., pp. 316–17.

25 The Kaiser personally launched both the first and last in the series; the second, the *Kronprinz Wilhelm*, was launched by his son and the ship's namesake, the Crown Prince Wilhelm. The Kaiser did not launch the ship bearing his own name, but instead supervised as the champagne was released by Fräulein Weigand, daughter of the ship's owner. That the Kaiser launched a ship bearing the name of his living and very popular daughter-in-law Cecilia speaks volumes for the deliberately reduced role of women in the Hohenzollern monarchy. He did the same at another launching ceremony that year for the *Kaiserin Auguste Victoria*, named after his wife, who accompanied him to watch the launch.

26 *Our Future Lies upon the Water* by Arthur Heinrich Wilhelm Fitger, displayed at the Victoria and Albert Museum's 'Ocean Liners: Speed and Style' exhibition; author's visit, 6 March 2018. The piece was on loan at that time from the Mariners' Museum and Park, Newport News, VA.

27 Cf. William H. Miller, *Famous Ocean Liners: The Story of Passenger Shipping, from the Turn of the Century to the Present Day* (Wellingborough: Patrick Stephens, 1987), p. 133.

28 The *Great Eastern*, designed by Isambard Kingdom Brunel and launched in 1858, had arguably been the first 'super-ship', but it had been a commercial disaster to the extent that no ship was tempted to outstrip her gross tonnage until 1901, with the maiden voyage of White Star's *Celtic*.

29 Gerald Aylmer, *R.M.S. 'Mauretania': The Ship and her Record* (London: Percival Mansion, 1935), pp. 14–15.

30 Bowen, *A Century of Atlantic Travel, 1830–1930,* pp. 232–3.

31 Brinnin, *Sway of the Grand Saloon,* p. 330.

32 Ibid., pp. 330–5.

33 Aylmer, *Mauretania*, p. 15; Bowen, *Century of Atlantic Travel*, p. 244.

34 The *Lusitania*, named after the ancient Roman province covering modern Portugal and parts of Spain, was built at the John Clyde & Co. shipyard in Clydebank, Scotland; the *Mauretania*, named after Roman Morocco, at the Swan, Hunter & Wigham Richardson yards in Tyne and Wear.

35 The *Kronprinzessin Cecilie* weighed in at approximately 19,400 tons; the *Mauretania* was 32,000 tons.

36 Her record was broken by the maiden voyage of a German liner, the *Bremen*, in 1929.

37 *Southampton Times*, 18 May 1912.

38 Lawrence Beesley, *The Loss of the S.S. Titanic: Its Story and its Lessons*, facsimile of the 1912 edition (Whitefish, MT: Kessinger Publishing, 2010), pp. 118–19.

39 Company correspondence, from both White Star and Harland and Wolff, proves that the decision to change the name had been taken before the *Titanic* left Belfast – minutes from meetings held on 19 and 26 May 1911 referred to the third ship as the *Britannic*, as did a Harland and Wolff order book entry for 17 October in the same year, by which point construction on the *Imperator* had begun. The most likely explanation is that *Gigantic* had been considered by White Star, until it was rejected by the company around the spring or summer of 1911, a move which they only made firm steps to publicise a year later after being pressured to by rumours regarding a by then ill-sounding name in the aftermath of the *Titanic*'s sinking. See Mark Chirnside and Paul Lee, 'The *Gigantic* Question', *Titanic Commutator* (Spring 2008), vol. 31, no. 180, pp. 181–92. Frustratingly, the minutes for the two May 1911 meetings at Harland and Wolff are not extant. However, they, and their use of the name *Britannic*, were mentioned at the British inquiry into the *Titanic* disaster in questions to the Rt Hon. Alexander Carlisle, former Chairman of the Harland and Wolff Board of Directors. We know from that question that the *Britannic* reference was apparently on page 21 of the now lost minutes. Some of the newspapers that continued to describe the ship incorrectly as the *Gigantic* after May 1912 include the *Scientific American* on 24 August 1912 and the *Weekly Irish Times* on 14 December 1912. Construction work on the *Imperator* began in the spring of 1910.

40 Interview with Paul Louden-Brown, 'Five *Titanic* Myths Spread by Films', *BBC News*, 2 April 2012.

41 My assessment of Ismay's character is based on the convincing yet balanced rehabilitation offered by Frances Wilson in her biography of him, *How to Survive the Titanic, or, The Sinking of J. Bruce Ismay* (London: Bloomsbury, 2012).

42 *Yale Daily News*, 11, 12 and 18 April 1912; Judith Schiff, 'When the *Titanic* Went Down', *Yale Alumni Magazine* (March/April 2012).

43 Brewster, *Gilded Lives*, p. 30.

44 Death notices in the *New York Times*, 20 May 1897 and 4 May 1912.

45 Preston Remington, 'Two Gobelin Tapestries', *Bulletin of the Metropolitan*

Museum of Art (1955), pp. 155–8. The original was kept by the Mobilier National, but a copy had produced an exact replica for the *Titanic*.

46 This description of the Reception Room is based on deck plans and specifications given in Beveridge et al., *Ship Magnificent*, II, pp. 354–61, and figs 9-7, 9-13, 90-16.

47 Letter from the Dowager Countess of Rothes to Walter Lord, 7 August 1955 (LMQ7/7/20).

48 Elmer Zebley Taylor, *Jigsaw Picture Puzzle of People Whom I Have Known and Sundry Experiences from 1864 to 1949*, (privately reprinted, 2017), p. 173.

49 Relatively accurate recreations of the Saloon formed prominent set pieces in *A Night to Remember* (1958) and *Titanic* (1997).

50 John Malcolm Brinnin, *Beau Voyage: Life Aboard the Last Great Ships* (New York: Barnes & Noble Books, 1981), p. 56.

51 Letter from Ewart Burr to Ethel Burr, 10 April 1912 (B25).

52 *The Shipbuilder*, p. 32.

53 This description of the *Titanic*'s Dining Saloon is based on a compilation from ibid., pp. 32–3; Beveridge et al., *Ship Magnificent*, II, pp. 361–5, figs 9-17 and 9-20; Chirnside, *Olympic*, Appendix III, 'Cunard's Spy', pp. 304–8.

54 Beveridge et al., *Ship Magnificent*, II, pp. 166–9.

55 Fitch, Layton and Wormstedt, *On a Sea of Glass*, p. 95.

Chapter 5: *A Safe Harbour for Ships*

1 The name Celtic Sea was not bestowed until 1921 when the marine biologist Ernest W. L. Holt announced it at a Dublin-based conference of fishery experts from England, France, Ireland, Scotland and Wales. Those attending the conference concluded that the area had needed a proper name for years.

2 Fitch, Layton and Wormstedt, *On a Sea of Glass*, p. 96.

3 White Star Line passenger information for the *Olympic* stated, 'The Lounge will be closed at 11.30 p.m. and the Reception Room at 11 p.m.'

4 Zebley Taylor, *Jigsaw Picture Puzzle*, p. 173.

5 Fletcher, *Travelling Palaces*, p. 259. There is some debate over the length of Farthing's service to the family. Joan Adler, Executive Director of the Straus Historical Society, doubts that he was in Isidor's employ for as long as twenty years, as some modern accounts of the disaster have stated, on the grounds that Farthing is infrequently mentioned in Isidor's letters; a telegram from Percy Straus to Maurice Rothschild, 27 April 1912 (SHS), implies strongly that he was unsure on the details of Farthing's appearance, and that he is not listed in the 1910 US Census as a resident in the Straus household. It is possible that he was working for Isidor by 1910, since he was married and his

wife did not live in the Straus home with him. Correspondence between the author and Joan Adler, 27 August and 12 November 2018.

6 Letter from Ida Straus to Rose Abraham, 30 March 1912 (SHS).

7 Ibid.; McCash, *Titanic Love Story*, pp. 181–2.

8 Ellen Bird's cabin was C-97. Her age and occupation are based on the entries for her in the 1891 and 1901 British censuses.

9 Purser Charles Spedding, *Reminiscences of Transatlantic Travellers* (London: T. Fisher Unwin, 1926), p. 61.

10 Moss and Hume, *Shipbuilders to the World*, pp. 146–7.

11 Unless otherwise stated, this chapter's description of the weather surrounding the *Titanic* between Cherbourg and Queenstown is based on comments made in letters, all written on 11 April 1912, by first-class passengers Ramon Artagaveytia (B46), Elizabeth Bonnell (which she misdated to 9 April) (B50), Margaretha Frölicher-Stehli (B61) and Adolphe Saalfeld (B76); second-class passengers Kate Buss (B26), Harvey Collyer (B55), Samuel James Hocking (B65) and Thomas Mudd (B73); and third-class passenger Henry Olsen (B74), as well as the memoirs of second-class passenger Lawrence Beesley, *Titanic*, p. 11.

12 Beesley, *Titanic*, p. 10; letter from passenger Ramon Artagaveytia to Adolfo Artagaveytia, 11 April 1912; passenger Margaret Brown in the *Newport Herald*, 28 May 1912.

13 *Evening Standard*, 24 April 1912; *Belfast Evening Telegraph*, 15 April 1912.

14 Fitch, Layton and Wormstedt, *On a Sea of Glass*, p. 96; a photograph by Francis Browne also shows the clouds shortly after sunrise.

15 Fitch, Layton and Wormstedt, *On a Sea of Glass*, p. 30.

16 Fletcher, *Travelling Palaces*, p. 262.

17 White Star's information for first-class passengers, 'Breakfast from 8 a.m. to 10 a.m.'.

18 Beesley, *Titanic*, p. 10.

19 The *síneadh fada* over the vowel in Cóbh is not always added today, but its absence alters the pronunciation significantly. My thanks to Scott De Buitléir for his advice on this.

20 Fletcher, *Travelling Palaces*, p. 236.

21 Fitch, Layton and Wormstedt, *On a Sea of Glass*, p. 99. The time of arrival at Queenstown was about 11.30 a.m.

22 Beesley, *Titanic*, p. 11.

23 William Garner, *Cobh: Architectural Heritage* (Dublin: An Foras Forbartha, 1979), pp. 5–6.

24 'When Erin First Rose', written c. 1795. Drennan's Andrews descendants did not share his politics and by the middle of the nineteenth century they were

firmly, if unsuccessfully, attempting to prevent his legacy's appropriation by Irish nationalists – see Ian McBride, 'Memory and Forgetting: Ulster Presbyterians and 1798', in Thomas Bartlett, David Dickson, Dáire Keogh and Kevin Whelan (eds), *1798: A Bicentenary Perspective* (Dublin: Four Courts Press, 2003), p. 489.

25 'That Jesuit on the *Titanic*', *L'Osservatore Romano*, 24 April 2012.

26 Jennifer Roche, 'How Holy Obedience Saved a Priest's Life on *Titanic*', *National Catholic Register*, 13 August 2017.

27 The best modern publication of Francis Browne's photographs of 11 April 1912 is E. E. O'Donnell, SJ (ed.), *Father Browne's Titanic Album: A Passenger's Photographs and Personal Memoir* (Dublin: Messenger Publications Jesuits in Ireland, 2011).

28 A letter from one of the *Titanic*'s Assistant Engineers, Albert Ervine, 11 April 1912 (B58), confirms that Andrews' inspection took place in the morning, before the stop at Queenstown.

29 Fitch, Layton and Wormstedt, *On a Sea of Glass*, p. 106.

30 David Blair's letter was auctioned by Henry Aldridge in 2007 and bought by an unnamed bidder.

31 Testimony of Frederick Fleet to the US Senate inquiry, 23 April 1912.

32 Fitch, Layton and Wormstedt, *On a Sea of Glass*, Appendix C, 'The Question of Binoculars', pp. 288–90. In a piece for the *New York Times*, on 8 May 1912, one of the *Titanic*'s survivors, Lawrence Beesley, also questioned 'whether they [the binoculars] would have helped to avert the disaster . . . The ship was nearly a sixth of a mile long, and at the speed she was travelling it is doubtful whether she could be turned away from an object half a mile away without some part of her touching.'

33 Fletcher, *Travelling Palaces*, p. 262; Beesley, *Titanic*, p. 12.

34 Tea was also served in the Lounge, Café Parisian and Reception Room.

35 The musician was Eugene Patrick Daly (1883–1965), who was travelling to attend the May 1912 Gaelic Feis in Queens, New York. 'Erin's Lament' was strongly anti-landlord in its sentiment, as well as critical of Irish people perceived as having betrayed their country by supporting legislation that either favoured the Ascendancy or tied the island politically closer to Great Britain. The song seems to have been written shortly after the Great Potato Famine. 'A Nation Once More' is generally associated with the Young Irelanders' movement in the 1840s and attributed to Thomas Osborne Davis (1814–45), one of the movement's early founders.

36 *The Shipbuilder*, p. 41; Beveridge et al., *Ship Magnificent*, II, pp. 248–56, fig. 6-42.

Chapter 6: *The Lucky Holdup*

1 Beveridge et al., *Ship Magnificent*, II, p. 44n.

2 *Titanic* ticket numbers 24160 and 17760, respectively. Allen was travelling in stateroom B-5 and Young in C-32. Both women survived the sinking of the *Titanic*; Allen, by then Elisabeth Mennell, died in Tunbridge Wells in 1967 and Young in New York in 1959. Ethel Roosevelt came out into DC Society in 1909; Peter Collier, with David Horowitz, *The Roosevelts: An American Saga* (London: André Deutsch, 1995), pp. 123–4, 147.

3 In First Class, cabins E-1 through to E-42 were usually classed as first-class accommodation, as they were for the April 1912 voyage, but they could be switched over to Second Class, if the need arose. In Second Class, cabins E-43 to E-68 were typically Second Class but could be used for First, as was the case for the *Titanic*'s maiden voyage.

4 Most memorably, the idea that the *Titanic* was fully booked formed a major plot-point for the 1953 movie, *Titanic*, the first major English-language motion picture about the disaster. In it, the fictitious millionaire Richard Sturges (played by Clifton Webb) has to haggle for a third-class ticket at Cherbourg in order to get on the at-capacity ship in the hopes of reconciling with his estranged wife, Julia (Barbara Stanwyck), who is travelling with his children in First Class. It was also central to the story of the less well-known television mini-series *Titanic* (1996), in which Captain Smith was played by George C. Scott, with various fictitious passengers and crew depicted by Catherine Zeta-Jones, Eva Marie Saint, Peter Gallagher and Tim Curry.

5 Lynch and Marschall, *Titanic:* p. 33.

6 Chirnside, *Olympic*, p. 78.

7 Hays did not survive the sinking of the *Titanic* and, because of this, the Laurier's proposed opening on 26 April was rescheduled and scaled down for 12 June.

8 *Titanic* ticket number 111320. Gee was one of those who lost their lives four days later.

9 Helen Churchill Candee, 'Sealed Orders', *Collier's Weekly*, 4 May 1912.

10 Randy Bryan Bigham, *Finding Dorothy: A Biography of Dorothy Gibson* (Raleigh, NC: Lulu Press, 2012), p. 9.

11 The two stars' salaries are sometimes incorrectly presented as comparable at this stage in their careers. Pickford had been on $225 during her brief stint with the Majestic Company in Chicago, but in December 1911 she re-signed with Biograph, accepting a drop to $150 in her weekly pay in order to pursue

more challenging roles; see Scott Eyman, *Mary Pickford: America's Sweetheart* (New York: Donald I. Fine, 1990), pp. 58–9.

12 John A. Brown's death certificate, B1195959, New Jersey State Archives.

13 Pauline Gibson's passport application (number 27124) to the State of New York in 1921 gives her date of birth as 30 June 1866.

14 For this overview of her career see 'A New Harrison Fisher Girl: Miss Dorothy Gibson', *New York Sunday American* (c.1909); 'Harrison Fisher Girls Tell their Stories', *New York Morning Telegraph* (c.1911); 'Mr. Fisher Believes in Every Woman's Beauty', *New York Herald* (c.1911); 'Harrison Fisher Discovered a New Type of Beauty', *New York Times*, 22 January 1911; a profile of Jules Brulatour published in *New York Dramatic Mirror*, 31 January 1911; a profile of Harry Raver in the *Moving Picture World*, 1 October 1910; Benjamin B. Hampton, *A History of the Movies* (New York: Covici Friede Publishers, 1931), p. 134; Bigham, *Finding Dorothy*, pp. 5–11, 13–14, 16–26, 31, 33–5, 39, 47–52; and Philip Gowan and Brian Meister, 'The Saga of the Gibson Women', *Atlantic Daily Bulletin* (2002), vol. 3, pp. 10–12.

15 One of Marie Antoinette's ladies-in-waiting described the historical inspiration for Dorothy's scene as taking place at one of Versailles' 'entertainments, when the most beautiful woman out of three hundred was selected to place a crown of laurels upon the white head of the American philosopher': see Jeanne-Louise-Henriette Campan, *La Vie privée de Marie-Antoinette* (New York: 1500 Books, 2006), p. 162.

16 The argument that Pitcher is an amalgam of several individuals is cogently expressed in Ray Raphael, *Founding Myths: Stories That Hide Our Patriotic Past*, rev. edn (New York: New Press, 2004), pp. 49–71.

17 Passenger Edith Rosenbaum in *Cassells* magazine, 1913. My gratitude to Randy Bryan Bigham for sharing his research with me, establishing that the ladies Rosenbaum spoke with must have been Dorothy and Pauline Gibson.

18 Andrew Britton, *SS Nieuw Amsterdam* (Stroud: The History Press, 2015), p. 14.

19 Beveridge et al., *Ship Magnificent*, II, pp. 137–9, 142–3.

20 The description of Dorothy and Pauline Gibson's cabin is based on ibid., pp. 395–7, and the relevant deck plans in figs 10-7 and 10-8. For the calmer weather on 11 April, see Beesley, *Titanic*, p. 10.

21 Dorothy and Pauline Gibson were travelling on ticket number 112378.

Chapter 7: A Decent Wee Man

1 Captain Smith's reply to Captain Caussin of *La Touraine* mentioned the 'fine weather' of the day, as does a surviving diary entry by third-class passenger

Jakob Johansson, who wrote of 'beautiful weather [and] no wind' (B90). See also Beesley, *Titanic*, pp. 12–13, and Thayer, *Titanic*, p. 333.

2 Eaton and Haas, *Titanic*, Appendix 1, '*Titanic*'s American Flag', p. 228; Fitch, Layton and Wormstedt, *On a Sea of Glass*, p. 63.

3 Fitch, Layton and Wormstedt, *On a Sea of Glass*, p. 109; *La Touraine*'s warning arrived at 5.46 p.m., ship time.

4 Thayer, *Titanic*, p. 333.

5 Descriptions of the *Titanic*'s Reading and Writing Room are based on reports in *The Shipbuilder*, p. 45, and Beveridge et al., *Ship Magnificent*, II, pp. 237–41.

6 *The Shipbuilder*, p. 40.

7 Ibid., p. 43.

8 Fletcher, *Travelling Palaces*, p. 255.

9 Brinnin, *Sway of the Grand Saloon*, pp. 464–5.

10 Fletcher, *Travelling Palaces*, p. 255.

11 Moss and Hume, *Shipbuilders to the World*, p. 157.

12 Jessop, *Titanic Survivor*, pp. 139–40.

13 Beveridge et al., *Ship Magnificent*, II, p. 408.

14 Jessop, *Titanic Survivor*, p. 132.

15 Beveridge et al., *Ship Magnificent*, II, pp. 392, 408.

16 Bullock, *Thomas Andrews*, p. 59. This was the galley that served the first-class à la carte Restaurant on B-Deck, which is discussed in fuller detail in Chapter 11.

17 This was Lutie Parrish (1852–1930), who was travelling in Second Class with her daughter, Imanita Shelley (1887–1954).

18 *Titanic* ticket number 17595. Ann Elizabeth Isham (1862–1912) lost her life in the sinking of the *Titanic*.

19 Bullock, *Thomas Andrews*, pp. 59–64; Thayer, *Titanic*, p. 332; Jessop, *Titanic Survivor*, p. 132; Fitch, Layton and Wormstedt, *On a Sea of Glass*, pp. 107–10; Beveridge et al., *Ship Magnificent*, II, pp. 155n, 157–66, 184n, 388–95, and fig. 10-4.

20 Fitch, Layton and Wormstedt, *On a Sea of Glass*, p. 107n.

21 Bullock, *Thomas Andrews*, p. 59.

22 Jessop, *Titanic Survivor*, pp. 113–14, 131–2.

23 Robin Gardiner and Dan van der Vat, *The Riddle of the Titanic* (London: Weidenfeld & Nicolson, 1995), p. 99.

24 Ibid., p. 94.

25 Robin Gardiner, *Titanic: The Ship That Never Sank?* (Shepperton: Ian Allan, 1998), pp. 266–7.

26 *Conspiracies: The Ship That Never Sank?*, first broadcast on Sky One on 16 September 2004.

27 Gardiner, *The Ship That Never Sank?*, p. 265.

28 For a full list of the differences between the *Olympic* and the *Titanic*, see Steve Hall, Bruce Beveridge and Art Braunschweiger, *Titanic or Olympic: Which Ship Sank?* (Stroud: The History Press, 2012), Appendix I, 'Almost Identical Sisters', pp. 157–213. There is also strong evidence recently discussed by *Titanic* experts to suggest that there was another significant difference between the two sisters when it came to their propellers, with the *Olympic*'s central propeller having four blades, while the *Titanic*'s had three – see Mark Chirnside, 'The Mystery of the *Titanic*'s Central Propeller' in *Voyage* (Spring 2008), no. 63, pp. 123–8.

29 Gardiner and van der Vat, *Riddle of the Titanic*, p. 261.

30 Ibid., pp. 98–9.

31 Bowen, *Century of Atlantic Travel*, pp. 235–6, 241.

32 Hall, Beveridge and Braunschweiger, *Titanic or Olympic*, p. 156.

33 This refutation of Gardiner's theories, in both his individual and his collaborative publications, is based on Hall, Beveridge and Braunschweiger's *Titanic or Olympic*, which is the most thorough published critique of each point made in *The Riddle of the Titanic* and *The Ship That Never Sank?*. See also Mark Chirnside, '*Olympic & Titanic*: An Analysis of the Robin Gardiner Conspiracy Theory' (BA thesis, University of Leicester, 2005); Chirnside, *Olympic*, pp. 91–110, 141–8, 257–64; Fitch, Layton and Wormstedt, *On a Sea of Glass*, pp. 7, 39; Beveridge et al., *Ship Magnificent*, II, pp. 216, 219, 222, 225, 286–7, 355, 416–25, and figs 5-3, 5-17, 5-39; Mark Chirnside, 'The Forward A-Deck Promenade', an online lecture delivered for the Titanic Channel, accessed 2017; and Parks Stephenson, 'The Identity Conspiracy', an online lecture delivered for the Titanic Channel, accessed 2017.

34 Cameron, *Belfast's Own*, p. 92.

35 Fitzpatrick, *Descendancy*, p. 275.

36 Letter from Mary Sloan to her mother, written from the SS *Lapland*, 27 April 1912, cit. Bullock, *Thomas Andrews*, pp. 63–4.

37 The description of this meeting in the Reception Room on Friday 12 April is based on ibid.

Chapter 8: *A Kind of Hieroglyphic World*

1 A menu for this dinner is one of the more potentially gruesome mementoes of the *Titanic* disaster – it was either retrieved from the flotsam and jetsam or from the corpse of a victim recovered by the SS *Mackay Bennett*. It was auctioned in New York as lot 2041 by Bonhams on 15 April 2012, the centenary of the sinking, for $35,250 (approximately £23,800).

2　Letter from Gladys Cherry, 18 April 1912 (B123).

3　Beesley, *Titanic*, p. 12.

4　Respectively, they were Margaretha Emerentia Frölicher-Stehli (1864–1955) and her daughter, Hedwig Margaritha Frölicher (1889–1972), Hélène Baxter (1862–1923) and Thomson Beattie (1875–1912). Jakob Johansson's diary entry for 13 April (B93) mentions a few cases of seasickness in Third Class, and in Second Class Esther Hart's letter of 14 April (B94), written to a friend in Essex but never posted, mentions that she had felt 'very bad all day yesterday', but concedes that the crew thought the ship was having a 'wonderful passage'. That the nausea was not caused by adverse weather was corroborated in a letter from Hedwig Frölicher, dated 18 April, in which she states, 'I took to my cabin and for three days was unbearably seasick, although the weather was beautiful and the sea calm.'

5　Cynthia Asquith, *Remember and be Glad* (London: Barrie 1952), p. 165.

6　Paul Poiret, *My First Fifty Years* (London: Victor Gollancz, 1931), p. 73; Laird Borrelli-Persson, 'Poiret is being revived a century after its heyday – will it matter to fashion audiences in 2018?', *Vogue*, 30 January 2018.

7　Evans, *Titanic Style*, pp. 28–32; Dorothy later submitted a claim to the White Star Line for the gloves she had bought in Paris and lost in the sinking.

8　United States District Court, Southern District of New York, *In the Matter of the Petition of the Oceanic Steam Navigation Company, Limited, for Limitation of its Liability as Owner of the Steamship 'TITANIC' – the Claim of The Rt. Hon. Lucy-Noel Dyer Martha, Countess of Rothes*, 13 January 1913.

9　Robert Farquharson, *The House of Commons from Within, and Other Memories* (London: Williams and Norgate, 1912), pp. 211–12.

10 Eaton and Haas, *Titanic*, pp. 56–7.

11 Peter Engberg and Andrew Williams, 'Mr Percy William Fletcher', *Encyclopedia Titanica* (August 2017).

12 The other styles were Old and New Dutch, Renaissance, Tudor, Jacobean, William and Mary, Queen Anne, Georgian, Adams, Chippendale, Sheraton, Louis XIV, Louis XV, Louis XVI, Italian Renaissance and the First Empire.

13 These descriptions of the Countess of Rothes' stateroom are based on Beveridge et al., *Ship Magnificent*, II, p. 326 and figs 7-28 and 8-16, and Tom McCluskie, *Anatomy of the Titanic* (London: PRC Publishing, 1998), pp. 146–8.

14 This is made from compiling accounts in 1870 and 1911 editions of ladies' maid guides.

15 Ibid., pp. 61–2.

16 Tessa Boase, *The Housekeeper's Tale: The Women Who Really Ran the English Country House* (London: Aurum Press, 2015), p. 110.

17 Letter from Gladys Cherry, 18 April 1912.

18 Roberta Maioni, *Daily Express* (1926).

19 Bigham, 'A Matter of Course'.

20 *The Eton Register: Part VI, 1889–1899* (Eton: Spottiswoode, 1910), p. 39; *The Eton Register: Part VIII, 1909–1919* (London: W. H. Smith & Son, 1932), p. 142.

21 Brendon and Whitehead, *The Windsors*, p. 259.

22 Correspondence between Randy Bryan Bigham and Ian Leslie, 21st Earl of Rothes.

23 Douglas Sutherland, *The Yellow Earl: The Life of Hugh Lowther, 5th Earl of Lonsdale, K.G., G.C.V.O., 1857–1944* (London: Cassell, 1965), pp. 165–7.

24 Rose, *George V*, pp. 100–1.

25 Cannadine, *Decline and Fall*, p. 65.

26 David Cannadine, *Aspects: Grandeur and Decline in Modern Britain* (New Haven and London: Yale University Press, 1994), p. 171.

27 Cannadine, *Aspects of Aristocracy*, pp. 171, 182–3; G. Elliot Smith, *Tutankhamen and the Discovery of his Tomb by the Late Earl of Carnarvon and Mr Howard Carter* (London: George Routledge & Sons, 1923), pp. 28–9.

28 United States District Court, Southern District of New York, *In the Matter of the Petition of the Oceanic Steam Navigation Company, Limited, for Limitation of its Liability as Owner of the Steamship 'TITANIC' – the Claim of The Rt. Hon. Lucy-Noel Dyer Martha, Countess of Rothes*, 13 January 1913.

29 *New York Times*, 6 June 1911.

30 Fitch, Layton and Wormstedt, *On a Sea of Glass*, p. 61.

31 Zebley Taylor, *Jigsaw Picture Puzzle*, p. 174.

32 Gracie, *Titanic*, p. 7; Roberta Maioni, *Daily Express* writing competition (1926); an article in the *Boston Globe*, dated 5 July 1911 and discussing Virginia Vanderbilt's crossing to France on the *Olympic*, refers to the Reception Room as the ship's ballroom. (Courtesy of the Mike Poirier Collection).

33 Gracie, *Titanic*, p. 7.

34 Fitch, Layton and Wormstedt, *On a Sea of Glass*, pp. 87–9.

35 Lady Duff Gordon also later designed part of the trousseau for Lady Elizabeth Bowes-Lyon when she married into the British Royal Family in 1923. In 1996, Duff Gordon's biographer, Randy Bryan Bigham, contacted the bride, by then Queen Elizabeth the Queen Mother, who wrote back that she could remember Duff Gordon's beautiful designs in her trousseau but, unfortunately, at the distance of seven decades could not recall with precision what the pieces had been. My thanks to Randy Bryan Bigham for sharing with me details of his correspondence with Queen Elizabeth the Queen Mother via her lady-in-waiting, Lady Angela Oswald, 6 January 1996.

36 *Vogue*, 15 April 1910; *Vogue*, 15 April 1912; Randy Bryan Bigham, *Lucile: Her Life by Design* (London: Lulu Press, 2014), pp. 82–3. The April 1912 *Vogue* article on Lady Duff Gordon hit the newsstands on the day the *Titanic* sank.

37 Fitch, Layton and Wormstedt, *On a Sea of Glass*, pp. 93, 107.

38 Zebley Taylor, *Jigsaw Picture Puzzle*, p. 173; Fletcher, *Travelling Palaces*, p. 148.

39 Senan Molony, 'Sun Yat Sen Will Eat Again', *Encyclopedia Titanica* (2004); 'Woman's Cult of The Dog – No. 1 – The Pekingese', *Illustrated London News*, 19 April 1913. In various instances, the latter article confused the Pekingese with the Chow-Chow.

40 Sergio Martínez Costos-Alvarín, 'Victor Peñasco, a Spanish tragedy' online, *Titanic Passengers and Crew Research* (6 July 2012). Peñasco was a maternal nephew of José Canalejos y Méndez, who served as Prime Minister of Spain from February 1910 until his assassination in November 1912.

41 *Het Laatste Nieuws*, cit. in John Baxter, Alan Hustak and Herman DeWulf, 'Mlle Berthe Antonine Mayné', *Encyclopedia Titanica*, 23 November 2018.

42 *Titanic* ticket number 17482.

43 *Titanic* ticket numbers 17593 and 17477. Guggenheim was in B-82 and Aubart in B-35.

44 Fletcher, *Travelling Palaces*, p. 148.

45 Jessop, *Titanic Survivor*, pp. 114, 135.

46 Fletcher, *Travelling Palaces*, p. 147.

47 A particularly beautiful cover of Candee's 1912 *The Tapestry Book* is currently part of the private collection of historian Randy Bryan Bigham.

48 Brewster, *Gilded Lives*, pp. 110–12. For a defence of Hugh Woolner, see Senan Molony, 'The Fleecing of Hugh Woolner', *Encyclopedia Titanica* (February 2007).

49 Ibid., pp. 92–7.

50 Correspondence between the author and Gavin Cameron Bell, 5 July 2018.

51 Courtesy of the Mike Poirier Collection.

52 Elizabeth Wharton Drexel Lehr, *'King Lehr' and the Gilded Age* (New York: J. B. Lippincott, 1935), p. 164.

53 Wilson, *Astors*, pp. 206–7; Brewster, *Gilded Lives*, p. 75; Fitch, Taylor and Wormstedt, *On a Sea of Glass*, p. 113.

54 Jessop, *Titanic Survivor*, p. 133.

55 *The Unsinkable Molly Brown* (MGM, 1964), directed by Charles Walters and starring Debbie Reynolds (Margaret Brown), Harve Presnell (James Joseph Brown) and Martita Hunt (the Grand Duchess Elise).

56 Passenger Margaret Brown in the *Newport Herald*, 28 May 1912.

57 Lucy, Lady Duff Gordon, *Discretions and Indiscretions* (London: Frederick A. Stokes, 1932), p. 147.

Chapter 9: *Its Own Appointed Limits Keep*

1 Fitch, Layton and Wormstedt, *On a Sea of Glass*, p. 116.

2 John Martin Robinson, *The Dukes of Norfolk: A Quincentennial History* (Oxford and New York: Oxford University Press, 1982), pp. 143, 213–17. During the Popish Plot crisis (1678–81), the 7th Duke of Norfolk publicly conformed to the Church of England and attended Anglican services. He opposed James II's alleged promotion of Catholicism between 1685 and 1688 and served as a Privy Councillor to William III and Mary II. However, privately he remained a Roman Catholic and received the Last Rites from a Catholic priest on his deathbed in 1701.

3 Robinson, *The Dukes of Norfolk*, pp. 218–19; Gareth Russell, *The Emperors: How Europe's Rulers were Destroyed by the First World War* (Stroud: Amberley, 2014), pp. 162, 208–9.

4 Bigham, *Finding Dorothy*, p. 5.

5 Gracie, *Titanic*, p. 6.

6 William Whiting, 'Eternal Father, Strong to Save' (1860).

7 Hasia R. Diner, *A New Promised Land: A History of the Jews in America* (Oxford and New York: Oxford University Press, 2003), p. 32.

8 McCash, *Titanic Love Story*, pp. 174–5; correspondence between the author and Joan Adler, Executive Director of the Straus Historical Society, concerning the Strauses' summer cottage in Canada, 12 November 2018.

9 Letter from Frank H. Tabor to Isidor Straus, 17 November 1909 (SHS).

10 Letter from Jacob H. Schiff to C. S. Mellon, 15 April 1912 (SHS); Nathan Straus thought his sister-in-law had looked 'less [well], as she had had a recent attack of her ailment', when he saw her at Cap Martin that February: see McCash, *Titanic Love Story*, p. 173.

11 Letter from Jesse Straus to Herbert Straus, 28 March 1912 (SHS) mentions his recent exhaustion and a desire to introduce Beatrice to European languages as reasons for the trip.

12 McCash, *Titanic Love Story*, p. 175.

13 Letter from Isidor Straus to Oscar Straus, 12 March 1912 (SHS).

14 Gracie, *Titanic*, p. 7; McCash, *Titanic Love Story*, p. 192.

15 McCash, *Titanic Love Story*, p. 192.

16 Beveridge et al., *Ship Magnificent*, II, pp. 241–2.

17 Gracie, *Titanic*, p. 3.

18 Ibid., pp. 3–4.

19 Ibid., p. 4.

20 Letter from Ambrose Bierce to Colonel Archibald Gracie IV, dated 9 March 1911, cit. in Ambrose Bierce, *Phantoms of a Blood-Stained Period: The Complete*

Civil War Writings of Ambrose Bierce (Amherst, MA: University of Massachusetts Press, 2002), p. 202.

21 Amanda Foreman, *A World on Fire: An Epic History of Two Nations Divided* (London: Penguin, 2011), pp. 540–3; Gracie, *Titanic*, p. 7.

22 Gracie, *Titanic*, p. 7.

23 Isidor Straus, *The Autobiography of Isidor Straus* (New York: The Straus Historical Society, 2011), p. 1.

24 Ibid. The manuscript was archived and then first published by the Straus Historical Society in 1955.

25 Michael Davie, *The Titanic: The Full Story of a Tragedy* (London: Guild Publishing, 1986), p. 48.

26 Straus, *Autobiography*, p. 3; McCash, *Titanic Love Story*, p. 25.

27 Hans Joachim Hahn, *The 1848 Revolutions in German-Speaking Europe* (London: Pearson, 2001), pp. 186–7; Thomas Nipperdey, *Germany from Napoleon to Bismarck, 1800–1866*, trans. Daniel Nolan (Dublin: Gill & Macmillan, 1996), p. 528.

28 McCash, *Titanic Love Story*, pp. 24–6.

29 Karolina Straus was the only sibling who chose to stay in Germany rather than join Sara when she brought the rest of the children to the United States in 1854.

30 Diner, *Promised Land*, pp. 23–4.

31 Straus, *Autobiography*, pp. 4–5.

32 McCash, *Titanic Love Story*, p. 33.

33 Straus, *Autobiography*, p. 5.

34 Robert N. Rosen, 'Jewish Confederates', in Jonathan D. Sarna and Adam Mendelsohn (eds), *Jews and the Civil War: A Reader* (New York and London: New York University Press, 2010), pp. 230–2.

35 Ibid., p. 229; McCash, *Titanic Love Story*, pp. 38–9.

36 McCash, *Titanic Love Story*, p. 14.

37 Bertram W. Korn, 'Jews and Negro Slavery in the Old South, 1789–1865', in Sarna and Mendelsohn (eds), *Jews and the Civil War*, p. 117.

38 Ibid., p. 116.

39 Ibid., p. 113.

40 James M. McPherson, *For Cause and Comrades: Why Men Fought in the Civil War* (Oxford and New York: Oxford University Press, 1997), p. 107; Korn, 'Jews and Negro Slavery', p. 113.

41 Korn, 'Jews and Negro Slavery', p. 113.

42 Straus, *Autobiography*, p. 3.

43 Korn, 'Jews and Negro Slavery', p. 95.

44 Oscar S. Straus, *Under Four Administrations: From Cleveland to Taft* (Smithtown, NY: The Straus Historical Society, 2017), p. 13.

45 Straus, *Under Four Administrations*, p. 12.

46 The attendance of both boys is discussed in McCash, *Titanic Love Story*, p. 41, who received her information from one of the Strauses' descendants. I am grateful to Joan Adler at the Straus Historical Society for the suggestion that the most likely author of the final decision to buy the pregnant woman was Nathan.

47 Ibid., p. 41.

48 Straus, *Under Four Administrations*, pp. 12–13.

49 I am grateful to Joan Adler at the Straus Historical Society for information on the argument that the number of slaves owned by the family was less than thirteen.

50 Rosen, 'Jewish Confederates', p. 233.

51 McPherson, *Cause and Comrades*, p. 77.

52 Mrs Abraham Levy, 'To the Israelites of the South', circular from the Hebrew Ladies' Memorial Association, published at Richmond, VA, 5 June 1866, a copy of which is currently kept at the Beth Ahabah Museum and Archives in Richmond, VA.

53 Diner, *Promised Land*, p. 35.

54 Rosen, 'Jewish Confederates', p. 228.

55 McCash, *Titanic Love Story*, p. 50.

56 Straus, *Autobiography*, pp. 19–20.

57 For the draft's impact on New York in the immediate aftermath of Gettysburg, see James M. McPherson, *Battle Cry of Freedom: The Civil War Era* (Oxford: Oxford University Press, 1988), p. 609.

58 McCash, *Titanic Love Story*, pp. 52–7; *New York Times*, 14 July 1863.

59 Letter from Isidor Straus to Lazarus Straus, 14 November 1863 (SHS).

60 McPherson, *Cause and Comrades*, p. 107.

61 That Grant, rather than a deputy, was personally responsible for the 'sweeping order' is the contention of his current biographer, see Ronald C. White, *American Ulysses: The Life of Ulysses S. Grant* (New York: Random House, 2016), pp. 251–2.

62 Diner, *Promised Land*, p. 37.

63 Straus, *Autobiography*, p. 16; Robert N. Rosen, *The Jewish Confederates* (Columbia, SC: University of South Carolina Press, 2000), p. 270.

64 Adam Mendelsohn, 'Before Korn: A Century of Jewish Historical Writing about the American Civil War', in Sarna and Mendelsohn (eds), *Jews and the Civil War*, p. 3.

65 Thomas D. Clark, 'The Post-Civil War Economy in the South', in Sarna and Mendelsohn (eds), *Jews and the Civil War*, p. 387.

66 Letter from Isidor Straus to Ida Straus, 18 July 1904 (SHS); McCash, *Titanic Love Story*, pp. 79–81; Straus, *Autobiography*, p. 41.

67 McCash, *Titanic Love Story*, p. 168.

68 Ibid., p. 84.

69 Letter from Ida Straus to Isidor Straus, 29 July 1891 (SHS).

70 McCash, *Titanic Love Story*, pp. 171–2.

71 Ibid., p. 92.

72 Ibid., p. 15.

73 Letter from Isidor Straus to Ida Straus, 18 July 1904 (SHS).

74 Straus, *Autobiography*, pp. 145–7.

75 *New York Times*, 15 October 1912; *Atlanta Constitution*, 10 August 1913.

76 McCash, *Titanic Love Story*, p. 6.

77 Edvard Radzinsky, *Alexander II: The Last Great Tsar*, trans. Antonina W. Bouis (New York: Simon & Schuster, 2005), p. 449.

78 Grand Duke Alexander Mikhailovich of Russia, *Once a Grand Duke* (New York: Farrar & Reinhart, 1932), p. 59.

79 Radzinsky, *Alexander II*, p. 419; Simon Sebag Montefiore, *The Romanovs, 1613–1918* (London: Weidenfeld & Nicolson, 2016), p. 450.

80 Sebag Montefiore, *Romanovs*, p. 452.

81 Hermann von Samson-Himmelstjerna, *Russia under Alexander III: and in the Preceding Period*, trans. J. Morrison (London: T. F. Unwin, 1893), p. 12.

82 Ibid., p. 60.

83 Diner, *Promised Land*, pp. 43–4.

84 Robert K. Massie, *Nicholas and Alexandra* (London: Victor Gollancz, 1968), p. 15.

85 Serhii Plokhy, *Lost Kingdom: A History of Russian Nationalism from Ivan the Great to Vladimir Putin* (London: Allen Lane, 2017), p. 152.

86 Diner, *Promised Land*, pp. 31–2.

87 *New York Times*, 11 September 1910; *Jewish Chronicle*, 7 June 1912. My thanks to Joan Adler, Executive Director of the Straus Historical Society, for access to this latter piece. The poem continues:

> How long wilt thou, O Russia! thy cruel burdens bear!
> How long wilt thou meekly succumb to dull despair!
> Rise up, throw off thy shackles, strike for the right to live!
> For freedom, justice, tolerance, thy people's wrongs retrieve!
> And thou wilt surely triumph, for tyrants cowards are,
> They shrink beneath the radiance of Liberty's bright star.

For thee will dawn an era of brighter, happier days,

And all thy lamentations will change to songs of praise;

Thy present chaos, misrule, which now so hopeless seem,

Will then be but a memory, a nightmare in a dream,

Once more among the nations thou wilt take thy place,

And with their march towards progress and culture keep apace.

Thy people will be blessed o'er all thy broad domain,

When Law and Order shall prevail, and peace supreme shall reign! . . .

88 Allen W. Trelease, *White Terror: The Ku Klux Klan Conspiracy and Southern Reconstruction* (Baton Rouge, LA: Louisiana State University Press, 1999), p. 422.

89 McCash, *Titanic Love Story*, p. 173.

90 Letter from Isidor Straus to Oscar Straus, 8 October 1907 (SHS).

91 McCash, *Titanic Love Story*, p. 13.

92 Letter from President Grover Cleveland to Isidor Straus, 11 January 1896 (SHS). The letter mentions that the President had uttered the phrase 'a thousand times' to Straus.

93 Testament from Isidor Straus to his children, 6 February 1892 (SHS).

94 McCash, *Titanic Love Story*, p. 15.

95 Gracie, *Titanic*, p. 12.

96 Fitch, Layton and Wormstedt, *On a Sea of Glass*, p. 118.

Chapter 10: *Two More Boilers*

1 Testimony of Joseph B. Ismay to the British inquiry, 4 June 1912.

2 Fitch, Layton and Wormstedt, *On a Sea of Glass*, p. 116.

3 Beesley, *Titanic*, p. 10.

4 Fitch, Layton and Wormstedt, *On a Sea of Glass*, p. 112.

5 Senan Molony, quoted in Rachael Pells, '*Titanic* sank due to an enormous uncontrollable fire, not iceberg, claim experts', *Independent*, 1 January 2017.

6 Documentary, *Titanic: The New Evidence*, first broadcast on the Smithsonian Channel, 21 January 2017; R. H. Essenhigh, 'What Sank the *Titanic*?: The Possible Contribution of the Bunker Fire', paper delivered to Geological Society of America, Denver annual meeting, 7 November 2004; Ian Griggs and Paul Bignell, '*Titanic* doomed by fire below decks, says new theory', *Independent*, 13 April 2008.

7 Tim Foecke, *Metallurgy of the* RMS Titanic (Gaithersburg, MD: US Department of Commerce and National Institute of Statistics and Technology, 1998), p. 16.

8 Fitch, Layton and Wormstedt, *On a Sea of Glass*, p. 142.

9 Ibid., p. 113.

10 Ibid., p. 151.

11 Brinnin, *Sway of the Grand Saloon*, pp. 347–51.

12 *Edmonton Daily Chronicle,* 22 April 1912 (Courtesy of the Mike Poirier Collection).

13 Fletcher, *Travelling Palaces*, p. 169.

14 Beesley, *Titanic*, p. 14.

15 Thayer, *Titanic*, p. 334; Testimony at the Limitation of Liability Hearings, as reported in the *New York Times*, 25 June 1915.

16 Thayer, *Titanic*, pp. 333–4.

17 Ibid., p. 334.

18 Ibid., pp. 332, 334.

19 Albert J. Churella, *The Pennsylvania Railroad*, vol. I: *Building an Empire, 1846–1917* (Philadelphia: University of Pennsylvania Press, 2013), pp. 647, 684.

20 Ibid., p. 719.

21 Letter from Ida Straus to Lilian Burbidge, 10 April 1912 (LMQ/7/2/30); Gracie, *Titanic*, p. 3.

22 Genesis 11:1–9.

23 Morgan Robertson, *The Wreck of the Titan, or Futility* (Springfield, IL: Monroe St Press, 2015), pp. 1–2.

24 Bowen, *Century of Atlantic Travel*, pp. 188–9.

25 Fletcher, *Travelling Palaces*, p. 24.

26 Bowen, *Century of Atlantic Travel*, p. 241; Miller, *Famous Ocean Liners*, p. 13.

27 Aylmer, *Mauretania*, pp. 40–2; Duncan Haws, *Merchant Fleets: White Star Line (Oceanic Steam Navigation Company)* (Newport: Starling Press, 1990), p. 14.

28 Bowen, *Century of Atlantic Travel*, p. 294; Beesley, *Titanic*, p. 13; George Behe, *On Board RMS Titanic: Memories of the Maiden Voyage* (Stroud: The History Press, 2017), p. 29.

29 Fletcher, *Travelling Palaces*, p. 239.

30 Henry Martyn Hart, *Recollections and Reflections* (New York: Gibb Bros. & Moran, 1916), p. 107.

31 *New York Times*, 17 April 1912.

32 Passenger Margaret Brown in the *Newport Herald*, 28 May 1912.

33 Fitch, Layton and Wormstedt, *On a Sea of Glass*, p. 120.

34 *Yale Daily News*, 12 April 1912.

35 Years later, Florence confirmed this herself in a conversation with her grand-daughter, Pauline Matarasso, see Matarasso, *A Voyage Closed and Done*, pp. 24–5.

36 Fitch, Layton and Wormstedt, *On a Sea of Glass*, pp. 120–1; affidavit of Emily

Ryerson to the US Senate inquiry into the loss of the *Titanic*, 16 May 1912; passenger Mahala Douglas, interviewed in the *Los Angeles Times,* 21 April 1912.

Chapter 11: *A Thousand Uneasy Sparks of Light*

1 Wilson, *Ismay*, p. 199.

2 Thayer, *Titanic*, p. 334.

3 Fletcher, *Travelling Palaces*, pp. 252–3.

4 Beveridge et al., *Ship Magnificent*, II, pp. 282–7.

5 Stefan Zweig, *Marie Antoinette: Portrait of an Average Woman* (New York: The Viking Press, 1933), p. 106.

6 Ernest Townsley, *Daily Express*, 16 April 1912.

7 J. Bruce Ismay's testimony to the US Senate inquiry, 30 April 1912.

8 Passenger May Futrelle, *Philadelphia Evening Bulletin*, 29 April 1912.

9 Fitch, Layton and Wormstedt, *On a Sea of Glass*, p. 113.

10 Passenger May Futrelle, *Atlanta Constitution,* 26 May 1912.

11 Fitch, Layton and Wormstedt, *On a Sea of Glass*, pp. 128–9.

12 Duff Gordon, *Discretions and Indiscretions*, pp. 150–1.

13 McCash, *Titanic Love Story*, p. 193.

14 William Thornton Carter II was twelve years old at the time.

15 *Palestine Daily Herald*, 23 July 1904; *Times Despatch*, 29 April 1912.

16 Debs received 5.99 per cent of the popular vote in November 1912. At the time of writing, this remains the highest percentage achieved by a socialist candidate in an American presidential election.

17 Emmerson, *1913*, p. 146.

18 Ibid., pp. 142–3.

19 Ron Chernow, *The House of Morgan: An American Banking Dynasty and the Rise of Modern Finance* (New York: Grove Press, 2010), pp. 146–7.

20 Morris, *Tycoons*, pp. 235, 278–9.

21 The Constitution of the United States of America, Amendment XVI.

22 Morris, *Tycoons*, p. 278.

23 Brewster, *Gilded Lives*, p. 80; George Behe, *A Death on the 'Titanic': The Loss of Major Archibald Butt* (Morrisville, NC: Lulu, 2011), pp. 141–2.

24 Letter from Marian Thayer to President William Howard Taft, 21 April 1912 (B251).

25 *Argus*, 16 March 1912.

26 For Butt's immediate response to the attempted assassination, see Behe, *A Death on the 'Titanic'*, pp. 194–6. The Italian royal children in 1912 were Princess Yolanda (1900–86); Princess Mafalda, who died as an inmate at

Buchenwald concentration camp in 1944; the future King Umberto II (1904–83); and Princess Giovanna (1907–99). The fifth and last child, Princess Maria-Francesca, was not born until 1914.

27 *Argus*, 16 March 1912.

28 Behe, *A Death on the 'Titanic'*, pp. 194–6.

29 The Mass was to mark the anniversary of the late King's birth on 14 March. King Umberto I of Italy (1844–1900) had been assassinated by anarchist Gaetano Bresci during a visit to Monza on 29 July.

30 Andreas Kopasis, Prince of Samos, was appointed Governor by Sultan Abdul Hamid II in 1908 and served until he was murdered in Vathy on 22 March 1912.

31 *Daily Telegraph*, 7 January 1899; Marguerite Cunliffe-Owen, *The Martyrdom of an Empress* (New York: Harper, 1899), pp. 274–82; *New York Times*, 10 November 1898.

32 The assassinations referenced are of Marie François Sadi Carnot (1837–94), President of France, murdered in Lyon by an anarchist; Antonio Cánovas del Castillo (1828–97), Prime Minister of Spain, assassinated by an anarchist in Mondragón; Elisabeth of Bavaria (1837–98), Empress Consort of Austria and Queen Consort of Hungary, stabbed by an anarchist during her visit to Geneva; Dmitri Sipyagin (1853–1902), Minister of the Interior, killed by a revolutionary socialist in St Petersburg; King Alexander I of Serbia (1876–1903) and his wife, Queen Draga (1864–1903), who were both lynched during a nationalist coup in Belgrade; Vyacheslav von Plehve (1846–1904), Minister of the Interior, killed by a revolutionary socialist in St Petersburg; Nicholas Bobrikov (1839–1904), Governor-General of Finland, assassinated in Helsinki by a revolutionary socialist; Grand Duke Sergei Alexandrovich of Russia (1857–1905), killed in a bomb attack by a socialist revolutionary five weeks after resigning as Governor-General of Moscow; Theodoros Deligiannis (1820–1905), Greek Prime Minister, murdered by a political opponent in Athens in 1905; Prime Minister Dimikar Petkov of Bulgaria (1858–1907), shot by an anarchist in Sofia; King Carlos I of Portugal (1863–1908), shot by a republican in Lisbon, dying twenty minutes before his son and heir, who thus achieved the sad distinction of the shortest reign in European history as King Luís-Filipe (1887–1908). Finally, the Russian Prime Minister, Pyotr Stolypin (1862–1911), was murdered by a revolutionary socialist while attending a performance of the opera in Kiev.

33 This was the wedding of King Alfonso XIII to Princess Victoria-Eugenia of Battenberg in Madrid on 31 May 1906.

34 Behe, *Death on the 'Titanic'*, p. 177.

35 Ibid., pp. 203–6.

36 Ibid., p. 207; *New York Times*, 3 June 1935; letter from Marian Thayer to President William Howard Taft, 21 April 1912.

37 Letter from Marian Thayer to President William Howard Taft, 21 April 1912.

38 Behe, *Butt*, p. 578.

39 Behe, *Death on the 'Titanic'*, pp. 21–2, 164–6.

40 Brewster, *Gilded Lives*, pp. 37–43.

41 Jonathan Ned Katz, *Love Stories: Sex between Men before Homosexuality* (Chicago and London: University of Chicago Press, 2001), p. 355.

42 Brewster, *Gilded Lives*, pp. 6–7.

43 Carl Sferrazza Anthony, *Nellie Taft: The Unconventional First Lady of the Ragtime Era* (New York: William Morrow, 2005), pp. 309–10, 483n–484n; James Gifford, 'Archie Butt and Edwardian Homosexuality', *Out* (April 2012). The First Lady was also friends with Millet.

44 Letter from Francis Millet to Alfred Parsons, 11 April 1912 (B72).

45 *Titanic* ticket number 13509.

46 *Titanic* ticket number 113050.

47 Fitch, Layton and Wormstedt, *On a Sea of Glass*, p. 130.

48 Letter from Daisy Minahan to Senator William Alden Smith (R-MI), 11 May 1912.

49 *Washington Herald*, 21 April 1912.

50 Letter from Mary Sloan to her sister, 27 April 1912.

51 Fitch, Layton and Wormstedt, *On a Sea of Glass*, p. 109.

52 Letter from Eleanor Cassebeer to Walter Lord, 9 November 1955 (Courtesy of the Mike Poirier Collection).

53 Passenger Eleanor Cassebeer in the *Binghamton Press*, 7 May 1912 (Courtesy of the Mike Poirier Collection).

54 Interview with passenger Vera Dick, printed in Bullock, *Thomas Andrews*, p. 42.

55 They were Hudson Allison and his wife Bessie (née Daniels), travelling in a suite of rooms, C-22, C-24, C-26, on ticket number 113781. They and their daughter, Loraine, lost their lives in the sinking of the *Titanic*.

56 The pigeon was referred to as Roast Squab. This description is based on the Saloon menu for Sunday 14 April that was sold at auction in Dallas, TX, by Heritage Auctions for $188,000 on Saturday 7 November 2015.

57 Letter from Gladys Cherry to her mother, 17 April 1912 (B113).

58 Ibid.; letter from the Dowager Countess of Rothes to Walter Lord, 7 August 1955.

59 Bullock, *Thomas Andrews*, p. 64. It is the current author's belief that the special bread would have been an Ulster speciality.

60 Bullock, *Thomas Andrews*, p. 134; interview with passengers Albert and Vera Dick, published in the *Calgary Herald*, 30 April 1912 (Courtesy of the Mike

Poirier Collection). Contemporary confusion over the Reception Room's proper name may explain why the *Calgary Herald* reported that Andrews and the Dicks initially planned to take coffee in 'what was called the Parisian cafe [*sic*], or the palm room'.

61 Bigham, *Finding Dorothy*, p. 189.

62 Behe, *On Board*, p. 376.

63 *New York World*, 20 April 1912; interview with Dorothy Gibson for the *New York Telegraph*, 21 April 1912.

64 Letter from John Badenoch to Percy Straus, 24 April 1912 (SHS).

65 Milton Clyde Long's United States passport application, 1910. Retrieved from *Encyclopedia Titanica*, 14 November 2017.

66 Long was berthed in stateroom D-6, ticket number 113501; see also Thayer, *Titanic*, p. 334.

67 Thayer, *Titanic*, p. 334.

68 Fitch, Layton and Wormstedt, *On a Sea of Glass*, p. 141.

69 Thayer, *Titanic*, p. 334.

70 Ibid.

71 Ibid., p. 335; Statement made by Jack Thayer to the first vice-president of Pennsylvania Lines West of Pittsburgh, 20 April 1912 (B250).

72 Thayer, *Titanic*, p. 335.

Chapter 12: *Going Up to See the Fun*

1 Fitch, Layton and Wormstedt, *On a Sea of Glass*, pp. 141–3.

2 Behe, *On Board*, pp. 84–5; passenger Frederick Hoyt in the *Springfield Union*, 20 April 1912 (Courtesy of the Mike Poirier Collection).

3 These were the recollections of Lady Lucy Duff Gordon in A-20, Nelle Snyder in B-45 and Elmer Taylor in C-126.

4 Beesley, *Titanic*, p. 22.

5 Second-class passenger Elizabeth Watt, *Portland Oregonian*, 24 April 1912; testimony by passenger Major Arthur Peuchen to the US Senate inquiry, 23 April 1912.

6 Letter from the Dowager Countess of Rothes to Walter Lord, 7 August 1955.

7 Thayer, *Titanic*, pp. 335–6.

8 Davie, *Titanic*, p. 101.

9 Letter from Gladys Cherry to her mother, 17 April 1912; letter from the Dowager Countess of Rothes to Walter Lord, 7 August 1955.

10 Letter from the Dowager Countess of Rothes to Walter Lord, 7 August 1955.

11 Thayer, *Titanic*, p. 336.

12 Ibid., p. 336 only mentions John Thayer as an accompanying parent. However,

the account of the sinking dictated by Jack Thayer on 20 April 1912 to the Pennsylvania Lines West of Pittsburgh Board references both parents on deck. See also Fitch, Layton and Wormstedt, *On a Sea of Glass*, p. 165.

13 *New York Morning Telegraph*, 21 April 1912.

14 Andrew Wilson, *Shadow of the Titanic: The Extraordinary Stories of Those Who Survived* (London: Simon & Schuster, 2011), pp. 28–9.

15 Passenger William Sloper's account, written on 18 April 1912 and published in the *Hartford Times*, 19 April 1912.

16 Ibid.

17 Ibid.

18 Passenger A. A. Dick in the *Calgary Herald*, 30 April 1912 (Courtesy of the Mike Poirier Collection).

19 Wilson, *Shadow*, p. 33.

20 Fitch, Layton and Wormstedt, *On a Sea of Glass*, p. 153.

21 Ibid., p. 151.

22 Behe, *On Board*, p. 148.

23 Passenger William Sloper's account, written on 18 April 1912 and published in the *Hartford Times*, 19 April 1912 (Courtesy of the Mike Poirier Collection).

24 Fitch, Layton and Wormstedt, *On a Sea of Glass*, pp. 151 n.226, 160, 397.

25 Ibid., Appendix F, 'The Iceberg Damage', pp. 295–7.

26 Testimony of Stewardess Annie Robinson to the British inquiry, 20 May 1912.

27 Fitch, Layton and Wormstedt, *On a Sea of Glass*, p. 186.

28 Testimony of Joseph Boxhall to the British inquiry, 22 May 1912.

29 Letter from the Dowager Countess of Rothes to Walter Lord, 7 August 1955.

30 This seems to disprove Lady Rothes' recollection in an otherwise generally accurate account, which she imparted to Walter Lord in 1955, that they received this warning from the ship's Purser, Hugh McElroy, who also told them to hurry. Gladys Cherry's version of the same events, which she wrote down while on the *Carpathia* two days after the sinking of the *Titanic*, seems the more probable of the two.

31 Passenger William Sloper's account, written on 18 April 1912 and published in the *Hartford Times*, 19 April 1912.

32 Letter from John Badenoch to Percy Straus, 24 April 1912.

33 McCash, *Titanic Love Story*, p. 194.

34 Letter from John Badenoch to Percy Straus, 24 April 1912.

35 Ibid.

36 Gracie, *Titanic*, p. 16. Later, Gracie could not remember if it was at this point or some time later that 'I had heard them discussing that if they were going to die they would die together.' If such a conversation did take place, it would likely have been later that night.

Chapter 13: *Music in the First-Class Lounge*

1 Letter from Gladys Cherry to her mother, 17 April 1912.
2 Letters from Gladys Cherry, one to her mother and the other to an unknown recipient, respectively dated 17 and 18 April 1912.
3 Letter from the Dowager Countess of Rothes to Walter Lord, 7 August 1955.
4 Fitch, Layton and Wormstedt, *On a Sea of Glass*, p. 184.
5 Nick Barratt, *Lost Voices from the Titanic: The Definitive Oral History* (London: Preface, 2009), p. 161.
6 Fitch, Layton and Wormstedt, *On a Sea of Glass*, p. 187.
7 Passenger Henry Harper in *Harper's Weekly*, 27 April 1912.
8 Helen Churchill Candee, *Sealed Orders*, 4 May 1912.
9 This account of the Thayer party was reached through compiling recollections of Martha Stephenson and Elizabeth Eustis (B247); account of the sinking dictated by Jack Thayer on 20 April 1912 to the Pennsylvania Lines West of Pittsburgh Board, and Thayer, *Titanic*, pp. 337–9.
10 Thayer, *Titanic*, p. 338.
11 Ibid., p. 339.
12 Fitch, Layton and Wormstedt, *On a Sea of Glass*, p. 184.
13 Thayer, *Titanic*, p. 339.
14 Passenger Gilbert Tucker in *Times Union*, 19 April 1912 (Courtesy of the Mike Poirier Collection).
15 Passenger William Sloper's account, written on 18 April 1912 and published in the *Hartford Times*, 19 April 1912 (Courtesy of the Mike Poirier Collection).
16 Wilson, *Shadow*, p. 35.
17 Passenger William Sloper's account, written on 18 April 1912 and published in the *Hartford Times*, 19 April 1912.
18 Ibid.
19 Wilson, *Shadow*, p. 244.
20 Fitch, Layton and Wormstedt, *On a Sea of Glass*, p. 194.
21 Passenger William Sloper's account, written on 18 April 1912 and published in the *Hartford Times*, 19 April 1912.
22 Fitch, Layton and Wormstedt, *On a Sea of Glass*, p. 165.
23 Passenger Margaret Brown to the *New York Times*, 22 April 1912.
24 Passenger Eleanor Cassebeer to the *Binghamton Press*, 29 April 1912.
25 Testimony of Officer Herbert Pitman to the US Senate inquiry, 23 April 1912.
26 Fitch, Layton and Wormstedt, *On a Sea of Glass*, p. 199.
27 Passenger Eleanor Cassebeer to the *Binghamton Press*, 29 April 1912.

Chapter 14: *Vox faucibus haesit*

1 Lady Rothes later told the writer Walter Lord that she did not hear the band at any point during the evacuation, which means she must have bypassed the Lounge, where the band were still playing throughout the time it took for her to leave the *Titanic*.

2 Letter from the Dowager Countess of Rothes to Walter Lord, 7 August 1955; Charles Herbert Lightoller, *Titanic and Other Ships* (Oxford: Oxford City Press, 2010), p. 85.

3 Letter from the Dowager Countess of Rothes to Walter Lord, 7 August 1955.

4 The roar from the funnels stopped at about 12.50 a.m.

5 The Countess of Rothes in the *New York Daily Herald*, 22 April 1912.

6 Letter from the Dowager Countess of Rothes to Walter Lord, 7 August 1955.

7 Ibid.

8 Ibid.

9 There seems to me no reason whatsoever to believe that it was a mystery trawler or an unidentified ship, when the *Californian* was within range and behaved precisely as several eyewitnesses described. For a thorough discussion of the debate see Fitch, Layton and Wormstedt, *On a Sea of Glass*, Appendix R, 'The *Californian* Affair', pp. 365–7.

10 Letter from the Dowager Countess of Rothes to Walter Lord, 7 August 1955.

11 *New York World*, 20 April 1912.

12 Letter from the Dowager Countess of Rothes to Walter Lord, 7 August 1955.

13 Gracie, *Titanic*, p. 16.

14 McCash, *Titanic Love Story*, p. 196.

15 Davie, *Titanic*, p. 48.

16 Passenger May Futrelle in the *Philadelphia Evening Bulletin*, 29 April 1912.

17 Duff Gordon, *Discretions and Indiscretions*, p. 154.

18 Ibid.

19 This was a lugubriously recurring trope in stories of shipwrecks, with similar misleading anecdotes reported around the loss of the Cunard Line's *Lusitania* (1915), the White Star–Royal Navy's *Britannic* (1916), the American cruise ship *Morro Castle* (1934) and the Northern Irish ferry *Princess Victoria* (1953). The latter of which was told to the author by his grandmother by whom, it must be said, no amount of contrary evidence has as yet been accepted as a convincing rebuttal.

20 My thanks to Mrs Laura Woodward for this anecdote.

21 Letter from third-class passenger Daniel Buckley to his mother, written c. 18 April 1912 (B110).

22 George Bernard Shaw, letter to the *Daily News*, 4 May 1912.

23 Sir Arthur Conan Doyle, letter to the *Daily News*, 8 May 1912.

24 Passenger Ellen Bird in the *New York World*, 20 April 1912.

25 My thanks to Joan Adler, Executive Director of the Straus Historical Society, for confirming this anecdote.

26 *New York World*, 20 April 1912.

27 Letter from the Dowager Countess of Rothes to Walter Lord, 7 August 1955, and letter from Gladys Cherry to her mother, 17 April 1912.

28 Ibid.

29 The best modern recreations of the sinking broadly concur with survivors' accounts that the water had reached the ship's nameplate by about 1.15 a.m.

30 Passenger May Futrelle in the *Seattle Daily Times*, 22 April 1912.

31 Passenger Hugh Woolner in the *New York Sun*, 19 April 1912.

32 Testimony of second-class passenger Imanita Shelley to the US Senate inquiry, 25 May 1912.

33 Ibid.

34 Fitch, Layton and Wormstedt, *On a Sea of Glass*, p. 211.

35 Letter from Imanita Shelley to Edith Harper, undated, in the summer of 1912 (B238).

36 Ibid.

37 Testimony of Colonel Archibald Gracie IV to the US Senate inquiry, 30 April 1912.

38 Letter from Imanita Shelley to Edith Harper, undated, in the summer of 1912.

39 Testimony by crew member August Weikman to the US Senate inquiry, 24 April 1912.

40 Letter from crew member Mary Sloan to her sister, 27 April 1912 (B241).

41 Beveridge et al., *Ship Magnificent*, II, pp. 292–4, 336–40, 370, figs 7-45, 9-32, 9-33, 9-34; *The Shipbuilder*, pp. 47–53, describes the second-class Smoke Room's decoration as 'a variation of [the] Louis XVI. period'. Apart from a few pieces of decoration on the doors, however, it is hard to see any decorating touches in common with the Louis Seize style.

42 Daniel Buckley (1890–1918) was born in Manchester, but moved as a child to Kingwilliamstown, Ireland (renamed Ballydesmond after Irish independence). He was killed on active service with the US Army during the First World War.

43 Testimony of third-class passenger Daniel Buckley to the US Senate inquiry, 3 May 1912.

44 Ibid.

45 Ibid.

46 Ibid.

47 Ibid; another third-class passenger, Victor Sunderland, mentioned the crew's

help – interview with the *Cleveland Plain Dealer*, 26 April 1912 (Courtesy of the Mike Poirier Collection).

48 Letter from third-class passenger Olaus Abelseth to his father, 19 April 1912 (B137).

49 Testimony of third-class passenger Daniel Buckley to the US Senate inquiry into the loss of the *Titanic*, day 13.

50 Fitch, Layton and Wormstedt, *On a Sea of Glass*, Appendix Q, 'J. "Brute" Ismay', pp. 364–5; Chuck Anesi, 'The *Titanic* Casualty Figures and What They Mean' (http://www.anesi.com/titanic.htm, 2018); British Parliamentary Papers, *Shipping Casualties (Loss of the Steamship 'Titanic'): Report of a formal investigation into the circumstances attending the foundering on the 15th April, 1912, of the British Steamship 'Titanic,' of Liverpool, after striking ice in or near Latitude 41° 46' N., Longitude 50° 14' W., North Atlantic Ocean, whereby loss of life ensued*, cmd 6352 (London: His Majesty's Stationery Office, 1912), p. 42.

51 This is based on compiling the respective nationalities of the passengers – First Class had 89 per cent of passengers from English-speaking nations (212 Americans, 48 British subjects, 27 Canadians); Second Class had 79 per cent (51 Americans, 1 Australian, 168 British subjects, 2 Canadians and 4 South Africans); Third Class had 39 per cent (43 Americans, 1 Australian, 231 from the United Kingdom, 5 Canadians and 1 South African).

52 The source for this particular rumour is apparently a comment Jack Thayer made at a 1915 insurance hearing and reported in the *New York Press*, 23 June 1915 (Courtesy of the Mike Poirier Collection). Jack allegedly said, 'My father and I went along to about eight different boats and inquired of the men in charge which boat would take first-class passengers, but each officer would send us to another boat, so finally we gave up.' This seems to suggest uncertainty in lifeboat allocation, rather than an assumption that they would be boarded ahead of others because they were in First Class.

53 Thayer, *Titanic*, p. 339 misidentifies this man, Steward Charles Dodd, as the Chief Dining Saloon Steward.

54 Fitch, Layton and Wormstedt, *On a Sea of Glass*, p. 221.

55 Thayer, *Titanic*, p. 339.

56 Gavin Cameron Bell, Philip Gowan, Bob Smith, Hermann Snölder, Brian J. Ticehurst, 'Miss Kate Buss', *Encyclopedia Titanica*, 23 November 2018.

57 Fitch, Layton and Wormstedt, *On a Sea of Glass*, pp. 178–9.

58 These were lifeboats 6, 16, 14, 12 and 2 from the port side, and 9, 11, 13 and 15 from starboard.

59 Account of second-class passenger Charlotte Collyer, 1912 (B162).

60 Fitch, Layton and Wormstedt, *On a Sea of Glass*, p. 211.

61 Testimony of Officer Harold Lowe to the US Senate inquiry, 24 April 1912.

62 Fitch, Layton and Wormstedt, *On a Sea of Glass*, p. 221.

63 For the lowering of Lifeboat 4, see Gracie, *Titanic*, pp. 19–20; Fitch, Layton and Wormstedt, *On a Sea of Glass*, pp. 222–3; passenger Kornelia Andrews' interview with the *Hudson Evening Register*, 20 April 1912; affidavit of Emily Ryerson to the US Senate inquiry, 16 May 1912; Behe, *Death on the 'Titanic'*, pp. 247–51, and the recollections of Martha Stephenson which she sent to Colonel Gracie and can be found in Gracie, *Titanic*, pp. 126-8.

64 Gracie, *Titanic*, p. 27; for the original quote and its translation, see Virgil, *Aeneid*, ii.774, and John O'Brien, 'Vox Faucibus Haesit' in *Symposium* (1996), 49, pp. 297–306.

65 Letter from the Dowager Countess of Rothes to Walter Lord, 7 August 1955.

Chapter 15: *Be British*

1 It was not, as is frequently stated, *The Approach to the New World*, another Wilkinson, which was on display in the *Olympic*'s Smoking Room.

2 Beveridge et al., *Ship Magnificent*, II, pp. 244–8.

3 Bullock, *Thomas Andrews*, p. 216.

4 Most memorably in the movies *A Night to Remember* (1958) and *Titanic* (1997), where Andrews was played by Michael Goodliffe and Victor Garber, and the television series *S.O.S. Titanic* (1979), in which he was played by Geoffrey Whitehead. The latter scene, with the Steward replaced by Stewardess Mary Sloan, played by Helen Mirren, was omitted from some of the later television broadcasts of *S.O.S. Titanic*.

5 Fitch, Layton and Wormstedt, *On a Sea of Glass*, Appendix L, 'Thomas Andrews' Fate', p. 322.

6 Sir Horace Plunkett (1854–1932), former MP for South Dublin, penned the foreword to the resultant biography of Thomas Andrews by Shan Bullock, *Thomas Andrews: Shipbuilder*, published in Dublin in December 1912.

7 Letter from crew member Mary Sloan to her sister, 27 April 1912.

8 Fitch, Layton and Wormstedt, *On a Sea of Glass*, p. 229.

9 Cameron, *Belfast's Own*, p. 93.

10 Bullock, *Thomas Andrews*, p. 74 records the 'final and grandest sight of him, throwing deck chairs overboard to the unfortunates in the water below'.

11 Bullock, *Thomas Andrews*, p. 4.

12 Bowen, *Century of Atlantic*, pp. 282–3.

13 Preston, *Wilful Murder*, pp. 471–3.

14 Richard Howells, *The Myth of the Titanic* (London: Macmillan Press, 1999), p. 101.

15 Passenger Frederick Hoyt in the *Springfield Union*, 20 April 1912 (Courtesy of the Mike Poirier Collection).

16 Howells, *Myth of the Titanic*, p. 111.

17 Ibid., p. 100.

18 Ibid., p. 101.

19 *Daily Graphic*, 20 April 1912 ('Titanic In Memoriam Number'), p. 9.

20 Howells, *Myth*, p. 101.

21 Ibid. The memorial is in Lichfield. The full text reads,

'COMMANDER
EDWARD JOHN SMITH R.D. R.N.R.
BORN JANUARY 27 1850 DIED APRIL 15 1912
BEQUEATHING TO HIS COUNTRYMEN
THE MEMORY & EXAMPLE OF A GREAT HEART
A BRAVE LIFE AND A HEROIC DEATH
"BE BRITISH"'

22 Ibid., p. 112.

23 Ibid., pp. 117–19.

24 George Bernard Shaw, *Daily News and Leader*, 14 May 1912, p. 9; Howells, *Myth*, p. 114.

25 Letter from the Dowager Countess of Rothes to Walter Lord, 7 August 1955.

26 Marian Thayer's affidavit, cit. Gracie, *Titanic*, pp. 125–6.

27 Fitch, Layton and Wormstedt, *On a Sea of Glass*, p. 197.

28 Howells, *Myth*, pp. 106, 114.

29 Third-class passenger Victor Sunderland in the *Cleveland Plain Dealer*, 26 April 1912 (Courtesy of the Mike Poirier Collection).

30 Statement made by Jack Thayer to the first vice-president of Pennsylvania Lines West of Pittsburgh, 20 April 1912.

31 Interview with passenger Charles E. Stengel in the *New York Evening Globe*, 19 April 1912; interview with third-class passenger Victor Sunderland in the *Cleveland Plain Dealer*, 26 April 1912 (Courtesy of the Mike Poirier Collection).

32 Interview with Wallace Hartley, reprinted in the *Manchester Guardian*, 22 April 1912.

33 Joey Butler, 'Did Faith Drive the *Titanic*'s Musicians?' (Queen's University Belfast circular, 2011).

34 Behe in Fitch, Layton and Wormstedt, *On a Sea of Glass*, Appendix J, 'The Music of the *Titanic*'s Band', p. 304.

35 Account of third-class passengers Ellen Mocklare and Bertha Moran in the *Evening World*, 22 May 1912.

36 Fitch, Layton and Wormstedt, *On a Sea of Glass*, p. 229; third-class passenger Victor Sunderland in the *Cleveland Plain Dealer*, 26 April 1912 (Courtesy of the Mike Poirier Collection).

37 Father Graham Smith, 'Devotion to a heroic priest who died on the *Titanic* is growing', *Catholic Herald*, 7 April 2016; *Hampshire Telegraph*, 3 May 1912 (Courtesy of the Mike Poirier Collection); account of third-class passengers Ellen Mocklare and Bertha Moran in the *Evening World*, 22 May 1912.

38 Letter from third-class passenger August Wennerström to his brother, 1 May 1912, cit. Fitch, Layton and Wormstedt, *On a Sea of Glass*, p. 229. Wennerström's article in the left-wing newspaper *Gula Faran* was not the first time that periodical had carried a piece in favour of a republic; however, his attracted widespread attention, and criticism, for the intensity of its attack on the personality of the late King, Oscar II (1829–1907).

39 Fitch, Layton and Wormstedt, *On a Sea of Glass*, p. 229.

Chapter 16: *Over the Top Together*

1 Captain Lawrence V. Wade, 'Lookouts: The Human Perspective', *Encyclopedia Titanica*, 28 August 2003.

2 Fitch, Layton and Wormstedt, *On a Sea of Glass*, p. 198.

3 Wilson, *Shadow*, p. 256.

4 Ibid., p. 255.

5 Ibid., p. 244.

6 Fitch, Layton and Wormstedt, *On a Sea of Glass*, p. 229.

7 Statement made by Jack Thayer to the first vice-president of Pennsylvania Lines West of Pittsburgh, 20 April 1912.

8 Ibid.

9 Crew member Cecil Fitzpatrick's testimony to the *Liverpool Journal of Commerce*, 30 April 1912.

10 Ibid.; Fitch, Layton and Wormstedt, *On a Sea of Glass*, Appendix L, 'Thomas Andrews' Fate', pp. 321–3.

11 Lightoller, *Titanic and Other Ships*, p. 188.

12 Statement by Colonel Archibald Gracie IV to the *New York Evening Globe*, 19 April 1912.

13 Statement made by Jack Thayer to the first vice-president of Pennsylvania Lines West of Pittsburgh, 20 April 1912.

14 Deck plans of A-Deck, drawn by Bruce Beveridge, printed in Fitch, Layton and Wormstedt, *On a Sea of Glass*, pp. 442–3.

15 Passenger Elizabeth Nye in the *Folkestone Herald*, 4 May 1912.

16 Thayer, *Titanic*, p. 343.

17 Ibid.

18 Ibid.

19 Statement made by Jack Thayer to the first vice-president of Pennsylvania Lines West of Pittsburgh, 20 April 1912; Thayer, *Titanic*, pp. 344–5. There are various recollections, although none with significant deviations from one another, of what Milton and Jack said to each other at that moment.

20 Thayer, *Titanic*, p. 344.

21 Statement made by Jack Thayer to the first vice-president of Pennsylvania Lines West of Pittsburgh, 20 April 1912.

22 Lightoller, *Titanic and Other Ships*, p. 191; Thayer, *Titanic*, p. 345.

23 Thayer, *Titanic*, p. 346.

24 Statement made by Jack Thayer to the first vice-president of Pennsylvania Lines West of Pittsburgh, 20 April 1912.

25 Thayer, *Titanic*, pp. 347–8.

Chapter 17: *The Awful Spectacle*

1 Interview given by Eleanor Danforth to the *New York Evening World*, 19 April 1912; Colonel Gracie saw Thayer move aft with George Widener and mentioned this to passenger May Futrelle, who repeated it in the *Seattle Times* on 23 April 1912.

2 Letter from third-class passenger Daniel Buckley to his mother, 18 April 1912.

3 Gracie, *Titanic*, p. 36.

4 *Washington Post Semi-Monthly Magazine*, 26 May 1912.

5 Passenger May Futrelle, *Seattle Times*, 23 April 1912; Fitch, Layton and Wormstedt, *On a Sea of Glass*, p. 238.

6 Testimony of Charles Lightoller to the British inquiry, 21 May 1912.

7 Gracie, *Titanic*, p. 38.

8 *Titanic* (20th Century Fox, 1953), directed by Jean Negulesco and starring Barbara Stanwyck, Clifton Webb, Richard Wagner, Brian Aherne and Thelma Ritter; *A Night to Remember* (The Rank Organisation and Paramount Studios, 1958), directed by Roy Baker, based on the novel by Walter Lord and starring Kenneth More, Honor Blackman, Tucker McGuire and Michael Goodliffe.

9 *Titanic* (20th Century Fox and Paramount, 1997), directed by James Cameron and starring Kate Winslet, Leonardo DiCaprio, Gloria Stuart, Billy Zane, Kathy Bates, Victor Garber, Rochelle Rose and Frances Fisher.

10 Letter from third-class passenger Bertha Mulvihill to her sister, written on 17 or 18 April 1912 (B114).

11 Second-class passenger Nellie Becker to the *Madras Mail*, 22 May 1912.

12 Letter from Gladys Cherry to her mother, 17 April 1912; letter from the Dowager Countess of Rothes to Walter Lord, 7 August 1955.

13 Statement made by Jack Thayer to the first vice-president of Pennsylvania Lines West of Pittsburgh, 20 April 1912.

14 Ibid.

15 Letter from passenger Hedwig Margaritha Frölicher to her brother, 18 April 1912 (B126).

16 Statement made by Jack Thayer to the first vice-president of Pennsylvania Lines West of Pittsburgh, 20 April 1912.

17 Wilson, *Shadow*, p. 244.

18 Bigham, *Finding Dorothy*, p. 63.

19 Dorothy Gibson's interview in the *Morning Telegraph*, 21 April 1912.

20 Testimony of Sir Cosmo Duff Gordon to the British inquiry, 17 May 1912.

Chapter 18: *Grip Fast*

1 Letter from Gladys Cherry to her mother, 17 April 1912.

2 Letter from the Dowager Countess of Rothes to Walter Lord, 7 August 1955.

3 Letter from Gladys Cherry to Thomas Jones, 19 April 1912.

4 Ibid.

5 Ibid.

6 British inquiry, question 11109.

7 Testimony of second-class passenger Imanita Shelley to the US Senate inquiry, 25 May 1912.

8 Brinnin, *Sway of the Grand Saloon*, p. 339.

9 Fitch, Layton and Wormstedt, *On a Sea of Glass*, p. 238.

10 Wilson, *Shadow*, pp. 253–4.

11 Letter from Gladys Cherry to her mother, 17 April 1912.

12 Letter from the Dowager Countess of Rothes to Walter Lord, 7 August 1955.

13 Davie, *Titanic*, p. 285.

14 The Countess of Rothes in the *New York Daily Herald*, 22 April 1912.

15 Letter from the Dowager Countess of Rothes to Walter Lord, 7 August 1955.

16 Ibid.

17 Fitch, Layton and Wormstedt, *On a Sea of Glass*, p. 240.

18 Letter from the Dowager Countess of Rothes to Walter Lord, 7 August 1955.

19 Letter from Gladys Cherry to her mother, 18 April 1912.

20 Letter from the Dowager Countess of Rothes to Walter Lord, 7 August 1955.

21 Ibid.

22 Fitch, Layton and Wormstedt, *On a Sea of Glass*, p. 247.

23 Third-class passenger Victor Sunderland in the *Cleveland Plain Dealer*, 26 April 1912 (Courtesy of the Mike Poirier Collection).

24 Letter from the Dowager Countess of Rothes to Walter Lord, 7 August 1955.

25 Passenger Juliette Taylor in the *Newburgh Daily* News, 19 April 1912 (Courtesy of the Mike Poirier Collection); passenger Elizabeth Nye in the *Folkestone Herald*, 4 May 1912.

26 Letter from Gladys Cherry to her mother, 17 April 1912.

Chapter 19: *Where's Daddy?*

1 Fitch, Layton and Wormstedt, *On a Sea of Glass*, pp. 254–5.

2 Thayer, *Titanic*, pp. 345, 354.

3 Gavin Bell, Michael A. Findlay and Philip Gowan, 'Mrs Marian Longstreth Thayer', *Encyclopedia Titanica* (accessed 22 March 2017).

4 Thayer, *Titanic*, pp. 354–5.

5 Lightoller, *Titanic and Other Ships*, p. 194.

6 Thayer, *Titanic*, p. 355.

7 *Hampshire Telegraph*, 3 May 1912 (Courtesy of the Mike Poirier Collection).

8 Fitch, Layton and Wormstedt, *On a Sea of Glass*, p. 242.

9 Ibid., p. 245.

10 Debate remains over whether Jack Phillips ever made it to Collapsible B, although he and Bride did jump from the *Titanic* at the same time.

11 Testimony of Assistant Cook John Collins to the Senate inquiry, 25 April 1912.

12 Gracie, *Titanic*, p. 61.

13 Thayer, *Titanic*, p. 352.

14 Gracie, *Titanic*, p. 69.

15 Ibid., pp. 61–2.

16 Ibid., p. 63; Fitch, Layton and Wormstedt, *On a Sea of Glass*, pp. 247–8. In his 1940 account of the sinking, Jack Thayer does not mention the lifeboat transfer, one of several omissions.

17 Gracie, *Titanic*, pp. 72–3.

18 Ibid., p. 66.

19 Logan Marshall, *The Sinking of the Titanic and Great Sea Disasters* (London: L. T. Meyer, 1912), p. 74. My thanks to the staff at the Linen Hall Library, Belfast, for allowing me to view this book while it was part of a display on the loss of the *Titanic*.

20 Thayer, *Titanic*, p. 351.

21 Ibid., p. 355.

22 Testimony of Captain Arthur Rostron to the US Senate inquiry, 21 June 1912.

23 Fitch, Layton and Wormstedt, *On a Sea of Glass*, pp. 255–6.

24 Ibid., p. 255.

25 Letter from second-class passenger Bertha Watt to Walter Lord, 10 April 1963 (LMQ/7/2/37).

26 Fitch, Layton and Wormstedt, *On a Sea of Glass*, p. 256.

27 Ibid., Appendix P, 'Buried at Sea', p. 362.

28 Ibid., pp. 244–5.

29 Ibid., pp. 241–2.

30 *The Book of Common Prayer* (1662), 'Forms of Prayer to be used at Sea'.

31 Jessop, *Titanic Survivor*, p. 161.

32 Wilson, *Shadow*, p. 59.

33 Karl Behr, 'Titanic Disaster', reprinted in *The Titanic Commutator*, no. 176 (Indian Orchard, MA: Titanic Historical Society, 2006).

34 Fitch, Layton and Wormstedt, *On a Sea of Glass*, p. 252.

35 Ibid., p. 254. This was Bertha Mulvihill (1886–1959).

36 Ibid.

37 The two identified suicide risks were Mathilde Weisz (1874–1953) and Jane Laver Herman (1861–1937); letter from second-class passenger Dagmar Bryhl to her uncle, April 1912 (B150).

38 Wilson, *Shadow*, p. 57.

39 Ibid., p. 55.

40 Tribute from second-class passenger Sylvia Caldwell (B158).

41 Wilson, *Shadow*, p. 52.

42 Letter from John A. Badenoch to Percy Straus, 24 April 1912 (the Straus Historical Society).

43 Bigham, 'A Matter of Course'; passenger Frederick Hoyt in the *Springfield Union*, 20 April 1912 (Courtesy of the Mike Poirier Collection).

44 Letter from the Dowager Countess of Rothes to Walter Lord, 7 August 1955.

45 Letter from Gladys Cherry to her mother, 17 April 1912.

46 Letter from first-class passenger Gladys Cherry, 18 April 1912 (B123).

47 Letters from first-class passenger Dr Alice Leader to Mrs Sarah Babcock, 16 April 1912, and third-class passenger Olaus Abelseth to various family members, 19 April 1912.

48 Christened Margaretta Spedden (1872–1950), but nearly always known as Daisy Spedden.

49 Letter from first-class passenger Margaretta Spedden, 18 April 1912.

50 Fitch, Layton and Wormstedt, *On a Sea of Glass*, p. 255.

51 Lightoller, *Titanic and Other Ships*, p. 195.

52 Eugene Abbott's age is sometimes given as thirteen, but in an interview given by his mother to the *Pawtucket Times* on 22 May 1912, she gives his age as eleven (Courtesy of the Mike Poirier Collection).

53 Fitch, Layton and Wormstedt, *On a Sea of Glass*, p. 252.

54 In her subsequent interviews, it was unclear whether Rossmore's rejection prompted Rhoda to delay fleeing with Eugene or if she had intended to try to get her youngest into a boat, only to be hampered by the chaos on deck during the *Titanic*'s final moments.

55 Rhoda Abbott, *Pawtucket Times*, 22 May 1912 (Courtesy of the Mike Poirier Collection).

56 Correspondence between Randy Bryan Bigham and the late Ian Leslie, 21st Earl of Rothes.

57 Letter from second-class passenger Amelia Brown to her mother, 17 April 1912.

58 Letter from Gladys Cherry, 17 April 1912; first-class passenger Dr Harry Frauenthal, *American Medicine*, May 1912 (B179).

59 Fitch, Layton and Wormstedt, *On a Sea of Glass*, p. 255.

60 Letter from second-class passenger Olga Lundin, 16 April 1912 (B102).

61 Letter from Gladys Cherry, 17 April 1912.

62 Letter from second-class passenger Elizabeth Nye, 16 April 1912; letter from first-class passenger Kornelia Andrews, written 16–18 April 1912, during her time on board the *Carpathia*.

63 Letter from second-class passenger Ethel Beane to her father, written during her time on board the *Carpathia*; Fitch, Layton and Wormstedt, *On a Sea of Glass*, p. 257.

64 From the extended letter from second-class passenger Kate Buss to her parents, entry for 16 April 1912.

65 Ibid., entry for 17 April 1912.

66 Passenger Margaret Brown, *Newport Herald*, 28–29 May 1912.

67 This was published in the *Toronto World*, 20 April 1912.

68 Wilson, *Shadow*, p. 61.

69 Fitch, Layton and Wormstedt, *On a Sea of Glass*, p. 252.

70 Passenger Margaret Brown, *Newport Herald*, 28–29 May 1912.

71 Ibid..

72 Fitch, Layton and Wormstedt, *On a Sea of Glass*, p. 251.

73 Thayer, *Titanic*, p. 356.

74 Letter from the Dowager Countess of Rothes to Walter Lord, 7 August 1955.

75 Bigham, *Finding Dorothy*, p. 64.

76 Ibid., pp. 63–4.

77 Fitch, Layton and Wormstedt, *On a Sea of Glass*, pp. 256–7.

78 Bigham, *Finding Dorothy*, p. 64.

79 Second-class passenger Sylvia Caldwell, *Women of the 'Titanic' Disaster* (B153).

80 Behe, *On Board*, p. 137.

81 Article by second-class passenger Ruth Becker, published in the *St. Nicholas Magazine*, 1913.
82 Fitch, Layton and Wormstedt, *On a Sea of Glass*, p. 262.
83 Ibid., p. 263.
84 Bigham, *Finding Dorothy*, p. 66.
85 Wilson, *Shadow*, p. 60.
86 Bigham, 'A Matter of Course'.
87 Ibid. Gladys's letters to her mother and Tom Jones are addressed from the Great Northern, while the Countess either went straight away to the Ritz or had moved there to celebrate her anniversary at that hotel by the following day.
88 Fitch, Layton and Wormstedt, *On a Sea of Glass*, p. 263.
89 Wilson, *Shadow*, p. 61.

Chapter 20: *Extend Heartfelt Sympathy to All*

1 Thayer, *Titanic*, p. 352. In the same section of his memoir, Jack was unsure of Lightoller's rank on the *Oceanic*, 'either Chief Officer or First'; he was First.
2 Fitch, Layton and Wormstedt, *On a Sea of Glass*, pp. 269–70. This was the Norddeutscher Lloyd's *Bremen*, which they operated from 1897 to 1914. She was seized as war reparations by the British government, who gifted her to P&O, who later sold her for work on the route from New York to Greece where she was eventually renamed the *King Alexander* and retired in 1929.
3 *St Louis Post Dispatch*, 1 May 1912 (Courtesy of the Mike Poirier Collection).
4 Fitch, Layton and Wormstedt, *On a Sea of Glass*, pp. 270–2.
5 Ibid., p. 272.
6 Lightoller, *Titanic and Other Ships*, p. 195.
7 *New York Times*, 29 May 1912, for a précis of British criticism of Senator Smith.
8 Lightoller, *Titanic and Other Ships*, p. 195.
9 Fitch, Layton and Wormstedt, *On a Sea of Glass*, p. 275.
10 Wilson, *Ismay*, p. 23.
11 Fitch, Layton and Wormstedt, *On a Sea of Glass*, p. 256.
12 Wilson, *Ismay*, pp. 5–6.
13 *Hampshire Telegraph*, 3 May 1912 (Courtesy of the Mike Poirier Collection).
14 For J. Bruce Ismay's later life, see William E. Carter, *The Times*, 22 April 1912; TRNISM 1/1; Lord Mersey's statements at the British Board of Trade inquiry into the loss of the *Titanic*; Matarasso, *A Voyage Closed and Done*, pp. 23–6; Wilson, *Ismay*, pp. 6, 19–20, 30, 202–4, 207, 209–10, 216–17, 219, 225–7, 249, and Wilson, *Shadow*, pp. 191, 213–14, 217–18.

15 Thayer, *Titanic*, p. 352.

16 Bigham, 'A Matter of Course'.

17 Ibid.

18 Letter from the Dowager Countess of Rothes to Walter Lord, 7 August 1955. The *Washington Post*, 4 May 1913, names the Countess as the guest at a party given by Lady Jane Williams-Taylor, wife of the General Manager of the Bank of Montreal. Some doubt has existed for years over where the Countess was when she experienced this horrible flashback to the *Titanic*. I am grateful to Randy Bryan Bigham for his time in allowing me to discuss my theories about it having been at the Ritz, rather than the Savoy, and for bringing the *Washington Post* piece to my attention.

19 Gosling, *Debutantes and the London Season*, pp. 15–18, 39.

20 Jasper Ridley, *Napoleon III and Eugénie* (London: Constable, 1979), p. 639.

21 Anne de Courcy, *Circe: The Life of Edith, Marchioness of Londonderry* (London: Sinclair-Stevenson, 1992), pp. 96–8 – the Lady Londonderry in question in 1914 was Edith's mother-in-law, Theresa; 'Obituary of Lady Mairi Bury', *Daily Telegraph*, 13 January 2010; Adrian Tinniswood, *The Long Weekend: Life in the English Country House between the Wars* (London: Jonathan Cape, 2016), p. 56.

22 Mark Bence-Jones, *Twilight of the Ascendancy* (London: Constable, 1987), pp. 156, 159, 162–3.

23 *Newtownards Chronicle*, 6 February 1915; Cameron, *Belfast's Own*, p. 93.

24 Cameron, *Belfast's Own*, p. 93.

25 Sir Horace Plunkett's foreword in Bullock, *Thomas Andrews*, p. xx, quotes the letter but for decency's sake considered the rest of the document 'too intimate to publish'.

26 Plunkett in ibid., pp. xiii, xviii–xix.

27 The current author's great-grandfather remembered and sang the first song; ibid., p. 47.

28 Coryne Hall, *Little Mother of Russia: A Biography of Empress Marie Feodorovna* (London: Shepheard-Walwyn, 1999), p. 247; Rappaport, *Four Sisters*, pp. 208–9.

29 Morton, *Thunder at Twilight*, pp. 1–2.

30 King and Woolmans, *Assassination of the Archduke*, p. 188.

31 Russell, *The Emperors*, p. 67.

32 Interview with the Earl and Countess of Rothes, published in the *Washington Post*, 22 April 1912 (Courtesy of the Mike Poirier Collection).

33 Bigham, 'A Matter of Course'.

34 Ibid.

35 Correspondence between the late Ian Leslie, 21st Earl of Rothes, and the historian Randy Bryan Bigham.

36 *Buildings at Risk: Register for Scotland - Leslie House with Conservatory, Garden and Walls*, Building Number 9693.

37 Bigham, 'A Matter of Course'.

38 This is based on the estimate of just over 19,000 men being killed in service on the Somme's first day. Popular legend sometimes identifies the first sinking to exceed the *Titanic*'s casualty figures as that of the Austrian liner, *Linz*, which struck a mine in the Adriatic during the spring of 1918. The official death toll from the loss of the *Linz* was 697 and while it is possible that she was carrying several non-registered passengers, most likely Austro-Hungarian soldiers, it is impossible that it was enough to bring the figure of lives lost to 2,700 as has subsequently been stated on very little evidence.

39 Interview with Vera Morrison, daughter of Helen Harland (née Barbour, prev. Andrews), BBC Newsline Northern Ireland, 12 April 2012.

40 'Elizabeth Andrews' in *CQD* magazine, no. 56 (December 2017).

41 *Ulster's New Prime Minister*, Pathé, 28 November 1940.

42 Correspondence between the author and Joan Adler, Executive Director of the Straus Historical Society, 12 November 2018.

43 Letters from Isidor Straus to the Rev. H. H. Redgrave, 9 April 1912, and from the Rev. H. H. Redgrave to Jesse Straus, 13 September 1934 (SHS).

44 II Samuel 1:23.

45 Song of Solomon 8:7.

Chapter 21: *The Spinner of the Years*

1 Dr J. C. H. Beaumont, *Ships – and People* (New York: Frederick A. Stokes Company, 1930), p. 282.

2 Dorothy Gibson interviewed in the *New York Dramatic Mirror*, 1 May 1912 (Courtesy of the Mike Poirier Collection).

3 The movie's title anglicised the name of Grand Duke Sergei Alexandrovich of Russia (1857–1905).

4 It was the last piece she filmed; a movie she had shot before her trip to France and Italy in 1912, *The Revenge of the Silk Masks*, was the last to be released.

5 For the later years of Dorothy Gibson's life, see Philip Gowan and Brian Meister, 'The Saga of the Gibson Women', *Encyclopedia Titanica* (2002); Bigham, *Finding Dorothy*, pp. 67–112; Wilson, *Shadow*, pp. 257–363.

6 *Philadelphia Evening Bulletin*, 14 April 1932.

7 Thayer, *Titanic*, p. 337.

8 Ibid., p. 333.

9 Lightoller, *Titanic and Other Ships*, p. 169.

10 Wilson, *Shadow*, p. 237.

NOTES

11 *The Times*, 12 July 1913.

12 *Boston Daily Globe*, 11 October 1914.

13 For the Countess of Rothes' life after 1912, the letter from the Dowager Countess of Rothes to Walter Lord, 7 August 1955; Bigham, 'A Matter of Course'; Gavin Cameron Bell et al., 'Thomas William Jones', *Encyclopedia Titanica* (2 November 2018).

14 Interview between James Cameron and Dr Robert Ballard, 'Why you won't find bodies on the *Titanic*', *National Geographic* (26 November 2017).

15 Davie, *Titanic*, p. 48.

16 Third-class passenger Victor Sunderland in the *Cleveland Plain Dealer*, 26 April 1912.

17 Wilson, *Ismay*, p. 49.

18 Letter from Gladys Cherry to her mother, 17 April 1912.

19 Brian Fagan, *The Little Ice Age: How Climate Made History, 1300–1850* (New York: Perseus Books, 2000), p. 4.

20 Thayer, *Titanic*, pp. 328–30.

21 Miller, *Famous Ocean Liners*, p. 29.

22 The British Seafarers' Union was founded on 6 October 1911 and was dissolved in 1922 following its merger with the Amalgamated Marine Workers' Union.

BIBLIOGRAPHY

Ahamed, Liaquat, *Lords of Finance: The Bankers Who Broke the World* (New York: Penguin, 2009)

Allday, Elizabeth, *Stefan Zweig: A Critical Biography* (London: W. H. Allen, 1972)

Anthony, Carl Sferrazza, *Nellie Taft: The Unconventional First Lady of the Ragtime Era* (New York: William Morrow, 2005)

Aronson, Theo, *Crowns in Conflict: The Triumph and the Tragedy of European Monarchy, 1910–1918* (London: Thistle Publishing, 2015)

Aronson, Theo, *Prince Eddy and the Homosexual Underworld* (London: John Murray, 1994)

Asquith, Cynthia, *Remember and be Glad* (London: Barrie, 1952)

Aylmer, Gerald, *R.M.S. 'Mauretania': The Ship and her Record* (London: Percival Mansion, 1935)

Baltzell, E. Digby, *The Protestant Establishment: Aristocracy and Caste in America* (New Haven and London: Yale University Press, 1964)

Bardon, Jonathan, *A History of Ulster* (Dundonald: The Blackstaff Press, 1992)

Bardon, Jonathan, and Henry V. Bell, *Belfast: An Illustrated History* (Dundonald: The Blackstaff Press, 1982)

Barratt, Nick, *Lost Voices from the Titanic: The Definitive Oral History* (London: Preface, 2009)

Bartlett, Thomas, David Dickson, Dáire Keogh and Kevin Whelan (eds), *1798: A Bicentenary Perspective* (Dublin: Four Courts Press, 2003)

Bartlett, W. B., *Titanic: 9 Hours to Hell, the Survivors' Story* (Stroud: Amberley, 2010)

Battiscombe, Georgina, *Queen Alexandra* (London: Constable, 1969)

Beaumont, Dr J. C. H., *Ships – and People* (New York: Frederick A. Stokes Company, 1930)

Becker, Seymour, *Nobility and Privilege in Late Imperial Russia* (DeKalb, IL: Northern Illinois University Press, 1985)

Beckett, J. C., and R. E. Glasscock (eds), *Belfast: The Origin and Growth of an Industrial City* (London: British Broadcasting Corporation, 1967)

Beesley, Lawrence, *The Loss of the S.S. Titanic: Its Story and its Lessons*, facsimile of the 1912 edition (Whitefish, MT: Kessinger Publishing, 2010)

Behe, George, *A Death on the 'Titanic': The Loss of Major Archibald Butt* (Morrisville, NC: Lulu, 2011)

Behe, George, *On Board RMS Titanic: Memories of the Maiden Voyage* (Stroud: The History Press, 2017)

Behe, George, *Voices from the Carpathia: Rescuing RMS Titanic* (Stroud: The History Press, 2015)

Bell, G. K. A., *Randall Davison, Archbishop of Canterbury* (Oxford: Oxford University Press, 1935)

Beller, Stephen, *Francis Joseph* (London and New York: Longman, 1996)

Beloff, Max, *Imperial Sunset: Britain's Liberal Empire, 1897–1921* (London: Methuen, 1969)

Bence-Jones, Mark, *Life in an Irish Country House* (London: Constable, 1996)

Bence-Jones, Mark, *Twilight of the Ascendancy* (London: Constable, 1987)

Bence-Jones, Mark, and Hugh Montgomery-Massingberd, *The British Aristocracy* (London: Constable, 1979)

Berg, A. Scott, *Wilson* (London: Simon & Schuster, 2013)

Betts, Raymond F., *The False Dawn: European Imperialism in the Nineteenth Century* (St Paul, MN: University of Minnesota Press, 1975)

Beveridge, Bruce, et al., *Titanic: The Ship Magnificent*, 2 vols, 5th edn (Stroud: The History Press, 2016)

Bew, John, *The Glory of Being Britons: Civic Unionism in Nineteenth-Century Belfast* (Dublin and Portland, OR: Irish Academic Press, 2009)

Bew, Paul, *Ideology and the Irish Question: Ulster Unionism and Irish Nationalism, 1912–1916* (Oxford: Oxford University Press, 1994)

Biagini, Eugenio F., and Mary E. Daly (eds), *The Cambridge Social History of Modern Ireland* (Cambridge: Cambridge University Press, 2017)

Bierce, Ambrose, *Phantoms of a Blood-Stained Period: The Complete Civil War Writings of Ambrose Bierce* (Amherst, MA: University of Massachusetts Press, 2002)

Biggs-Davison, John, and George Chowdharay-Best, *The Cross of Saint Patrick: The Catholic Unionist Tradition in Ireland* (Abbotsbrook: The Kensal Press, 1984)

Bigham, Randy Bryan, *Finding Dorothy: A Biography of Dorothy Gibson* (Raleigh, NC: Lulu Press, 2012)

Bigham, Randy Bryan, *Lucile: Her Life by Design* (London: Lulu Press, 2014)

Bigham, Randy Bryan, 'A Matter of Course', *Encyclopedia Titanica* (April 2006)

Bingham, Caroline, *James V: King of Scots* (London: William Collins, 1971)

Binnington, Ian, *Confederate Visions: Nationalism, Symbolism, and the Imagined South in the Civil War* (Charlottesville, VA, and London: University of Virginia Press, 2013)

Black, Jeremy, *The British Seaborne Empire* (New Haven and London: Yale University Press, 2004)

Blackwood, William (ed.), *The New Statistical Account of Scotland* (Edinburgh: William Blackwood & Sons, 1836)

Blum, Jerome, *The End of the Old Order in Rural Europe* (Princeton, NJ: Princeton University Press, 1978)

Boardman, Kay, and Christine Kinealy (eds), *1848: The Year the World Turned?* (Newcastle: Cambridge Scholars Publishing, 2007)

Boase, Tessa, *The Housekeeper's Tale: The Women Who Really Ran the English Country House* (London: Aurum Press, 2015)

Bogle, James and Joanna Bogle, *A Heart for Europe: The Lives of Emperor Charles and Empress Zita of Austria-Hungary* (Leominster: Gracewing, 2000)

Bottomore, Stephen, *The Titanic and Silent Cinema* (Uckfield: Windmill Press, 2000)

Bowen, Frank C., *A Century of Atlantic Travel, 1830–1930* (London: Sampson Low, Marston, 1932)

Brendon, Piers and Philip Whitehead, *The Windsors: A Dynasty Revealed, 1917–2000* (London: Pimlico, 2000)

Brett, C. E. B., *Buildings of Belfast, 1700–1914*, 2nd edn (Belfast: Friar's Bush Press, 1985)

Brewster, Hugh, *Gilded Lives, Fatal Voyage: The 'Titanic's' First-Class Passengers and their World* (New York: Broadway Paperbacks, 2012)

Brinnin, John Malcolm, *Beau Voyage: Life Aboard the Last Great Ships* (New York: Barnes & Noble Books, 1997)

Brinnin, John Malcolm, *The Sway of the Grand Saloon: A Social History of the North Atlantic*, 2nd edn (New York: Barnes & Noble Books, 2000)

Britton, Andrew, *SS Nieuw Amsterdam* (Stroud: The History Press, 2015)

Bromley, Michael L., *William Howard Taft and the First Motoring Presidency, 1909–1913* (Jefferson, NC: McFarland, 2007)

Brook-Shepherd, Gordon, *The Last Empress: The Life and Times of Zita of Austria-Hungary, 1892–1989* (London: HarperCollins, 1991)

Brook-Shepherd, Gordon, *Royal Sunset: The Dynasties of Europe and the Great War* (London: Weidenfeld & Nicolson, 1987)

Brown, Wallace, *The Good Americans: The Loyalists in the American Revolution* (New York: William Morrow, 1969)

Brown, Wallace, *The King's Friends: The Composition and Motives of the American Loyalist Claimants* (Providence, RI: Brown University Press, 1965)

Brownlow, Kevin, *Behind the Mask of Innocence* (London: Jonathan Cape, 1990)

Buchan, John, *The King's Grace: 1910–1935* (London: Hodder & Stoughton, 1935)

Buckle, George Earle (ed.), *The Letters of Queen Victoria, Third Series:*

BIBLIOGRAPHY

A Selection from Her Majesty's Correspondence and Journal between the Years 1886 and 1901 (London: John Murray, 1932)

Bullock, Shan F., *Thomas Andrews: Shipbuilder* (Dublin and London: Maunsel, 1912)

Burk, Kathleen, *The Lion and the Eagle: The Interaction of the British and American Empires, 1783–1972* (London: Bloomsbury, 2018)

Burton, David H., *The Learned Presidency: Theodore Roosevelt, William Howard Taft, Woodrow Wilson* (London and Toronto: Associated University Presses, 1988)

Bush, M. L., *The English Aristocracy: A Comparative Synthesis* (Manchester: Manchester University Press, 1984)

Cameron, Stephen, *Titanic: Belfast's Own* (Dublin: Wolfhound Press, 1998)

Campbell, Aidan, *Belfast Through Time* (Stroud: Amberley, 2016)

Campbell, Aidan, 'South Belfast – Through Time', *South Belfast Life* (Spring/Summer 2017)

Canfield, Cass, *The Incredible Pierpont Morgan: Financier and Art Collector* (London: Hamish Hamilton, 1974)

Cannadine, David, *Aspects of Aristocracy: Grandeur and Decline in Modern Britain* (New Haven and London: Yale University Press, 1994)

Cannadine, David, *Class in Britain* (New Haven and London: Yale University Press, 1998)

Cannadine, David, *The Decline and Fall of the British Aristocracy*, 2nd edn (London: Picador, 1992)

Cannadine, David, *Ornamentalism: How the British Saw their Empire* (London: Allen Lane, 2001)

Card, James, *Seductive Cinema: The Art of Silent Cinema* (New York: Alfred A. Knopf, 1994)

Cashman, Sean Dennis, *America in the Gilded Age: From the Death of Lincoln to the Rise of Theodore Roosevelt*, 2nd edn (New York and London: New York University Press, 1988)

Cecil, David, *The Cecils of Hatfield House* (London: Constable, 1973)

Cecil, Lamar, *Albert Ballin: Business and Politics in Imperial Germany, 1888–1918* (Princeton, NJ: Princeton University Press, 1967)

Cecil, Lamar, *Wilhelm II: Emperor and Exile, 1900–1941* (Chapel Hill, NC, and London: University of North Carolina Press, 1996)

BIBLIOGRAPHY

Cecil, Lamar, *Wilhelm II: Prince and Emperor, 1859–1900* (Chapel Hill, NC, and London: University of North Carolina Press, 1989)

Chambers, Robert, *Domestic Annals of Scotland from the Reformation to the Revolution* (Edinburgh: W. & R. Chambers, 1859)

Channon, Henry, *The Ludwigs of Bavaria* (London: John Lehman, 1952)

Chauncey, George, *Gay New York: Gender, Urban Culture, and the Making of the Gay Male World, 1890–1940* (New York: Perseus Books, 1994)

Cherchi Usai, Paolo, *Silent Cinema: An Introduction* (London: British Film Institute, 2000)

Chernow, Ron, *The House of Morgan: An American Banking Dynasty and the Rise of Modern Finance* (New York: Grove Press, 2010)

Chirnside, Mark, '*Olympic* & *Titanic*: An Analysis of the Robin Gardiner Conspiracy Theory' (BA thesis, University of Leicester, 2005)

Chirnside, Mark, *Olympic, Titanic, Britannic: An Illustrated History of the 'Olympic' Class Ships* (Stroud: The History Press, 2014)

Chirnside, Mark, *RMS Olympic: Titanic's Sister*, 2nd edn (Stroud: The History Press, 2015)

Christie, O. F., *The Transition from Aristocracy, 1832–1867* (London: Seeley, Service, 1927)

Churella, Albert J., *The Pennsylvania Railroad*, vol. I: *Building an Empire, 1846–1917* (Philadelphia: The University of Pennsylvania Press, 2013)

Clarke, Peter, *Hope and Glory: Britain, 1900–1990* (London: Penguin, 1996)

Clarke, Richard, *The Royal Victoria Hospital, Belfast: A History, 1797–1997* (Belfast: The Blackstaff Press, 1997)

Claydon, Tony, *William III* (London: Pearson, 2002)

Collier, Peter, with David Horowitz, *The Roosevelts: An American Saga* (London: André Deutsch, 1995)

Compton, Nic, *Titanic on Trial: The Night the Titanic Sank Told through the Testimonies of her Passengers and Crew* (London: Bloomsbury, 2012)

Constant, Stephen, *Foxy Ferdinand, 1861–1948: Tsar of Bulgaria* (London: Sidgwick & Jackson, 1979)

404

Cook, Petronelle, *Queen Consorts of England: The Power Behind the Throne* (New York: Facts on File, 1993)

Cooper Jr, William J., *Jefferson Davis, American* (New York: Alfred A. Knopf, 2000)

Corti, Count Egon Caesar, *Ludwig I of Bavaria*, trans. Evelyn B. Graham Stamper (London: Thornton Butterworth, 1938)

Courcy, Anne de, *Circe: The Life of Edith, Marchioness of Londonderry* (London: Sinclair-Stevenson, 1992)

Cowles, Virginia, *The Astors: The Story of a Transatlantic Family* (London: Weidenfeld & Nicolson, 1979)

Cox, Frank, 'The Untimely Death of James Dobbin: Shipwright', *Encylopedia Titanica* (May 2012)

Crain, Esther, *The Gilded Age in New York, 1870–1910* (New York: Black Dog & Leventhal, 2016)

Cross, Colin, *The Fall of the British Empire, 1918–1968* (London: Book Club Associates, 1968)

Cunliffe-Owen, Marguerite, *The Martyrdom of an Empress* (New York: Harper, 1899)

Cust, Lionel, *King Edward VII and his Court: Some Reminiscences* (London: John Murray, 1930)

Dangerfield, George, *The Damnable Question: A Study in Anglo-Irish Relations* (London: Quartet Books, 1979)

Davenport-Hines, Richard, *Titanic Lives: Migrants and Millionaires, Conmen and Crew* (London: HarperPress, 2012)

Davie, Michael, *The Titanic: The Full Story of a Tragedy* (London: Guild Publishing, 1986)

Davis, Jefferson, *The Rise and Fall of the Confederate Government* (New York: D. Appleton, 1881)

Diggle, E. G., *The Romance of a Modern Liner* (London: Sampson Low, Marston, 1930)

Diner, Hasia R., *A New Promised Land: A History of the Jews in America* (Oxford and New York: Oxford University Press, 2003)

Dixon, Thomas, *Weeping Britannia: Portrait of a Nation in Tears* (Oxford: Oxford University Press, 2015)

Donaldson, Gordon, *All the Queen's Men: Power and Politics in Mary*

Stewart's Scotland (London: Batsford Academic and Educational, 1983)

Douglas-Home, Jessica, *A Glimpse of Empire* (Norwich: Michael Russell Publishing, 2011)

Doyle, Mark, *Fighting Like the Devil for the Sake of God: Protestants, Catholics and the Origins of Violence in Victorian Belfast* (Manchester and New York: Manchester University Press, 2009)

Duberman, Martin, Martha Vicinus and George Chauncey Jr (eds), *Hidden from History: Reclaiming the Gay and Lesbian Past* (New York: Penguin, 1989)

Dudley Edwards, Ruth, *Patrick Pearse: The Triumph of Failure* (Swords, Co. Dublin: Poolbeg Press, 1977)

Duff, David, *Alexandra: Princess and Queen* (London: William Collins, 1980)

Duff Gordon, Lucy, Lady, *Discretions and Indiscretions* (London: Frederick A. Stokes, 1932)

Dunn, Laurence, *Famous Liners of the Past: Belfast Built* (London: Adlard Coles, 1964)

Eaton, John P., and Charles A. Haas, *Titanic: A Journey through Time* (Yeovil: Patrick Stephens, 1999)

Edgerton, David, *The Rise and Fall of the British Nation: A Twentieth-Century History* (London: Allen Lane, 2018)

Edwards, Anne, *Matriarch: Queen Mary and the House of Windsor* (London: Rowman & Littlefield, 2015)

Elliott, Marianne, *The Catholics of Ulster: A History* (London: Penguin, 2000)

Elliott, Marianne, *When God Took Sides: Religion and Identity in Ireland: Unfinished History* (Oxford: Oxford University Press, 2009)

Emmerson, Charles, *1913: The World before the Great War* (London: The Bodley Head, 2013)

Eton Register: Part VI, 1889–1899, The (Eton: Spottiswoode, 1910)

Eton Register: Part VIII, 1909–1919, The (Eton: Spottiswoode, 1932)

Evans, Eli N., *Judah P. Benjamin: The Jewish Confederate* (New York: The Free Press, 1988)

Evans, Grace, *Titanic Style: Dress and Fashions on the Voyage* (Ludlow: Moonrise Press, 2011)

Eyman, Scott, *Mary Pickford: America's Sweetheart* (New York: Donald I. Fine, 1990)

Fagan, Brian, *The Little Ice Age: How Climate Made History, 1300–1850* (New York: Basic Books, 2000)

Farquharson, Robert, *The House of Commons from Within, and Other Memories* (London: Williams and Norgate, 1912)

Ferguson, Niall, *Colossus: The Rise and Fall of the American Empire* (London: Penguin, 2004)

Ferguson, Niall, *Empire: How Britain Made the Modern World* (London: Penguin, 2004)

Ferry, Julie, *The Transatlantic Marriage Bureau: Husband Hunting in the Gilded Age: How American Heiresses Conquered the Aristocracy* (London: Aurum Press, 2017)

Fink, Leon (ed.), *Major Problems in the Gilded Age and the Progressive Era* (Lexington, MA: D. C. Heath, 1993)

Fitch, Tad, J. Kent Layton and Bill Wormstedt, *On a Sea of Glass: The Life and Loss of the RMS Titanic*, 3rd edn (Stroud: Amberley, 2015)

Fitzpatrick, David, *Descendancy: Irish Protestant Histories since 1795* (Cambridge: Cambridge University Press, 2014)

Fitzpatrick, Rory, *God's Frontiersmen: The Scots-Irish Epic* (London: Weidenfeld & Nicolson, 1989)

Fleming, N. C., *The Marquess of Londonderry: Aristocracy, Power and Politics in Britain and Ireland* (London and New York: Tauris Academic Studies, 2005)

Fletcher, R. A., *Travelling Palaces: Luxury in Passenger Steamships* (London: Sir Isaac Pitman & Sons, 1913)

Foecke, Tim, *Metallurgy of the* RMS Titanic (Gaithersburg, MD: US Department of Commerce and National Institute of Statistics and Technology, 1998)

Foote, Shelby, *The Civil War, a Narrative: Red River to Appomattox* (New York: Vintage Books, 1986)

Foreman, Amanda, *A World on Fire: An Epic History of Two Nations Divided* (London: Penguin, 2011)

Fry, Paul (ed.), *Methodist College Belfast 1st XV: 1875–76 to 1993–94* (Belfast: Methodist College Belfast, 1994)

Gailey, Andrew, *Ireland and the Death of Kindness: The Experience of Constructive Nationalism, 1890–1905* (Cork: Cork University Press, 1987)

Gallagher, Lyn, *The Grand Opera House Belfast* (Dundonald: The Blackstaff Press, 1995)

Gardiner, Robin, *Titanic: The Ship That Never Sank?* (Shepperton: Ian Allan, 1998)

Gardiner, Robin, and Dan van der Vat, *The Riddle of the Titanic* (London: Weidenfeld & Nicolson, 1995)

Garner, William, *Cobh: Architectural Heritage* (Dublin: An Foras Forbartha, 1979)

Georgiou, Ioannis, 'The Forgotten Drills Aboard Titanic', *Encyclopedia Titanica* (2018)

Gibbs, C. R. Vernon, *Passenger Liners of the Western Ocean: A Record of the North Atlantic Steam and Motor Passenger Vessels from 1838 to the Present Day* (New York: P. Staples, 1952)

Glancy, Mark, 'The *Titanic*: Three Films', *History Extra* online, 12 April 2012

Gosling, Lucinda, *Debutantes and the London Season* (Oxford: Shire Publications, 2013)

Gould, Lewis L., *Four Hats in the Ring: The Birth of Modern American Politics* (Lawrence, KS: University of Kansas Press, 2008)

Gowan, Philip, and Brian Meister, 'The Saga of the Gibson Women', *Atlantic Daily Bulletin* (2002)

Gracie, Colonel Archibald, *Titanic: A Survivor's Story* (Stroud: The History Press, 2008)

Gray, Annie, *The Greedy Queen: Eating with Victoria* (London: Profile Books, 2017)

Gray, John, *City in Revolt: James Larkin and the Belfast Dock Strike of 1907* (Dundonald: The Blackstaff Press, 1985)

Gregg, Edward, *Queen Anne* (London: Routledge & Kegan Paul, 1980)

Gribben, Crawford, and Andrew R. Holmes (eds), *Protestant Millennialism, Evangelicalism, and Irish Society, 1790–2005* (Basingstoke: Palgrave Macmillan, 2006)

Guy, John, *My Heart is my Own: The Life of Mary Queen of Scots* (London: Harper Perennial, 2004)

Gwynn, Denis, *The Life of John Redmond* (London: George G. Harrap, 1932)

Gwynne, S. C., *Rebel Yell: The Violence, Passion, and Redemption of Stonewall Jackson* (New York: Simon & Schuster, 2014)

Hahn, Hans Joachim, *The 1848 Revolutions in German-Speaking Europe* (London: Pearson, 2001)

Haines, Keith, *Campbell College* (Stroud: Tempus Publishing, 2004)

Halévy, Elie, *A History of the English People, 1905–1915* (London: Ernest Benn, 1934)

Hall, Coryne, *Little Mother of Russia: A Biography of Empress Marie Feodorovna* (London: Shepheard-Walwyn, 1999)

Hall, Steve, Bruce Beveridge and Art Braunschweiger, *Titanic or Olympic: Which Ship Sank?* (Stroud: The History Press, 2012)

Hamann, Brigitte, *The Reluctant Empress: A Biography of Empress Elisabeth of Austria*, trans. Ruth Hein (New York: Alfred A. Knopf, 1986)

Hamilton, Lord Frederic, *The Vanished World of Yesterday* (London: Hodder & Stoughton, 1950)

Hampton, Benjamin B., *A History of the Movies* (New York: Covici Friede Publishers, 1931)

Harris, Jose, *Private Lives, Public Spirit: A Social History of Britain, 1870–1914* (Oxford: Oxford University Press, 1993)

Harris, Ruth, *Lourdes: Body and Spirit in the Secular Age* (London: Allen Lane, 1999)

Harrison, Brian, *Separate Spheres: The Opposition to Women's Suffrage in Britain* (London: Croom Helm, 1978)

Hart, Eva, and Ronald C. Denney, *The Shadow of the Titanic: A Survivor's Story*, 2nd edn (Sevenoaks: Chadwell Publishers, 2007)

Hart, Henry Martyn, *Recollections and Reflections* (New York: Gibb Bros. & Moran, 1916)

Hawks, Ellison, *The Romance of the Merchant Ship* (London: George G. Harrap, 1931)

Haws, Duncan, *Merchant Fleets: White Star Line (Oceanic Steam Navigation Company)* (Newport: Starling Press, 1990)

Heffer, Simon, *The Age of Decadence: Britain, 1880 to 1914* (London: Random House Books, 2017)

Henderson, J. W., *Methodist College Belfast, 1868–1938: A Survey and Retrospect* (Belfast: Privately published by and for the Governors of Methodist College, 1939)

Hibbert, Christopher, *Edward VII: A Portrait* (London: Penguin, 1976)

Hibbert, Christopher, *Wellington: A Personal History* (London: HarperCollins, 1997)

Hoensch, Jörg, *A History of Modern Hungary, 1867–1994*, trans. Kim Traynor, 2nd edn (London: Longman, 1996)

Holmes, Geoffrey, *British Politics in the Age of Anne* (New York: St Martin's Press, 1967)

Hostettler, John, *Sir Edward Carson: A Dream Too Far* (Chichester: Barry Rose Law Publishers, 1997)

Hough, Richard, *Edward and Alexandra: Their Private and Public Lives* (London: Hodder & Stoughton, 1992)

Howells, Richard, *The Myth of the Titanic* (London: Macmillan Press, 1999)

Hume, Robert, 'When Spanish Flu Hit Britain', *BBC History Magazine* (January 2018)

Industries of Ireland: Part I – Belfast and the Towns of the North, The (Belfast: W. H. Crawford, 1986)

Jamieson, John, *The History of the Royal Belfast Academical Institution, 1810–1960* (Belfast: William Mullan and Son, 1959)

Jasanoff, Maya, *The Dawn Watch: Joseph Conrad in a Global World* (London: William Collins, 2017)

Jess, Mervyn, *The Orange Order* (Dublin: The O'Brien Press, 2007)

Jessop, Violet, *Titanic Survivor: The Memoirs of Violet Jessop, Stewardess*, ed. John Maxtone-Graham (Stroud: The History Press, 2010)

Judson, Pieter M., *The Habsburg Empire: A New History* (Cambridge, MA, and London: Harvard University Press, 2016)

Katz, Jonathan Ned, *Love Stories: Sex between Men before Homosexuality* (Chicago and London: University of Chicago Press, 2001)

Kavaler, Lucy, *The Astors: A Family Chronicle* (London: George G. Harrap, 1966)

Kendle, John, *Ireland and the Federal Solution: The Debate over the United Kingdom Constitution, 1870–1921* (Kingston and Montreal: McGill-Queen's University Press, 1989)

King, Greg, and Sue Woolmans, *The Assassination of the Archduke: Sarajevo 1914 and the Murder that Changed the World* (London: Macmillan, 2013)

Klier, John, with Helen Mingay, *The Quest for Anastasia: Solving the Mystery of the Lost Romanovs* (London: Smith Gryphon, 1996)

Larkin, John Francis (ed.), *The Trial of William Drennan on a Trial for Sedition, in the Year 1794 and his Intended Defence* (Dublin: Irish Academic Press, 1991)

Larmour, Paul, *Belfast: An Illustrated Architectural Guide* (Belfast: Friar's Bush Press, 1987)

Larson, Erik, *Dead Wake: The Last Crossing of the Lusitania* (London: Transworld, 2015)

Layton, J. Kent, *The Edwardian Superliners: A Trio of Trios* (Stroud: Amberley, 2013)

Lee, Hermione, *Edith Wharton* (New York: Alfred A. Knopf, 2007)

Lee, J. J., *Ireland, 1912–1985: Politics and Society* (Cambridge: Cambridge University Press, 1989)

Lee, Raymond M., 'Intermarriage, Conflict and Social Control in Ireland: The Decree "Ne Temere"', *Economic and Social Review* (October 1985)

Lehr, Elizabeth Wharton Drexel, *'King Lehr' and the Gilded Age* (New York: J. B. Lippincott, 1935)

Leighton, John M., *History of the County of Fife*, illus. Joseph Swan (Glasgow: George Brookman, 1840)

Levine, Philippa, *The British Empire: Sunrise to Sunset*, 2nd edn (Harlow: Pearson, 2007)

Lewis, Geoffrey, *Carson: The Man Who Divided Ireland* (London and New York: Hambledon & London, 2005)

Lewis, R. W. B., *Edith Wharton: A Biography* (London: Constable, 1975)

Lightoller, Charles Herbert, *Titanic and Other Ships* (Oxford: Oxford City Press, 2010)

Lodge's Peerage, Baronetage, Knightage & Companionage of the British Empire for 1912, with which is incorporated Foster's Peerage, Baronetage and Knightage, 81st edn (London: Kelly's Directories, 1912)

Longford, Elizabeth, *Victoria R.I.* (London: Weidenfeld & Nicolson, 1998)

Lord, Walter, *A Night to Remember* (London: Penguin, 2012)

Ludwig, Emil, *Kaiser Wilhelm II* (London and New York: G. P. Putnam's Sons, 1927)

Lurie, Jonathan, *William Howard Taft: The Travails of a Progressive Conservative* (Cambridge and New York: Cambridge University Press, 2012)

Lynch, Don, and Ken Marschall, *Titanic: An Illustrated History* (London: Hodder & Stoughton, 1992)

Lynch, John, *Belfast Built Ships* (Stroud: The History Press, 2012)

Macaulay, James, *The Classical Country House in Scotland, 1660–1800* (London: Faber & Faber, 1987)

MacDonogh, Giles, *Frederick the Great: A Life in Deed and Letters* (London: Weidenfeld & Nicolson, 1999)

MacDonogh, Giles, *The Last Kaiser: William the Impetuous* (London: Weidenfeld & Nicolson, 2000)

MacDougall, Norman, *James III: A Political Study* (Edinburgh: John Donald, 1982)

MacGibbon, David, and Thomas Ross, *The Castellated and Domestic Architecture of Scotland: From the Twelfth to the Eighteenth Century* (Edinburgh: David Douglas, 1889)

Mack Smith, Denis, *Italy and its Monarchy* (New Haven and London: Yale University Press, 1989)

Mackay, James, *In the End is my Beginning: A Life of Mary Queen of Scots* (Edinburgh and London: Mainstream, 1999)

MacKnight, Thomas, *Ulster as It Is, or, Twenty-Eight Years' Experience as an Irish Editor* (New York: Macmillan, 1896)

MacLaran, Andrew, *Dublin: The Shaping of a Capital* (London and New York: Belhaven Press, 1993)

MacNeice, John Frederick, *Carrickfergus and its Contacts: Some Chapters in the History of Ulster* (London: Simpkin Marshall, 1928)

Madsen, Axel, *John Jacob Astor: America's First Multimillionaire* (New York: John Wiley & Sons, 2001)

Magnus, Katie, Lady, *Outlines of Jewish History: from B.C.E. 586 to C.E. 1885* (London: Myers, 1924)

Marshall, Logan, *The Sinking of the Titanic and Great Sea Disasters* (New York: L. T. Meyer, 1912)

Marshall, P. J., *The Making and Unmaking of Empires: Britain, India, and America, c. 1750–1783* (Oxford: Oxford University Press, 2005)

Marshall, Ronald, *Methodist College Belfast: The First Hundred Years* (Belfast: Methodist College Belfast, 1968)

Marshall, Rosalind K., *Scottish Queens, 1034–1714* (East Linton: Tuckwell, 2003)

Massie, Robert K., *Nicholas and Alexandra* (London: Victor Gollancz, 1968)

Matarasso, Pauline, *A Voyage Closed and Done* (Norwich: Michael Russell, 2005)

Matthew, H. C. G., *The Liberal Imperialists: The Ideas and Politics of a Post-Gladstonian Elite* (Oxford: Oxford University Press, 1973)

Maume, Patrick, *The Long Gestation: Irish Nationalist Life, 1891–1918* (Dublin: Gill & Macmillan, 1999)

Maylunas, Andrei, and Sergei Mironenko (eds), *A Lifelong Passion: Nicholas and Alexandra, Their Own Story*, trans. Darya Galy (London: Weidenfeld & Nicolson, 1996)

Mayo, Jonathan, *Titanic: Minute by Minute* (London: Short Books, 2016)

McCash, June Hall, *A Titanic Love Story: Ida and Isidor Straus* (Macon, GA: Mercer University Press, 2012)

McCluskie, Tom, *Anatomy of the Titanic* (London: PRC Publishing, 1998)

McCluskie, Tom, Michael Sharpe and Leo Marriott, *Titanic and her Sisters Olympic and Britannic* (London: Parkgate Books, 2000)

McDonough, Terrence (ed.), *Was Ireland a Colony?: Economics, Politics and Culture in Nineteenth-Century Ireland* (Dublin and Portland, OR: Irish Academic Press, 2005)

McGladdery, Christine, *James II* (Edinburgh: John Donald, 1990)

McIntosh, Gillian, *Belfast City Hall: One Hundred Years* (Belfast: The Blackstaff Press, 2006)

McNeill, Ronald, *Ulster's Stand for Union* (London: John Murray, 1922)

McPherson, James, *Battle Cry of Freedom: The American Civil War* (Oxford: Oxford University Press, 1988)

McPherson, James, *For Cause and Comrades: Why Men Fought in the Civil War* (Oxford and New York: Oxford University Press, 1997)

Miller, William H., *Famous Ocean Liners: The Story of Passenger Shipping, from the Turn of the Century to the Present Day* (Wellingborough: Patrick Stephens, 1987)

Miller, William H., *Great Passenger Ships, 1910–1920* (Stroud: The History Press, 2011)

Mitchell, Walter F., *Belfast Rowing Club, 1880–1982* (Belfast: Belfast Rowing Club, 1994)

Molony, Senan, 'The Fleecing of Hugh Woolner', *Encyclopedia Titanica* (February 2007)

Molony, Senan, 'Sun Yat Sen – Will Eat Again', *Encyclopedia Titanica* (2004)

Moore, George, *Hail and Farewell!: Ave* (London: William Heinemann, 1911)

Moore, Mary, Sadie Turkington, Norah Watts and Kathleen White, *Victoria College Belfast: Centenary, 1859–1959* (Belfast: Victoria College Board of Governors, 1959)

Morris, Charles R., *The Tycoons: How Andrew Carnegie, John D. Rockefeller, Jay Gould, and J. P. Morgan Invented the American Supereconomy* (New York: Henry Holt, 2005)

Morris, Lloyd R., *Incredible New York: High Life and Low Life from 1850 to 1950* (New York: Syracuse University Press, 1996)

Morton, Frederic, *Thunder at Twilight: Vienna, 1913–1914* (Boston: Da Capo Press, 2014)

Moskowitz, Eli, *The Jews of the Titanic: A Reflection of the Jewish World on the Epic Disaster* (New York: Hybrid Global, 2018)

Moss, Michael, and John R. Hume, *Shipbuilders to the World: 125 Years of Harland and Wolff, Belfast, 1861–1986* (Dundonald: The Blackstaff Press, 1986)

Nairn, T., 'The Glamour of Backwardness', *The Times Higher Education Supplement*, 11 January 1985

Nevis, Allan, *Grover Cleveland: A Study in Courage* (New York: Dodd, Mead, 1932)

Nicolson, Harold, *King George the Fifth: His Life and Reign* (London: Constable, 1952)

Nipperdey, Thomas, *Germany from Napoleon to Bismarck, 1800–1866*, trans. Daniel Nolan (Dublin: Gill & Macmillan, 1996)

O'Brien, John, 'Vox Faucibus Haesit', *Symposium* (1996), no. 49

O'Donnell, SJ, E. E. (ed.), *Father Browne's Titanic Album: A Passenger's Photographs and Personal Memoir* (Dublin: Messenger Publications Jesuits in Ireland, 2011)

Pakula, Hannah, *The Last Romantic: A Biography of Queen Marie of Roumania* (London: Phoenix, 1996)

Palmer, Alan, *Twilight of the Habsburgs: The Life and Times of the Emperor Francis Joseph* (London: Weidenfeld & Nicolson, 1994)

Paludan, Philip Shaw, *The Presidency of Abraham Lincoln* (Lawrence, KS: University Press of Kansas, 1994)

Parkinson, Alan F., *Belfast's Unholy War: The Troubles of the 1920s* (Dublin: Four Courts Press, 2004)

Pattullo, Nan, *Castles, Houses and Gardens of Scotland* (Edinburgh and London: William Blackwood & Sons, 1967)

Paul, Sir James Balfour, *The Scots Peerage: Founded on Wood's Edition of Sir Robert Douglas's Peerage of Scotland* (Edinburgh: David Douglas, 1910)

Pelly, Patricia, and Andrew Tod (eds), *Elizabeth Grant of Rothiemurchus: The Highland Lady in Dublin, 1851–1856* (Dublin: New Island, 2005)

Plokhy, Serhii, *Lost Kingdom: A History of Russian Nationalism from Ivan the Great to Vladimir Putin* (London: Allen Lane, 2017)

Plumptre, George, *Edward VII* (London: Pavilion Books, 1995)

Poiret, Paul, *My First Fifty Years* (London: Victor Gollancz, 1931)

Powell, David, *The Edwardian Crisis: Britain, 1901–1914* (London: Macmillan Press, 1996)

Preston, Diana, *Wilful Murder: The Sinking of the Lusitania* (London: Corgi Books, 2003)

Purdue, Olwen (ed.), *Belfast: The Emerging City, 1850–1914* (Dublin and Portland, OR: Irish Academic Press, 2013)

Purdue, Olwen, *The Big House in the North of Ireland: Land, Power and Social Elites, 1878–1960* (Dublin: University College Dublin Press, 2009)

Radzinsky, Edvard, *Alexander II: The Last Great Tsar*, trans. Antonina W. Bouis (New York: Simon & Schuster, 2005)

Ramsden, John (ed.), *Real Old Tory Politics: The Political Diaries of Sir Robert Sanders, Lord Bayford, 1910–35* (London: The Historians' Press, 1984)

Raphael, Ray, *Founding Myths: Stories That Hide Our Patriotic Past*, rev. edn (New York: New Press, 2004)

Rappaport, Helen, *Four Sisters: The Lost Lives of the Romanov Grand Duchesses* (London: Pan Macmillan, 2014)

Rees, Philip, *Biographical Dictionary of the Extreme Right since 1890* (New York: Simon & Schuster, 1990)

Rees, Russell, *Ireland, 1905–25*, vol. 1: *Text and Historiography* (Newtownards: Colourpoint Books, 1998)

Ribeiro, Aileen, *Clothing Art: The Visual Culture of Fashion, 1600–1914* (New Haven and London: Yale University Press, 2017)

Richards, Jeffrey, *A Night to Remember: The Definitive Titanic Film* (London: I. B. Tauris, 2003)

Ridley, Jane, *Bertie: A Life of Edward VII* (London: Chatto & Windus, 2012)

Ridley, Jasper, *Napoleon III and Eugénie* (London: Constable, 1979)

Roach, John, 'Titanic Was Found During Secret Cold War Navy Mission', *National Geographic*, 21 November 2017

Robertson, Morgan, *The Wreck of the Titan, or Futility* (Springfield, IL: Monroe St Press, 2015)

Robinson, John Martin, *The Dukes of Norfolk: A Quincentennial History* (Oxford and New York: Oxford University Press, 1982)

Röhl, John C. G., *Wilhelm II: Into the Abyss of War and Exile, 1900–1941*, trans. Sheila de Bellaigue and Roy Bridge (Cambridge: Cambridge University Press, 2014)

Röhl, John C. G, *Wilhelm II: The Kaiser's Personal Monarchy, 1888–1900*, trans. Sheila de Bellaigue (Cambridge: Cambridge University Press, 2004)

Röhl, John C. G., *Young Wilhelm: The Kaiser's Early Life, 1859–1888*, trans. Jeremy Gaines and Rebecca Wallach (Cambridge: Cambridge University Press, 1998)

Rose, Kenneth, *King George V* (London: Weidenfeld & Nicolson, 1983)

Rose, Kenneth, *The Later Cecils* (London: Weidenfeld & Nicolson, 1975)

Rosen, Robert N., *The Jewish Confederates* (Columbia, SC: University of South Carolina Press, 2000)

Russell, Gareth, *The Emperors: How Europe's Rulers were Destroyed by the First World War* (Stroud: Amberley, 2014)

Russia, Grand Duke Alexander Mikhailovich of, *Once a Grand Duke* (New York: Farrar & Reinhart, 1932)

St Aubyn, Giles, *Edward VII: Prince and King* (London: Collins, 1979)

Samson-Himmelstjerna, Hermann von, *Russia under Alexander III: and in the Preceding Period*, trans. J. Morrison (London: T. F. Unwin, 1893)

Sarna, Jonathan D., and Adam Mendelsohn (eds), *Jews and the Civil War: A Reader* (New York and London: New York University Press, 2010)

Schleswig-Holstein, Princess Marie Louise of, *My Memories of Six Reigns* (London: Evan Brothers, 1957)

Schorske, Carl E., *Fin-de-Siècle Vienna: Politics and Culture* (New York: Random House, 1981)

Sebag Montefiore, Simon, *The Romanovs, 1613–1918* (London: Weidenfeld & Nicolson, 2016)

Seward, Ingrid, *The Last Great Edwardian Lady* (London: Random House, 1999)

Shanks, Amanda N., *Rural Aristocracy in Northern Ireland* (Aldershot: Gower Publishing, 1988)

Simmons, Allan, *Joseph Conrad* (London: Palgrave Macmillan, 2006)

Smith, Douglas, *Former People: The Last Days of the Russian Aristocracy* (London: Macmillan, 2013)

Smith, G. Elliot, *Tutankhamen and the Discovery of his Tomb by the Late Earl of Carnarvon and Mr Howard Carter* (London: George Routledge & Sons, 1923)

Smith, Gene, *Maximilian and Carlota: The Habsburg Tragedy in Mexico* (London: George G. Harrap, 1974)

Snyder, Timothy, *The Red Prince: The Secret Lives of a Habsburg Archduke* (New York: Perseus, 2008)

Spedding, Charles, *Reminiscences of Transatlantic Travellers* (London: T. Fisher Unwin, 1926)

Spring, D., 'Land and Politics in Edwardian England', *Agricultural History*, 58 (1984)

Stewart, A. T. Q., *Belfast Royal Academy: The First Century, 1785–1885* (Belfast: Belfast Royal Academy, 1985)

Stewart, A. T. Q., *Edward Carson* (Belfast: The Blackstaff Press, 1997)

Straus, Isidor, and Sara Straus Hess, *The Autobiography of Isidor Straus* (Smithtown, NY: The Straus Historical Society, 2011)

Straus, Oscar S., *Under Four Administrations: From Cleveland to Taft* (Smithtown, NY: The Straus Historical Society, 2017)

Suchet, John, *The Last Waltz: The Strauss Dynasty and Vienna* (New York: St Martin's Press, 2015)

Sutherland, Douglas, *The Yellow Earl: The Life of Hugh Lowther, 5th Earl of Lonsdale, K.G., G.C.V.O., 1857–1944* (London: Cassell, 1965)

Taylor, James, *The Great Historic Families of Scotland* (London: J. S. Virtue, 1890)

Thayer, John B., *The Sinking of the S.S. Titanic* (Chicago: Academy Chicago Publishers, 2010)

Thompson, F. M. L., *English Landed Society in the Nineteenth Century* (Toronto: University of Toronto Press, 1963)

Thompson, Francis, *A History of Chatsworth: Being a Supplement to the Sixth Duke of Devonshire's Handbook* (London: Country Life, 1949)

Thurley, Simon, *Hampton Court: A Social and Architectural History* (New Haven and London: Yale University Press, 2003)

Tinniswood, Adrian, *The Long Weekend: Life in the English Country House between the Wars* (London: Jonathan Cape, 2016)

Trelease, Allen W., *White Terror: The Ku Klux Klan Conspiracy and Southern Reconstruction* (Baton Rouge, LA: Louisiana State University Press, 1999)

Tripp, C. A., *The Intimate World of Abraham Lincoln*, ed. Lewis Gannett (New York: The Free Press, 2005)

Uglow, Jenny, *A Gambling Man: Charles II and the Restoration, 1660–1670* (London: Faber & Faber, 2009)

Valente, Joseph, *The Myth of Manliness in Irish National Culture, 1880–1922* (Champaign, IL: University of Illinois Press, 2011)

Vickers, Hugo, *Elizabeth, the Queen Mother* (London: Arrow, 2006)

Vickers, Hugo, *Gladys, Duchess of Marlborough* (New York: Holt, Reinhart & Winston, 1979)

Walpole, Horace, *Memoirs of King George II*, ed. John Brooke (New York and London: Yale University Press, 1985)

Watson, Robert P., *The Nazi Titanic: The Incredible Untold Story of a Doomed Ship in World War II* (Cambridge, MA: Da Capo Press, 2016)

Weatherall, Norman, and David Evans (illus.), *South Belfast: Terrace and Villa* (Donaghadee: Cottage Publications, 2002)

Weatherall, Norman, and George E. Templeton, *South Belfast* (Dublin: Nonsuch Publishing, 2008)

Welch, David, *Propaganda and the German Cinema, 1933–1945* (Oxford: Oxford University Press, 1983)

Welch, Frances, *The Imperial Tea Party: Family, Politics and Betrayal: The Ill-Fated British and Russian Royal Alliance* (London: Short Books, 2018)

Welch Jr, Richard E., *The Presidencies of Grover Cleveland* (Lawrence, KS: University Press of Kansas, 1988)

Wells, John, *The House of Lords: From Saxon Wargods to a Modern Senate* (London: Hodder & Stoughton, 1997)

White, Ronald C., *American Ulysses: A Life of Ulysses S. Grant* (New York: Random House, 2016)

White Star Line: Royal Mail Triple-Screw Steamers 'Olympic' and 'Titanic' (Holywood, Co. Down: Ulster Folk and Transport Museum, 1987)

Wilson, A. N., *Victoria: A Life* (London: Atlantic Books, 2015)

Wilson, Andrew, *Shadow of the Titanic: The Extraordinary Stories of Those Who Survived* (London: Simon & Schuster, 2011)

Wilson, Derek, *The Astors: The Life and Times of the Astor Dynasty, 1763–1992* (London: Weidenfeld & Nicolson, 1993)

Wilson, Frances, *How to Survive the Titanic, or, The Sinking of J. Bruce Ismay* (London: Bloomsbury, 2012)

Winchester, Simon, *Their Noble Lordships: The Hereditary Peerage Today* (London: Faber & Faber, 1981)

Woodcock, Thomas, and John Martin Robinson, *Heraldry in Historic Houses of Great Britain* (London: National Trust Enterprises, 2000)

BIBLIOGRAPHY

Zahra, Tara, *The Great Departure: Mass Migration from Eastern Europe and the Making of the Free World* (New York: W. W. Norton, 2016)

Zebley Taylor, Elmer, *Jigsaw Picture Puzzle of People Whom I Have Known and Sundry Experiences from 1864 to 1949* (privately reprinted, 2017)

Zweig, Stefan, *Marie Antoinette: The Portrait of an Average Woman* (New York: Atrium Press, 1984)

Zweig, Stefan, *The World of Yesterday*, trans. Anthea Bell (London: Pushkin Press, 2010)

IMAGE CREDITS

Picture section

(Lucy) Noel Martha Leslie (née Edwardes, later Mrs Macfie), Countess of Rothes by Bassano Ltd (© *National Portrait Gallery*)

Dunallan House – the former home of Thomas and Helen Andrews in Malone, Belfast (© *All rights reserved by John McDonald*)

Thomas, Helen and Elizabeth Andrews, c.1910 (*Public domain, by an unknown photographer*)

Poster advertising the White Star Line, 1911 (*Cauer Collection, Germany/Bridgeman* Images)

Lusitania 'ballroom' (*Pictures Now/Alamy Stock Photo*)

The Dining Saloon (First Class) on the RMS *Titanic* (*By permission of the Mary Evans Picture Library Ltd*)

Belfast, UK – c.June 2018 – SS *Nomadic*, tender ship of the White Star Line in the Titanic Quarter (*stockeurope/Alamy Stock Photo*)

John Thayer III, c.1913 – believed to have been taken from a yearbook at the University of Pennsylvania (*Public domain, by an unknown photographer*)

Dorothy Gibson, sketched by Harrison Fisher, 1911 (© *The Randy Bryan Bigham Collection*)

Georgian-style suite, B-77, on the *Olympic* (*By kind permission of Daniel Klistorner from his personal collection*)

White Star steamship *Olympic* Grand Staircase, second landing, photographed by William Herman Rau *(Niday Picture Library/Alamy Stock Photo)*

Colin Campbell Cooper, *Rescue of the Survivors of the Titanic by the Carpathia (History and Art Collection/Alamy Stock Photo)*

Luxuries versus lifeboats, date: 8 May 1912 *(Chronicle/Alamy Stock Photos)*

Underwater shot of the *Titanic* from documentary 'Ghosts of the Abyss', directed by James Cameron *(Entertainment Pictures/ Alamy Stock Photos)*

Leslie House, May 2018 (© *Neil Henderson*)

Integrated images

p. 4, Countess of Rothes. Unknown photographer *(The Picture Art Collection/Alamy Stock Photo)*

p. 9, sovereign funeral *(The Protected Art Archive/Alamy Stock Photo)*

p. 13, Countess of Rothes, 1911 (© *The Randy Bryan Bigham* Collection)

p. 16, launch of the RMS *Titanic* at Belfast, 31 May 1911 *(By kind permission of Daniel Klistorner from his personal collection)*

p. 26, Thomas Andrews Jr *(Historic Images/Alamy Stock Photos)*

p. 31, panoramic view from the corner of Donegall Square West, by Robert John Welch (© *National Museums NI*)

p. 32, Queen's Island workmen homeward bound, by Robert John Welch (© *National Museums NI*)

p. 40, the completed steamship *Titanic* at Belfast, Ireland *(Science History Images/Alamy Stock Photos)*

p. 53, view from the first-class gangplank of the RMS *Titanic* at approximately 11.30 a.m. on Wednesday 10 April 1912, as photographed by passenger, Father Francis Browne, SJ *(Science & Society Library/Father Browne Collection)*

p. 56, sitting room of first-class parlour suite on the *Olympic*, by Robert John Welch (© *National Museums NI*)

p. 60, the near-collision of the RMS *Titanic* and the SS *New York*, 10 April 1912 *(Trinity Mirror/Mirropix/Alamy Stock Photo)*

p. 65, John Borland Thayer *(Granger Historical Picture Archive/Alamy Stock Photo)*

p. 72, ocean liner *Kaiser Wilhelm der Große*, photographed *c*.1897 *(The Library of Congress)*

p. 85, the *Titanic* at anchor in Queenstown (Cóbh), photographed by Father Francis Browne, SJ, 11 April 1912 *(Science and Society Picture Library/Father Browne Collection)*

p. 92, Dorothy Gibson, 1911 *(© The Randy Bryan Bigham Collection)*

p. 97, Jules Brulatour *(© The Randy Bryan Bigham Collection)*

p. 109, the *Olympic* and the *Titanic* at Belfast, Ireland *(Science History Images/Alamy Stock Photo)*

p. 112, White Star SS *Olympic* entering New York Harbor on first trip *(State Historical Society of Columbia, 1949, gift to the Library of Congress)*

p. 112, RMS *Titanic* in profile *(By kind permission of Daniel Klistorner from his personal collection)*

p. 124, Countess of Rothes with her son Malcolm, Viscount Leslie, later the 20th Earl of Rothes, *c*.1907 *(© The Randy Bryan Bigham Collection)*

p. 146, last known photograph of Isidor and Ida Straus, *c*.1910–11 *(© From the Photo Archives of the Straus Historical Society)*

p. 169, silver wedding anniversary Straus family photograph, 12 July 1896 *(© From the Photo Archives of the Straus Historical Society)*

p. 179, J. Bruce Ismay *(Granger Historical Picture Archive/Alamy Stock Photo)*

p. 184, Colman's Mustard advertisement for use in the *Olympic* and *Titanic*'s first-class restaurants, *c*.1911 *(Author's Own)*

p. 190, Marian Thayer *(Historic Images/Alamy Stock Photo)*

p. 194, William Howard Taft out for a stroll with Archibald Butt, military aide, and Charles Dewey Hilles, secretary to the president, *c*.1910 *(Harris & Ewing Collection at the Library of Colorado)*

p. 201, cabins C-66-68 on the *Olympic* (*By kind permission of Daniel Klistorner from his personal collection*)

p. 210, cabin C-59 on the Harland and Wolff steamer, *Olympic* (© *Ray Lepien Collection*)

p. 214, the *Olympic*-class First Class Lounge (*By kind permission of Daniel Klistorner from his personal collection*)

p. 224, view from the first-class section of the *Titanic*'s Boat Deck, 11 April 1912, photographed by Father Francis Browne, SJ (© *Irish Examiner*)

p. 239, *Titanic*, sinking, life boats, contemporary painting (*Interfoto/Alamy Stock Photo*)

p. 243, the *Olympic*-class First Class Smoking Room (*By kind permission of Daniel Klistorner from his personal collection*)

p. 246, Captain Smith on the *Titanic*'s Bridge (*By kind permission of Daniel Klistorner from his personal collection*)

p. 257, the *Olympic*-class's boilers (*By kind permission of Daniel Klistorner from his personal collection*)

p. 277, *Titanic* survivors on lifeboat approaching the *Carpathia* (*Granger Historical Picture Archive/Alamy Stock Photo*)

p. 284, survivors aboard the *Carpathia* (*Chronicle/Alamy Stock Photos*)

p. 308, HMHS *Britannic* (*History and Art Collection/Alamy Stock Photo*)

p. 318, Dorothy Gibson in a promotional still for *Saved from the Titanic* (© *The Randy Bryan Bigham Collection*)

p. 321, Dorothy Gibson, c.1930 (© *The Randy Bryan Bigham Collection*)

p. 325, the late Father Giovanni Barbareschi (© *The Randy Bryan Bigham Collection*)

INDEX

A Living Memory (movie), 99
'A Nation Once More' (song), 8
A Night to Remember (movie), 262, 333
A Night to Remember (novel), 330,
 332–3
Abbott, Eugene, 285
Abbott, Rhoda, 285–6, 292
Abbott, Rossmore, 285
Abdul Hamid II, Ottoman Sultan, 145,
 192
Abelseth, Karen, 232
Abelseth, Olaus Jørgensen, 232–4,
 316–7
Abercorn, James Hamilton, 2nd Duke
 of, 305
Abernerthy, Bessie, 26
Adelaide of Saxe-Meiningen, Queen of
 the United Kingdom, 25
Albert I, King of the Belgians, 7
Alexander I, King of Serbia, 192
Alexander I, King of Yugoslavia, 8
Alexander II, Emperor of Russia, 163–4
Alexander III, Emperor of Russia, 145,
 163–5
Alexandra Feodorovna, Empress of
 Russia, 306
Alexandra of Denmark, Queen of the
 United Kingdom, 4, 7, 8, 311
Alfonso XIII, King of Spain, 7, 192, 322
Algerine (trailer), 294
Alice (ship), 157
Allen, Elisabeth, 89, 262

Allison family, 199
America (tender), 84
American Line, 48
The Americanisation of the World (book),
 133
Amerika (liner), 147–8, 168–9
Anderson, Harry, 186, 198, 207
Andrews, Eliza, 117, 199, 305
Andrews, Elizabeth ('Elba'), 26, 117,
 199, 312–3
Andrews, Helen, 26, 28, 44–5, 48, 199,
 305, 312
Andrews, James, 27, 313
Andrews, John, 27, 313
Andrews, Kornelia, 240
Andrews, Thomas
 ancestry, 28–9
 childhood, 27, 29
 education, 27
 work on *Oceanic*, 49, 293
 wedding, 39
 household in Belfast, 24, 26
 work on *Olympic*, 33–4, 106
 attends *Titanic*'s launch, 15–16
 oversees *Titanic*'s sea trials, 39, 45
 work in Southampton (1912), 47–8
 receives gifts from crew, 108
 suffers from homesickness, 24, 117–8
 describes *Titanic* as unsinkable,
  172–3, 207
 conversations with the Thayers, 177,
  327–8

conversations with Mary Sloan,
116–18, 213–4, 242–4, 250
inspects damage from iceberg, 206–9
helps load lifeboats, 221, 244
during evacuation, 213–14, 230,
242–4, 250
rumoured last sighting, 242–4, 248
death, 257–8, 280
1912 biography, 243–3, 305
as father, 26, 199
and employees, 27, 48, 106, 117,
213–14, 306
friendship with Dr O'Loughlin,
116–18
friendship with the Dicks, 200, 206
religious views, 143
political views, 34, 37, 41, 43
sporting interests, 27–8, 244
beekeeping, 244
memorials, 304
as symbol of Ulster unionism, 305
cinematic portrayals, 243
Andrews, Thomas Sr., 29, 117, 305
Andrews, William (TA's brother), 27
Andrews, William (TA's uncle), 29
Anichkov Palace, 306
Animated Weekly (newsreel), 316
Anna Karenina (novel), 164
Anne, Queen of Great Britain and
Ireland, 12
Aosta, Emanuele Filiberto, 2nd Duke
of, 8
Aquitania (liner), 74, 306
Arnaud, Étienne, 318
Asquith, Cynthia, 8, 120
Asquith, Herbert, 1st Earl of Oxford
and, 7, 12–13
Assassination of the Grand Duke Sergius
(movie), 319
Astor, Caroline, 67
Astor, John Jacob (IV), 64, 66, 91,
139–41, 175, 186, 219–21, 240–1
Astor, Madeleine, 64, 139–41, 186,
219–21, 240, 275, 280, 292, 300
Atlanta Constitution (newspaper), 162
Atlantic (movie), xvii
Aubart, Léontine, 135

Audacious (warship), 115
Augusta Victoria of Schleswig-Holstein,
German Empress, 32
The Awakening (movie), 99
Aylmer, Gerald, 73

B'nai Jeshurun, Manhattan (synagogue),
167
Badenoch, John, 282–3
Ballard, Robert, xv
Balmoral Castle, 24–5
Baltic (liner), 169, 174, 174n, 275
Bankers' Crisis (1907), 187–8
Barbareschi, Giovanni, 324
Barkworth, Algernon, 138, 278, 288
Baron von Hirsch (cemetery), 295
Barrett, Frederick, 170
Battier, George, 94, 320
Baxter, Hélène, 120, 135
Baxter, Quigg, 134–5
Bayford, Robert Sanders, 1st Baron, 18
Beaton, David, Cardinal, 22
Beattie, Thomson, 120
Bébé (dog), 219
Becker, Nellie, 264
Beerbohm, Sir Henry ('Max'), 127
Beesley, Lawrence, 75, 84, 262
Behe, George, 194, 252
Behr, Karl, 132–3, 221, 280
Belfast and County Down Railway
Company, 29
Belfast Chamber of Commerce, 30
Belfast City Hall, 30, 43
Belfast Dock Riots (1907), 34–5
Belfast News-Letter, 17
Bell, Gavin, 138
Belmonte, Gennaro di, Cardinal, 19
Benedictines, 3, 331
Berengaria (liner) see *Imperator*
Beresford, Charles de la Poer, 1st
Baron, 248
Beresford, Lady Lily see Marlborough
Bessborough, Blanche Ponsonby,
Countess of, 204
Bessborough, Edward Ponsonby, 8th
Earl of, 204
Beveridge, Bruce, 115

Bigham, Randy Bryan, 93, 286, 322, 324
Billboard (magazine), 316
Bird, Ellen, 59, 81, 210–11, 219, 228, 283, 313
Bishop, Dickinson, 219
Bismarck (liner) see Majestic (1922)
Björnström-Steffansson, Mauritz Håkan, 137
Blair, David, 86–7
Blood Libel, myth of, 165
Blue Riband, 71, 74, 177, 286
Bobrikov, Nicholas, 192
Bonnell, Caroline, 262
Boris Vladimirovich, Grand Duke of Russia, 322
Bovaradej, Prince of Siam, 8
Bowen, Grace Scott, 76, 239
Boxhall, Joseph, 206, 262–3
Boyne, battle of the, 40
Brandywine, battle of, 97
Braunschweiger, Art, 115
Bremen (liner), 293–4
Bresci, Gaetano, 191
Brewster, Hugh, 194
Bride, Harold, 276–8, 289
Brideshead Revisited (novel), 127
Bridge (movie), 99
Britannic (liner), 32–3, 74–5, 129, 235, 306, 308–9
British Miners' Federation, 48
British Seafarers' Trade Union, 337
Brooms and Pans (movie), 100
Brown, Ernest, 290
Brown, James Joseph, 141
Brown, John, 93
Brown, Margaret, 140–1
Browne, Francis, 85–6
Brulatour, Clara, 98–9, 316, 320
Brulatour, Claude, 98
Brulatour, Hope, 323
Brulatour, Jules, 98–100, 256, 289–90, 316–18
Brulatour, Marie, 98
Brulatour, Ruth, 98
Buchanan Cassatt, Lois see Thayer
Buckingham Palace, 4, 6, 43

Buckley, Daniel, 227, 231–3
Buggery Act (1533), 133–4
Bullock, Shan, 305–6
Burbidge, Lilian, 57, 61–2
Burbidge, Richard, 57
Bureik, Hamad Hassam, 134
Burr, Ewart, 78, 199
Bute, John Crichton-Stuart, 4th Marquess of, 20
Butt, Archibald, 64, 189–97, 238, 240, 286, 290, 300–1
Butt, Arrington, 193
Butt, Edward, 193
Butt, Pamela, 193
Byles, Thomas, 144, 253
Bystander (magazine), 5

Caesar (dog), 7
Caldwell, Sylvia, 280–1, 290
Californian (ship), 225, 268, 296
Cambridge, University of, 137
Cameron, James, 129, 263
Campbell College, Belfast, 27–8
Campbell, Henry, 27–8
Canalejas y Méndez, José, 134
Candee, Helen Churchill, 91–2, 136, 215
Cap Arcona (liner), xvii
Cardeza, Charlotte Drake, 135–6, 297
Carlisle, Alexander, 312
Carlos I, King of Portugal, 192
Carnarvon, George Herbert, 5th Earl of, 128
Carnegie Steel Company, 66
Carnot, Marie François Sadi, President, 192
Caronia (liner), 59
Carpathia (ship), xv, 272–92, 295, 297, 309, 318
Carruthers, Francis, 39, 45
Carson, Edward, Baron, 41, 43
Carter, Lucile, 186
Carter, William, 186
Carter, William Thornton (II), 186
Case, Howard Brown, 240
Cassebeer, Eleanor, 198–9, 206–7, 214, 221–2

Castillo, Antonio Cánovas del, 192
Castlereagh, Edith, Viscountess *see*
  Londonderry
Cecilia of Mecklenburg-Schwerin,
  German Crown Princess, 72
Cedric (liner), 297
Chadwick, French Ensor, 335
Charles I, King of England, Scotland
  and Ireland, 22
Charles II, King of England, Scotland
  and Ireland, 22
Charles X, King of France, 19
Chasse de Guise (tapestry), 77
Château de Rétival, 352
Château de Versailles, 20, 97, 148
Château Laurier, 91
Chaudanson, Victorine, 76, 239
Chelsea Flower Show, 303
Cherry, Charles, 52, 292
Cherry, Gladys, 52–3, 122–4, 200, 204,
  209, 212, 223, 228, 234, 264,
  268–71, 273, 283–6, 292, 335
Chickamauga, battle of, 149
Children's Guild, 6
Chirnside, Mark, 111
Chotek, Countess Henriette, 367
'Christ's Kirk on the Green' (poem), 2
Citizen Kane (movie), 323
Clara de Hirsch Home for Working
  Girls, Manhattan, 162
Clark, James Beauchamp ('Champ'),
  186–7
Cleopatra VII, Pharaoh of Egypt, xv
Cleveland, Grover, President, 149, 161,
  168
Collins, John, 276
Collyer, Charlotte, 280–1
Collyer, Marjorie, 280–1
Connellan, Marguerite, 324
Constantine I, King of the Hellenes, 8
Corkey, William, 38
Cosmopolitan (magazine), 96
Cottam, Harold, 289, 318
Countess of Rothes Voluntary Aid
  Detachment, 5
Craig, James *see* Craigavon
Craigavon, James, 1st Viscount, 43

Criminal Law Amendment Act (1885),
  133
Crosby, Harriette, 139
Croÿ, Karl, 13th Prince von, 69–70
Croÿ, Nancy, Princess von, 69–70
Crozier, John (archbishop), 324
Crundall, Alexander, 311
Cunard Line, 56, 73–4, 129, 175, 245
Cunard-White Star Line, 330
Curzon of Kedleston, George Curzon,
  1st Marquess, 303
Cusani Confalonieri, Luigi, Marquis of,
  250
Czolgosz, Leon, 191–2

D'Alba, Antonio (anarchist), 191
Daily Express, 331n
Daily Mail, 296, 298
Daily Telegraph, 313
Dairymaids (play), 94
Daly, Eugene, 88
Danilo, Crown Prince of Montenegro, 8
Davenport-Hines, Richard, 194
David, King of Israel and Judah, 314
Davidson, Randall (archbishop), 303
Davies, Marion, 323
Davis Cup, 133
Daz Herz von Königen (movie), xvii
De La Warr, Constance Sackville,
  Countess of, 6
Deacon, Gladys *see* Marlborough
Debs, Eugene, 187, 189
Deligiannis, Theodoros, 192
Delta Psi (fraternity), 303
Der Fuchs von Glenarvon (movie), xvii
Deramore, Thomas Bateson, 1st Baron,
  25
Dettingen, battle of, 23
Deutschland (liner), 72. 177–8
Deutschland (tanker), 180
Devlin, Joseph, 34
Devonian (liner), 329
Devonshire, Evelyn Cavendish, Duchess
  of, 6
Devonshire, William Cavendish, 7th
  Duke of, 127–8
Dick, Vera and Albert, 198, 206·

Dillon, Thomas, 262
Divine Comedy (poem), 67, 215
Divorcons (movie), 99
Dobbin, James, 15
Dolan, Pauline, 292
Donegall, marquesses of, 25, 30
Donoughmore, Elena Hely-Hutchinson, Countess of, 304
Donoughmore, Richard Hely-Hutchinson, 6th Earl of, 304
Doria-Pamphilj, Prince Alfonso, 19
Douglas, Mahala, 297
Douglas, Mary Hélène, 135
Down County Council, 29
Doyle, Arthur Conan, 277–8
Drachstedt, Baron Alfred von *see* Nourney
Draga, Queen of Serbia, 192
Dramatic Mirror (magazine), 100
Drennan, William, 85
Drexel, Elizabeth Wharton, 139
Dublin Mean Time, 83
Duff Gordon, Lucy, Lady, 131–2, 135, 142, 185–6, 226–7, 322
Duff Gordon, Sir Cosmo, 131–2, 135, 226–7, 267
Dufferin and Ava, Hariot Hamilton-Temple-Blackwood, Marchioness of, 31–2
Dyer-Edwardes, Clementina, 3, 52–3, 77, 331
Dyer-Edwardes, Thomas, 5, 52–3, 77, 331

The Easter Bonnet (movie), 100
Easter Rising (1916), 83n
Eastman Kodak Company, 99
Educational Alliance, 162
Edward I, King of England, 21
Edward III, King of England, 21
Edward VII, King of the United Kingdom, 6, 7, 10–11, 29, 71
Edward VIII, King of the United Kingdom, 59n
Elena of Montenegro, Queen of Italy, 191
Elisabeth of Bavaria, Empress of Austria and Queen of Hungary, 192

Elisabeth of Bavaria, Queen of the Belgians, 19
Elizabeth Bowes-Lyon, Queen of the United Kingdom, 303n
Elizabeth I, Queen of England and Ireland, xvii, 78, 122
Elizabeth II, Queen of the United Kingdom, 125
Empress of Ireland (liner), xvi
'Erin's Lament' (song), 88
Etches, Harry, 213–14
'Eternal Father, Strong to Save' (hymn), 145
Eton College, Berkshire, 67, 125, 311
Eustis, Elizabeth, 200, 215, 236, 238

Fairview (cemetery), 295
Farley, John, Cardinal, 312
Farquharson, Robert, 121
Farthing, John, 59, 81, 210–11, 283
Fayre Court, Gloucestershire, 331
Federation of Jewish Farmers of America, 162
Ferdinand I, King of Romania, 8
Ferdinand I, Tsar of Bulgaria, 7–8, 19
Festival of Empire (1911), 14
Fife, Louise, Duchess of *see* Louise
Fifth of October Revolution (Portugal), 192
Finnegans Wake (novel), 85
First Assembly Ball, 183
First Baptist Church, Hoboken, 144, 291
Fitch, Ted, xx
Fitzpatrick, Cecil, 257–8
Fleet, Frederick, 87
Fleming, Margaret, 184, 215, 291
Fletcher, Percy, 122
Fletcher, Richard, 50, 106
Flodden, battle of, 21
Florida (ship), 173
Foreman, Benjamin, 198
Fossoli (internment camp), 323
Fragonard, Jean-Honoré, 57
Francatelli, Laura, 185
France (liner), 74
Francis (shop), 128

Franco, Francisco, 322
Franco, Nicolás, 322
François II, King of France, 22
Franklin, Benjamin, 97
Franz Ferdinand, Archduke of Austria-
    Este, 8, 19, 66, 307
Franz Josef, Emperor of Austria and
    King of Hungary, 19, 66
Frauenthal, Henry, 221, 287
Frederick VIII, King of Denmark, 7
Friedrich II, King of Prussia, 25
Frohman, Charles, 94
Frölicher, Hedwig, 120
Frölicher-Stehli, Margaretha, 120
Frost, Archibald, 174
Froude, James Anthony, 73
Fry, Richard, 299
Fushimi Sadanaru, Prince of Japan, 8
Futility (novel), 175–6
Futrelle, Jacques, 133, 139, 182, 226
Futrelle, Lily ('May'), 185, 226, 229

Gaelic Revival, 36
Gailor, Thomas (bishop), 153
Gardiner, Robin, 109–10, 114
Gatti, Luigi, 184
Gee, Arthur, 91
General Order No. 11 (1863), 158–9
Geological Society of America, 171
George I, King of the Hellenes, 7
George II, King of Great Britain and
    Ireland, 23
George III, King of the United
    Kingdom, 20
George V, King of the United Kingdom,
    xx, 7, 11–12, 14–15, 18, 44, 126,
    329
George VI, King of the United
    Kingdom, 313
Gestapo, xviii, 323–4
Getting Dad Married (movie), 99
Gettysburg, battle of, 157–8
Gibson, Dorothy
    early life, 93–4
    acting career, 94–100
    musical career, 94, 320
    modelling career, 95–6

first marriage, 94–5
affair with Jules Brulatour, 98–100,
    316
suffers exhaustion (1912), 99–100
visit to Genoa (1912), 100–1
shopping trip in Paris (1912), 101,
    121
boards Titanic, 101
accommodation on Titanic, 101–2,
    129
movements on Sunday 14 April,
    200–1
during collision, 205–6
conversation with TA, 206
fear during evacuation, 209, 218–19
leaves Titanic, 217–20
behaviour in lifeboats, 220, 255–6,
    266
on Carpathia, 289
return to New York (1912), 291, 316
films Saved from the Titanic, 318–19
first divorce, 320
travels on La Provence (1912), 320
involved in hit and run, 320
second divorce, 321
moves to Europe, 321–2
later life (1920s and 1930s), 322–3
stepfather's funeral, 321
begins affair with Emilio Ramos, 322
mocked in Citizen Kane, 323
arrested by Nazis, 323–4
imprisoned in Italy, 324
death and burial, 325–6
will, 325
inspiration for Il generale Della Rovere,
    326
relationship with mother, 93, 98–100,
    321, 323
relationship with stepfather, 93, 321
appearance, 91–2
salary, 93, 101
religious views, 95, 144, 324
attitude to fascism, 316, 332–3, 325
taste in fashion, 121
reviews, 94, 100, 320
discrepancies in testimonies, 200–1,
    266, 316–17

Gibson, Leonard, 93, 102, 291, 321
Gibson, Pauline, 91, 93, 98, 100–2, 144, 217–18, 291, 321–3, 325
Giovanna of Savoy, Tsaritsa of Bulgaria, 191
Glyn, Elinor, 132
Goebbels, Josef, xvii–xix
Gone with the Wind (novel), 150
Gontaut-Biron, Martha, Comtesse de, 69
Government of Ireland Act (1914), 14, 44
Gowan, Philip, 322
Gracie, Archibald (III), 58, 149
Gracie, Archibald (IV), 58, 130–1, 148–50, 168, 225, 240, 251, 258, 272, 276–8, 288
Grand Opera House, Belfast, 30
Grand Trianon, Versailles, 66
Grand Trunk Pacific Railway, 91
Grant, Ulysses S., President, 158
Great Eastern (liner), 157
Grey, Edward, 1st Viscount, 6
The Guardian Angel (movie), 99
Guggenheim, Benjamin, 64, 135

Haakon VII, King of Norway, x
Haddon Hall, Derbyshire, 79, 196
Haldane, Richard, 1st Viscount, 11
Hall, Steve, 115
Hamburg-Amerika Line, 49, 175
Hamilton, Thompson, 48
Hampton Court Palace, 20
Hands Across the Sea (movie), 97–8
Harald Hardrada, King of Norway, 335
Harcourt, William, 133
Harland and Wolff, 15, 32–5, 133, 147, 171, 173
Harland, Henry Pierson, 312
Harper, Henry, 134, 215
Harper's Bazaar (magazine), 95
Harris, Henry, 282
Harris, Irene, 185, 282
Harrison, William, 299
Harrods, 31, 57
Harrow School, London, 67
Hartley, Wallace, 131

Harvard University, 280
Hatfield House, Hertfordshire, 78
Haverford School, PA, 67
Hawke (warship), 47, 61, 109–10, 115
Hays, Charles, 91, 175–6
Hays, Margaret, 219
Hearst, William Randolph, 296–7, 323
Heart of the Antarctic (book), 210
Hebrew Ladies' Memorial Association for Confederate Dead, 155–6
Hebrew Orphans Society, 162
Hendrickson, Charles, 170
Henley Royal Regatta, 303
Henry of Mecklenburg-Schwerin, Prince Consort of the Netherlands, 8
Henry VI, King of England, 125
Henry VIII, King of England and Ireland, 21, 133, 331
Hess, Sarah Straus, 161, 313
Hitchcock, Alfred, xvii
Hitchens, Robert, 203
Hitler, Adolf, 322
Hogg, George, 255, 266
Hohenberg, Duchess of *see* Sophie
Hohenberg, Maximilian, Duke of, 307
Hohenberg, Prince Ernst von, 307
Hohenberg, Princess Sophie von, 307
Home Rule Bill, Third *see* Government of Ireland Act
Hook, Knowles & Co., 121
The House of Commons from Within (memoir), 136
House of Lords Act (1911) *see* Parliament Act
How Women May Earn a Living (book), 136
Hoyt, Frederick, 247
Hoyt, William, 276
Huntsman the Tailor, 20
Hurlingham Polo Club, 304
Hutton, Thomas, xix
Hyde Park, 7

Il generale Della Rovere (novel and movie), 326
Il Vittoriano, Rome, 190
Île de France (liner), 106

Immaculate Conception (Denver), Cathedral of the, 141
Imperator (liner), xvi, 49, 63, 74, 315
In Nacht und Eis (movie), xvi
Independent (newspaper), 171
Independent Motion Picture Company, 96
The Industries of Ireland (book), 29
Infantry Division, 79th (US), 326
International Ice Patrol, 110, 296
International Mercantile Marine, 16, 76, 110
Ireland (tender), 84
Irish Rebellion of 1641, 41
Irving, Washington, 100
Isabella (née von Croÿ), Archduchess of Austria, 70
Isham, Ann, 107
Ismay, Joseph Bruce, xviii, xix–xxii, 16, 75–6, 82, 107, 174, 174n, 180–1, 220–2, 288, 296–301, 328
Ismay, Julie ('Florence'), 16, 180, 199, 301
Ismay, Thomas H., 301
It Pays to Be Kind (movie), 99

Jaffe, Otto, 33
Jaime de Borbón, Duke of Madrid and Anjou, 19
James II, King of Scots, 21
James IV, King of Scots, 21
James V, King of Scots, 2, 21–2
James VI & I, King of England, Scotland and Ireland, 22, 106
James VII & II, King of England, Scotland and Ireland, 40
Jenkins, John Card, 146
Jenny (cat), 107
'Jerusalem' (hymn), 251
Jessop, Violet, xx, 58, 107–8, 135–6, 140, 280
John Bull (magazine), 298
John XXII, Pope, 21
Johnstown Flood (1889), 336
Jonathan, Prince of Israel, 314
Jones, Thomas (sailor), 268–9, 272, 332
Joyce, James, 85

Kaiser Wilhelm der Große (liner), 71, 93, 115, 177, 304
Kaiser Wilhelm II (liner), 72
Karl I, Emperor of Austria and King of Hungary, 19
Katherine Parr, Queen of England and Ireland, 14
Kensington Palace, 20
Kiev pogroms, 165
Knickerbocker Crisis *see* Bankers' Crisis
The Kodak Contest (movie), 99
Korn, Betram, 153
Kronprinz Wilhelm (liner), 72
Kronprinzessin Cecilie (liner), 63, 72

La Provence (liner), 320
La Touraine (liner), 105
Labouchère Amendment, 133–4
Labouchère, Henry, 133
Lady Rothes (lifeboat), 310
'Land of Hope and Glory' (song), 251
Larkin, James, 34
Layton, J. Kent, xx
'Lead, Kindly Light' (hymn), 272
Lee, Robert E., 157
The Legend of Sleepy Hollow (movie, 1912), 100
Leinster, dukes of, 126
Leishman, John, 69–70, 193
The Leopard (novel), 127
Leslie House, Fife, 2, 5, 15, 20, 22–3, 310–11, 311n, 330–1
Leslie Town Hall, Fife, 5, 311
Leslie, Bartholomew, 21, 271
Leslie, John (d. 1991), 5, 125
Leslie, Malcolm (d. c. 1176), 21
Leviathan (liner) *see Vaterland*
Lightoller, Charles, 86, 219, 223–4, 226, 240, 244, 258, 262, 275–6, 278, 285, 293, 295–6, 328
Lincoln Memorial, D. C., 64, 190
Lincoln, Abraham, President, 64, 159
Livadia Palace, 18
Lloyd's of London, 110
Londonderry, Charles Vane-Tempest-Stewart, 7th Marquess of, 13

Londonderry, Edith Vane-Tempest-Stewart, Marchioness of, 13
Londonderry, Theresa Vane-Tempest-Stewart, Marchioness of, 304
Londsale, Hugh Lowther, 5th Earl of, 126
Long, Charles, 201
Long, Milton, 201, 216, 236–7, 256, 258–9
Lord, Stanley, 225
Lord, Walter, 279, 330–2
The Loss of the S. S. Titanic (memoir), 262
Lost Cause, myth of (US), 160
Louden-Brown, Paul, 76
Louis Seize (style), 183
Louis XV, King of France, 106
Louis XVI, King of France, 96–7, 184
Louise, Princess Royal and Duchess of Fife, 6
Love Finds a Way (movie), 99
Lowe, Harold, 222, 237–8, 250–1
Loyal Orange Institution, 40–3
Lubin Studios, 96
The Lucky Holdup (movie), 91, 100
Ludwig I, King of Bavaria, 151
Luís Filipe, King of Portugal, 192
Lusitania (liner), xv, 51, 63, 74, 79, 245, 302, 309
Luxemburg, Rosa, 19
LV-117 (lightship), 115

Macfie, Claud, 331, 333
Mackay-Bennett (trawler), 294
MacNeice, Louis, 116
Macy's, 57, 146, 161
Mafalda of Savoy, Landgravine of Hesse, 191
Magnes, Judah, 167
Mahan, Alfred Thayer, 300
The Maiden Tribute of Modern Babylon (articles), 133
Maioni, Robert ('Cissy'), 52–3, 55, 61, 101, 120, 123–4, 223, 271, 284, 292, 331n
Maison Lucille, 131
Majestic (liner, 1889), 48

Majestic (liner, 1922), 315
Malcolm III, King of Scots, 21
Mamie Bolton (movie), 99
Manhattan Hospital, 162
Manuel II, King of Portugal, 7
Maréchal, Pierre, 219
Margaret of Connaught, Crown Princess of Sweden, 132
Margaret of Wessex (saint), Queen of Scots, 21, 271
Marie Antoinette of Austria, Queen of France, 97, 183–4
Marie de Guise, Queen of Scots, 22
Marie Feodorovna (of Denmark), Empress of Russia, 8, 163, 306
Marion Cricket Club, 67. 303
Marlborough College, Wiltshire, 137
Marlborough, Charles Spencer-Churchill, 9th Duke of, 20
Marlborough, Consuelo Spencer-Churchill, Duchess of, 6
Marlborough, Gladys Spencer-Churchill, Duchess of, 20
Marlborough, Lily Spencer-Churchill, Duchess of, 31
Martin, Nicholas, 63
Mary of Modena, Queen of England, Scotland and Ireland, 22
Mary of Teck, Queen of the United Kingdom, xx, 6, 8, 14, 18, 329
Mary, Queen of Scots, xvii, 22
Matthias, Paul, 207–8
Maud of Wales, Queen of Norway, 8
Mauretania (liner), xvi, 17, 63, 74, 79, 177–8, 309
Maximilian II, King of Bavaria, 151
Maxtone-Graham, John, xx
Mayflower (ship), xv
Mayné, Berthe, 135
The Mayor and the Manicure (play), 94
McCann case (1910), 38
McElroy, Hugh, 56, 78, 90, 198, 213, 331
McGee, Francis, 283–4, 288–9, 300
McKelway, Virginia, 162
McKinley, William, President, 192
Mein Leben für Irland (movie), xvii

Mersey, John Bigham, 1st Viscount, 262, 296, 296n, 298
Methodist College, Belfast, 27
Metropolitan Comic Opera Company, 94
Meyer, Leila, 185
Miguel I, King of Portugal, 19
Mikhail Alexandrovich, Grand Duke of Russia, 8
Mikhail Mikhailovich, Grand Duke of Russia, 8
Millet, Francis, 64, 190, 194–7, 238, 241
Millet, Elizabeth, 195
Minahan, Ida ('Daisy'), 197–8
Minahan, William Edward, 197
Miners' strike (1912), 48, 147
Minia (trawler), 294
Miss Masquerader (movie), 98–9
Miss Spence's School, New York, 139
Monmouth, battle of, 97
Montanelli, Indro, 323–4, 326
Montefiore Home for Chronic Invalids, Bronx, 162
Montgamny (trailer), 294
Moody, James, 203, 252
Moore, Clarence, 134
Morgan, John Pierpont, 16, 73, 187–8
Mornington, Anne Wellesley, Countess of, 25
Most Holy Redeemer, Belfast, Church of the, 35
Most Illustrious Order of St Patrick, 29
Motion Picture Distributing and Sales Company Ball, 98
Motion Picture News, 97
Mount Olivet (cemetery), 295
Mount Vernon (plantation), 97
Moving Picture News, 102, 316, 319
Murdoch, William, 86, 202–3, 208, 217–18, 226, 244, 255–6, 286
The Musician's Daughter (movie), 99
Mussolini, Benito, 323

Nagel, Charles, 290
National Mercantile Marine Fund, 302
National Milk Hostels, 6

Ne Temere (decree), 37–8
'Nearer, My God, to Thee' (hymn), 251–2
Nelson, Horatio, 1st Viscount, 249
Nesbitt, Evelyn, 138
New York (liner), 48–9, 61, 63, 80, 149, 328
New York American, 297
New York City Draft Riots (1863), 158
New York Dramatic Mirror, 317
New York Evening Post, 335
New York Sun, 317
New York Telegraph, 200
New York Times, 94, 129, 162, 165–6
New York World, 200
Newsom, Helen, 280
Nicholas II, Emperor of Russia, 18–19, 163, 165–6, 192, 306
Nieuw Amsterdam (liner), 101
Noah (patriarch), xv
Nomadic (tender), 63–4, 68, 76, 92
Norddeutscher Lloyd, 71–2
Norfolk, dukes of, 144
Normandie (liner), 116
Nourney, Alfred, 134, 219, 287, 289
Nripendra Narayan, Maharajah of Cooch-Behar, 32
Nuremberg Rally (1937), 322

'O God, Our Help in Ages Past' (hymn), 145
O'Brien, Thomas J., 191
O'Loughlin, William, 116–18, 120, 185, 198, 280
Objectivist historiography *see* Reconciliationist
Oceanic (liner), 48, 165, 177, 293–5
Odessa pogrom, 165
Offenbach, Jacques, 200
Ohio State University, 171
Ohm Krüger (movie), xvii
Olga Nikolaevna, Grand Duchess of Russia, 18–19
Olympic (liner), xvi, 16–18, 47–49, 57n, 61–3, 79, 82, 86, 105, 107, 116, 129, 147–8, 178, 199, 217, 308, 316, 330

On a Sea of Glass (book), xx
Orange Order *see* Loyal Orange
    Institution
Orange Riots, New York (1871), 161
Order of St Benedict *see* Benedictines
Osborne House, 25
Os-Saltaneh, Prince Samad Khan
    Momtaz, 8
Ostriche, Muriel, 291
Our Future Lies Upon the Water
    (painting), 72

Pains of Youth (play), 127
Pankhurst, Charles, 334
Paris (liner), 116
Parliament Act (1911), 10–14, 188
Parrish, Lutie, 230
Parsons, Alfred, 195
Parsons, Louella, 323
Pathé, 313
Pearl Harbor attacks, 323
Pearse, Pádraig, 44
Peñaranda, Hernando Fitz-James Stuart,
    14th Duke of, 304
Peñasco, María-Josefa de, 134, 224,
    235, 241, 271, 283, 292, 332
Peñasco, Victor de, 134, 224, 228
Pennsylvania Railroad, 65, 175
Pennsylvania Senate Railroad
    Committee, 175
Pennsylvania, University of, 303, 326,
    329
Peruschitz, Joseph, 253
Peskett, Leonard, 79, 79n
Petersburg, siege of, 58
Petit Trianon, Versailles, 66
Petkov, Dimikar, 192
Peuchen, Arthur, 226–7, 287
Philadelphia (liner), 48
Philadelphia Evening Bulletin, 327
Philip of Greece and Denmark, Duke of
    Edinburgh, 125
Pichon, Stephen, 9
Pickford, Mary, 93, 99
Pirrie, Margaret, Viscountess, 15, 298
Pirrie, William, 1st Viscount, 15, 27,
    29, 34, 107

Pitcher, Molly, 97
Pitman, Herbert, 221–2, 262–3, 282
Pius VI, Pope, 38
Pius X, Pope, 37–8, 193
Plehve, Vyacheslav von, 192
Plunkett, Horace, 243, 305
Plymouth Harbour (painting), 242
Pobedonostsev, Constantine, 164
Poiret, Paul, 120
Polk, James, President, 186
Poppe, Johann, 71
Port Hudson, siege of, 158
Portland, Winifred Cavendish-Bentinck,
    Duchess of, 304
Princeton University, 67, 303
Prinknash Abbey (prev. Park), 3, 331
Puccini, Giacomo, 185
'Pull for the Shore' (hymn), 272

Queen Mary (liner), 78, 330
Queen Victoria School, Dunblane, 6
Quirinal Palace, 191

Ramos, Emilio Antonio, 322, 324–5
Randolph Wemyss Memorial Hospital,
    Fife, 6
Ranelagh Polo Club, 304
Raphall, Morris J., 156
Rasmussen, Rita, 96
Raver, Harry, 98, 100, 318
Reconciliationist historiography, 160
Recreation Rooms and Settlement,
    Brooklyn, 162
Red Cross, 5, 127, 291, 331
Redgrave, H. H., 313
Redmond, John, 43
Rembrandt, 22
Republic (liner), 173, 177, 208, 218
Republican National Convention
    (1912), 190
The Revenge of the Silk Masks (movie),
    100
Reynolds, Debbie, 140
Reynolds, Joshua, 23
Richman, Julia, 162
The Riddle of the Titanic (book), 109,
    114–15

Rijn, Rembrandt Harmenszoon van *see* Rembrandt
'The Roast Beef of Old England' (song), 122
Robert I, King of Scots, 21
Robertson, Morgan, 175–6
Robinson and Cleaver, 31
Robinson, Annie, 213, 231, 329
Roehampton Polo Club, 304
Roosevelt, Ethel, 89
Roosevelt, Franklin D., President, 324
Roosevelt, Theodore, President, 9, 89, 136, 145, 186, 189, 191
Rose Tree Fox Hunt, 326
Rosebery, Archibald Primrose, 5th Earl of, 303
Rosenbaum, Edith, 68. 101, 292
Rosenkrantz, Baroness Rebecca, 193
Rostron, Arthur, 275, 279, 288, 300, 309
Rothes, Andrew Leslie, 5th Earl of, 21–22
Rothes, George Leslie, 4th Earl of, 21, 77
Rothes, Ian Leslie, 21st Earl of, 286, 310, 333
Rothes, John Leslie, 10th Earl of, 23
Rothes, John Leslie, 1st Duke and 7th Earl of, 22
Rothes, Lucy Noëlle Martha Leslie, Countess of
early life, 3
as debutante, 3–4
wedding, 2–4
life at Leslie House, 2, 20, 23, 310
social life, 4–6, 15, 20, 303–4
boards *Titanic*, 51–3, 55
accommodation on board, 53, 55–7, 122–3
dinners on board, 78, 129, 199
reaction to collision, 200, 204, 209
warned by Captain Smith, 209
struggles to find life belt, 212
during evacuation, 213, 223–4
leaves *Titanic*, 225, 228
behaviour in lifeboats, 241, 252n, 264, 269–72
rescue, 272–3
on *Carpathia*, 272, 283–6, 292, 332
remembers last concert on the *Titanic* (1913), 200, 304
attends 1914 London Season, 303–4
during First World War, 309–11
loss of Leslie House, 311
loss of Prinknash Park, 330–1
widowhood, 330–1
interviews on the *Titanic*, 252n, 309–10
correspondence with Walter Lord, 330–2
second marriage, 331
death and burial, 333
relationship with Lord Rothes, 3–4, 309–11
as mother, 5, 125, 283, 331
as employer, 124
as nurse, 5, 127, 284, 292, 309–10
aristocratic friendships, 6, 20, 126
and María-Josefa de Peñasco, 224, 228, 241, 271, 283, 292
and Thomas Jones, 268–9, 272, 332
and Rhoda Abbott, 285–6
manners, 55
appearance, 3, 5
religious faith, 144, 272, 333
political views, 13–14, 126, 310
racial views, 249
attitude to Catholicism, 312
taste in fashion, 51, 128
jewellery, 128
philanthropy, 5, 303, 311
Rothes, Malcolm Leslie, 20th Earl of, 5, 125, 283, 311, 331
Rothes, Mary Haworth-Leslie, Countess of, 125
Rothes, Norman Leslie, 19th Earl of, 2, 4, 9, 12, 15, 23, 51, 125, 128, 270, 309–11, 330–1, 333
Rothes, William Leslie, 3rd Earl of, 11
Rothschild, Amanda, 157
Roxburghe, Mary Innes-Ker, Duchess of, 303
Royal Academy Private View, 303
Royal Air Force, xix

Royal Ascot, 303

Royal Belfast Academical Institute, 27, 30

Royal Caledonian Ball, 5, 303

Royal Caledonian Educational Trust, 5

Royal College of Surgeons of Ireland, 116

Royal Cork Yacht Club, 87

Royal Hospital, Chelsea, 303

Royal Irish Constabulary, 44

Royal Navy Reserve, 104–5

Royal Opera House, London, 303

Royal Society for the Protection of Birds, 304

Royal Victoria Hospital, Belfast, 15

Russell, Edith *see* Rosenbaum

Ryerson, Arthur Jr., 76, 179

Ryerson, Arthur Sr., 76, 178–80, 238–9, 301

Ryerson, Emily, 76–7, 180, 238–9, 280, 299–301

Ryerson, Emily (younger), 76–7, 238–9

Ryerson, John ('Jack'), 76–7, 238–9

Ryerson, Suzette, 76–7, 238–9

Saale (liner), 116

Saint-Germain-en-Laye (cemetery), 326

Saks (store), 185

Saks, Andrew, 185

Salvation Army, 133, 291–2

Samos, Andreas Kopasis, Prince of, 192

San Francisco Earthquake (1906), 335

San Vittore (prison), 323, 326

Sanders, Robert *see* Bayford

Sanssouci Palace, 25

'The Sash' (song), 41–2

Saturday Evening Post, 96

Saved from the Titanic (movie), xvi, 318–20

Scheftel, Vivian, 60n, 161

Schuster, Ildefonso, Cardinal, 324

Schutzstaffel ('SS'), xix, 324

The Scots Peerage, 21

Scotsman (newspaper), 5

Segregation, racial (US), 160

Sehzade Yusuf Izzedin, Ottoman Crown Prince, 8

Selpin, Herbert, xviii

Selzick, David, xvii

Sergei Alexandrovich, Grand Duke of Russia, 165, 192, 319

Seward, Frederic, 198, 200, 217–18

Shackleton, Ernest, 200

Shaw, George Bernard, 227–8, 249

Shelley, Imanita, 107, 229–30

Shipbuilder (magazine), 17–18, 192

Shubert Brothers (agency), 94

The Sinking of the S. S. Titanic (memoir), 327

Sipyagin, Dmitri, 192

Sixteenth Amendment (US), 188–9

Sloan, Mary, 116n, 116–18, 120, 198, 213–14, 231, 244

Sloper, William, 200, 205, 217–18, 220, 256

Smith, Edward, 61, 76, 80, 86, 105, 129–30, 143, 145, 172–3, 172n, 178, 180, 197–8, 206, 208–9, 217, 222, 224, 233–4, 247–50, 257, 263, 268, 286, 298, 316, 335

Smith, James, 137–8, 240–1

Smith, William Alden, 232–3, 295–6

Société Française des Films et Cinématographes Éclair, 96–100, 317, 320

Soldiers and Sailors Fund, 311

Solly-Flood, Richard, 304

Solway Moss, battle of, 21

Somme, battle of, 312

'Songe d'Automne' (waltz), 251

Sophie, Duchess of Hohenberg, 19, 307

Soto y Tova, Manuel Peréz de, 332

Spectator, 319

Spencer, Marie-Eugenie, 139

Spencer, William, 139

Sporting Days (play) –94

St Anne's Cathedral, Belfast, 30

St Bernard's Academy, New York, 146

St Canice's Cathedral, Kilkenny, 304

St Colman's Cathedral, Cóbh, 84

St Louis (liner), 48

St Mark's Episcopal Church, Philadelphia, 179

St Mary Abbots Church, Kensington, 4
St Mary's Church, Fairford, 333
Stanwyck, Barbara, 330
Stead, William T., 133, 198, 230
Steffansson, Erik, 137
Stephenson, Martha, 200, 215, 236, 238
Stewart, John, 242–3
Stimson, Henry, 136
Stoddard, Charles Warren, 195
Stolypin, Pytor, 192
Strathmore and Kinghorne, Cecilia Bowes-Lyon, Countess of, 303
Straus, Beatrice, 147, 168
Straus, Clarence, 161
Straus, Herbert, 146, 161
Straus, Hermine, 151–2
Straus, Ida (Rosalie)
  early life, 58, 157
  wedding, 161
  death of second son, 161
  criticism of Tsar Nicholas II, 165–6
  travels on *Caronia*, 59, 82
  trips to France, 20, 59, 147
  stays at Claridge's (1912), 81
  troubles with maids, 59, 81
  accommodation on board, 57, 57n, 60, 81–3
  letter to Lilian Burbidge, 61–2
  dinners on board, 129, 186
  telegrams son from *Titanic*, 168–9
  during collision, 200–1, 210
  during evacuation, 211, 225, 228
  gift to Ellen Bird, 228
  later sightings, 229–30, 251, 258
  death confirmed, 282–3
  as mother, 161, 168–9
  as grandmother, 146
  experiences anti-Semitism, 145
  personality, 59
  health, 149, 225, 269
  religious views, 167–8
  love of Paris, 58
  philanthropy, 162–3, 313
  memorials, 312–14
Straus, Irma, 147, 168

Straus, Isidor
  early life, 58, 150–3
  emigrates to USA, 152
  service to the Confederacy, 58, 156–7
  visit to New York (1863), 58, 157
  wedding, 161
  travels on *New York*, 161
  as co-owner of Macy's, 57, 147
  political career, 57
  writes memoirs, 149–50
  travel on *Caronia*, 59, 82
  stays at Claridge's (1912), 81, 313
  accommodation on board, 57, 57n, 60, 81–3
  witnesses *New York* incident, 61–2
  dinners on board, 129, 186
  during collision, 200–1, 210
  during evacuation, 211, 225, 228
  later sightings, 229–30, 251, 258
  death, 258
  death confirmed, 282–3
  recovery of body, 295, 313
  as father, 147, 162, 168–9
  as grandfather, 146
  generosity to siblings, 145
  experiences anti-Semitism, 145–6, 159–60
  friendship with Col. Gracie, 58–9, 148–9
  friendship with President Cleveland, 149, 168
  wealth, 59, 162
  religious views, 145, 167–8
  patriotism, 168
  views on slavery, 154
  opposition to Zionism, 157
  love of London, 58
  philanthropy, 162, 313
  memorials, 313–14
Straus, Jakob, 151–2
Straus, Jesse, 147, 149–50, 161, 315–15
Straus, Karolina, 151
Straus, Lazarus, 150–5, 159–60
Straus, Lina, 59n
Straus, Minnie *see* Weil

Straus, Nathan 59n, 145–6, 151–2, 154, 166, 167
Straus, Oscar, 145, 151–4
Straus, Percy, 161, 282
Straus, Sara *see* Hess
Straus, Sara (Isidor's mother), 151–3
Straus, Vivian *see* Scheftel
Suevic (liner), 177
Sun Yat-sen (dog), 134, 215
Sutherland, Cromartie Sutherland-Leveson-Gower, 4th Duke of, 12
Sutherland, Millicent Sutherland-Leveson-Gower, Duchess of, 6, 12, 303

Taft, Hellen ('Nellie'), 195
Taft, William, President, xx, 186, 189, 191–3, 289–90
Talbot, Edward (bishop), 334
Talbott, Margaret, 292, 329–30
The Tales of Hoffmann (opera), 200, 304
Tatiana Nikolaevna, Grand Duchess of Russia, 306
Taylor, Elmer, 130–2
Tchaikovsky, Pyotr Ilyich, 185
Temple Emanu-El, Manhattan, 167
Teutonic (liner), 71
Thackera, Alexander Montgomery, 20, 69
Thaw, Harry, 137–8
Thayer, Alexander, 326
Thayer, Edward, 326, 329
Thayer, John Borland
education, 67
marriage, 67
career, 65, 175
visit to Switzerland (1911–12), 175
visit to Berlin (1912), 19–20, 69–70
boards *Titanic*, 76–7
accommodation on board, 77, 201–2
conversations with Thomas Andrews, 174, 327–8
conversations with Ismay, 174, 180–1
attends Wideners' dinner party, 185–90
during collision, 202
during evacuation, 204, 215–16, 236–7

helps load lifeboats, 238–40
discusses possibility of death, 240–1
death, 261
friendship with Arthur Ryerson, 76, 178–81
and Martha Stephenson and Elizabeth Eustis, 200, 215
appearance, 65
wealth, 65, 182
mental health, 175, 193
religious views, 144
political views, 175
anglophile sympathies, 67
athleticism, 67
cricketing, 67
Thayer, John (III) ('Jack')
education, 67–8, 303
accommodation on board, 77, 201–2
explores *Titanic*, 104
conversations with Thomas Andrews, 174, 327–8
conversations with Ismay, 174, 288
attends Sunday concert, 201
during collision, 202
during evacuation, 204, 215–16, 236, 256
loses sight of parents, 236–7
leaves the *Titanic*, 258–60
experience in lifeboats, 261, 265–7, 272, 276–8
rescue, 274–6
on *Carpathia*, 277–80, 288, 292
testimony on *Titanic* (1912), 327
conversations with Charles Lightoller, 293, 328
trip to Europe (1914), 293, 295, 302–3
testimony on *Titanic* (1915), 327
marriage, 326
military service, 326
career, 326
article on *Titanic* (1932), 327
writes memoir, 327–8
son's death, 329
suicide, 329
and Milton Long, 201, 216, 236–7, 256, 258–9

appearance, 67
mental health, 328–30
athleticism, 67
discrepancies in testimonies, 327–8
eulogises Edwardian era, 335–6
Thayer, John (IV), 326
Thayer, Julie, 326, 329
Thayer, Lois (Jack's daughter), 326
Thayer, Lois (Jack's wife), 303, 326
Thayer, Margaret *see* Talbott
Thayer, Marian
ancestry, 67
wedding, 67
social life in Philadelphia, 67
visit to Switzerland (1911–12), 175
visit to Berlin (1912), 69–71
boards *Titanic*, 76–7
accommodation on *Titanic*, 77, 201–2
during collision, 201–2
notices *Titanic*'s list, 204–5
during evacuation, 215–16, 236–7
leaves *Titanic*, 238–40
experience in lifeboat, 278
on *Carpathia*, 274, 280, 288, 291–2
grief at widowhood, 291–2, 300
defends Smith and Ismay, 197–8,
    299–300
files insurance claim, 301–2
travels on *Lusitania* (1914), 302
later life, 328–9
death, 329
friendship with Emily Ryerson, 76–7,
    180–1, 299
friendship with Lady Duff Gordon,
    132
friendship with Archibald Butt,
    189–91, 193–4, 197, 300–1
friendship with Ismay, 180–1,
    299–302
protestantism, 144
racism, 249–50
taste in fashion, 132, 182
interest in homeopathy, 193
spiritualist beliefs, 193, 328–9
Thayer, Pauline (Jack's daughter), 326
Thayer, Pauline (Jack's sister) *see* Dolan
The Times, 3

Thomas Andrews Memorial Hall,
    Comber, 304–5
Thomas Andrews: Shipbuilder (biog-
    raphy), 305
Titanic (liner)
Construction and voyage
symbol of Anglo-American coopera-
    tion, xvii, xx, 17
deaths during construction, 15
launch, 15–17
sea trials, 39–40, 44
Board of Trade inspections, 39, 45,
    47
fire on board, 39, 45, 48, 170–1
quality of steel, 171–2
rivets, 171
rudder, 171–2
strength of, 17. 172, 257
design flaws, 235
lack of binoculars on board, 86–7
lack of preparedness for maiden
    voyage, 47–8
stay in Southampton, 46–8
departure from Southampton, 60–2
stay in Cherbourg, 63–4, 68
stay in Queenstown, 83–8
mail contract, 84
speed, xv, 80, 82, 104, 170, 174–5
collision with iceberg, xv, 202–4,
    207–8

On board
Gymnasium, 54, 195, 221
Grand Staircase, 129, 131, 185,
    205–7, 209, 236–7, 258
Lounge, 80, 104–5, 113, 122, 148–9,
    169, 200–1, 205, 215–16, 221,
    236–7, 251–2, 264, 266
Reading and Writing Room, 104, 113,
    122, 148, 258, 195n, 258
Smoking Room (First Class), 104,
    113, 122, 148, 185, 195–6, 207,
    242–4. 258, 264
Verandah Cafés, 88, 242, 165
Café Parisian, 47–8, 112–13, 200
Restaurant, 112–13, 183–5
Purser's Office, 55–6, 128, 213

Dining Saloon (First Class), xviii, 77–9, 107, 264
Turkish Bath, 54, 105, 113–15, 195, 334
electric baths, 105
Squash Court, 54, 195, 209, 218, 223
Swimming Pool, 54, 105, 328
First Class cabins, 48, 54–7, 81–2
Second Class public rooms, 231
Second Class cabins, xvi, 107
Third Class public rooms, 234
Third Class cabins, 108, 232
accommodation for crew, 108
watertight compartments, 86, 170, 173, 203, 295–6
lifeboats, 46–7, 216–17
differences from *Olympic*, 112–14
differences from *Britannic*, 235

Sinking
order given to evacuate, 209
distress rockets, 216, 224
music during evacuation, 215, 237, 251–2
treatment of third-class passengers, xxii, 231–6
collapse of funnels, 259–60
splits apart, 262–5
disappearance, 265
casualty figures, xv–xvi

After 1912
inquiries into, xv, 267, 295–6
cinematic portrayals, xvi, 263, 318–20, 333
use in Nazi propaganda, xvii–xix
wreck, xv, 262, 264, 337
theory of switch with *Olympic*, 112–16
centenary of sinking, xx

Titanic (movie, 1943), xvii–xix
Titanic (movie, 1953), 263, 330
Titanic (movie, 1997), 76, 129, 263
Titanic and Other Ships (memoir), 328
Titanic: The Ship That Never Sank? (book), 110
'To the Tsar' (poem), 165–6

Tolstoy, Count Leo, 164
Traffic (tender), 64
Tranby House, East Riding, 138
Travelling Palaces (book), 105–6
Treaty of London (1839), 307
Tredegar, viscounts, 126
Trent (ship), 157
Trinity College, Dublin, 116
A Trip to Japan (play), 95
Triton Fish and Game Club, 146
The Truth about Chickamauga (book), 149
The Truth about the Titanic (memoir), 262
Turing, Alan, 133
Tutankhamen, Pharaoh of Egypt, 128
Twain, Mark, 69, 195
Two Nations Theory (Irish), 36

U-20 (submarine), xvi, 245
Ulster Journal of Archaeology, 36–7
Ulster Liberal Unionist Association, 29
Ulster Covenant, 43
Ulster Volunteer Force, 42–3
Umberto I, King of Italy, 191–2
Umberto II, King of Italy, 191
United States Coast Guard, 145, 296
United States Institute of Statistics and Technology, 172
United States Lines, 315
United States Marine Corps, 145
The Unsinkable Molly Brown (musical), 140

Vacani's School of Dancing, Knightsbridge, 304
Val, Rafael Merry del, Cardinal, 193
Vanity Fair (magazine), 128
Variety (magazine), 316
Vat, Dan van der, 104, 114–15
Vaterland (liner), 75, 306, 315
Vernon, Anne, 326
Vespucci, Amerigo, 184
Vicksburg, siege of, 158
Victor Emmanuel II, King of Italy, 190
Victor Emmanuel III, King of Italy, 191
Victoria College, Belfast, 27

Victoria, Princess Royal and German Empress, 71
Victoria, Queen of the United Kingdom, 6, 29–31, 84
Victoria-Eugenia of Battenberg, Queen of Spain, 132, 192
Vienna Bank Employees' Club Ball, 306–7
Vienna Derby, 19
Village Clubs Association, 6
Vogue (American), 132, 320

Waldo, Rheinlander, 291
Washington Post, 4
Washington, George, President, 97
Weil, Minnie, 59, 161
Welles, Orson, 323
Wellington College, Belfast, 25
Wellington, Arthur Wellesley, 1st Duke of, 25
Wellington, Katherine Wellesley, Duchess of, 6
Wennerström, August, 253
Westminster Confession of Faith (1646), 143
Wharton, Edith, 19
Wharton, Edward, 19
'When Erin First Rose' (poem), 85
The White Aprons (movie), 99, 318
White Star Line, xv, 46, 68–9, 73, 79, 110, 112, 129, 137–8, 173, 175–6, 245, 287
White, Ella, 77, 89–90, 270–1
White, Stanford, 137–8
Whitehaven Pit Disaster (1910), 126
Whiting, Richard (martyr), 331
Widener, Eleanor, 91, 183, 189, 275, 280, 300
Widener, George, 91, 183, 240, 251, 280, 286
Widener, Harry, 186, 280
Widener, Peter, 91
Wilde, Henry, 86, 286, 298
Wilde, Oscar, 43, 133

Wilding, Edward, 39, 45, 48
Wilhelm I, German Emperor, 70–1
Wilhelm II, German Emperor, 7, 32, 71, 74
Wilkinson, Norman, 242
William III, King of England, Scotland and Ireland, 20, 42
William IV, King of the United Kingdom, 25
Williams, Richard Norris (II), 280
Wilson, Frances, 299
Wilson, Woodrow, President, 66, 187
Wimbledon Championships, 133, 303
Winchester College, Hampshire, 67
Winchester, marquesses of, 126
Windsor Castle, 7, 24, 67
Wisniewska, Faustina, 66
Women's Unionist Association, Fife, 310
Women's Wear Daily, 183
Woodlawn, Bronx (cemetery), 313
Woolner, Hugh, 137, 229
Woolner, Thomas (sculptor), 138
Wormstedt, Bill, xx
The Wrong Bottle (movie), 99

Xinhai Revolution, 134

Yale Daily News, 179
Yale University, 76, 179
Yat-sen, Sun, President, 134
Yolanda of Savoy, Countess of Bergolo, 191
Yorktown, battle of, 97
Young Men's Christian Association, 5
Young, Marie, 89
Yurievskaya, Princess Catherine, 163

Zaitao, Prince of China, 8
Zerlett-Olfenius, Walter, xviii
Zita of Bourbon-Parma, Empress of Austria and Queen of Hungary, 19
Zuleika Dobson (novel), 127
Zweig, Stefan, 183–4
Zyrot en Cie, 51